'Go for it!'

'It'll be all right on the night.'

'It's only rock 'n roll.'

'The end of civilization as we know it.'

'The real nitty gritty.'

'Ahh Bisto!'

'Beam me up Scotty.'

'Don't call us, we'll call you.'

The **BLOOMSBURY DICTIONARY OF POPULAR PHRASES** by Nigel Rees is a compendium of catch phrases, clichés, colloquialisms, format phrases, idioms, nicknames, sayings, slogans and stock phrases, current or remembered at the start of the 1990s. It explains what they mean, details (where possible) their origins and gives illustrative examples and includes many phrases never before documented. Extensive cross-references.

The **DICTIONARY** is based on over 15 years' research by writer and broadcaster Nigel Rees. He is probably best known as the deviser and presenter of Radio 4's long-running *Quote … Unquote* programme. He has written over 20 books, including three novels. His special interest is in the popular use of the English language.

DICTIONARY OF POPULAR PHRASES

NIGEL REES

BLOOMSBURY

First published in Great Britain 1990
This paperback edition published 1991

Copyright © 1990 by Nigel Rees
Bloomsbury Publishing Limited, 2 Soho Square, London W1V 5DE

British Library Cataloguing in Publication Data

A CIP catalogue record for this book
is available from the British Library

ISBN 0 7475 0989 1

Designed by Malcolm Smythe

Typeset by Discript, London

Printed in Great Britain by Clays Ltd, St Ives Plc

There is no bigger peril either to thinking or to education than the popular phrase.

(Frank Binder, *Dialectic*, 1932)

Idiom is held in little esteem by schoolmasters and old-fashioned grammarians, but good writers love it . . . It may be regarded as the sister of poetry, for like poetry it retranslates our concepts into living experiences, and breathes that atmosphere of animal sensation which sustains the poet in his flights.

(Logan Pearsall Smith, *English Idioms*,
S.P.E. Tract No. xii, 1923)

INTRODUCTION

Why 'Popular Phrases'?

Well, Eric Partridge called his great work *A Dictionary of Slang and Unconventional English*, but I always felt that was too apologetic a way of describing what is the liveliest, richest and most frequently used area of the English language. Partridge also compiled *A Dictionary of Catch Phrases* and *A Dictionary of Clichés*, books with which this one is more directly comparable, but neither of these titles would completely describe what I have tried to produce.

A Dictionary of Popular Phrases is a selective examination of 1,500 contemporary catch phrases, clichés, idioms, popular sayings and slogans. The ones I have chosen to include are those about which there is something interesting to say with regard to their origins and use. As a rule of thumb, I have only written about those phrases which are in popular use now as we enter the 1990s, or which are still remembered from a few decades back. I have also made a special effort to discuss phrases not tackled previously by myself or others.

In fact, Paul Beale, Partridge's reviser, with my permission, drew very heavily on two earlier books of mine, *Very Interesting . . . But Stupid! – A Book of Catchphrases from the World of Entertainment* (1980) and *Slogans* (1982). I, too, have drawn on them, but only, I hope, where I have something to add or to correct.

Let me explain a little more clearly what I mean by 'Popular Phrases'. In each case I have tried to categorize the phrase, though I must emphasize at once that, for the most part, these categories are not exclusive. It is possible for a phrase to be a catch phrase *and* a slogan, an idiom *and* a cliché, and it isn't worth agonizing too hard over what the status is at a particular moment.

I have also invented two new categories – what I call 'format phrases' and 'stock phrases' – because they describe rather better certain types of popular phraseology. By 'format phrase', I mean something like ONE SMALL STEP FOR ——, ONE GIANT LEAP FOR —— where the sentence structure can be adapted to suit the speaker's purpose.

By 'stock phrase', I mean a well-known phrase – for example, a broadcaster's verbal mannerism by which he or she is well-known but which can't be said to have 'caught on' with the public as a proper catch phrase should. It also refers to phrases which get regularly trotted out but which, again, cannot be said to have passed into the language generally.

Let me briefly define what I mean by the various categories of popular phrases used in this dictionary:

Catch Phrase: simply a phrase that has 'caught on' with the public and is, or has been, in frequent use. It might have originated with a named entertainer – like LOADSAMONEY – or it might not be traceable to a particular source – like AND BOB'S YOUR UNCLE!

Cliché: a worn or hackneyed phrase. WINTER OF DISCONTENT was a bright phrase when Shakespeare first minted it in *King Richard III* but it has become devalued by frequent repetition in other contexts. AT THE END OF THE DAY must also once have been rather a good way of describing something, but not now. I could not argue that 'in the final analysis', for example, was ever a good phrase.

There are some who would say that the clichés of journalism are used in such a way that they amount to a special language – journalese – which does not deserve to be condemned. I disagree.

Colloquialism: I have used this term to describe any form of familiar speech or writing which does not readily fit into any of the other categories.

Format Phrase: a basic phrase or sentence structure capable of infinite variation by the insertion of new words.

Idiom: a picturesque expression that is used to convey a metaphorical meaning different to its literal one – or, as *The Oxford Dictionary of Current Idiomatic English* puts it, that has a meaning 'not deducible from those of the separate words'. For example, if I say someone is a SQUARE PEG IN A ROUND HOLE it is obvious he or she cannot literally be such a thing. My hearers will know exactly what I mean, although I have not told them directly.

Like the term 'catch phrase', 'idiom' could be applied to most of the phrases in this book, but I have tried to restrict its use to those which conform to the above definition.

Nickname: a pithy, descriptive additional or substitute name.

Saying: this is what is sometimes called 'a well-known phrase or saying' (as in 're-arrange these words into a well-known phrase or saying') but, unlike a formal 'quotation', is probably not attributable to a precise source, be it speaker, book or show. Proverbial expressions most commonly fall into this category.

Slogan: a phrase designed to promote a product, idea or cause – or which has this effect. However, at times I have employed it rather loosely to cover any phrase that is used in advertising – in headlines, footnotes, but not necessarily in a selling line that names the product. BODY ODOUR/B.O. could hardly be described as a slogan in itself, but as an advertising line it did help to promote a product.

Stock Phrase: a regularly used phrase that can't be said to have 'caught on' like a full-blooded catch phrase.

I must repeat that there is considerable overlap between these categories. Indeed, it is possible for a phrase to be several things at once – catch phrase, slogan, idiom, or whatever. The symbol > is used to indicate a definite shift from one state to another. For example, NICE ONE, CYRIL! started off as a *Slogan* > *Catch Phrase*.

On the whole, I have chosen to define a 'phrase' as an expression made up of more than one word, though a one-word catch phrase is a possibility. Apart from which, popular single words tend to be adequately dealt with by the ever-growing number of word dictionaries, phrases less so.

Dating: Partridge was always game (as someone once put it) to try and pinpoint when a phrase came into use, though many of his stabs at it were no more than guesses. Using the citations available in the *Oxford English Dictionary* and its *Supplement* I have tried to be a little more precise in this area. When I say that a phrase was '*Current* in 1975', I mean that I simply have a record of its use then – *not* that I think it was first used in that year. It may also have been current long after that date. When I say that a phrase was '*Quoted* in 1981', I mean precisely that – not that it was originated in that year. It might have been coined long before.

Cross references to other entries are made in SMALL CAPITALS. Because it saves repetition of basic information, I have grouped some radio and TV catch phrases under the name of the show they came from (eg *MONTY PYTHON'S FLYING CIRCUS*). The swung dash symbol ~ is used in cross references to indicate the headword.

Alphabetical order: the phrases are listed in 'letter by letter' order – in other words, in alphabetical order of letters within the whole phrase and not just of the first word. Thus, for example, **nicely** appears before **nice one, Cyril!** and **moving** before **Mr**.

I am most grateful to all those people mentioned in the text who have responded to my queries over the years. In the preparation of this ***Dictionary of Popular Phrases*** I have also been assisted on specific points by: Nicholas Comfort; Donald Hickling; Ian Messiter; Derek Robinson; the London Bureau of the *New York Times*; the British Library Newspaper Library, Colindale, and the BBC Central Reference Library. I am also much indebted to the authors and publishers of books quoted in the text and to the editors and journalists of the many newspapers and magazines who have unwittingly provided citations.

NIGEL REES

Abbreviations

Bartlett	*Bartlett's Familiar Quotations* (15th ed.), 1980
Bible	The Authorized Version, 1611 (except where stated otherwise)
Brewer	*Brewer's Dictionary of Phrase and Fable*, 1975
CODP	*The Concise Oxford Dictionary of Proverbs*, 1982
DOAS	*Dictionary of American Slang*, 1960 (1975 revision)
Ewart	Neil Ewart, *Everyday Phrases*, 1983
Flexner	Stuart Berg Flexner, *I Hear America Talking*, 1976
Halliwell	Leslie Halliwell, *Halliwell's Film Guide* (6th ed.), 1987
Longman/*Register*	John Ayto, *The Longman Register of New Words* (1989)
Mencken	*H.L. Mencken's Dictionary of Quotations*, 1942
Morris	William and Mary Morris, *Morris Dictionary of Word and Phrase Origins*, 1977
ODCIE	*The Oxford Dictionary of Current Idiomatic English* (2 vols.), 1985
ODQ	*The Oxford Dictionary of Quotations* (3rd ed.), 1979
ODP	*The Oxford Dictionary of Proverbs* (3rd ed.), 1970
OED	*The Compact Edition of the Oxford English Dictionary*, 1987
OED Supp.	*A Supplement to the Oxford English Dictionary* (4 vols.), 1972–86
Partridge/*Catch Phrases*	Eric Partridge, *A Dictionary of Catch Phrases* (2nd ed., edited by Paul Beale), 1985
Partridge/*Slang*	Eric Partridge, *A Dictionary of Slang and Unconventional English* (8th ed., edited by Paul Beale), 1984
Polite Conversation	Jonathan Swift, *A Complete Collection of Genteel and Ingenious Conversation &c.*, 1738
Prayer Book	*The Book of Common Prayer*, 1662
Safire	William Safire, *Safire's Political Dictionary*, 1978
Shakespeare	The Arden Shakespeare (in the most recent editions available in 1989)

A

The phrases are listed in alphabetical order of letters
within the whole sentence and not just of the first word.
Cross references to other entries are made in
SMALL CAPITALS.

about. See THAT'S WHAT —— IS ALL ~.

**accident waiting to happen, this was
an.** Saying > Cliché. Frequently uttered
in the wake of disasters, this is the survivors' and experts' way of pointing to
what, to them, seems a foreseeable, inevitable result of lax safety standards
which should have been corrected in advance but will now probably only be corrected as a result of the tragedy. Much
used in relation to the late 1980s spate of
UK disasters (Bradford City football
ground fire, Zeebrugge ferry overturn-
ing, Piper Alpha oil-rig explosion, Kings
Cross Tube fire, Hillsborough football
stadium crowd deaths). Used as the title
of a book on the subject by Judith Cook
(1989).

acclamation. See DESPERATION . . .

action. See INDUSTRIAL ~.

actress. See AS THE BISHOP . . . under AS THE
ART MISTRESS SAID . . .

actual. See YOUR ACTUAL under *ROUND THE
HORNE*.

adjust. See DO NOT ~ YOUR SET; PLEASE ~ YOUR
DRESS . . .

advertise. See IT PAYS TO ~.

advertisement. See THIS ~ DEGRADES
WOMEN.

affairs. See DISCUSSING UGANDAN ~.

Africa. See OUT OF ——.

after you, Claude!/no, after you, Cecil!
Catch Phrase. One of the most enduring

phrases from the radio show *ITMA*, this exchange was spoken originally by Horace Percival and Jack Train playing two over-polite handymen, Cecil and Claude respectively. It still survives in pockets as an admirable way of overcoming social awkwardness in such matters as deciding who should go first through a door.

again. See NEVER ~!; PLAY IT ~, SAM.

age before beauty! *Catch Phrase.* A phrase used (like AFTER YOU . . .) when inviting another person to go through a door before you. In the famous story, Clare Boothe Luce said it to Dorothy Parker, ushering her ahead. Parker assented, saying, 'Pearls before swine'. (Mrs Luce described this account as completely apocryphal in answer to a question from John Keats, Parker's biographer, quoted in *You Might as Well Live*, 1970).

I have no idea how the saying originated – presumably when people first started going through doorways. It does not occur in Swift's *Polite Conversation* (1738), as one might expect.

A variant reported to me from New Zealand (1987) was, 'Dirt before the broom', though Partridge/*Catch Phrases* has this as the *response* to 'Age before beauty' (which it describes as a 'mock courtesy').

age of the train. See under WE'RE GETTING THERE.

agony, Ivy. See under *RAY'S A LAUGH*.

a good idea . . . son! See under *EDUCATING ARCHIE*.

ahead. See GO ~, MAKE MY DAY; IF YOU WANT TO GET ~ . . .

ahh Bisto! *Slogan.* Bisto gravy browning has been promoted with this cry since 1919. The name of the product is a hidden slogan, too. When the Cerebos company first put it on the market in 1910, the product did not have a name. According to legend, the initial letters of the proposed slogan 'Browns, Seasons, Thickens In One' were rearranged to give it one.

The Bisto Kids, drawn by Will Owen, first appeared in 1919, sniffing a wisp of gravy aroma and murmuring, 'Ahh Bisto!' This is a phrase much played with in cartoon captions over the years – 'Ah, Blitzo!'; 'Ah, Bizerta!'; 'Ah, Crippso!'; 'Ah! Winston!'; 'Ah! Coupon free!'

ah, Woodbine – a *great* little cigarette! *Slogan.* Current in 1957. Norman Hackforth – the Mystery Voice from radio's *Twenty Questions* – spoke the line memorably in TV ads.

ain't. See AND THAT ~ HAY; ~ IT A SHAME? (under *ITMA*); THINGS ~ WHAT THEY USED TO BE.

Aladdin. See IT WAS LIKE AN ~'s CAVE.

alarm. See SET ~ BELLS RINGING; SPREADING ~ AND DESPONDENCY.

Alice. See PASS THE SICK-BAG, ~ under I THINK WE SHOULD BE TOLD.

alive. See COME ALIVE . . .

alive and well and living in ——. *Format Phrase.* It probably began in a perfectly natural way – 'What's happened to old so-and-so?' 'Oh, he's alive and well and living in Godalming' etc. In the preface to *His Last Bow* (1917) Conan Doyle wrote: 'The Friends of Mr Sherlock Holmes will be glad to learn that he is still alive and well . . .'

The extended form was given a tremendous fillip when the Belgian-born songwriter and singer Jacques Brel (1929–78) was made the subject of an off-Broadway musical show entitled *Jacques Brel is Alive and Well and Living in Paris* (1968–72). Quite why M. Brel should have merited the WHERE ARE THEY NOW? treatment, I have never been too sure.

But the format caught on. It was used as part of religious sloganeering – 'God is not dead . . . he's alive and well and living in your heart' – and in jokes: 'God is not dead – but alive and well and working on a much less ambitious project' (quoted in 1979); 'Jesus Christ is alive and well and signing copies of the Bible at Foyles' (quoted in 1980).

A film in 1975 was lumbered with the title *Sheila Devine Is Dead and Living in New York.*

all animals are equal, but some are more equal than others. *Slogan.* A fictional slogan from George Orwell's *Animal Farm* (1945), a commentary on the totalitarian excesses of Communism. It had been anticipated: Hesketh Pearson recalled in his biography of the actor/manager Sir Herbert Beerbohm Tree that Tree wished to insert one of his own epigrams in a play by Stephen Phillips called *Nero,* produced in 1906. It was: 'All men are equal – except myself.'

The saying alludes, of course, to Thomas Jefferson's 'All men are created equal and independent', from the Preamble to the American Declaration of Independence (1776). It has, perhaps, the makings of a *Format Phrase* in that it is more likely to be used to refer to humans than to animals. Only the second half of the phrase need actually be spoken, the first half being understood: 'You-Know-Who [Mrs Thatcher] is against the idea [televising parliament]. There aren't card votes at Westminster, but some votes are more equal than others' (*Guardian*, 15 February 1989).

all dressed up and nowhere to go. *Catch Phrase.* The *OED Supp.* has this phrase starting life in a song by 'G. Whiting' (1912), 'When You're All Dressed Up and have No Place to Go'. But Lowe's *Directory of Popular Music* (ASCAP 4th ed.) ascribes it to Silvio Hein and Benjamin Burt. It goes:

When you're all dressed up and no place to go,
Life seems dreary, weary and slow.
My heart has ached as well as bled
For the tears I've shed,
When I've had no place to go
Unless I went back to bed . . .

Cole Porter wrote a parody in 1914 concluding with the words '. . . and don't know Huerto Go'. But the song appears to have been chiefly popularized by the American comedian Raymond Hitchcock in *The Beauty Shop* (New York, 1914) and *Mr Manhattan* (London, 1915). The words gained further emphasis when they were used by William Allen White to describe the Progressive Party following Theodore Roosevelt's decision to retire from presidential competition in 1916. He said they were 'All dressed up with nowhere to go.'

allergy. See DREADED LERGY under *GOON SHOW.*

all human life is there. *Slogan*. The only reference to this phrase in the *ODQ* appears under Henry James, 'Madonna of the Future' (1879): 'Cats and monkeys, monkeys and cats – all human life is there.' What is the connection, if any, with the *News of the World* which used the line to promote itself *c* 1958–9?

In 1981, Maurice Smelt, the advertising copywriter, told me: ' "All human life is there" was my idea, but I don't, of course, pretend that they were my words. I simply lifted them from the *Oxford Dictionary of Quotations*. I didn't bother to tell the client that they were from Henry James, suspecting that, after the "Henry James – WHO HE?" stage, he would come up with tiresome arguments about being too high-hat for his readership. I did check whether we were clear on copyright, which we were by a year or two . . . I do recall its use as baseline in a tiny little campaign trailing a series that earned the *News of the World* a much-publicized but toothless rebuke from the Press Council. The headline of that campaign was: " 'I've been a naughty girl', says Diana Dors". The meiosis worked, as the *News of the World* knew it would. They ran an extra million copies of the first issue of the series.'

alligator. See SEE YOU LATER, ~.

all in the mind. See under *GOON SHOW*.

all is fair in love, war and ——. *Saying > Format Phrase*. The basic proverb here is, of course, 'All's fair in love and war' which *CODP* finds in the form 'Love and war are all one' by 1620 and well-established by the nineteenth century. But nowadays I would say that the extended form – to include almost anything that the speaker might wish – is more common.

'The Shadow Chancellor, Mr John Smith . . . said he did not expect to receive any special favours from his political opponents. "All is fair in love, war and parliamentary politics," he added' – *Guardian*, 23 January 1989.

all kid gloves and no drawers. *Idiom*. Describing a certain kind of woman, this is given as an example of colourful cockney bubble-pricking by Kenneth Williams in *Just Williams* (1985). He says it was used in his youth (1930s) to denote the meretricious.

Another version I have encountered in a Welsh context (1988) is, **(all) fur coat and no knickers** (which was also the title of a play that toured the UK in the same year).

all publicity is good publicity. *Saying* – almost proverbial. I would date this from the 1960s (which was when I first heard it) but probably it's as old as the public relations industry. Alternative forms include: 'There's no such thing as bad publicity', 'There's no such thing as over-exposure – only bad exposure', 'Don't read it – measure it' and 'I don't care what the papers say about me as long as they spell my name right'. The latter saying has been attributed to the American Tammany leader 'Big Tim' Sullivan.

CODP includes it in the form 'Any publicity is good publicity' but finds no example before 1974.

all right. See BUT I'M ~ NOW under *ITMA*; IT'LL BE ~ . . .

all the news that's fit to print. *Slogan.* This was devised by Adolph S. Ochs when he bought the *New York Times* and it has been used in every edition since – at first on the editorial page, on 25 October 1896, and from the following February on the front page near the masthead. It became the paper's war-cry in the 1890s battle against formidable competition from the *World*, the *Herald* and the *Journal*. It has been parodied by Howard Dietz as 'All the news *that fits* we print' – and at worst sounds like a slogan for the suppression of news. However, no newspaper prints everything.

all the world and his wife. *Idiom.* A popular way of saying 'everybody', though in decline now after the feminism of the 1970s. The *ODQ* cites Christopher Anstey's use of the phrase in *The New Bath Guide* (1766):

You may go to Carlisle's, and to Al-mack's too;
And I'll give you my head if you find such a host,
For coffee, tea, chocolate, butter, and toast:
How he welcomes at once all the world and his wife,
And how civil to folk he ne'er saw in his life.

But the phrase was quite clearly an established one by 1738 when Swift included it in *Polite Conversation*: 'Who were the Company? – Why; there was all the World and his Wife.'

There is an equivalent French expression: 'All the world and his father.'

all we want is the facts, ma'am. See under *DRAGNET*.

alone. See I WANT TO BE ~; YOU'RE NEVER ~ WITH A STRAND.

alternative. See THERE IS NO ~.

always a bridesmaid. See OFTEN A BRIDES-MAID.

always merry and bright. *Catch Phrase.* The comedian Alfred Lester (1872–1925) – who was always lugubrious – was associated with this phrase, although it crops up in all sorts of other places. Peter Doody, a lugubrious jockey in the Lionel Monckton/Howard Talbot/Arthur Wimperis musical comedy *The Arcadians* (1909) had it as his motto in a song, 'My Motter'. Somerset Maugham in a letter to a friend (1915) wrote: 'I am back on a fortnight's leave, very merry and bright, but frantically busy – I wish it were all over.' An edition of the *Magnet* from 1920 carries an ad for *Merry and Bright* – a comic paper. And Larry Grayson suggests that it was used as the billing for Billy Danvers, the music-hall entertainer.

Amami. See FRIDAY NIGHT IS ~ NIGHT.

ambition. See SAVAGE STORY OF LUST AND ~.

America. See LET'S GET ~ MOVING AGAIN; ONLY IN ~ . . .

American way. See TRUTH, JUSTICE AND THE ~ under *SUPERMAN*.

am I right, or am I right? *Colloquialism.* Brooking no debate. Ex-American showbiz, I suspect. It is in the script of the US film *Shampoo* (1975).

Amplex. See SOMEONE ISN'T USING ~ under EVEN YOUR BEST FRIENDS . . .

anatomy of ——, the. *Format Phrase.* Fritz Spiegl in his *Keep Taking the Tabloids* (1983) points out that this journalist's cliché really dates back to *The Anatomy of Melancholy* (1621) by Robert Burton. That book used the word 'anatomy' in an appropriate manner, its subject being a medical condition (*anatome* is the Greek word for dissection). The modern vogue for 'anatomies' of this and that, began with Anthony Sampson's *Anatomy of Britain*, first published in 1962 and revised a number of times since. However, the book *Anatomy of a Television Play* was published that same year and the film *Anatomy of a Murder* had come out in 1959.

and all because the lady loves Milk Tray. *Slogan.* Cadbury's Milk Tray chocolates have been promoted with this line since 1968. On TV, it is the pay-off to action adverts showing feats of James Bond daring which lead up to the presentation of a box of the chocolates to a suitably alluring female.

and a special goodnight to *you.* *Stock Phrase.* David Hamilton (*b* 1939) was an announcer with a number of ITV companies, including Tyne Tees, ABC and Thames, before becoming a DJ on radio. In the days when TV programmes ended round about midnight, his romantic sign-off became so distinctive that he even made a record with the title 'A Special Goodnight to You' (*c* 1967). The sign-off was used by Barry Aldiss ('B.A.') on Radio Luxembourg at about the same time and subsequently by several other broadcasters.

and awa-a-aay we go! *Stock Phrase.* On the *Jackie Gleason Show* on US television (1952–70), the rotund comic hosted variety acts, and used this phrase to lead into the first sketch. He had a special pose to accompany it – head turned to face left, one leg raised ready to shoot off in the same direction. Gleason's other stock (perhaps catch) phrase was **how sweet it is!** and he popularized the word 'labonza' for posterior, as in 'a kick in the labonza'.

and I don't mean maybe! *Colloquialism.* An intensifier, to show that you have just issued a command, not expressed a wish. Mencken lists it as an 'American saying *c* 1920'. The second line of the song 'Yes, Sir, That's My Baby' (1922/5) is: '. . . No, sir, don't mean maybe'.

and now a word from our sponsor. *Stock Phrase.* One of the various ways of getting into a commercial break, taken from American radio and television and much employed in British parodies of same – though never used in earnest (for the simple reason that sponsored TV has not yet been allowed). Known here from the 1950s onwards.

and now for something completely different . . . *Catch Phrase.* From MONTY PYTHON'S FLYING CIRCUS and used as the title of the comedy team's first cinema feature in 1971. Usually delivered by John Cleese as a dinner-jacketed BBC announcer, seated before a microphone on a desk in some unlikely setting, the phrase was taken from a slightly arch 'link' much-loved by magazine programme presenters. These people were thus deprived of a very useful phrase. When I introduced Radio 4's breakfast-time *Today* programme in the mid-1970s, I sorely regretted this. After all, if you are introducing a magazine programme there's not much else you can say to get from an interview with the Prime Minister to an item about beer-drinking budgerigars.

and so we say farewell . . . *Stock Phrase.* The travelogues made by James A. Fitzpatrick (*b* 1902) were a supporting feature of cinema programmes from 1925 onwards. With the advent of sound, the commentaries to 'Fitzpatrick Traveltalks' became noted for their closing words:

> And it's from this paradise of the Canadian Rockies that we reluctantly say farewell to Beautiful Banff . . .
> And as the midnight sun lingers on the skyline of the city, we most reluctantly say farewell to Stockholm, Venice of the North . . .
> With its picturesque impressions indelibly fixed in our memory, it is time to conclude our visit and reluctantly say farewell to Hong Kong, the hub of the Orient . . .

Frank Muir and Denis Norden's notable parody of the genre – 'Bal-ham – Gateway to the South' – first written for radio *c* 1948 and later performed on record by Peter Sellers (1958) accordingly contained the words, 'And so we say farewell to the historic borough . . .'

(Compare SO, FAREWELL THEN.)

and that ain't hay! *Catch Phrase.* The title of the Abbot and Costello 1943 film which is said to have popularized this

(almost exclusively American) exclamation was *It Ain't Hay*. But in the same year, Mickey Rooney exclaimed 'And that ain't hay!' as he went into the big 'I Got Rhythm' number (choreographed by Busby Berkeley) in the film *Girl Crazy* (the scene being set, appropriately, in an agricultural college).

It means 'And that's not to be sniffed at/ not negligible', usually with reference to money. The *OED Supp.* finds it – also in 1943 – in Raymond Chandler's *The Lady in the Lake*.

and that's the way it is. *Stock Phrase.* Walter Cronkite (*b* 1916) retired from anchoring the CBS TV Evening News after 19 years – for most of which he had concluded with these words. On the final occasion, he said: 'And that's the way it is, Friday March 6, 1981. Goodnight.'

and the best of luck! *Catch Phrase.* Ironic encouragement. Frankie Howerd, the comedian (*b* 1922), claims in his autobiography, *On the Way I Lost It* (1976), to have given this phrase to the language: 'It came about when I introduced into radio *Variety Bandbox* (late 1940s) those appallingly badly sung mock operas starring . . . Madame Vera Roper (soprano) . . . Vera would pause for breath before a high C and as she mustered herself for this musical Everest I would mutter, "And the best of luck!" Later it became, "And the best of British luck!" The phrase is so common now that I frequently surprise people when I tell them it was my catch phrase on *Variety Bandbox*.'

Partridge/*Catch Phrases* suggests, however, that the 'British' version had already been a Second World War army phrase meaning the exact opposite of what it appeared to say, and compares it with a line from a First World War song: 'Over the top with the best of luck/Parleyvoo' (though that was not ironic).

and the next object is ——. *Stock Phrase.* In the radio quiz *Twenty Questions,* broadcast by the BBC from 1947 to 1976, a mystery voice – most memorably Norman Hackforth's – would inform listeners in advance about the object the panellists would then try to identify by asking no more than twenty questions. 'And the next object is "The odour in the larder" (or some such),' Hackforth would intone in his deep, fruity voice.

The game appears to have been based on a popular nineteenth-century parlour game.

See also ANIMAL, VEGETABLE OR MINERAL.

and the next *Tonight* **will be tomorrow night . . .** *Stock Phrase.* The concluding phrase of the original BBC TV early evening magazine so called (1957–65) was 'And the next Tonight will be tomorrow night . . . good night!' Cliff Michelmore, who used to say it, told me in 1979: 'The combined brains of Alasdair Milne, Donald Baverstock, myself and three others were employed to come up with the phrase. There were at least ten others tried and permed. At least we cared . . . !'

and thereby hangs a tale. *Colloquialism.* As a story-telling device, this is still very much in use – we might use it to indicate that some tasty tit-bit is about to be revealed. It occurs a number of times in Shakespeare. In *As You Like It* (II.vii.28) Jaques, reporting the words of a motley fool (Touchstone), says:

And so from hour to hour, we ripe and ripe,
And then, from hour to hour, we rot and rot:
And thereby hangs a tale.

Other examples occur in *The Merry Wives of Windsor* (I.iv.143) and *The Taming of the Shrew* (IV.i.50). In *Othello* (III.i.8), the Clown says, 'O, thereby hangs a tail', emphasizing the innuendo that may or may not be present in the other examples.

and there's more (where that came from). *Catch Phrase.* In the GOON SHOW, this was sometimes said by Major Denis Bloodnok (Peter Sellers) and occasionally by Wallace Greenslade (a BBC staff announcer who, like his colleague, John Snagge, was allowed to let his hair down on the show). Perhaps it was also said by Moriarty and others, too?

The origins of the phrase probably lie in some music-hall comedian's patter, uttered after a particular joke had gone well. Charles Dickens in Chapter 11 of *Martin Chuzzlewit* (1843–4) shows that the phrase was established in other contexts first: 'Mr Jonas filled the young ladies' glasses, calling on them not to spare it, as they might be certain there was plenty more where that came from.'

Jimmy Cricket, a later comedian, was exclaiming simply, 'And there's *more!*', by 1986.

and they all lived happily ever after. *Catch Phrase > Cliché.* The traditional ending to 'fairy' tales is not quite so frequently used as ONCE UPON A TIME, but it is (more or less) present in five of *The Classic Fairy Tales* gathered in their earliest known English forms by Iona and Peter

Opie (1974). 'Jack and the Giants' (*c* 1760) ends: 'He and his Lady lived the Residue of their Days in great Joy and Happiness.' 'Jack and the Bean-Stalk' (1807) ends: 'His mother and he lived together a great many years, and continued always to be very happy.'

A translation of 'Snow White and the Seven Dwarfs' by the brothers Grimm (1823) ends: 'Snow-drop and the prince lived and reigned happily over that land many many years.' From the same year, a translation of 'The Frog-Prince' ends: 'They arrived safely, and lived happily a great many years.'

A Scottish version of 'Cinderella' (collected 1878) has: 'They lived happily all their days.'

and this is what you do! See under MORNING ALL!

and this is where the story *really* begins. See under *GOON SHOW*.

and when did you last see your father? *Catch Phrase*. There can be few paintings where the title is as important as (and as well known as) the actual picture. This one was even turned into a tableau at Madame Tussaud's where it remains to this day. It was in 1878 that William Frederick Yeames RA first exhibited his painting with this title at the Royal Academy; the original is now in the Walker Art Gallery, Liverpool.

In Roy Strong's book *And When Did You Last See Your Father? – The Victorian Painter and British History* (1978), he notes: 'The child . . . stands on a footstool about to answer an inquiry made by the Puritan who leans across the table towards him . . . To the left the ladies of the house . . . cling to each other in tearful emotion. They, it is clear, have not answered the dreaded question.'

All Yeames himself recalled of the origin of the painting was this: 'I had, at the time I painted the picture, living in my house a nephew of an innocent and truthful disposition, and it occurred to me to represent him in a situation where the child's outspokenness and unconsciousness would lead to disastrous consequences, and a scene in a country house occupied by the Puritans during the Rebellion in England suited my purpose.'

The title of the painting became a kind of joke catch phrase, often used allusively (compare the title of Christopher Hampton's 1964 play *When Did You Last See My Mother?*)

and when the music stops . . . See under ARE YOU SITTING COMFORTABLY? . . .

and with that, I return you to the studio. See under *BEYOND OUR KEN*.

animals. See ALL ~ ARE EQUAL . . . ; NEVER WORK WITH CHILDREN OR ~.

animal, vegetable or mineral. *Stock Phrase*. Not a quotation from anyone particular, so far as I can tell, merely a way of describing three types of matter. And yet, why does the phrase trip off the tongue so? Why not 'animal, *mineral*, vegetable'? Or '*vegetable*, animal, mineral'? Perhaps because these variants are harder to say, although in W.S. Gilbert's lyrics for *The Pirates of Penzance* (1879), Major-General Stanley does manage to sing:

But still in matters vegetable, animal, and mineral,
I am the very model of a modern Major-General.

For television viewers in the 1950s, the order was clearly stated in the title of the long-running archaeological quiz *Animal, Vegetable and Mineral* in which eminent university dons had to identify ancient artefacts just by looking at them.

The trio of words was also evoked in the long-running radio series *Twenty Questions*. This originated on the Mutual Radio Network in the US in 1946, having been created by Fred Van De Venter and family – who transferred with the show to NBC TV, from 1949 to 1955. The programme ran on BBC radio from 1947 to 1976, though I'm not sure it was ever tried out on British TV. Panellists simply had to guess the identity of a 'mystery object' by asking up to twenty questions. A fourth category – 'abstract' – was added in time. In 1973/4 I recall taking part as a panellist in a version of the game made for BBC World Service which was actually called *Animal, Vegetable or Mineral*.

The key to the matter is that the original American show was admittedly based on the old parlour game of 'Animal, Vegetable or Mineral'. This seems to have been known on both sides of the Atlantic in the nineteenth century. In *Charles Dickens: His Tragedy and Triumph* by Edgar Johnson, we find (1839–41): 'Dickens was brilliant in routing everybody at "Animal, Vegetable, or Mineral," although he himself failed to guess a vegetable object mentioned in "mythological history" and belonging to a queen, and was chagrined to have it identified as the tarts made by the Queen of Hearts.'

In the same book, in a chapter on the period 1858–65, we also read: '(Dickens) was swift and intuitive in "Twenty Questions" . . . On one occasion, he failed to guess "The powder in the Gunpowder Plot", although he succeeded in reaching Guy Fawkes.'

Presumably, then, the game was known by both names, though Dickens also refers to a version of it as 'Yes and No' in *A Christmas Carol* (1843). 'Twenty Questions' is referred to as such in a letter from Hannah Moore as early as 1786.

Anne. See QUEEN ~ IS DEAD.

another. See THERE'LL NEVER BE ~.

another little drink wouldn't do us any harm. *Catch Phrase*. This boozer's jocular justification for another snort is, in fact, rather more than a catch phrase. I first became aware of the phrase through the allusion to it made in Edith Sitwell's bizarre lyrics for 'Scotch Rhapsody' in *Façade* (1922):

There is a hotel at Ostend
Cold as the wind, without an end,
Haunted by ghostly poor relations . . .
And 'Another little drink wouldn't do us
     any harm,'
Pierces through the sabbatical calm.

The actual origin is in a song with the phrase as title, written by Clifford Grey to music by Nat D. Ayer, and sung by George Robey in *The Bing Boys Are Here* (1916). The song includes a reference to the well-known fact that Prime Minister Asquith was at times the worse for drink when on the Treasury Bench:

Mr Asquith says in a manner sweet and
     calm:

And another little drink wouldn't do us any harm.

another page turned in the book of life. *Idiom > Cliché.* The first funeral I ever went to (in Liverpool, 1962) was a sparsely attended affair at a crematorium. A cracked record of 'The Lord is My Shepherd' was used to supplement our hymn-singing and the minister Uriah-Heeped his way through the service. When we went home for the wake, one of the dear departed's contemporaries sighed deeply and declared to all and sundry, 'Well, that's another page turned in the book of life.' As such, it is one of the numerous clichés of bereavement, designed to keep the awfulness of death at bay.

answer. See I THINK THE ~ LIES IN THE SOIL under *BEYOND OUR KEN*; THERE'S NO ~ TO THAT! under *MORECAMBE AND WISE SHOW*.

anyone for tennis? *Stock Phrase > Catch Phrase.* This perkily expressed inquiry from a character entering through French windows and carrying a tennis racquet has become established as typical of the 'teacup' theatre of the 1920s and 1930s (as also in the forms **who's for tennis?** and **tennis, anyone?**) A clear example of it being used has proved elusive, however, although there is any number of near-misses. The opening lines of Part II of Strindberg's *Dance of Death* (1901) are (in translation): 'Why don't you come and play tennis?' A *very* near miss occurs in the first act of Shaw's *Misalliance* (1910) in which a character asks: 'Anybody on for a game of tennis?' An informant assures me that the line was used in one of the shows presented by Edward Laurillard and George Gross-mith – which must have been in the years 1914–21. Teddie in Somerset Maugham's *The Circle* (1921) always seems on the verge of saying it, but only manages, 'I say, what about this tennis?' Myra in Noël Coward's *Hay Fever* (1925) says, 'What a pity it's raining, we might have had some tennis.' Another inform-ant assured me I could find it in Terence Rattigan's *French Without Tears* (1936) – which sounded a very promising source – but it does not occur in the printed text.

Perhaps it was just another of those phrases which was never actually said in the form popularly remembered? Unfortunately, a terrible wild-goose chase was launched by Jonah Ruddy and Jonathan Hill in their book *Bogey: The Man, The Actor, The Legend* (1965). Describing Humphrey Bogart's early career as a stage actor (*c* 1921) they said: 'In those early Broadway days he didn't play me-nace parts. "I always made my entrance carrying a tennis racquet, baseball bat, or golf club. I was the athletic type, with hair slicked back and wrapped in a blazer. The only line I didn't say was, 'Give me the ball, coach, I'll take it through'. Yes, sir, I was Joe College or Joe Country Club all the time."

'It was hard to imagine him as the orig-inator of that famous theatrical line – "Tennis anyone?" – but he was.'

It is clear from this extract that the authors were adding their own gloss to what Bogart had said. Bartlett (1968) joined in and said it was his 'sole line in his first play'. But Bogart (who died in 1957) had already denied ever having said it (quoted in Goodman, *Bogey: The Good-Bad Boy* and in an ABC TV film of 1974 using old film of him doing so.) Alistair Cooke in *Six Men* (1977) is more cautious: 'It is said he appeared in an ascot and blue blazer and tossed off the invitation "Tennis, anyone?" ' – and adds that Bogart probably did not coin the phrase.

In British show business, I have heard it suggested that Leon Quatermaine, a leading man of the 1920s and 30s who was at one time married to Fay Compton, was the first man to say it. Alan Melville, the playwright and revue artist, told me (1983): 'I know who *claimed* to have said it in a play first: Freddy Lonsdale. But he was such a delightful liar he probably invented the invention. Years ago, just after the war, down in the South of France, he maintained that he'd first put it in a play – when quizzed, he couldn't remember which one – and was quite miffed that it had gone into general circulation without due acknowledgement being made to him as the creator.' Alas, Frances Donaldson, Lonsdale's daughter, told me in 1983 that she was pretty sure he hadn't coined the phrase – or even used it, as 'it's not his style'.

In the form 'Anyone for Tennis?' the phrase was used by J.B. Priestley as the title of a 1968 television play, and in 1981 it was converted into *Anyone for Denis?* by John Wells as the title of a farce guying Margaret Thatcher's husband.

anything can happen and probably will. See under *TAKE IT FROM HERE*.

any time, any place, anywhere. *Slogan.* From Martini ads, since the early 1970s. Barry Day of the McCann-Erickson advertising agency which coined the phrase agrees there is more than a hint of Bogart in the line: 'As a Bogart fan of some standing, with my union dues all paid up,

I think I would have known if I had lifted from one of his utterances, but I honestly can't place it.' Two popular songs of the 1920s were 'Anytime, Any Day, Anywhere' and 'Anytime, Anywhere, Any Place – I Don't Care'.

In April 1987, a woman called Marion Joannou was jailed at the Old Bailey for protecting the man who had strangled her husband. She was nicknamed 'Martini Marion' because, apparently, she would have sex 'any time, any place, anywhere'.

appreciate. See 2–4–6–8, WHO DO WE ~.

Archers, The. The BBC's agricultural soap-opera – 'an everyday story of country-folk' – has been running on national radio since 1951. The nearest it has come to a catch phrase has been **oooo arr, me ol' pal, me ol' beauty!** said distinctively by Chriss Gittins (*d* 1988) in the part of the old yokel Walter Gabriel (and, no doubt, simply adopted from traditional yokel-ese).

Norman Painting, who has written many of the episodes as well as playing Phil Archer all through, told me (1983) that a number of expository cliché/catch phrases have crept in, namely, **why are you telling me all this?** and **I see what you mean.**

are there any more at home like you? *Catch Phrase.* Partridge/Catch Phrases traces this chat-up line to the musical comedy *Floradora* (1900) which contains the song, 'Tell me, pretty maiden, are there any more at home like you?' (written by Leslie Stuart). Partridge adds that the line was 'obsolete by 1970 – except among those with long memories.' Well, not quite. Tom Jones may be heard saying it to a member of the audience on the LP Tom Jones Live at Caesar's Palace Las Vegas (1971).

are yer courtin? See under HAVE A GO.

are you looking for a punch up the bracket? See under HANCOCK'S HALF-HOUR.

are you ready, Eddie? *Slogan*. Not one of the immortals, but worth mentioning for what it illustrates about advertising agencies and the way they work. In 1986, *Today*, a new national newspaper using the latest production technology, was launched by Eddie Shah, hitherto known as a union-busting printer and publisher of provincial papers. In its collective wisdom, the Wight Collins Rutherford Scott agency, charged with promoting the new paper's launch, built the whole campaign round the above slogan. Why had they chosen it? Starting with the name 'Eddie' – he being thought of as a folk-hero in some quarters – they found that it rhymed with 'ready'. So the man was featured in TV ads surrounded by his staff being asked this important question.

Unfortunately, the ad agency had homed in all too well on the most pertinent aspect of the paper's launch. *Today* was *not* ready, and the slogan echoed hollowly from the paper's disastrous start to the point at which Mr Shah withdrew to lick his wounds.

The same rhyme occurred in **ready for Freddie**, meaning 'ready for the unexpected, the unknown or the unusual' (*DOAS*), an American phrase that came out of the 'L'il Abner' comic strip. 'Are You Ready for Freddy?' was used as a slogan to promote *Nightmare on Elm Street – Part 4* (1989) – referring to Freddy Krueger, a gruesome character in the film.

are you sitting comfortably? Then I'll/we'll begin. *Stock Phrase*. This was the customary way of beginning a story on BBC radio's daily programme for small children, *Listen with Mother*. The phrase was used from the programme's inception in January 1950. Julia Lang, the original presenter, recalled in 1982: 'The first day it came out inadvertently. I just said it. The next day I didn't. Then there was flood of letters from children saying, "I couldn't listen because I wasn't ready".' It remained a more or less essential part of the proceedings until the programme was threatened with closure in 1982.

From the same programme, I also remember the stock phrase **and when the music stops**, [Daphne Oxenford, or some other] **will be here to tell you a story.**

arf a mo, Kaiser! *Catch Phrase*. A recruiting poster in the First World War showed a British 'Tommy' lighting a pipe prior to going into action, with this caption underneath. The catch phrase took off from there.

I have also seen a photograph of a handwritten sign from the start of the Second World War saying, ''Arf a mo, 'itler!'

arm. See IT'S WHAT YOUR RIGHT ~'S FOR; LONG ~ OF THE LAW.

army. See F.T.A.; JOIN THE ~ ...

arrived. See I'VE ~ AND TO PROVE IT ... under *EDUCATING ARCHIE*.

Arthur. See BIG-HEARTED ~ under *BAND WAGGON.*

art mistress. See AS THE ~ SAID . . .

as busy as a one-armed paperhanger with the itch. *Colloquialism.* Mencken listed this in 1942 as an 'American saying'. I suspect that most of these colourful comparisons are American in origin. The supply is endless, but here are a few more:

as useless as a chocolate kettle (of a UK football team, quoted on *Quote . . . Unquote* 1986).

as scarce as rocking-horse manure (an example from Australia).

as lonely as a country dunny (ditto).

as mad as a gumtree full of galahs (ditto).

as inconspicuous as Liberace at a wharfies' picnic (ditto).

as easy as juggling with soot.

as jumpy as a one-legged cat in a sandbox.

as much chance as a fart in a windstorm.

as likely as a snow-storm in Karachi.

See also LIKE TAKING MONEY FROM BLIND BEGGARS; NO MORE CHANCE THAN A SNOWBALL IN HELL; QUEER AS A CLOCKWORK ORANGE.

'as 'e bin in, whack? *Stock Phrase. Club Night* was a radio comedy series from the BBC's North Region in 1955/6 and was hosted by the pebble-lensed 'manager', Dave Morris. He would be pestered repeatedly by an eccentric figure who asked, "As 'e bin in, whack?' ('E never 'ad, of course.) Morris also originated the saying **meet the wife – don't laugh!**

What the real Mrs Morris thought of this is something we may perhaps never know.

as every schoolboy knows. *Catch Phrase > Cliché.* Bishop Jeremy Taylor (1613–67) used the expression 'every schoolboy knows it'. In the next century, Jonathan Swift used 'To tell what every schoolboy knows'. But the most noted user of this rather patronizing phrase was Lord Macaulay, the historian, who would say things like, 'Every schoolboy knows who imprisoned Montezuma, and who strangled Atahualpa' (*Lord Clive*, essay, January 1840). But do they still?

as if I cared . . . *Catch Phrase.* From *ITMA.* 'Sam Fairfechan' (Hugh Morton) would say, 'Good morning, how are you today?' and immediately add, 'As if I cared . . .' The character took his name from Llanfairfechan, the seaside resort in North Wales, where Ted Kavanagh, *ITMA*'s scriptwriter, lived when the BBC Variety Department was evacuated to nearby Bangor during the early part of the Second World War.

as it happens. *Stock Phrase.* A verbal tic of the disc-jockey Jimmy Savile OBE (*b* 1926). He used it as the title of his autobiography in 1974. However, when the book came out in paperback it had been changed to *Love is an Uphill Thing* because (or so it was explained) the word 'love' in a title ensured extra sales.

After dance-hall exposure, Savile began his broadcasting career with Radio Luxembourg in the 1950s. His other stock phrase **how's about that then, guys and gals?** started then.

asked. See I ONLY ARSKED.

ask the Man from the Pru. *Slogan.* The Prudential Assurance Co. Ltd was founded in 1848. The phrase 'The Man from the Pru' evolved naturally from what people would call the person who came to collect life-insurance premiums. It had become a music-hall joke by the end of the century but there was no serious use of it as a company slogan until the late 1940s, when it appeared in ads as 'Ask the Man from the Pru'.

as pleased as Punch. *Idiom.* The earliest citation for this phrase in *OED* is in a letter from Thomas Moore to Lady Donegal in 1813: 'I was (as the poet says) as pleased as Punch.'

Obviously this alludes to the appearance of Mr Punch, a character known in England from the time of the Restoration. As his face is carved on wood, it never changes expression and is always beaming. But the *Longman Dictionary of English Idioms* (1979) is wrong in attributing the *origin* of the phrase to 'the cheerful pictures of the character Punch, who appeared on the covers of *Punch* magazine in the 1840s.'

Even earlier than this, there appears to have been the expression, 'As *proud* as Punch'. A description of a visit by George III and his Queen to Wilton House in 1778 is contained in a letter from a Dr Eyre to Lord Herbert, dated 1 January 1779. He says: 'The Blue Closet within was for her Majesty's private purposes, where there was a red new velvet Close Stool, and a very handsome China Jordan, which I had the honour to produce from an old collection, & you may be sure, I am proud as Punch, that her Majesty condescended to piss in it.'

This version – 'as proud as Punch' – would now seem to have died out.

as the art mistress said to the gardener! *Catch Phrase.* 'Monica' (Beryl Reid), the posh schoolgirl friend of Archie Andrews in *EDUCATING ARCHIE* used this as an alternative to the traditional **as the Bishop said to the actress!** for turning a perfectly innocent remark into a *double entendre* (eg 'I've never seen a female "Bottom" ... as the Bishop said to the actress').

—— **as we know it.** *Format Phrase > Cliché.* 'Politics as we know it will never be the same again' – *Private Eye*, 4 December 1981.

See also END OF CIVILIZATION AS WE KNOW IT.

at, where it's. See under —— IS THE NAME OF THE GAME.

at 60 miles an hour the loudest noise in this new Rolls-Royce comes from the electric clock. *Slogan.* The best-known promotional line there has ever been for a motor car was devised not by a copywriter but came from a car test of the 1958 Silver Cloud by the technical editor of *The Motor*. David Ogilvy, who had the idea of using it in advertisement copy, recalls presenting it as a headline to a senior Rolls-Royce executive in New York who shook his head sadly and said: 'We really ought to do something about that damned clock'.

Even the anonymous motoring journalist had not been entirely original. A 1907 review of the Silver Ghost in *The Autocar* read: 'At whatever speed the car is driven, the auditory nerves when driving are troubled by no fuller sound than emanates from the 8-day clock.'

Rolls-Royce originally used (and sometimes still do), **the Best Car in the World** (current by 1929, and also quoting a journalist – in a 1908 edition of *The Times*.)

attention all shipping! *Stock Phrase*. For many years on BBC radio, the shipping (weather) forecasts were preceded by this call when rough seas were imminent. Then: 'The following Gale Warning was issued by the Meterological Office at 0600 hours GMT today . . .' (or similar).

at the end of the day. *Colloquialism > Cliché.* This must have been a good phrase once – alluding perhaps to the end of the day's fighting or hunting. It appeared, for example, in Donald O'Keeffe's 1951 song, 'At the End of the Day, I Kneel and Pray'. But it was used in epidemic quantities during the 1970s and 1980s, and was particularly beloved of trade unionists and politicians, indeed anyone wishing to tread verbal water.

Anthony Howard, a journalist, interviewing some BBC big-wig in *Radio Times* (March 1982), asked, 'At the end of the day one individual surely has to take responsibility, even if it has to be after the transmission has gone out?'

Patrick Bishop, writing in the *Observer* (4 September 1983), said: 'Many of the participants feel at the end of the day, the effects of the affair (the abortion debate in the Irish Republic) will stretch beyond the mere question of amendment.'

And, heavens, Her Majesty the Queen, opening the Barbican Centre in March 1982, also used it. But it *is* the Queen's

English, so perhaps she is entitled to do what she likes with it.

at this moment/point in time. *Colloquialism > Cliché.* Ie 'now'. Ranks with the previous entry at the top of the colloquial clichés poll. From its periphrastic use of five words where one would do, I suspect an American origin. Picked up with vigour by trade unionists in ad lib wafflings. Only occasionally to be found committed to paper – eg in R. McGowan and J. Hands, *Don't Cry for me, Sergeant Major*, 1983: 'The Marines, of course, had other ideas, but fortune was not favouring them at this moment in time.'

I once thought that clichés, to qualify as such, must have been good phrases once. But no. There was never any point to this one.

Auntie/Aunty BBC (or plain **Auntie/Aunty**). *Nickname.* The BBC was mocked in this way by newspaper columnists, TV critics and her own employees, most noticeably from about 1955 at the start of commercial television – the BBC supposedly being staid, over-cautious, prim and unambitious by comparison. A BBC spokesman countered with, 'An Auntie is often a much-loved member of the family.' The corporation assimilated the nickname to such effect that when arrangements were made to supply wine to BBC clubs in London direct from vineyards in Burgundy, it was bottled under the name *Tantine*.

In 1979, Arthur Askey suggested to me that he had originated the term during the *Band Waggon* programme as early as the late 1930s. While quite probable, the widespread use of the nickname is more likely to have occurred at the time suggested above. Wallace Reyburn in his book *Gilbert Harding – A Candid Portrayal* (1978) ascribed the phrase to the 1950s radio and TV personality. The politician Iain Macleod used it when editing the *Spectator* in the 1960s. Jack de Manio, the broadcaster, entitled his memoirs *To Auntie With Love* (1967).

average. See SMARTER THAN THE ~ BEAR.

avoid 'five o'clock shadow'. *Slogan.* The expression 'five o'clock shadow' for the stubbly growth that some dark-haired men acquire on their faces towards the end of the day would appear to have originated in adverts for Gem Razors and Blades in the US before 1939. A 1937 advert added: 'That unsightly beard growth which appears prematurely at about 5 pm looks bad.'

The most noted sufferer was Richard Nixon who may have lost the TV debates in his US presidential race against John F. Kennedy in 1960 as a result. In his *Memoirs* (1978) he wrote: 'Kennedy arrived . . . looking tanned, rested and fit. My television adviser, Ted Rodgers, recommended that I use television make-up, but unwisely I refused, permitting only a little "beard stick" on my perpetual five o'clock shadow.'

avoid —— like the plague, to. *Cliché.* Ie to avoid completely, to shun. The *OED Supp.* finds the poet Thomas Moore in 1835 writing, 'Saint Augustine . . . avoided the school as the plague'. I am told that the fourth-century St Jerome is also said to have quipped, 'Avoid as you

would the plague, a clergyman who is also a man of business.'

It may have been Arthur Christiansen, one of the numerous former editors of the *Daily Express*, who once posted a sign in the office saying: 'ALL CLICHES SHOULD BE AVOIDED LIKE THE PLAGUE.'

Avon calling! *Slogan.* First used in the US in 1886. The first Avon Lady, Mrs P.F.A. Allre, was employed by the firm's founder, D.H. McConnell, to visit customers at home and sell them cosmetics.

away. See AND AWA-A-AAY WE GO!; GET ~ FROM IT ALL; UP, UP AND AWA-A-A-AY under *SUPERMAN.*

aw, don't embarrass me! *Stock Phrase.* Ventriloquist Terry Hall (*b* 1926) first created his doll, Lenny the Lion, from a bundle of fox-fur and papier mâché – with a golf-ball for a nose – in 1954. He gave his new partner a gentle lisping voice, and added a few mannerisms and a stock phrase which emerged thus:

He's ferocious! *(drum roll)*
He's courageous! *(drum roll)*
He's the king of the jungle! *(drum roll)*
– Aw, don't embarrass me! *(said with a modest paw over one eye).*

Unusually for the originator of a successful phrase, Terry Hall told me (1979) that he made sure he didn't over-use it and rested it from time to time.

awful. See OOOH, YOU ARE ~ . . .

aye, aye, that's yer lot! *Catch Phrase.* Jimmy Wheeler (1910–73) was a Cockney comedian with a fruity voice redolent of beer, jellied eels and winkles. He would appear in a bookmaker's suit, complete with spiv moustache and hat, and play a violin. At the end of his concluding fiddle piece, he would break off his act and intone these words.

ay thang yew! See under *BAND WAGGON*.

baby. See BURN, ~, BURN!; WHO LOVES YA, ~?; YOU'VE COME A LONG WAY, ~.

backing. See I LIKE THE ~ under I'LL GIVE IT FOIVE.

backs to the wall. *Idiom* bordering on the *Cliché*. This phrase, meaning 'up against it' – which dates back to 1535, at least, according to the *OED* – was most memorably used when, on 21 March 1918, the Germans launched their last great offensive of the First World War. On 12 April, Sir Douglas Haig (1861–1928), the British Commander-in-Chief on the Western Front, issued an order for his troops to stand firm: 'Every position must be held to the last man: there must be no retirement. With our backs to the wall, and believing in the justice of our cause, each one us must fight on to the end. The safety of our Homes and the Freedom of mankind alike depends on the conduct of each one of us at this critical moment.'

A.J.P. Taylor in his *English History 1914–45* (1966) commented: 'In England this sentence was ranked with Nelson's last message. At the front, the prospect of staff officers fighting with their backs to the walls of their luxurious chateaux had less effect.'

back to square one. *Idiom.* Meaning 'back to the beginning'. This appears to have gained currency in the 1930s onwards through its use by British radio football commentators. *Radio Times* used to print a map of the football field divided into numbered squares, to which commentators would refer thus: 'Cresswell's going to make it – FIVE. There it goes, slap into the middle of the goal – SEVEN. Cann's header there – EIGHT. The ball comes out to Britton. Britton man-oeuvres. The centre goes right in – BACK TO EIGHT. Comes on to Marshall – SIX' (an extract from the BBC commentary on the 1933 Cup Final between Everton and Manchester City). The idea had largely been abandoned by 1940.

Partridge/*Catch Phrases* prefers, how-ever, an earlier origin in the children's game of hopscotch or in the board game Snakes and Ladders. The commentators may have done no more than build on this use.

back to the land. *Slogan*. The cry 'Back to the land!' was first heard at the end of the nineteenth century when it was realized that the Industrial Revolution and the transfer of the population towards non-agricultural labour had starved farming of labour. At about this time, a Wickham Market farmer wrote to Sir Henry Rider Haggard, who was making an inventory of the decline, published as *Rural England* (1902): 'The labourers "back to the land". That is the cry of the press and the fancy of the people. Well, I do not think that they will ever come back; certainly no legislation will ever bring them. Some of the rising generation may be induced to stay, but it will be by training them to the use of machinery and paying them higher wages. It should be remembered that the most intelligent men have gone: these will never come back, but the rising generation may stay as competition in the town increases, and the young men of the country are better paid.'

The *OED Supp.* cites an 1894 formula-tion of the idea, from *The Times* (25 October): 'All present were interested in the common practice that it was desir-able, if possible, to bring the people back to the land.' By 1905, the *Spectator* (23 December) was saying: ' "Back-to-the-land" is a cry full not only of pathos, but of cogency.'

In the 1980s, a TV comedy series was called *Backs to the Land*, playing on the phrase to provide an innuendo about its heroines – 'Land Girls', members of the Women's Land Army conscripted to work on the land during the Second World War (though the WLA was first established in the First World War).

bag, paper. See under COULDN'T RUN A WHELK-STALL.

Balfour must go. See —— MUST GO!

ball game. See WHOLE NEW ~.

balls. See GREAT ~ OF FIRE.

banana. See HAVE A ~.

Band Waggon. Arthur Askey (1900–82) had a good claim to be the father of the British radio catch phrase. He had such a profusion of them from *Band Waggon* onwards that he may be said to have popularized the notion that broadcast comedians were somehow incomplete *without* a catch phrase.

'There had been radio comedians before this who used catch phrases,' he told me in 1979, 'like Sandy Powell, but ours was the first show which really made a thing of them. I was the one who was on the air most and kept banging them in.'

Band Waggon was the first comedy show specifically tailored for radio – as opposed to being one made up of variety acts. The basic format was that of a ma-gazine, but the best-remembered segment was that in which Arthur shared a flat with Richard Murdoch (*b* 1907) on the top of Broadcasting House in London, bringing added meaning to the term 'resident comedians'.

A catch phrase that stayed with Askey for the rest of his life was spoken in the first edition of *Band Waggon* on 5 January 1938: **Big-hearted Arthur, that's me!** – 'I have always used this expression – even when I was at school. When playing cricket, you know, if the ball was hit to the boundary and nobody would go and fetch it – I would . . . saying "Big-hearted Arthur, that's me!"'

Another early coinage was **hello, playmates!** though, as Askey pointed out, this was originally **hello, folks!** When he used 'Hello, folks!' in the first broadcast of *Band Waggon*, he received a call from Tommy Handley telling him to lay off as the other comedian considered it to be *his* catch phrase. So, Askey changed it to 'Hello, playmates!' instead (with *Hello Playmates!* becoming the title of another of his radio shows in the mid-1950s).

Handley continued to use 'Hello, folks!' throughout *ITMA*. After which, the Goons took up the cry and gave it a strangulated delivery. Harry Secombe extended this to **hello, folks, and WHAT ABOUT THE WORKERS?!** and Eric Morecambe gave it a sexual connotation when he referred to **a touch of hello folks and what about the workers?!**

Askey's third most illustrious phrase was **ay thang yew!** – a distinctive pronunciation of 'I thank you!' picked up from the cry of London bus conductors. 'I didn't know I was saying it till people started to shout it at me.' Later, as *I Thank You*, it became the title of one of Askey's films (1941).

Other *Band Waggon* coinages included:

doesn't it make you want to spit! Askey was rapped over the knuckles for introducing this 'unpleasant expression': '[Sir John] Reith [the BBC Director-General] thought it a bit vulgar but I was in the driving seat. The show was so popular, he couldn't fire me. I suppose I said it all the more!'

happy days! Sighed by Askey and Murdoch in unison when reminiscing about their early days in the flat.

it'll be all right with a bit of doing up. Askey, clearing out the flat at the top of Broadcasting House: 'Shall we throw this out?' 'No, it'll be all right with a bit of doing up.'

light the blue touchpaper and retire immediately The firework instruction was first used on a Guy Fawkes night broadcast and subsequently when withdrawing from any confrontation with Mrs Bagwash.

serve that lady with a crusty loaf! 'Why I said that, I've no idea,' Askey told me. 'It came out of the blue when some woman was laughing very loud in the studio audience. Perhaps it goes back to the days when I used to do the shopping for my mum in Liverpool and picked it up then.'

what would you do, chums? A regular feature of *Band Waggon* was a tale told by the actor Syd Walker (1887–1945) in the character of a junkman. He would pose some everyday dilemma and end with this query – or a variation upon it. It was used as the title of a film in 1939.

you silly little man! As, for example: *Murdoch (instructing Askey how to court Nausea Bagwash, with whom*

he was supposed to be in love): You say, 'Darling Nausea, your lips are like petals ...'
Askey: Nausea, darling, your lips are like petals. Bicycle petals.
Murdoch: No, no, no, you silly little man!
The final edition of *Band Waggon* was broadcast on 2 December 1939. See also HERE AND NOW, BEFORE YOUR VERY EYES; SPEAK AS YOU FIND, THAT'S MY MOTTO.

bang. See BIG ~.

bang goes saxpence! *Catch Phrase.* The origins of this lie in a *Punch* cartoon of 1868. A Scotsman who has just been on a visit to London says: 'Mun, a had na' been the-rre abune two hours when – bang – went saxpence!' It was repopularized by Sir Harry Lauder, the professional stage Scotsman.

bang to rights. *Catch Phrase.* As in 'You've got me bang to rights!' said by a criminal to an arresting policeman, this is an alternative to 'It's a fair cop!' ('You are quite right to have caught me, constable!'). There is also an element of 'You've caught me red-handed', too. Partridge/*Slang* dates this from the 1930s, but the *OED Supp.* finds an American example in 1904.
I have always thought it a very odd, contrived expression. However, one might note the somewhat rare Americanism 'bang' for a criminal charge or arrest, as in 'it's a bum bang'. Does this have some connection with the banging of the cell door?

bank. See COME AND TALK TO THE LISTENING ~.

ban the bomb. *Slogan.* One of the simplest and best-known alliterative slogans, current in the US from 1953 and some time marginally afterwards in the UK. The Campaign for Nuclear Disarmament – whose semi-official slogan it became – was not publicly launched until February 1958. The phrase was in use by 1960. (Richard Crossman refers to 'Scrap the Bomb' in a 1957 press article.)

bark. See DOGS ~ ...

barn. See LET'S DO THE SHOW ...

Barnet. See WOGS BEGIN AT ~.

Barney. See GIVE 'IM THE MONEY, ~! under *HAVE A GO.*

bash/flog the bishop, to. *Idiom.* Meaning 'to masturbate'. Partridge/*Slang* dates this from the late nineteenth century and suggests it derives from the resemblance between the penis and a bishop in ecclesiastical mitre or a chess bishop.
It was unfortunate, therefore, that Labour MPs should have accused the Conservative minister, John Selwyn Gummer MP, of 'bishop-bashing' when he was involved in criticisms of various Anglican bishops in March 1988.
The suffix '-bashing' had been used before, of course – as in the practice of 'Paki-bashing' *c* 1970 (ie subjecting Pakistani immigrants to physical assault), and as in the old 'square-bashing' (army slang for drill).

bath, early. See under UP AND UNDER.

Batman. Batman and Robin were characters created by Bob Kane and featured in comic books for over thirty years before being portrayed by Adam West and Burt Ward in a filmed series for TV (1966–8). The putting of the prefix **Holy ——!** in exclamations was a hallmark of the programme – 'Holy flypaper!'/ 'Holy cow!'/ 'Holy schizophrenia!' etc. Also used were **quick thinking, Batman!** – a typically crawling remark from sidekick Robin – and **boy wonder!** – Batman's commendation in return.

(The subtitles 'Pow!' 'Biff!' 'Thwack!' 'Crunch!' 'Rakkk!' 'Oooofff!' and 'Bonk!' could also be said to be a kind of catch phrase.)

bats in the belfry, to have. *Idiom.* As in the simple 'bats' or 'batty', this means 'to be mad' and comes presumably from the idea of a disturbed person raving like bats disturbed by the ringing of bells. Stephen Graham wrote in *London Nights* (1925): 'There is a set of jokes which are the common property of all the comedians. You may hear them as easily in Leicester Square as in Mile End Road. It strikes the unwonted visitor to the Pavilion as very original when Stanley Lupino says of some one: "He has bats in the belfry". It is not always grasped that the expression belongs to the music-hall at large.'

Attempts have been made to derive 'batty' from the name of William Battie (1704–76), author of a *Treatise on Madness*, though this seems a little harsh, given that he was the psychiatrist and not the patient. On the other hand, there was a Fitzherbert Batty, barrister of Spanish Town, Jamaica, who made news when he was certified insane in London in 1839. I think, however, the names of these two

gentlemen merely, and coincidentally, reinforced the 'bats in the belfry' idea – though *OED Supp.* finds no example of either this term or 'batty' before 1900.

battle. See NEVER-ENDING ~ FOR TRUTH . . . under *SUPERMAN*.

BBC. See AUNTIE/AUNTY ~.

beam me up, Scotty. *Stock Phrase.* The TV science-fiction series *Star Trek* (1966–9), though short-lived, nevertheless acquired a considerable after-life through countless repeats (not least in the UK) and the activities of 'trekky' fans. It was the series whose spoken introduction proposed **to boldly go where no man has gone before!** (In one of the feature films that belatedly spun off from the series – the 1988 one – the split infinitive remained but feminism, presumably, decreed that it should be 'where no *one* has gone before'.)

Capt. Kirk (William Shatner) would say to Lt. Commander 'Scotty' Scott, the chief engineer, 'Beam me up, Scotty!' – which meant that he should transpose body into matter, or some such thing.

beans. See HOW MANY ~ MAKE FIVE?

Beanz Meanz Heinz. *Slogan.* For Heinz Baked Beans from 1967. It is the type of advertising line that drives teachers into a frenzy because it appears to condone wrong spelling. Johnny Johnson wrote the music for the jingle that went:
A million housewives every day
Pick up a tin of beans and say
Beanz meanz Heinz.
'I created the line at Young & Rubicam,' copywriter Maurice Drake told me in

1981. 'It was in fact written – although after much thinking – over two pints of bitter in the Victoria pub in Mornington Crescent.'

bear. See SMARTER THAN THE AVERAGE ~.

beat. See IF YOU CAN'T ~ 'EM . . . ; IT ~S AS IT SWEEPS . . .

beating. See WHEN DID YOU STOP ~ YOUR WIFE?

beautiful. See ~ DOWNTOWN BURBANK under *LAUGH-IN*; BLACK IS ~; BUT MISS —— YOU'RE ~; IF I SAID YOU HAD A ~ BODY; SMALL IS ~.

beautiful people, the. *Nickname.* Coinage of this term is credited in *Current Biography* (1978) to the American fashion journalist, Diana Vreeland (*c* 1903–89). Whether she deserves this or not is open to question, although she does seem to have helped launch the similar term 'Swinging London'.

The earliest *OED Supp.* citation is in the *Spectator* for 4 August 1967, with capital letters for each word. The *Supp.* makes it refer to ' "flower people", hippies' though I would prefer the 1981 *Macquarie Dictionary*'s less narrow 'fashionable social set of wealthy, well-groomed, usually young people'. The Lennon and McCartney song 'Baby You're a Rich Man' (released in July 1967) contains the line 'How does it feel to be one of the beautiful people?'

William Saroyan's play *The Beautiful People* had been performed long before all this, in 1941, and Oscar Wilde in a letter to Harold Boulton (December 1879), wrote: 'I could have introduced you to some very beautiful people. Mrs

Langtry and Lady Lonsdale and a lot of clever beings who were at tea with me.'

beauty. See AGE BEFORE ~; ME OL' ~! under *ARCHERS*.

because. See AND ALL ~ . . .

because it is there. *Catch Phrase.* As a flippant justification for doing anything, this makes use of a phrase chiefly associated with the mountaineer, George Leigh Mallory (1886–1924). He disappeared on his last attempt to scale Mount Everest. The previous year, during a lecture tour in the US, he had frequently been asked why he wanted to achieve his goal. He replied, 'Because it is there.'

In 1911, apparently, at Cambridge, A.C. Benson had urged Mallory to read Carlyle's life of John Stirling – a book that achieved high quality simply 'by being *there*'. Perhaps that is how the construction entered Mallory's mind. On the other hand, Tom Holzel and Audrey Salkeld in *The Mystery of Mallory and Irvine* (1986) suggest that 'the four most famous words in mountaineering' may have been invented for the climber by a reporter named Benson in the *New York Times* (18 March 1923).

A report in the *Observer* (2 November 1986) noted that Howard Somervell, one of Mallory's climbing colleagues in the 1924 expedition declared forty years later that the 'much-quoted remark' had always given him a 'shiver down the spine – it doesn't smell of George Mallory one bit'. Mallory's niece, Mrs B.M. Newton Dunn, claimed in a letter to the *Daily Telegraph* (11 November 1986) that the mountaineer had once given the reply to his sister (Mrs Newton Dunn's mother) 'because a silly question deserves a silly answer'.

The saying has become a catch phrase in situations where the speaker wishes to dismiss an impossible question about motives and also to express acceptance of a challenge that is in some way daunting or foolish.

There have been many variations (and misattributions). Sir Edmund Hillary repeated it regarding his own successful attempt on Everest in 1953.

Richard Ingrams of *Private Eye* once invented a reply for the Duke of Edinburgh to make to the question why he had married the Queen: 'Because she was there.'

bed. See I SHOULD OF STOOD IN BED under WE WUZ ROBBED!

Bedfordshire. See UP THE WOODEN HILL TO ~.

beef. See WHERE'S THE ~?

been. See 'AS 'E BIN IN, WHACK?

beer. See I'M ONLY HERE FOR THE ~.

beer and sandwiches at No. 10. *Idiom.* To denote the informal (and often eleventh-hour) negotiations held at senior level (and quite often at the Prime Minister's residence) between trade unionists and politicians to avert threatened strikes and stoppages. This form of negotiation only really took place under the Labour Prime Ministership of Harold Wilson (viz 1964–70, 1974–6). Nothing like it has been known under Margaret Thatcher, who has seldom if ever been known to converse with union leaders,

let alone offer them any form of hospitality.

Some called it 'pragmatism'; others viewed it less favourably. Phillip Whitehead (a one-time Labour MP) was quoted in the *Independent* (25 April 1988) as having said of Wilson that he, 'bought the hours with beer and sandwiches at No. 10 and the years with Royal Commissions'.

beers. See HEINEKEN REFRESHES THE PARTS . . .

before/as quick as one can say 'Jack Robinson'. *Idiom.* An old phrase. It appears to have been employed by Richard Brinsley Sheridan in the House of Commons (after 1780) to avoid using a fellow member's name (as was, and is partly still, the custom). Having made a derogatory reference to the Secretary to the Treasury, John Robinson, and been asked by members shouting 'Name, name' to disclose the person he was referring to, Sheridan said, 'You know I cannot name him, but I could as soon as I can say Jack Robinson.'

Clearly, Sheridan was alluding to an already established expression. Ewart cites the theory that it 'refers to an erratic [eighteenth-century] gentleman of that name who rushed around to visit his neighbours, rang the front-door bell, and then changed his mind and dashed off before the servant had time to announce his name'. Eric Partridge in his *Name Into Word* (1949) suggests that it was a made-up name using very common first and last elements.

Fanny Burney has 'I'll do it as soon as say Jack Robinson' in her novel *Evelina* (1778), so that pushes back the date somewhat. A promising explanation is that the phrase may have something to do with Sir John Robinson who was Officer Commanding the Tower of London from 1660–79. In that case, the original reference might have been to the speed of beheading with an axe (discussed in the *Observer*, 24 April 1988).

before your very eyes. See HERE AND NOW . . .

beggars. See LIKE TAKING MONEY FROM BLIND ~.

begin. See ARE YOU SITTING COMFORTABLY?; LIFE ~S AT FORTY.

behind. See ~ YOU! under OH NO, THERE ISN'T; I'M ALL ~ . . .

belfry. See BATS IN THE ~.

believed. See I'VE NEVER ~ IN ANYTHING SO MUCH . . .

believe it or not! *Catch Phrase.* This exclamation was used as the title of a long-running syndicated newspaper feature, and radio and TV series, in the US. Robert Leroy Ripley (1893–1949) created and illustrated a comic strip, *Ripley's Believe It or Not*, from c 1923 onwards. The researcher on the strip until 1975 was Norbert Pearlroth (who died aged 89 in 1983). He spent seven days a week in the New York Public Library unearthing 62,192 amazing facts and anecdotes, believe it or not.

One can't help but feel that the phrase must pre-date this specific use, but evidence is lacking.

believe only half of what you see and nothing that you hear. *Saying.* I first heard this piece of advice from an Anglican clergyman (and former padre in the Western Desert) at, oddly enough, confirmation class in 1958.

Mencken finds a much earlier quotation in *A Woman's Thoughts* by Dinah Mulock Craik (1858) where it is already described as a 'cynical saying, and yet less bitter than at first appears'. As such, it builds upon the simpler 'Don't believe all you hear' which *CODP* finds in some form before 1300, perhaps even as a proverb of King Alfred the Great's.

be like dad, keep mum. *Slogan.* (Another version was **keep mum, she's not so dumb** and showed a very un-Mum-like blonde being ogled by representatives of the three services.) It emanated from the Ministry of Information in 1941. The security theme was paramount in both the UK and US wartime propaganda. Civilians as well as military personnel were urged not to talk about war-related matters lest the enemy somehow got to hear.

belongs. See TOMORROW ~ TO ME.

bench. See NO MORE LATIN . . .

bend. See CLEAN(S) ROUND THE ~.

Bennett. See GORDON ~!

Bentley. See under *TAKE IT FROM HERE*.

be prepared. *Slogan.* The motto of the Boy Scout movement (founded 1908) had the same initials as the movement's founder Sir Robert Baden-Powell. With permission, the words were subsequently used as an advertising slogan for Pears' soap.

Bernie, the bolt! *Stock Phrase > Catch Phrase.* Some of the best popular phrases come about by accident, but according to Bob Monkhouse, who used to say this one on ATV's game *The Golden Shot*, it was carefully engineered like an industrial product. He explained in 1979: 'I dislike the notion of a conscientiously created catch phrase. The best, it appears to me, have been born spontaneously and have survived because of their multiple applications. This one broke all my own rules.

'Lew Grade had bought the Swiss-German TV success *The Golden Shot*. Jackie Rae, the original host, had to repeat one line in each show – the word of instruction to the technician to load the dangerous crossbow and simultaneously warn the studio of the fact that the weapon was armed. He said, "Heinz, the bolt!"

'When I took over in 1967 I increased the number of times he would have to load the crossbows from eight to fifteen. But a lucky chance saved me from finding fifty-seven ways of saying Heinz. Heinz went home. He stayed long enough to train an ATV technician, Derek Young. I said, " 'Derek, the bolt' sounds lousy. Let's make it alliterative. What's funny and begins with B?" Colin Clews, the producer, favoured Basil. I liked Bartholomew. We were reckoning without the man himself. Derek liked Derek. "Well, you think of a name that begins with B and won't embarrass you," I said. And Bernie it became. I found out later that his wife liked it. Certainly the audience did. Only blokes called Bernie grew to loathe it. Thousands of letters were addressed simply to "Bernie the Bolt, ITV". [The phrase stayed the same even when Derek was replaced by another technician.]

'I spoke the magic three little words for the last time on 13 April 1975. At a conservative estimate I had said them on network TV no less than 2500 times. On a May night in 1979 I found written in the dust on my car outside a Nottingham cabaret club, "BERNIE THE BOLT LIVES!" '

At one time, viewers watching the programme at home could ring and instruct the operator to aim the gun. Hence: **Left a bit, – stop! Down a bit, – stop! Up a bit, – stop! Fire!** This acquired a kind of catch phrase status, not least because of the possible *double entendre*.

be soon! See under SHE KNOWS, YOU KNOW!

best. See AND THE ~ OF LUCK!; ~ CAR IN THE WORLD under AT 60 MILES AN HOUR . . . ; EVEN YOUR ~ FRIENDS . . . ; I ALWAYS DO MY ~. . . under *ITMA*; PROBABLY THE ~ LAGER . . . ; YOU WANT THE ~ SEATS . . .

best possible taste. See IT'S ALL DONE . . .

better red than dead. *Saying* – with some of the force of a *Slogan*. Used by some (mainly British) nuclear disarmers. Bertrand Russell wrote in 1958: 'If no alternative remains except communist domination or the extinction of the human race, the former alternative is the lesser of two evils.' The counter cry, 'Better dead than red' may also have had some currency.

(In the 1964 film *Love With a Proper Stranger*, Steve McQueen proposed to Natalie Wood with a picket sign stating, 'Better Wed Than Dead'.)

Betty. See OOH, ~!

bet you can't eat just one. *Slogan.* Lay's potato chips used this in the US (quoted in 1981). By 1982, **bet you can't eat three** was being used by the cricketer Ian Botham to promote Shredded Wheat in the UK.

bet your sweet bippy. See under *LAUGH-IN.*

Beulah, peel me a grape! *Catch Phrase.* This expression of dismissive unconcern was first uttered by Mae West to a black maid in the film *I'm No Angel* (1933) after a male admirer had stormed out on her. It has had some wider currency since then but is perhaps, really, always used as a quotation.

bewdy Newk! *Catch Phrase.* Translated from the Australian, this means 'What a beauty, Newcombe!', referring to the tennis player, John Newcombe. **Life. Be in it** was the slogan of a campaign which began in the State of Victoria and then spread across Australia in the late 1970s, aiming to get people involved in healthy activities like tennis. One TV commercial showed 'Norm', a fat armchair sportsman (or 'couch potato', as he would later have been described), watching Newcombe and cheering him on with the phrase.

Beyond Our Ken. Kenneth Horne (1900–69) was a bald, benign and urbane figure who had little of show business about him. He was not a stand-up comedian. He seemed to have drifted into the radio studio from a busy life elsewhere as a company director (and until ill-health forced him to choose broadcasting instead of business, this might well have been the case).

From 1958–64, Horne presided over a radio show called *Beyond Our Ken.* This was basically a sketch show, scripted by Eric Merriman and Barry Took, and performed by some able supporting actors. One of these was Kenneth Williams (1926–88) who created a professional countryman figure with a loam-rich voice (perhaps based on Ralph Wightman or A.G. Street) and called 'Arthur Fallowfield' who appeared in an *Any Questions* spoof. **I think the answer lies in the soil** was his comment on every problem. He also had the lament, **I'm looking for someone to love.** In addition, Williams played an ancient gentleman who, when asked how long he had been doing anything, would reply, forthrightly, **thirty-five years!**

In the same show, Hugh Paddick played 'Cecil Snaith', a hush-voiced BBC outside broadcasts commentator. After some disaster in which he had figured, he would give, as the punchline, in a deadpan manner, **and with that, I return you to the studio!** Kenneth Horne apparently suggested the line. In its straight form, many TV and radio news reporters use the phrase in live spots even today.

Paddick and Williams also played two frightfully correct types who would greet each other with: **Hello, Rodney!/Hello, Charles!**

B.F.N. – bye for now! See under MORNING ALL!

big. See HE WAS A ~ MAN . . . ; MR ~.

Big Bang, the. *Nickname.* On 27 October 1986, the London Stock Exchange deregulated the British securities market in a move to which this light-hearted appellation was applied by those hoping for a 'boom' and fearing a 'bust' (which duly followed a year later).

The system of fixed commissions on stock trading was eliminated in favour of negotiated rates. At the same time, the practice of separating brokers (who take orders and execute trades on behalf of investors) from jobbers (who buy and sell stock on their own account in order to make a market in that stock) was abolished (information from *Time*, 25 August 1986).

The previous March, banks and brokerages, domestic and foreign, were allowed to become members of the exchange in a move dubbed 'Little Bang'.

Clearly, this 'Big Bang' echoes the so-called 'Big Bang' theory of the beginning of the universe – which by 1950 was being discussed by Fred Hoyle in his book *The Nature of the Universe*. Longman/ *Register* points out that the general metaphorical use of 'big bang', so derived, predates the specific application to deregulation in the City. It defines the phrase as, 'a fundamental and far-reaching set of changes introduced as a single package rather than piecemeal or gradually'.

Big Brother is watching you. *Catch Phrase*. From a fictional *Slogan*, in George Orwell's novel *Nineteen Eighty-Four* (1948). In a dictatorial state, every citizen is regimented and observed by a spying TV set in the home. The line became a popular catch phrase following the BBC TV dramatization of the novel in 1954 (which caused a sensation).

A possible source? Aspects of the Ministry of Truth in the novel were derived not only from Orwell's knowledge of the

BBC (where he worked) but also from his first wife, Eileen's work at the Ministry of Food, preparing 'Kitchen Front' broadcasts during the Second World War, *c* 1942–4. One campaign used the slogan 'Potatoes are Good for You' and was so successful that it had to be followed by 'Potatoes are Fattening'.

Big Chill generation, the. *Nickname*. Popular phrases coined on one side of the Atlantic are so frequently picked up on the other that it is the exceptions which are remarkable. Reading about Douglas Ginsburg's rejected nomination as a member of the US Supreme Court in *Time* (16 November 1987) I was puzzled by the following: 'Although Ginsburg's indiscretion may have been common among members of the Big Chill generation, his confessions fatally undermined his support among the Capitol Hill conservatives who had lobbied so hard for his nomination.'

What was this 'Big Chill generation'? Had it something to do with the cooling of the earth's temperature, the New Ice Age, and – if it did – why should one generation be so dubbed? Turning up the *Washington Post* for 1 August 1985, I came across: 'A performance by the Temptations or the Four Tops is always a big thrill for the "Big Chill" generation.' Note the quotation marks. So it was a synonym for 'sixties people'.

The answer is that in 1983 a film was released called *The Big Chill* – 'the story of eight old friends searching for something they lost, and finding that all they needed was each other'. It employed the slogan 'In a cold world you need your friends to keep you warm'. Halliwell called it 'a wry satirical comedy which seems to be nostalgic for the sixties . . . the movie was too American to become an international hit' – which may explain why neither the film nor the phrase cut much ice on this side of the Atlantic.

bigger. See CLOUD NO ~ THAN A MAN'S HAND; THIS THING IS ~ THAN BOTH OF US.

big-hearted Arthur, that's me! See under *BAND WAGGON*.

big money! See under LOADSAMONEY!

big one, the. *Nickname/Slogan.* This boast, beloved – in particular – of a certain type of advertiser, almost certainly dates back to 1907 when, in the US, Ringling Brothers Circus bought up its rival, Barnum and Bailey. The two together were billed, understandably, as 'The Big One'. When the outfit closed in 1956, the *New York Post* had the headline, 'THE BIG ONE IS NO MORE!'

DOAS points out that a 'big one' is also a thousand dollar bill (from gambling) and a nursery euphemism for a bowel movement. Partridge/*Slang* has 'big one' or 'big 'un' for 'a notable person' and dates it to 1800–50.

bike. See MIND MY ~; ON YOUR ~.

Bill. See BUNGALOW ~.

Billy. See SILLY ~.

bippy. See YOU BET YOUR SWEET ~ under *LAUGH-IN*.

bird. See IT'S A ~ under *SUPERMAN*.

birdie. See WATCH THE ~.

bishop. See AS THE ~ SAID under AS THE ART MISTRESS . . . ; BASH THE ~; DO YOU KNOW THE ~ OF NORWICH?

Bisto. See AHH, ~!

bit. See LEFT A ~ under BERNIE, THE BOLT!

black. See YOUNG, GIFTED AND ~.

black-coated workers. *Nickname.* For prunes as laxatives. This was popularized in the 1940s by the Radio Doctor (Charles Hill) who noted in his autobiography *Both Sides of the Hill* (1964): 'I remember calling on the Principal Medical Officer of the Board of Education . . . At the end of the interview this shy and solemn man diffidently suggested that the prune was a black-coated worker and that this phrase might be useful to me. It was.'

black is beautiful. *Slogan.* The Rev. Dr Martin Luther King Jr launched a poster campaign based on these words in 1967 but Stokely Carmichael had used the phrase at a Memphis civil rights rally in 1966. It may have its origins in the Song of Solomon 1:5, 'I am black, but comely.'

black mark, Bentley! See under *TAKE IT FROM HERE*.

black power. *Slogan.* Encompassing just about anything that people want it to mean, from simple pride in the Black race to a threat of violence. Adam Clayton Powell Jr, the Harlem congressman, said in a baccalaureate address at Howard University in May 1966: 'To demand these God-given rights is to seek black power – what I call audacious power – the power to build black institutions of splendid achievement.'

On 6 June the same year, James Meredith, the first Black to integrate the University of Mississippi (in 1962), was shot and wounded during a civil rights march. Stokely Carmichael, heading the Student Non-violent Coordinating Committee, continued the march, during which his contingent first used the phrase as a shout. Carmichael used it in a speech at Greenwood, Mississippi, the same month. It was also adopted as a slogan by the Congress for Racial Equality. However, the notion was not new in the 1960s.

Langston Hughes had written in *Simple Takes a Wife* (1953): 'Negro blood is so powerful – because just *one* drop of black blood makes a coloured man – *one* drop – you are a Negro! . . . Black is powerful.'

blind. See LIKE TAKING MONEY FROM ~ BEGGARS.

Blitz. See IT WAS WORSE THAN THE ~.

blonde bombshell. *Nickname* – and a journalistic *Cliché* now. Used to describe any blonde woman of dynamic personality, usually a film star, show business figure, or model. The original was Jean Harlow who appeared in the 1933 film *Bombshell*. In Britain – presumably so as not to suggest that it was a war film – the title was changed to *Blonde Bombshell*.

blow one's own trumpet, to. *Idiom.* Meaning 'to boast of one's own achievements', this is sometimes said to have originated with the statue of 'Fame' on the parapet of Wilton House, near Salis-

bury. The figure – positioned after a fire in 1647 – originally held a trumpet in each hand.

This is pushing it a bit. Why does one need a precise origin for such an obvious phrase? On the other hand, the *OED Supp.* cannot find a use earlier than 1854. Brewer states that the 'allusion is to heralds, who used to announce with a flourish of trumpets the knights who entered a list'.

Lord Beaverbrook used to say that, if you did not blow your own trumpet, no one else would do it for you (quoted in the *Observer*, 12 March 1989).

blow some my way. *Slogan.* Used, from 1926 (some would say suggestively) when a woman made her first appearance in US cigarette advertising. The brand was Chesterfield.

blow the whistle on, to. *Idiom > Cliché.* Meaning 'to call a halt to something by exposing it' (alluding to the police use of whistles). The *OED Supp.* finds a 1934 use in P.G. Wodehouse. More recently, the *Listener* of 3 January 1980 reported: 'English as she is murdered on radio became an issue once more. Alvar Lidell stamped his foot and blew the whistle in the *Listener*.' Sir Robert Armstrong was quoted in the *Observer* (2 March 1986) as saying: 'I do not think there could be a duty on a civil servant to blow the whistle on his Minister.'

blue. See ENOUGH ~ TO . . . ; LIGHT THE ~ TOUCHPAPER under *BAND WAGGON*.

blue pencil, to. *Idiom.* In the BBC wartime radio series *Garrison Theatre* (first broadcast 1939), Jack Warner as 'Private

Warner' helped further popularize this well-established synonym for censorship (the *OED Supp.*'s first citation is an American one from 1888). In reading blue-pencilled letters from his brother at the Front, expletives were deleted ('not blue pencil likely!') and Warner's actual mother boasted that, 'My John with his blue pencil gag has stopped the whole nation from swearing.'

In his autobiography, Warner recalled a constable giving evidence at a London police court about stopping 'Mr Warner', a lorry driver. The magistrate inquired, 'Did he ask what the blue pencil you wanted?' 'No, sir,' replied the constable, 'this was a different Mr Warner . . .'

B.O. See BODY ODOUR.

BOAC takes good care of you (all over the world). *Slogan.* For British Overseas Airways Corporation, from 1948, and adapted when the airline changed its name to British Airways to **we'll take more care of you**. Japan Air Lines began to say they would take 'Good care of you, too' but were persuaded to drop the line, although they had used the punning **love at first flight** a dozen years before BOAC took up the slogan. In its time, BA has ranged from the patriotic **fly the flag**, through **try a little VC 10derness** (echoing the song 'Try a Little Tenderness'(1933), to **the world's favourite airline** (still current in 1989).

Bob's your uncle!, and. *Catch Phrase.* Meaning 'And there you are/there you have it!'/ 'All will be well'/ 'It's as simple as that' – an almost meaningless expression of the type that takes hold from time to time. It was current by the 1880s but doesn't appear to be of any hard and fast origin. It is basically a British expression – and somewhat baffling to Americans. There is the story of one such who went into a London shop, had it said to him, and exclaimed, 'But how did you know – I do have an Uncle Bob!?'

In 1886, Arthur Balfour was appointed Chief Secretary for Ireland by his uncle, Robert Arthur Talbot Gascoyne-Cecil, 3rd Marquis of Salisbury, the Prime Minister. Is that where the phrase came from, as some people fervently believe?

body. See IF I SAID YOU HAD A BEAUTIFUL ~ . . . ; YOU, TOO, CAN HAVE A ~ LIKE MINE.

body odour (or **B.O.**) *Slogan.* A notable phrase given to the language by advertising. The new, worrying concept was used to promote Lifebuoy soap, initially in the US, and was current from 1933. On American radio in the 1930s, they used to sing the jingle:

Singing in the bathtub, singing for joy,
Living a life of Lifebuoy -
Can't help singing, 'cos I know
That Lifebuoy really stop B.O.

The initials 'B.O.' were sung *basso profundo*, emphasizing the horror of the offence. In the UK, TV ads showed pairs of male or female friends out on a spree, intending to attract partners. When one of the pair was seen to have a problem, the other whispered helpfully, 'B.O.'

bogey man. See HUSH, HUSH, HUSH, HERE COMES THE ~.

bold. See OOH, BOLD! under *ROUND THE HORNE*.

boldly go, to. See under BEAM ME UP, SCOTTY.

bolt. See BERNIE, THE ~!

bomb. See BAN THE ~.

bombshell. See BLONDE ~.

Booboo. See SMARTER THAN YOUR AVERAGE BEAR.

book. See ANOTHER PAGE TURNED IN THE ~ OF LIFE; EVERYBODY HAS ONE ~ IN THEM; READ ANY GOOD ~S. LATELY? under *MUCH BINDING IN THE MARSH*.

book 'em, Danno! *Stock Phrase.* From the American TV series *Hawaii Five-O* (1968–80). On making an arrest, Det. Steve McGarrett (Jack Lord) would say to Det. 'Danno' Williams (James MacArthur), 'Book 'em, Danno!' – adding 'Murder One' if the crime required that charge.

boom, boom! *Catch Phrase.* The verbal underlining to the punchline of a gag. Ernie Wise suggested to me (1979) that it was like the drum-thud or trumpet-sting used, particularly by American entertainers, to point a joke. Music-hall star Billy Bennett (1887–1942) may have been the first to use this device, in the UK, to emphasize his comic couplets. The *MORECAMBE AND WISE SHOW*, Basil Brush, and many others, took it up later.

born 1820 – still going strong. *Slogan.* Johnnie Walker whisky has used this line since 1910. There *was* a John Walker but he was not born in 1820 – that was the year he set up a grocery, wine and spirit business in Kilmarnock. In 1908, Sir Alexander Walker decided to incorporate a portrait of his grandfather in the firm's advertising. Tom Browne, a commercial artist, was commissioned to draw the firm's founder as he might have appeared in 1820. Lord Stevenson, a colleague of Sir Alexander's, scribbled the phrase 'Johnnie Walker, born 1820 – still going strong' alongside the artist's sketch of a striding, cheerful Regency figure. It has been in use ever since.

born yesterday. See I WASN'T ~.

boss, boss, sumpin' terrible's happened! See under *ITMA*.

bottle. See MILK'S GOTTA LOTTA ~.

bound. See WITH ONE ~ HE WAS FREE.

bountiful. See LADY ~.

Bovril prevents that sinking feeling. *Slogan.* On H.H. Harris's cheery poster of a pyjama-clad man astride a jar of Bovril (meat extract) at sea, this line first appeared in 1920. However, the slogan was born in a golfing booklet issued by Bovril in 1890 which included the commendation: 'Unquestionably, Bovril . . . supplies . . . the nourishment which is so much needed by all players at the critical intermediate hour between breakfast and luncheon, when the *sinking feeling* engendered by an empty stomach is so distressing, and so fruitful of deteriorated play.' It is said that Bovril had intended to use the phrase earlier but withheld it because of the *Titanic* disaster of 1912. With updated illustrations, it lasted until 1958.

Heading from the *Independent* (12 April 1989): 'Crucible challenge for a champion [Steve Davis, snooker player] who thinks rivals under the table before relishing that sinking feeling'.

box. See OPEN THE ~.

boy wonder! See under *BATMAN*.

bra. See BURN YOUR ~!; I DREAMED I . . .

bracing. See IT'S SO ~.

bracket. See PUNCH UP THE ~ under HAN-COCK'S HALF-HOUR.

brandy-y-y-y! under GOON SHOW.

bread. See GREATEST THING SINCE SLICED ~.

break a leg! *Catch Phrase*. A traditional theatrical greeting before a performance, especially a first night. It is supposed to be bad luck to wish anyone 'good luck' directly.

Partridge/*Slang* has 'to break a leg' as 'to give birth to a bastard', dating from the seventeenth century, but that is probably unconnected. As also is the fact that John Wilkes Booth, an actor, broke his leg after assassinating President Lincoln in a theatre.

Morris passes on a suggestion that it is based on a German good luck expression, *Hals-und-Beinbruch* [May you break your neck and your leg – lit. neck-and-bone-break]. Perhaps this entered theatrical speech (like several other expressions) via Yiddish?

Theatrical superstition is understandable, I suppose, in a profession so dependent on luck. However, the euphemism **the Scottish play**, invariably used for Shakespeare's *Macbeth*, is based on a well-documented history of bad luck

associated with productions of the play. Merely to utter the name of the play would thus be to invoke misfortune.

breakfast of champions. Slogan. Has been used to promote Wheaties breakfast cereal in the US, since 1950 at least. In the 1980s, a series of ads featuring sporting champions showed 'Jackie Robinson – one of the greatest names in baseball . . . this Dodgers star is a Wheaties man: "A lot of us ball players go for milk, fruit and Wheaties," says Jackie . . . Had *your* Wheaties today?'

Kurt Vonnegut used the phrase as the title of a novel (1973).

brewery. See under COULDN'T RUN A WHELK-STALL.

brick(s) short of a full load. See under FEW VOUCHERS.

bride. See OFTEN A BRIDESMAID . . .

bright. See ALWAYS MERRY AND ~.

Britain. See KEEP ~ TIDY.

Britain can take it. *Slogan*. During the Second World War, slogans rained down upon the hapless British as profusely as German bombs. The Ministry of Information, in blunderbuss fashion, fired away with as much material as possible in the hope of hitting something. Some of the slogans were brilliant, others were quite the reverse – hence the Ministry's abandonment of 'Britain can take it' in December 1941.

'While the public appreciated due recognition of their resolute qualities,' wrote Ian McLaine in *Ministry of Morale*

(1979), 'they resented too great an emphasis on the stereotyped image of the Britisher in adversity as a wise-cracking Cockney. They were irritated by the propaganda which represented their grim experience as a sort of particularly torrid Rugby match.'

The notion was resurrected by Winston Churchill in May 1945 in a tribute to Cockney fortitude: 'No one ever asked for peace because London was suffering. London was like a great rhinoceros, a great hippopotamus, saying: "Let them do their worst. London can take it." London could take anything.'

British justice. See THIS HAS RESTORED MY FAITH . . .

broken. See IF IT AIN'T ~.

bronzed. See LOOKING ~ AND FIT.

brother. See BIG ~.

brown. See DON'T SAY ~ . . . ; HOW NOW, ~ COW?

brownie points, to earn/win. *Idiom.* Originating in American business (I expect), this has nothing to do with Brownies, the junior branch of the Girl Guides, and the points they might or might not gain for doing their 'good deed for the day'. Oh no! This has a scatological origin, not unconnected with brown-nosing, brown-tonguing, arse-licking and other unsavoury methods of sucking up to someone important.

Note also the American term 'Brownie', an award for doing something *wrong*. According to *DOAS*, 'I got a pair of Brownies for that one' (1942) refers to a system

of disciplinary demerits on the railroads. The word was derived from the inventor of the system.

brush. See DAFT AS A ~.

buck stops here, the. *Saying.* President Truman had a sign on his desk bearing these words, indicating that the Oval Office was where the passing of the buck had to cease. It appears to be a saying of his own invention. 'Passing the buck' is a poker player's expression. It refers to a marker that can be passed on by someone who does not wish to deal. Later, Jimmy Carter restored Truman's motto to the Oval Office.

When President Nixon published his memoirs (1978), people opposed to its sale went around wearing buttons which said, 'The book stops here'.

Buggins's turn. *Idiom.* Buggins's turn is an appointment made because it is somebody's turn to receive it rather than because the person is especially well-qualified to do so. The name Buggins is used because it sounds suitably dull and humdrum. The earliest recorded use of the phrase is by Admiral Fisher, later First Sea Lord, in a letter of 1901. Later, in a letter of 1917 (printed in his *Memories*, 1919), he said: 'Some day the Empire will go down because it is Buggins's turn.' It is impossible to say whether Fisher coined the phrase, though he spoke and wrote in a colourful fashion.

But what do people with the name Buggins think of it? In February 1986, a Mr Geoffrey Buggins was reported to be threatening legal action over a cartoon which had appeared in the London

Standard. It showed the husband of Margaret Thatcher looking through the New Year's Honours List and asking, 'What did Buggins do to get an MBE?' She replies: 'He thought up all those excuses for not giving one to Bob Geldof' (the popstar and fund-raiser who only later received an Honorary KBE).

The real-life Mr Buggins (who had been awarded an MBE for services to export in 1969), said from his home near Lisbon, Portugal: 'I am taking this action because I want to protect the name of Buggins and also on behalf of the Muddles, Winterbottoms and the Sillitoes of this world.'

The editor of the *Standard* said: 'We had no idea there was a Mr Buggins who had the MBE. I feel sorry for his predicament, but if we are to delete Buggins's turn from the English language perhaps he could suggest an alternative.'

bull. See COCK AND ~ STORY; LIKE A RED RAG TO A ~.

bullet. See FASTER THAN A SPEEDING ~ under *SUPERMAN*.

bumper bundle, a. See under *FAMILY FAVOURITES*.

Bungalow Bill. *Nickname*. This was applied to a man called Bill Wiggins who achieved a certain amount of media fame in 1987/8 simply for being an amour of Joan Collins. 'The Continuing Story of Bungalow Bill' (a joke upon 'Buffalo Bill', of course) was the title of a Lennon and McCartney song (1968). However, it was explained that Mr Wiggins was so called because he did not have much up top.

Burbank. See THIS IS BEAUTIFUL DOWNTOWN ~ under *LAUGH-IN*.

burn, baby, burn! *Slogan*. A Black extremists' slogan that arose from the August 1965 riots in the Watts district of Los Angeles when thirty-four people were killed and entire blocks burnt. (The 1974 hit song by Hudson-Ford with this title had other connotations.)

burn your bra! *Slogan*. A feminist slogan from America c 1970, encouraging women to destroy an item of apparel quite clearly designed by a male chauvinist and likely to make a woman more of a sex object. The analogy is with the burning of draft-cards as a protest against the Vietnam War.

Burton. See GONE FOR A ~.

buses. See NEVER CHASE GIRLS OR ~.

business as usual. *Slogan*. The standard declaration when a shop has suffered some misfortune like a fire or is undergoing alterations. However, in the First World War the phrase was adopted in a more general sense. H.E. Morgan (later Sir Herbert Morgan) was an advertising man working for W.H. Smith & Sons. He promoted this slogan which had quite a vogue until it was proved to be manifestly untrue and hopelessly inappropriate. Morgan was an advertising consultant to H. Gordon Selfridge, the store owner, who also became associated with the slogan. On 26 August 1914, Selfridge said, ' "Business as usual" must be the order of the day.' In a Guildhall speech on 9 November, Winston Churchill said, 'The maxim of the British people is "Business as usual".'

busy. See AS BUSY AS . . .

but I'm all right now. See under *ITMA*.

butler. See WHAT THE ~ SAW.

butler did it! the. *Catch Phrase*. I have drawn an almost complete blank over the origins of this phrase as (an often ironic) suggested solution to detective stories of the – I suppose – 1920s and 30s. However, a correspondent did recall hearing it spoken by a member of the audience after a showing of the last episode of the film series *The Exploits of Elaine* at a London cinema in *c* 1916. Joseph R. Sandy told me (1983): 'The detective was called Craig Kennedy and the butler's name was Bennet. I do not remember who played the parts (except the heroine, who was Pearl White) or anything much more about the serial.'

So perhaps the phrase was current by that date. But why did it enter common parlance? One of the conventions of who-dunnit writing of the period we are talking about is that the butler or servants seldom, if ever, do 'do it'. Father Ronald Knox, compiling a list of rules for this kind of fiction in his introductions to *The Best Detective Stories of the Year, 1928*, noted: 'The only person who is really scratch on morals is the aged butler. I cannot off-hand recall any lapse of virtue on the part of a man who has been with the family for sixteen years. But I may be wrong; I have not read all the detective stories.'

The earliest use of the phrase I can give chapter and verse for is the film *My Man*

Godfrey (1957 – not the 1936 original) which is not even a whodunnit: 'The butler did it! He made every lady in the house, oh, so very happy!'

Alan Melville remembered (1983): 'Years ago, a repertory actor up in Scotland ruined every available Agatha Christie or other crime drama by saying the line straight out to the audience when he was slightly pissed – "No need to wait to the end, the butler did it." He was sacked, poor soul, but the sad thing is that the week he got his cards the play he was appearing in, however unsteadily, was one in which the butler really did do it.'

The Georgette Heyer thriller *Why Shoot a Butler?* (1933) manages to avoid any mention of the phrase. It became the title of an instrumental number written, and performed on drums, by Frank Butler – natch – in 1958.

but Miss ——, you're beautiful! *Cliché*. Of the cinema. Uttered by the boss when his hitherto bespectacled secretary reveals her true charms. I can't cite an actual example, but feel that Cary Grant was probably around at the time.

butter. See CAN YOU TELL STORK FROM ~?

buy. See STOP ME AND ~ ONE.

buy some for Lulu. See WOTALOTIGOT.

bye for now. See under MORNING ALL!

by half. See TOO CLEVER ~.

by hook or by crook. *Idiom*. 'By hook or by crook I'll be last in this book' is the cliché you append to the final page of an autograph book when asked to contribute a little something more than your signature. But why 'hook' and 'crook', apart from the rhyme? The *OED*, while finding a couple of references in the works of John Wycliffe around 1380, states firmly that while there are many theories, there is no firm evidence for the origin of the phrase.

In fact, the only theory is the one about peasants in feudal times being allowed only to take for firewood those tree branches which they could pull down 'by hook or by crook'. 'Crook' here meaning the hooked staff carried by shepherds (and also, symbolically, by bishops).

Brewer quotes the *Bodmin Register* (1525): 'Dynmure wood was ever open and common to the . . . inhabitants of Bodmin . . . to bear away upon their backs a burden of lop, crop, hook, crook, and bag wood.' Ewart, without giving a source, claims a precise origin in the granting of a right to collect wood in this way to a certain Purkiss, charcoal burner in the New Forest, at the time of William Rufus's death in 1100.

by jingo! *Catch Phrase.* Now a mild and meaningless oath, the phrase derived its popularity from G.W. Hunt's notable anti-Russian music-hall song 'We Don't Want to Fight' of 1877:

> We don't want to fight, but by Jingo if we do,
> We've got the ships, we've got the men, and got the money too,
> We've fought the Bear before, and while we're Britons true,
> The Russians shall not have Constantinople.

The song gave the words 'jingo' and 'jingoism' their modern meaning, but the oath had existed long before. Motteux in his version of Rabelais in 1694 put 'by jingo' for *'par dieu'* and there is some evidence to show that 'jingo' was conjuror's gibberish dating from a decade or two before.

by Jove, I needed that! *Catch Phrase.* Used, as though after long-awaited alcoholic refreshment, by several comedians. Ken Dodd has said it after a quick burst on the banjo, to relieve tension. It also appeared in the GOON SHOW.

cage. See PLAY THE MUSIC ... under MUM, MUM, THEY ARE LAUGHING AT ME.

Calabash. See GOODNIGHT, MRS ~.

Calais. See under WOGS BEGIN AT BARNET.

calamity. See OH, ~!

calibre. See A MAN OF MY ~ under *HANCOCK'S HALF-HOUR*.

call. See DON'T ~ US ... ; THEY ~ ——.

calling. See AVON ~!

calling all cars, calling all cars! *Catch Phrase.* From American cops and robbers films and TV series of the 1950s. What the police controller says on the radio to patrolmen. For some reason, the archetypal cop phrase of the period, and evo-

cative. However, the formula had obviously been known before this if the British film titles *Calling All Stars* (1937), *Calling All Ma's* (1937) and *Calling All Cars* (1954) are anything to go by.

Calvins. See YOU KNOW WHAT COMES BETWEEN ME AND MY ~?

Camay. See YOU'LL LOOK A LITTLE LOVELIER ...

came. See THEY ~ ... ; THIS IS WHERE WE ~ IN.

can a (bloody) duck swim! (sometimes **does/will a fish swim!**) *Idiom/Catch Phrase.* Meaning 'you bet!', 'of course what you say is to my liking'. *ODP* has 'Will a duck swim?' in 1842. The earliest use I have come across of the 'can' version is by Winston Churchill, who claimed he said it to Stanley Baldwin when Baldwin asked if he would accept the post of Chancellor of the Exchequer in the 1924 government. Lady Violet Bonham-Carter used Churchill's own phrase *to* him when he asked her to serve as a Governor of the BBC in 1941. Thence he proceeded to refer to her as his 'Bloody Duck' and she had to sign her letters to him, 'Your B.D.'

Candid Camera. See SMILE, YOU'RE ON ~.

can dish it out but can't take it in, (s)he. *Catch Phrase/Idiom.* Said of people who can't take the sort of criticism they dispense to others. A reader's letter to *Time* (4 January 1988) remarked of comedienne Joan Rivers's action in suing a magazine for misquoting her about her late husband: 'For years she has made big money at the expense of others with her caustic remarks. Obviously Rivers can dish it out but can't take it in.'

I think this is the basic form of the phrase. In the film *49th Parallel* (1941), Raymond Massey as a Canadian soldier apparently plays with the phrase when he says to a Nazi, 'When things go wrong, we can take it. We can dish it out, too.'

can I do you now, sir? *Catch Phrase.* One of the great catch phrases – from *ITMA*. Said by 'Mrs Mopp' (Dorothy Summers), the hoarse-voiced charlady or 'Corporation Cleanser', when entering the office of Tommy Handley, as the Mayor. Curiously, the first time Mrs Mopp used the phrase, on 10 October 1940, she said, 'Can I do *for* you now, sir?' This was soon replaced by the familiar emphases of 'Can I *do* you *now*, sir?' that people can still be heard using today.

Bob Monkhouse recalled (1979) Dorothy Summers saying: 'Oh, I do wish people wouldn't expect me to be only Mrs Mopp. That awful char. I never wanted to say it in the first place. I think it was rather distasteful.' She seems to have been the only person to detect any double meaning in it.

can you hear me, mother? *Catch Phrase.* 'It was in about 1932/3,' Sandy Powell, the comedian (1900–82), told me in 1979, 'when I was doing an hour's show on the radio, live, from Broadcasting House in London. I was doing a sketch called "Sandy at the North Pole". I was supposed to be broadcasting home and wanting to speak to my mother. When I got to the line, "Can you hear me, mother?" I dropped my script on the studio floor. While I was picking up the sheets all I could do was repeat the phrase over and over. Well, that was on a Saturday night. The following week I was appearing at the Hippodrome, Coventry, and the manager came to me at the band rehearsal with a request: "You'll say that, tonight, won't you?" I said, "What?" He said, " 'Can you hear me, mother?' Everybody's saying it. Say it and see." So I did and the whole audience joined in and I've been stuck with it ever since. Even abroad – New Zealand, South Africa, Rhodesia, they've all heard it. I'm not saying it was the first radio catch phrase – they were all trying them out – but it was the first to catch on.'

can *you* tell Stork from butter? *Slogan.* For Stork margarine, from *c* 1956. One of the earliest slogans on commercial TV, it invariably was alluded to in parodies of TV advertising. In the original ads, housewives were shown taking part in comparative tests and tasting pieces of bread spread with real butter and with Stork.

car. See BEST ~ IN THE WORLD under AT 60 MILES AN HOUR . . . ; CALLING ALL ~S; HOLE HEALS UP. . . . ; WOULD YOU BUY A USED ~ . . .

caravan. See DOGS BARK . . .

carborundum. See ILLEGITIMI NON ~.

care. See BOAC TAKES GOOD ~ OF YOU; TENDER LOVING ~.

cared. See AS IF I ~.

careful. See IF YOU CAN'T BE GOOD . . . .

carelessness kills. See KEEP DEATH OFF THE ROAD.

carry on, London! See IN TOWN TONIGHT.

Casbah. See COME WITH ME TO THE ~.

cash. See IN GOD WE TRUST . . .

cash/ throw in one's chips/checks, to. Idiom – verging on the Cliché. Meaning, originally, to stop gambling. But then 'to die', and, as DOAS has it: 'To terminate a business transaction, sell one's share of, or stock in, a business, or the like, in order to realize one's cash profits.'
It also may mean 'to make a final gesture' – Tom Mangold wrote in the Listener (8 September 1983), concerning the US arms race in space: 'Under malign command, a technological guarantee of invulnerability could induce the holder

to cash his chips and go for a pre-emptive first strike.'

cast of thousands, with a. Slogan. Now only used jokingly and ironically, this type of film promotion line may have made its first appearance in connection with the 1927 version of Ben Hur where the boast was, 'Cast of 125,000'!

cat, one-legged. See under AS BUSY AS . . .

Cecil. See AFTER YOU, CLAUDE . . .

Central Casting. See STRAIGHT OUT OF ~.

century. See —— OF THE ~.

champions. See BREAKFAST OF ~.

chance. See under AS BUSY AS . . . ; NO MORE ~ THAN A SNOWBALL IN HELL.

change. See NEVER SWAP HORSES IN MID-STREAM; WIND OF ~; YOU MUST HAVE SEEN A LOT OF ~.

changed. See ONLY THE NAMES HAVE BEEN ~ under DRAGNET.

charge. See I'M IN ~.

Charles, hello. See under BEYOND OUR KEN.

Charley. See CLAP HANDS, HERE COMES ~.

Charlie. See PROPER ~.

Charlie Farnsbarns. Nickname. Denoting a twit whose name one can't remember. Noting that this moderately well-known expression had passed by Partridge and his reviser, Paul Beale, I mentioned it to

Beale in November 1985, suggesting that it sounded military to me, even pre-Second World War, though I had heard the comedian Ronnie Barker use it in a monologue quite recently. He came back with: 'Charlie Farnsbarns was a very popular equivalent of eg "Mrs Thing" or "Old Ooja", ie "Old whatsisname". Much play was made with the name in MUCH BINDING IN THE MARSH, but whether Murdoch and Horne actually invented it, or whether they borrowed it "out of the air", I'm afraid I don't know. They would mention especially, I remember, a magnificent motorcar called a "Farnsbarns Special" or something like, say, a "Farnsbarns Straight Eight". This was in the period, roughly, 1945–50, while I was at school – I recall a very jolly aunt of mine who was vastly amused by the name and used it a lot.'

I suspect it came out of the services (probably RAF) in the Second World War. Denis Gifford, incidentally, in *The Golden Age of Radio* (1985), says the name was used by 'Sam Costa in *Merry-Go-Round* (1946)' – but the RAF edition of that show was the forerunner of MUCH BINDING IN THE MARSH.

A 'Charlie' (as in PROPER CHARLIE, RIGHT CHARLIE) was a slightly derogative name to apply to anyone. 'Farnsbarns' has the numbing assonance needed to describe a bit of a nonentity.

chattering classes, the. *Nickname.* For those newspaper journalists and broadcasters who are paid to discuss topics of current interest, the opinion-formers, but also those who simply like to discuss current events. I don't know when it was first used but I do know when I first registered the phrase. In the *Observer* (4

August 1985), Alan Watkins wrote: 'At the beginning of the week the *Daily Mail* published, over several days, a *mélange* of popular attitudes towards Mrs Thatcher. Even though it contained little that was surprising or new, it was much discussed among the chattering classes.'

Then the following weekend (on 11 August), a *Sunday Times* editorial went thus: 'The BBC and the weather have been the only two stories in town this silly season. But the outlook for British broadcasting is actually rather cheery, despite all the wailing and gnashing of teeth among the chattering classes.'

cheap. See PILE IT HIGH . . .

checks. See CASH ONE'S ~.

cheeky monkey! See under RIGHT MONKEY!

cheerful. See IT'S BEING SO ~ under *ITMA*.

cheerful Charlie. See PROPER CHARLIE.

cheers. See CUP THAT ~.

chew gum. See HE CAN'T FART AND ~ . . .

chicken. See IS THAT A ~ JOKE under *LAUGH-IN*.

chiefly, yourselves! See under YOUR OWN, YOUR VERY OWN!

children. See GOODNIGHT ~ EVERYWHERE; NEVER WORK WITH ~ OR ANIMALS; WOMEN AND ~ FIRST.

chill. See BIG ~ GENERATION.

Chinese. See DAMN CLEVER THESE ~ under *GOON SHOW*; OUT OF YOUR TINY ~ MIND.

chips. See CASH ONE'S ~.

chips with everything. *Catch Phrase.* Arnold Wesker's play with this title was about class attitudes in the RAF during National Service and was first performed by the English Stage Company at the Royal Court Theatre, London, in 1962. The title, I take it, alluded to the belief that the working classes tend to have chips as the accompaniment to almost any dish. Indeed, the play contains the line: 'You breed babies and you eat chips with everything.'

Partridge/*Catch Phrases* dates it *c* 1960 and says the phrase has 'been applied to that sort of British tourist abroad which remains hopelessly insular' – though I'm not sure whether that says it all.

I have come across 'Declaration', written in 1957 by the film director Lindsay Anderson, which states: 'Coming back to Britain is always something of an ordeal. It ought not to be, but it is. And you don't have to be a snob to feel it. It isn't just the food, the sauce bottles on the cafe tables, and the *chips with everything* [my italics]. It isn't just saying goodbye to wine, goodbye to sunshine . . . We can come home. But the price we pay is high.'

chocolate kettle. See under AS BUSY AS . . .

Christmas. See —— SHOPPING DAYS TO ~.

Christmas has come early this year. *Idiom > Cliché.* Meaning, 'we have had some welcome [usually, financial] news'. Beginning a report in the *Guardian* (8 April 1988), Michael Smith wrote of the

Volvo purchase of the Leyland Bus operation: 'Christmas has come early for management and staff at Leyland Bus, the sole UK manufacturers of buses which changed hands last week' – they stood to enjoy a windfall of £19 million.

The previous week, Lord Williams had said of another sale – that of Rover to British Aerospace: 'Christmas has come rather early this year.'

One wonders just how late in the year the phrase may safely be employed?

chums. See WHAT WOULD YOU DO, ~? under *BAND WAGGON*.

cigarette. See AH, WOODBINE . . .

Cinderella. See under COULD MAKE ANY ORDINARY GIRL . . .

circle. See WHEEL HAS COME FULL ~.

circumstances. See DUE TO ~ . . .

circus. See IF YOU CAN'T RIDE TWO HORSES . . .

city. See THIS IS THE CITY under *DRAGNET*.

civilization. See END OF ~ . . .

clanger. See DROP A ~.

Clapham omnibus. See MAN ON THE ~.

clap hands, here comes Charley. *Catch Phrase.* This apparently nonsensical catch phrase, popular at one time in Britain, appears to derive from its use in the signature tune of Charlie Kunz (1896–1958). Born in America, Kunz became a feathery-fingered, insistently-rhythmic pianist popular on British radio in the 1930s/40s.

The song went, 'Clap hands, here comes Charley . . . here comes Charley now.' With lyrics by Billy Rose and Ballard Mac-Donald, and music by Joseph Meyer, it was recorded in the US in 1925.

According to *The Book of Sex Lists*, the song was written 'in honour of a local chorine, first-named Charline, who had given many of the music publishers' contact men (song pluggers) cases of gonor-rhoea – a venereal disease commonly known as "the clap" '.

According to Partridge/*Slang*, 'to do a clap hands Charlie' was 1940s RAF slang for flying an aircraft in such a way as to make the wings seem to meet overhead.

classes. See CHATTERING ~.

classic. See IT WENT FROM FAILURE TO ~ . . .

Claude. See AFTER YOU, ~.

clean. See IT BEATS AS IT SWEEPS . . . ; MR ~.

clean(s) round the bend. *Slogan/Idiom.* Harpic lavatory cleaner used this line from the 1930s onwards, but it is not the origin of the idiom 'round the bend', meaning 'mad'. The *OED Supp.* cites F.C. Bowen in *Sea Slang* (1929) as defining it thus: 'an old naval term for anybody who is mad'.

clear. See I WANT TO MAKE IT PERFECTLY ~.

clever. See DAMN ~, THESE CHINESE under *GOON SHOW*; TOO ~ BY HALF.

click. See CLUNK, ~, EVERY TRIP.

clock. See under COULD MAKE ANY ORDINARY GIRL . . .

clockwork. See QUEER AS A ~ ORANGE.

clogs. See POP ONE'S ~.

closed. See I WENT TO NEW ZEALAND BUT . . . ; WE NEVER ~.

close encounter of the —— kind, a. *Format Phrase.* Following the title of the Steven Spielberg film *Close Encounters of the Third Kind* (1977), said to be taken from the categories used by the American services to denote UFOs. A 'close encounter 1' would be a simple UFO sighting; a 'close encounter 2' would be evidence of an alien landing; and a 'close encounter 3' would be actual contact with aliens. The categories were devised by a UFO researcher called J. Allen Hyhek (source: Rick Meyers, *The Great Science Fiction Films*).

Used allusively to describe intimacy: 'For a close encounter of the fourth kind, ring **** '; 'Polanski's new movie – Close Encounters with the Third Grade' – graffiti, quoted 1982.

closes. See ONE DOOR ~ . . .

closet. See OUT OF THE ~ . . .

close your eyes and think of England. *Catch Phrase.* The source that Partridge/*Catch Phrases* gives for this saying – in the sense of advice to women when confronted with the inevitability of sexual intercourse, or jocularly to either sex about doing anything unpalatable – is the *Journal* (1912) of Alice, Lady Hillingdon: 'I am happy now that Charles calls on my bedchamber less frequently than of old. As it is, I now endure but two calls a week and when I hear his steps outside my door I lie down on my bed, close my eyes, open my legs and think of England.'

There *was* an Alice, Lady Hillingdon (1857–1940). She married the 2nd Baron in 1886. He was Conservative MP for West Kent (1885–92) and, according to *Who's Who*, owned 'about 4500 acres' when he died (in 1919). A portrait of Lady Hillingdon was painted by Sir Frank Dicksee PRA in 1904. I believe the rose 'Climbing Lady Hillingdon' may have been named after her.

But where her journals are, if they were ever indeed published, I have not been able to discover.

Salome Dear, Not With a Porcupine (ed. Arthur Marshall, 1982) has it instead that the newly-wedded Mrs Stanley Baldwin was supposed to have declared: 'I shut my eyes tight and thought of the Empire.' I think we may discount Bob Chieger's assumption in *Was It Good for You, Too?* (1983) that 'Close your eyes and think of England' was advice given to Queen Victoria on her wedding night.

Sometimes the phrase occurs in the form 'lie back and think of England' but I think this comes from confusion with SHE SHOULD LIE BACK AND ENJOY IT.

clothes. See MOST FUN YOU CAN HAVE . . .

cloud no bigger than a man's hand, a. *Idiom*. When something is this, it is not yet very threatening – as though a man could obliterate a cloud in the sky by holding his hand between his face and it. In a letter to Churchill on 14 December 1952, Bob Boothby MP wrote of a dinner

at Chartwell: 'It took me back to the old care-free days when I was your Parliamentary Private Secretary, and there seemed to be no cloud on the horizon; and on to the fateful days when the cloud was no bigger than a man's hand, and there was still time to save the sum of things.'

clowns. See SEND IN THE ~.

clunk, click, *every* trip. *Slogan*. Accompanied by the sound of a car door closing and seat-belt being fastened, used as a slogan in road safety ads featuring Jimmy Savile from 1971. In 1979, someone wrote the slogan on a museum cabinet containing a chastity belt.

c'mon Colman's, light my fire. *Slogan*. For Colman's mustard, current 1979. A clear lift of the title of the Doors/Jim Morrison song '(Com' On, Baby,) Light My Fire' (1967) and used to accompany the picture of a voluptuous woman on a tiger rug.

coach and horses. See DRIVE A ~ THROUGH . . .

coat. See ALL FUR ~ . . . under ALL KID GLOVES; I WON'T TAKE MY ~ OFF . . .

cock and bull story, a. *Idiom*. Meaning a long, rambling, unbelievable one. The phrase is used notably in Laurence Sterne's *Tristram Shandy* (1760–7). The last words of the novel are: 'L—d! said my mother, what is all this story about? — A COCK and a BULL, said Yorick — And one of the best of its kind, I ever heard.'

Other suggested origins are that the phrase comes from: old fables in general which have animals talking, going right back to Aesop – confirmed perhaps by the equivalent French phrase '*coq à l'âne*' (lit. 'cock to donkey') – someone who hated having to listen to such fables was probably the first to dub them as such; Samuel Fisher's 1660 story about a cock and a bull being transformed into a single animal – which people may have thought pretty improbable; somehow from the Cock and Bull public houses, which are but a few doors apart in Stony Stratford, Buckinghamshire; generally confused tales told first in one pub, the Cock, and then retold in another, the Bull.

The *OED Supp.*'s earliest citation in this precise form is from the Philadelphia *Gazette of the United States* (1795): 'a long cock-and-bull story about the Columbianum' (a proposed national college).

cock a snook, to. *Idiom.* A snook is the derisive gesture made with thumb and hand held out from the nose. 'To take a sight' is a variation. Both were known by the mid-nineteenth century, indeed *OED* has 'cock snooks' in 1791. The game of 'snooker' derives its name not from this, but rather from the military nickname for a raw recruit.

cocoa. See GRATEFUL AND COMFORTING . . . ; I SHOULD ~.

cold. See —— WHO CAME IN FROM THE ~.

Colman's. See C'MON ~, LIGHT MY FIRE.

come. See YOU KNOW WHAT ~S BETWEEN ME AND MY CALVINS?; YOU'VE ~ A LONG WAY . . .

come alive – you're in the Pepsi generation. *Slogan.* In use in this form since 1964. The worldwide spread of the soft drinks Coca-Cola and Pepsi Cola has given rise to some difficulties in translating their slogans. It is said that 'Come alive with Pepsi' became in German, 'Come alive out of the grave,' and, in Chinese, 'Pepsi brings your ancestors back from the dead'.

When Coca-Cola started advertising in Peking, **put a smile on your face** was translated as 'Let Your Teeth Rejoice'. Odder still, the famous slogan **it's the REAL THING** came out as 'The Elephant Bites the Wax Duck'.

come and talk to the listening bank. *Slogan.* Used by the Midland Bank, from 1980. A slogan that turned sour when a twenty-one year old was *arrested* when she went to see her Midland manager about her overdraft.

come back. See I GO – I ~ under *ITMA*.

come back ——, all is forgiven. See under WHERE ARE THEY NOW?

come hell and/or high water. *Idiom.* Ie 'come what may'. This is mentioned in Partridge/*Slang* as a cliché but, as phrases go, is curiously lacking in citations. The *OED Supp.* finds no examples earlier than this century. And I have to admit defeat, too. *Come Hell or High Water* was used as the title of a book by yachtswoman Clare Francis in 1977 – she followed it in 1978 with *Come Wind or Weather. Hell and High Water* was the title of an American film in 1954.

Graeme Donald in *Today* (26 April 1986) linked it to punishments meted out to witches in the Middle Ages: 'Lesser transgressions only warranted the miscreant being obliged to stand in boiling water, the depth of which was directly proportional to the crime. Hence the expression "From Hell and high water, may the good Lord deliver us".'

This is rather fanciful, I think. Perhaps he was thinking of the so-called Thieves' Litany – 'From Hull, Hell and Halifax, good Lord deliver us' (because the gibbet was much used in these places in the sixteenth and seventeenth centuries)?

come on down! *Stock Phrase*. In the American TV consumer game *The Price is Right* (1957–), the host would appear to summon contestants from the studio audience by saying '[name], come on down!' This procedure was reproduced when the quiz was broadcast on ITV from 1984–8, with Leslie Crowther uttering the words.

come up and see me sometime. *Catch Phrase*. Mae West (1892–1980) had a notable stage hit on Broadway with her play *Diamond Lil* (first performed 9 April 1928). When she appeared in the 1933 film version entitled *She Done Him Wrong*, what she said to a very young Cary Grant (playing a coy undercover policeman) was: 'You know I always did like a man in uniform. And that one fits you grand. Why don't you come up some time and see me? I'm home every evening.'

As a catch phrase, the words have been rearranged to make them easier to say. That is how W.C. Fields says them *to* Mae West in the film *My Little Chickadee* (1939), and she herself took to saying them in the rearranged version.

come with me to the Casbah. *Catch Phrase*. A line forever associated with the film *Algiers* (1938) and its star, Charles Boyer. He is supposed to have said it to Hedy Lamarr. Boyer impersonators used it, the film was laughed at because of it, but nowhere is it said in the film. It was simply a Hollywood legend that grew up. Boyer himself denied he had ever said it and thought it had been invented by a press agent.

comfortably. See ARE YOU SITTING ~ . . . ?

comforting. See GRATEFUL AND ~ . . .

commandment. See ELEVENTH ~.

comment. See NO ~.

completely. See AND NOW FOR SOMETHING ~ DIFFERENT.

complexion. See KEEP THAT SCHOOLGIRL ~.

continong, sur le. See under MORNING ALL!

control. See DUE TO CIRCUMSTANCES . . .

cookie-wise. See THAT'S THE WAY IT CRUMBLES, ~.

cool as a mountain stream. *Slogan*. For Consulate (menthol) cigarettes, from the early 1960s.

cop. See I'M A ~ under *DRAGNET*.

coughs and sneezes spread diseases. *Slogan*. This was a Ministry of Health warning from *c* 1942, coupled with the line, 'Trap the germs in your handkerchief'.

could make any ordinary girl feel like a princess. *Cliché*. (Compare, could make you feel like Cinderella before the clock struck.) A testament to male prowess of one sort or another, though perhaps more likely to occur to journalists than mere mortals.

In February 1983, the Press Council reported on the curious case of Miss Carol Ann Jones and the *News of the World*. Miss Jones had been quoted as having said that Peter Sutcliffe, the Yorkshire Ripper, 'could make any ordinary girl from a mill town feel like a princess. Even now I have a place in my heart for him.'

The Press Council felt that 'some words attributed to her as direct quotations were ones she was unlikely to have used.'

couldn't run a whelk-stall. *Idiom*. This pleasantly obscure way of describing incompetence appears – until an earlier instance turns up – to have originated with John Burns, the Labour MP. In the *South-Western Star* for 13 January 1894 he is quoted as saying: 'From whom am I to take my marching orders? From men who fancy they are Admirable Crichtons ... but who have not got sufficient brains and ability to run a whelk-stall?'

Partridge/*Slang* has 'no way to run a whelk-stall' as the British equivalent of the US '[that's] a hell of a way to run a railroad' (see WHAT A WAY TO RUN A——), and dates it 'later C20'. The phrases couldn't organize a piss-up in a brewery and couldn't fight his/her way out of a paper bag are as likely, or more likely, to be employed nowadays.

country. See COUNTRY DUNNY under AS BUSY AS ... ; GOD'S OWN ~; THIS IS A FREE ~; YOUR ~ NEEDS YOU.

courting. See ARE YER COURTIN'? under *HAVE A GO*.

cow. See HOW NOW, BROWN ~; I'M ALL BEHIND ...

crackle. See SNAP! ~! POP!

crazy like a fox. *Catch Phrase*. Ie 'apparently crazy but with far more method than madness' (Partridge/*Catch Phrases*). Craziness is hardly a quality one associates with foxes, so the expression was perhaps merely formed in parallel with the older 'cunning as a fox'.

But foxes always seem to get into expressions like these. Interviewing the actress Judy Carne in 1980, I asked about Goldie Hawn, her one-time colleague on *Laugh-In*. Carne said: 'She's not a dizzy blonde. She's about as *dumb* as a fox. She's incredibly bright.'

Crazy Like a Fox was the title of a US TV series about a 'sloppy old private eye' and his 'smart lawyer son' (from 1984). Before that, it was used as the title of a book by S.J. Perelman (1945).

crazy, man, crazy! See GO, MAN, GO!

credit. See PLEASE DO NOT ASK FOR ~ ...

crikey. See NO LIKEY? OH, ~! under *ITMA*.

crook. See BY HOOK OR BY ~.

crown. See JEWEL IN THE ~.

crumbles. See THAT'S THE WAY IT ~ ...

crusty loaf. See SERVE THAT LADY WITH A ~ ... under *BAND WAGGON*.

cup that cheers, the. *Nickname*. For tea, in preference to alcohol. In William Cowper's *The Task* (1783), it's in the plural:

Now stir the fire, and close the shutters fast,
Let fall the curtains, wheel the sofa round,
And, while the bubbling and loud-hissing urn
Throws up a steamy column, and the cups,
That cheer but not inebriate, wait on each,
So let us welcome peaceful ev'ning in.
'The Winter Evening'

Partridge lists 'cups that cheer but not inebriate' as a cliché in his dictionary of same, and notes that in *Siris* (1744), Bishop Berkeley had earlier said of tar water that it had a nature 'so mild and benign and proportioned to the human constitution, as to warm without heating, to cheer but not inebriate'. Not a cliché now, just a pleasant archaism.

cure. See DOCTOR GREASEPAINT WILL ~ ME.

customer is always right, the. *Saying* – verging on the *Cliché*. H. Gordon Selfridge (1856–1947) was an American who, after a spell with Marshall Field & Co. came to Britain and introduced the idea of the monster department store. It appears that he was the first to say 'the customer is always right' and many another phrase now generally associated with the business of selling through stores.

See also —— SHOPPING DAYS TO CHRISTMAS.

cut off at the pass, to. *Idiom*. One of the milder sayings to have emerged from the transcripts of the Watergate tapes (published as *The White House Transcripts*, 1974) was 'to cut something/someone off at the pass'. This was a re-cycled phrase from Western films where the cry would be uttered, meaning 'to intercept, ambush'. As said by President Nixon it meant simply 'we will use certain tactics to stop them'. The phrase occurred in a crucial exchange in the White House Oval Office on 21 March 1973 between the President and his Special Counsel, John Dean:

P: You are a lawyer, you were a counsel ... What would you go to jail for?
D: The obstruction of justice.
P: The obstruction of justice?
D: That is the only one that bothers me.
P: Well, I don't know. I think that one ... I feel it could be cut off at the pass, maybe, the obstruction of justice.

cuts. See DEATH OF A THOUSAND ~.

Cyril. See NICE ONE, ~!

D

dad. See BE LIKE ~ . . . ; I'LL 'AVE TO ASK ME ~ under *ITMA*.

daddy, what did *you* do in the Great War? *Slogan > Catch Phrase.* This line was used on recruiting posters in the First World War. The accompanying picture showed an understandably appalled family man puzzling over what to reply to the daughter on his knee. It became a catch phrase in the form, WHAT DID *YOU* DO IN THE GREAT WAR, DADDY? and gave rise to such responses as 'Shut up, you little bastard. Get the Bluebell and go and clean my medals' (Partridge/*Catch Phrases*). *What Did You Do in the War, Daddy?* was the title of a film (US, 1966).

daft. See EE, AIN'T IT GRAND TO BE ~.

daft as a brush. *Catch Phrase.* Adapted from the northern expression 'soft as a brush' by the comedian Ken Platt. Said Ken in 1979, 'I started saying daft as a brush when I was doing shows in the Army in the 1940s. People used to write and tell me I'd got it wrong!' (Partridge/*Slang* suggests that 'daft . . .' was in use before this, however.)

See also I WON'T TAKE ME COAT OFF . . .

damage. See WHAT'S THE DAMAGE?

damn(ed) clever these Chinese! See under *GOON SHOW*.

dancing. See THERE'LL BE ~ IN THE STREETS TONIGHT.

dangerous age, the. *Idiom.* The title of an early (and very mild) Dudley Moore film comedy of 1967 was *Thirty Is a Dangerous Age, Cynthia.* This would seem to allude, however distantly and unknowingly, to *Den farlige alder* (The dangerous age), a book in Danish by Karin Michaelis (1910). In that case, the dangerous age was forty.

In the Moore film, as far as I can recall, it was very important for him to write a musical, or perhaps get married, before he was thirty. I think, however, that the 'dangerous age' can be more than one. It might be said of teenagers first encountering the opposite sex, 'Well, that's the dangerous age, of course' as much as it might be said of married folk experiencing the SEVEN YEAR ITCH.

Danno. See BOOK 'EM, ~.

dark. See KEEP IT ~; TALL, ~ AND HANDSOME; THEY ALL LOOK THE SAME IN THE ~.

darken. See NEVER ~ MY DOOR AGAIN.

darlings. See HELLO, MY ~.

daughter. See IT'S NOT FOR ME, IT'S FOR MY ~.

day. See AT THE END OF THE ~; GO AHEAD, MAKE MY ~; HAVE A NICE ~; P.O.E.T.S.' ~; QUEEN FOR A ~; WHAT A DIFFERENCE A ~ MAKES; HAPPIEST ~S OF YOUR LIFE; TODAY IS THE FIRST ~ . . .

day war broke out, the. *Catch Phrase.* From the radio monologues of Robb Wilton (1881–1957): 'The day war broke out . . . my missus said to me, "It's up to you . . . you've got to stop it." I said, "Stop what?" She said, "The war." ' Later, when circumstances changed, it became 'the day *peace* broke out'.

dead. See BETTER RED THAN ~; DROP ~; QUEEN ANNE'S ~; WHEN I'M ~ under THERE'LL NEVER BE ANOTHER!

dead as a door-nail, as. *Idiom.* In the Middle Ages, the door-nail was the knob on which the knocker struck: 'As this is frequently knocked on the head, it cannot be supposed to have much life in it' (Brewer). The phrase occurs as early as 1350, then in 1362 in Langland's *Piers Plowman* ('And dead as a door-nail'). Shakespeare uses it a couple of times, in the usual form and, as in *The Second Part of King Henry IV* (V.iii.117):

Falstaff: What, is the old king dead!
Pistol: As nail in door!

Dickens uses the phrase in *A Christmas Carol* (Stave i): 'Old Marley was as dead as a door-nail.'

dead parrot. *Idiom.* Meaning 'something that is quite incapable of resuscitation'. This expression derives from the most famous of all the MONTY PYTHON'S FLYING CIRCUS sketches (first shown on 14 December 1969) in which a man who has just bought a parrot that turns out to be dead, registers a complaint with the pet shop owner in these words: 'This parrot is no more. It's ceased to be. It's expired. It's gone to meet its maker. This is a late parrot. It's a stiff. Bereft of life it rests in peace. It would be pushing up the daisies if you hadn't nailed it to the perch. It's rung down the curtain and joined the choir invisible. It's an ex-parrot.'

In early 1988, there were signs of it becoming an idiom when it was applied to a controversial policy document drawn up as the basis for a merged Liberal/Social Democratic Party. Then the *Observer* commented (8 May 1988): 'Mr Steel's future – like his document – was widely regarded as a "dead parrot". Surely this was the end of his 12-year reign as Liberal leader?' Whether the phrase will have much further life, ONLY TIME WILL TELL.

Compare SICK AS A PARROT under OVER THE MOON.

death. See HIS ~ DIMINISHES US ALL; KEEP ~ OFF THE ROAD; KISS OF ~.

death of/by a thousand cuts. *Idiom.* Meaning 'the cumulative effect of sniping, rather than of one big blow'. I am not sure where this came from originally – bull-fighting? The earliest citation the *OED Supp.* has to offer is from 1974. In February 1989, Robert Runcie, Archbishop of Canterbury, told the General Synod: 'If the Government does not take the axe to the BBC, there is surely here the shadow of death by a thousand cuts.'

deed. NO GOOD ~ GOES UNPUNISHED.

deeply regret any embarrassment/ inconvenience caused. *Cliché.* Of apology. The standard apology goes something like: 'British Rail apologizes for the late running of this train and for any inconvenience that may have been caused' (never mind the pain of having to listen to the apology being trotted routinely out).

Incidentally, when giving apologies it is important never to be explicit as to the cause. If trains arrive late it is 'because of late departure' (but no apology for that); at airports, planes are late taking off 'because of the late arrival of the incoming plane'. Or, in other words, things happen – or, rather, don't happen, 'for operational reasons'.

Lt Col Sitiveni Rabuka, leader of a coup in Fiji (May 1987) was quoted as saying,

'We apologize for any inconvenience caused.'

degrades. See THIS AD INSULTS WOMEN.

deliberate. See DID YOU SPOT . . . ?

depends. See IT ALL ~ WHAT YOU MEAN BY . . .

deserting. See LIKE RATS ~ A SINKING SHIP.

desperation, pacification, expectation, acclamation, realization – 'it's Fry's'. *Slogan.* Ads for Fry's chocolate for many years after the First World War featured the faces of five boys anticipating a bite.

despondency. See SPREADING ALARM AND ~.

deviation. See WITHOUT HESITATION . . .

diamond. See DOUBLE ~ WORKS WONDERS.

diamond is forever, a. *Slogan.* In 1939, the South African-based De Beers Consolidated Mines launched a campaign to promote further the tradition of diamond engagement rings. The N.W. Ayer agency of Chicago (copywriter B.J. Kidd) came up with this line.

It passed easily into the language, having an almost proverbial ring. Anita Loos in *Gentlemen Prefer Blondes* (1925) had enshrined something like the idea in: 'Kissing your hand may make you feel very, very good but a diamond and safire bracelet lasts for ever.' Ian Fleming gave a variation of the phrase as the title of his 1956 James Bond novel *Diamonds are Forever*.

Technically speaking, however, they are not. It takes a very high temperature, but, being of pure carbon, diamonds *will* burn.

Dick. See SAY GOODNIGHT, ~ under *LAUGH-IN*.

dicky bird. See WATCH THE BIRDIE.

did I ever tell you about the time I was in Sidi Barrani? See under *MUCH BINDING IN THE MARSH*.

didn't he do well? See under *GENERATION GAME*.

did the earth move for you? *Catch Phrase*. Jokily addressed to one's partner after sexual intercourse, this appears to have originated as 'Did thee feel the earth move?' in Ernest Hemingway's *For Whom the Bell Tolls* (1940). I have not been able to find it in the 1943 film version, however. Headline from the *Sport* (22 February 1989): 'SPORT SEXCLU-SIVE ON A BONK THAT WILL MAKE THE EARTH MOVE'.

did you spot this week's deliberate mistake? *Stock Phrase > Catch Phrase*. As a way of covering up a mistake that was *not* deliberate, this expression arose from the BBC radio series *Monday Night at Seven* (later *Eight*) in *c* 1938. Ronnie Waldman had taken over as deviser of the 'Puzzle Corner' part of the programme which was presented by Lionel Gamlin. 'Through my oversight a mistake crept into "Puzzle Corner" one night,' Wald-man recalled in 1954, 'and when Broad-casting House was besieged by telephone callers putting us right, Harry Pepper [the producer] concluded that such "lis-tener participation" was worth exploiting

as a regular thing. "Let's always put in a deliberate mistake," he suggested.'

Waldman revived the idea when he himself presented 'Puzzle Corner' as a part of *Kaleidoscope* on BBC Television in the early 1950s and the phrase 'this week's deliberate mistake' has continued to be used jokingly as a cover for inepti-tude.

die. See EAT, DRINK AND BE MERRY . . . ; NEVER SAY ~; OLD SOLDIERS NEVER ~ . . .

difference. See WHAT A ~ A DAY MAKES.

different. See AND NOW FOR SOMETHING COM-PLETELY ~.

dig for victory. *Slogan*. Shortage of food-stuffs was an immediate concern in the UK upon the outbreak of the Second World War. On 4 October 1939, Sir Regi-nald Dorman Smith, the Minister of Agri-culture, broadcast these words: 'Half a million more allotments, properly worked, will provide potatoes and veget-ables that will feed another million adults and one and a half million children for eight months out of twelve . . . So, let's get going. Let "Dig for victory" be the motto of everyone with a garden and of every able-bodied man and woman ca-pable of digging an allotment in their spare time.'

A poster bearing the slogan showed a booted foot pushing a spade into earth. Consequently, the number of allotments rose from 815,000 in 1939 to 1,400,000 in 1943.

dim. See MY EYES ARE ~.

dirty. See YOU ~ ROTTEN SWINE, YOU! under GOON SHOW; YOU ~ RAT.

discontent. See WINTER OF ~.

discovered. See I THOUGHT —— UNTIL I ~.

discussing Ugandan affairs. *Idiom.* In *Private Eye* No. 293 (9 March 1973), there appeared a gossip item which launched a euphemism for sexual intercourse: 'I can reveal that the expression "Talking about Uganda" has acquired a new meaning. I first heard it myself at a fashionable party given recently by media-people Neal and Corinna Ascherson. As I was sipping my Campari on the ground floor I was informed by my charming hostess that I was missing out on a meaningful confrontation upstairs where a former cabinet colleague of President Obote was "talking about Uganda".

'Eager, as ever, to learn the latest news from the Dark Continent I rushed upstairs to discover the dusky statesman "talking about Uganda" in a highly compromising manner to vivacious former features editor, Mary Kenny . . . I understand that "Long John" and Miss Kenny both rang up later to ascertain each other's names.'

Later, references to 'Ugandan practices' or 'Ugandan discussions' came to be used – though whether far beyond the readership of *Private Eye*, I doubt. In a letter to *The Times* (13 September 1983), Corinna Ascherson (now signing herself Corinna Adam) identified the coiner of the phrase as the poet and critic James Fenton. She also claimed that the phrase had been included in 'The Oxford Dictionary of

Slang', whatever that might be. It is not in Partridge/*Slang*.

Richard Ingrams (editor of *Private Eye* at the time) added the interesting, er, footnote in the *Observer* (2 April 1989) that the original Ugandan was 'a one-legged former Minister in President Obote's Government. When the *New Statesman* found out that the *Eye* was going to refer to the incident, representations were made to the effect that the Minister, on the run from Obote, would be in danger if identified. The detail of the wooden leg was therefore omitted, but the expression passed into the language.'

As a further, er, footnote, Nicholas Wollaston wrote to the *Observer* (9 April 1989) and pointed out that the one-legged performer *wasn't* on the run from President Obote but 'the much-loved chairman of the Uganda Electricity Board, also of the Uganda Red Cross, and an exile for seven years from the tyranny of Idi Amin. When he died in 1986, it was reported that 10,000 people attended his funeral . . . and a memorial service at St Martin-in-the-Fields was packed with his friends, among them several who remembered their discussions on Uganda with him, the artificial limb notwithstanding, with much pleasure.'

diseases. See COUGHS AND SNEEZES . . .

disgusted, Tunbridge Wells. *Stock Phrase? > Catch Phrase.* When it was announced in February 1978 that a Radio 4 programme was to be launched with the title *Disgusted, Tunbridge Wells* (providing a platform for listeners' views on broadcasting), there was consternation in the Kent township (properly,

Royal Tunbridge Wells). The title was intended to evoke the sort of letter fired off to the press between the wars when the writer did not want to give his/her name – 'Mother of Three', 'Angry Rate-payer', 'Serving Policeman', etc. Tunbridge Wells has long been held as the source of reactionary, blimpish views. Derek Robinson, the presenter of the programme while disliking its title, told me (1989): 'Why Tunbridge Wells was considered to be stuffier than, say, Virginia Water or Maidenhead, I don't know. It's just one of those libels, like tightfisted Aberdeen, that some places get lumbered with.'

The *Kent Courier* (24 February 1978) reported the 'disgust' that the 'Disgusted' label had stirred up in the town. Some people interviewed thought the tag had originated with Richard Murdoch in MUCH BINDING IN THE MARSH in which 'he made much use of his connections with the town' and was always mentioning it. I think someone else suggested that the phrase – capturing a certain type of outraged tone of voice – might equally have arisen in TAKE IT FROM HERE. Can the phrase ever have been seriously used, however? That is why I hesitate to call it a *Stock Phrase*. Earlier citations are lacking.

dish. See CAN ~ IT OUT . . .

disposition. See NOT SUITABLE FOR THOSE . . .

diver. DON'T FORGET THE ~.

doc. See WHAT'S UP, ~?

doctor. See IS THERE A ~ IN THE HOUSE?

Doctor Greasepaint/Theatre will cure me. *Saying.* I do not know how widespread use of this expression is in the world of the theatre. Both versions were quoted in obituaries for the actress Irene Handl in November 1987 as a phrase used by her. It suggests that acting is not only a cure for ailments, but also implies that actors have to be well most of the time to perform their function.

dodgy! *Catch Phrase.* Rather as the upper classes tend to rely on two adjectives – 'fascinating' and 'boring' so, too, did the comedian Norman Vaughan (*b* 1927) in the 1960s. Accompanied by an upward gesture of the thumb, his **Swinging!** was the equivalent of upper-class 'fascinating' and (with a downward gesture of the thumb) his 'Dodgy!', the equivalent of 'boring'. Norman told me in 1979: 'The words "swinging" and "dodgy" came originally from my association with jazz musicians and just seemed to creep into everyday conversation. Then when I got the big break at the Palladium [introducing ITV's *Sunday Night at the London Palladium* in 1962] they were the first catch phrases that the papers and then the public seized upon.'

According to *The Making of the Prime Minister 1964* by Anthony Howard and Richard West, the Labour Party considered using the word 'swinging' with an upraised thumb as the basis of its advertising campaign prior to the 1964 General Election. However, doubts were expressed whether everyone would get the allusion and only the thumb was used. Although not, of course, the first person to use the word, Norman's use of 'swinging' helped to characterize an era – the SWINGING SIXTIES.

During his Palladium stint he also introduced the format phrase, **a touch of the** —— ('A touch of the Nelson Riddles' etc.) Later, he had a TV series called *A Touch of the Norman Vaughans*. This was established by May 1965 when I entitled an undergraduate revue at Oxford *A Touch of the Etceteras* ('The Etceteras' being a hoped-for Oxford equivalent of the Cambridge Footlights).

doesn't it make you want to spit! See under BAND WAGGON.

does she . . . or doesn't she? *Slogan > Catch Phrase*. This innuendo-laden phrase began life selling Clairol hair-colouring in 1955. The brain-child of Shirley Polykoff (who entitled her advertising memoirs *Does She . . . or Doesn't She?* in 1975), the question first arose at a party when a girl arrived with flaming red hair. Polykoff involuntarily uttered the line to her husband, George. As she tells it, however, her mother-in-law takes some of the credit for planting the words in her mind some twenty years previously. George told Shirley of his mother's first reaction on meeting her: 'She says you paint your hair. Well, do you?'

When Ms Polykoff submitted the slogan at the Foote Cone & Belding agency in New York (together with two ideas she wished to have rejected) she suggested it be followed by the phrase 'Only her mother knows for sure!' or 'So natural, only her mother knows for sure'. She felt she might have to change 'mother' to 'hairdresser' so as not to offend beauty salons, and **only her hairdresser knows for sure** was eventually chosen.

However, it was felt that the double meaning in the main slogan would cause the line to be rejected. Indeed, *Life* magazine would not take the ad. But subsequent research at *Life* failed to turn up a single female staff member who admitted detecting any innuendo and the phrases were locked into the form they kept for the next eighteen years.

'J' did find a double meaning, as shown by this comment from *The Sensuous Woman* (1969): 'Our world has changed. It's no longer a question of "Does she or doesn't she?" We all know she wants to, is about to, or does.' A New York graffito, quoted in 1974, stated: 'Only *his* hairdresser knows for sure.'

See also IS SHE . . . OR ISN'T SHE?

dog. See LOVE ME, LOVE MY ~.

dogs bark – but the caravan passes by, the. *Saying*. Sir Peter Hall, the theatre director, was given to quoting this 'Turkish proverb' during outbursts of public hostility in the mid-1970s. I'm not sure that it is a Turkish proverb, but who can say? The meaning is clear – critics make a noise, but it does not last. I have also seen it quoted as a favourite saying of Jan Smuts, the South African politician.

In *Within a Budding Grove* – the 1924 translation of Marcel Proust's *A l'Ombre des Jeunes Filles en Fleurs* (1918) – C.K. Scott Moncrieff has the 'fine Arab proverb, "The dogs may bark; the caravan goes on!" '

doing up. See IT'LL BE ALL RIGHT . . . under BAND WAGGON.

—— **do it** ——. *Format Phrase*. By 26 April 1979, the *Sun* was offering a variety of T-shirts with nudging 'do it' slogans inscribed upon them. The craze was said to have started in the US. Whatever the case, scores of slogans 'promoting' various groups appeared over the next several years on T-shirts, lapel-buttons and car-stickers. In my *Graffiti* books (1979–86) I recorded some seventy, among them: 'Charles and Di do it by Royal Appointment'; 'Donyatt Dog Club does it with discipline and kindness'; 'Linguists do it orally'; 'Footballers do it in the bath afterwards'; 'Gordon does it in a flash'; 'Chinese want to do it again after twenty minutes'; 'City planners do it with their eyes shut'; 'Builders do it with erections'; 'Windsurfers do it standing up'; 'Printers do it and don't wrinkle the sheets'.

All this from simple exploitation of the innuendo in the phrase 'do it', which had perhaps first been exploited by Cole Porter in the song 'Let's Do It, Let's Fall in Love' (1928):

In shady shoals, English soles do it,
Goldfish in the privacy of bowls do it . . .

and then in a more personal parody by Noël Coward (in the 1940s):

Our leading writers in swarms do it
Somerset and all the Maughams do it . . .

dollar. See SIXTY-FOUR ~ QUESTION.

do not adjust your set (there is a fault). *Stock Phrase.* In the early days of British television, particularly in the late 1940s and early 1950s, technical breakdowns were a common feature of the evening's viewing. The BBC's caption **normal service will be resumed as soon as possible** became a familiar sight. The wording is still sometimes used in other contexts. As standards improved, it was replaced by the (usually more briefly displayed) phrase, 'There is a fault – do not adjust your set'. The latter phrase was used as the title of a children's comedy series on ITV in 1968, devised in part by some of the future *Monty Python* team.

do not pass 'Go'. *Catch Phrase.* A *Sunday Mirror* editorial (3 May 1981) stated: 'The laws of contempt are the ones under which editors and other media folk can be sent straight to jail without passing Go.' A businessman said to a woman who had paid for her husband to be duffed up (report of trial, *The Times*, 30 November 1982): 'If the police find out you are paying, you will go to jail, directly to jail, you will not pass "go" or collect £200.'

These two citations are testimony to the enduring use of Monopoly phraseology. Monopoly is the name of a board game invented by an unemployed salesman, Charles Darrow, in 1929, the year of the Wall Street crash, and is based on fantasies of buying up real estate in Atlantic City. The UK version, in which players begin on the square marked 'Go', may possibly bring them back to that square to 'collect £200 salary as you pass', or let them land on the 'Go to jail' square, or draw a 'Chance' card with the penalty:

GO TO JAIL
MOVE DIRECTLY TO JAIL
DO NOT PASS 'GO'
DO NOT COLLECT £200.

don't be vague – ask for Haig. *Slogan.* For Haig whisky, since *c* 1936. The origin of this slogan is to some extent lost in a Scotch mist because many of the John Haig & Co. archives were destroyed during the Second World War. However, the agency thought to be responsible was C.J. Lytle Ltd. An ad survives from 1933 with the wording 'Don't be vague, order Haig';

another from 1935 with, 'Why be vague? Ask for Haig'; and it seems that the enduring form arose in about 1936.

It has been jocularly suggested that Haig's premium brand, Dimple (which is sold as Pinch in North America), should be promoted with the slogan, 'Don't be simple, ask for Dimple'.

don't call/ring us, we'll call you. *Catch Phrase* – verging on the *Cliché*. What theatre directors say to auditionees, the implication being that 'we' will never actually get round to calling 'you'. Now more widely applied to anyone unwelcome seen to be asking a favour. The *OED Supp.* finds no example before 1969.

don't do anything I wouldn't do. See under IF YOU CAN'T BE GOOD . . .

don't forget the diver! *Catch Phrase.* Of all the many, many catch phrases sired by *ITMA*, the one with the most interesting origin was spoken by Horace Percival as the Diver. It was derived from memories that the star of the show, Tommy Handley, had of an actual man who used to dive off the pier at New Brighton. 'Don't forget the diver, sir, don't forget the diver,' the man would say, collecting money. 'Every penny makes the water warmer, sir.'

The radio character first appeared in 1940 and no lift went down for the next few years without somebody using the Diver's main catch phrase or his other one, **I'm going down now, sir!**

But who was the original diver? James Gashram wrote to *The Listener* (21 August 1980):

My grandfather McMaster, who came from a farm near the small village of Rathmullen, in Co. Donegal, knew Michael Shaughnessy, the one-legged ex-soldier, in the late 1890s, before he left for the Boer War and the fighting that cost him his leg. About 1910, Shaughnessy, then married to a Chester girl, settled in Bebington on the Wirral peninsula . . . Before the internal combustion engine, (he) used to get a lift every weekday from Bebington to New Brighton in a horse-drawn bread-cart owned by the Bromborough firm of Bernard Hughes. The driver of that cart, apparently, was always envious of the 'easy' money Shaughnessy got at New Brighton – sometimes up to two pounds a day in the summer – and would invariably say to him on the return to Bebington, 'Don't forget the *driver*'. Shaughnessy rarely did forget. It was many years later, some time in the early 1930s, that, remembering the phrase so well, he adapted it to his own purposes by changing it to 'Don't forget the diver', and shouted it to the people arriving from Liverpool.

As for 'I'm going down now, sir', I am told that bomber pilots in the Second World War would use this phrase when about to make a descent. From *ITMA*'s VE-Day edition:

Effects: Knocking

Handley: Who's that knocking on the tank?

The Diver: Don't forget the diver, sir – don't forget the diver.

Handley: Lumme, it's Deepend Dan. Listen, as the war's over, what are you doing?

The Diver: I'm going down now, sir.

Effects: Bubbles.

don't forget the fruit gums, mum! *Slogan*. For Rowntree's Fruit Gums, 1958–61. Coined by copywriter Roger Musgrave at S.T. Garland. Market research showed that most fruit gums were bought by women but eaten by children. Later on, the line fell foul of advertising watchdogs keen to save parents from nagging. 'Mum' became 'chum'.

don't get me mad, see! *Catch Phrase*. Frequently used by those impersonating James Cagney in gangster mode, but I am unable to say which of his films he says it in.

don't go near the water. *Catch Phrase*. Meaning 'be careful'. Mencken quotes 'author unidentified':

Mother, may I go out to swim?
Yes, my darling daughter;
Hang your clothes on a hickory limb,
But/And don't go near the water.

Don't Go Near the Water was the title of a film (1957) about US sailors based on a South Pacific island – based on a William Brinkley novel. 'Yes, My Darling Daughter' was a popular song of 1941 – the Andrews Sisters recorded it – and there was also a play with the title in the late 1930s, subsequently filmed (US, 1939). *No, My Darling Daughter* was the title of a British film comedy, 1961. I take it (from 'hickory limb') that the rhyme is of American origin.

don't say Brown – say Hovis. *Slogan*. For Hovis bread, from the mid-1930s. One of the firm's paper bags of that period showed a radio announcer saying, 'Here's a rather important correction . . . I should have said Hovis and not just "brown".' The slogan was used in its final form from 1956 to 1964. It still reverberates: in May 1981, when a British golfer, Ken Brown, was deserted by his caddie during a championship, a *Sunday Mirror* headline was, 'Don't Say Brown, Say Novice'.

don't some mothers have 'em? *Catch Phrase*. Jimmy Clitheroe (1916–73) was a person of restricted growth with a high-pitched voice who played a naughty schoolboy until the day he died. The radio comedy programme *The Clitheroe Kid* which ran from 1957–1972 popularized an old Lancashire – and possibly general North Country – saying, 'Don't some mothers have 'em?' In the form, 'Some mothers do 'ave 'em', the phrase was used in the very first edition of TV's *Coronation Street* in 1960 and later as the title of a Michael Crawford TV series (1974–9).

don't spit – remember the Johnstown flood. *Catch Phrase*. Admonition against spitting – a turn of the century Americanism. The Johnstown flood of 31 May 1889 entered US folk-lore when a dam burst near Johnstown, Pennsylvania, and 2200 died. A silent film, *The Johnstown Flood*, was made in the US in 1926. Partridge/*Catch Phrases* finds that notices bearing this joke were exhibited in bars before Prohibition started in 1919.

Safire quotes William Allen White's comment on the defeat of Alfred Landon in the 1936 US presidential election: 'It was not an election the country has just undergone, but a political Johnstown flood.'

Mencken lists it as an 'American proverb'.

don't teach your grandmother to suck eggs. *Idiom.* Ie 'don't try to tell anyone things which, given the person's age and experience, he/she might be expected to know anyway'. According to Partridge/*Slang*, variations of this very old expression include advice against instructing grandmothers to 'grope ducks', 'grope a goose', 'sup sour milk', 'spin', and 'roast eggs'. In 1738, Swift's *Polite Conversation* has 'Go teach your grannam to suck eggs.'

I have heard it suggested that, in olden days, sucking eggs would be a particularly important thing for a grandmother to be able to do because, having no teeth, it would be all she was capable of.

don't worry, be happy. *Saying > Slogan.* Bobby McFerrin's song with this title became George Bush's unofficial campaign theme in the presidential election of 1988 and won the Grammy award for the year's best song. 'The landlord says the rent is late, he might have to litigate, but don't worry, be happy,' sang McFerrin, in a song which became a minor national anthem, reflecting a feeling in the US at the time.

The Times (8 March 1989) noted: 'The song has spawned a whole "happy" industry and re-launched the Smiley face emblem that emerged in America in the late 1960s and was taken up in Britain by the acid-house scene last year. Bloomingdales, the Manhattan department store, now features a "Don't worry, be happy shop".'

don't you know there's a war on? *Catch Phrase.* A response to complaints used by (Will) Hatton and (Ethel) Manners portraying a Cockney chappie and a Lanca-shire lass in their variety act of the 1940s. Fairly widely taken up, I feel sure – even, ironically, *after* the Second World War. Partridge/*Catch Phrases* has the similar 'Remember there's a war on' dating from the First World War.

doomed. See WE BE ~ under *ROUND THE HORNE*.

door. See EVER-OPEN ~; NEVER DARKEN MY ~ AGAIN; ONE ~ CLOSES . . . ; OPEN THE ~, RICHARD under *ITMA*; SHUT THAT ~.

door-nail. See DEAD AS A ~.

Dorothy. See IS SHE A FRIEND OF ~?

Double Diamond works wonders, a. *Slogan.* For Double Diamond beer, from 1952. The double alliteration may have a lot to do with it, but it was also the singing of this slogan to the tune of 'There's a Hole in my Bucket' that made it one of the best-known of all.

double your pleasure, double your fun. *Slogan.* For Wrigley's Doublemint chewing gum, in the US, from 1959. However, about the same time, the signature tune of ITV's *Double Your Money* quiz included the line, 'Double your money, and double your fun'. The show was first transmitted in 1955.

doubt. See IF IN ~ . . .

down a bit. See under BERNIE, THE BOLT!

down in the forest something stirred. *Catch Phrase.* A gently mocking suggestion merely that something has happened (perhaps after prolonged inactivity), and not without possible innuendo. The line comes from the song 'Down in the Forest' (1915) with music by Sir Landon Ronald and words by H. Simpson. And what was it that stirred? 'It was only the note of a bird.'

down memory lane. *Cliché.* Once a pleasant phrase, now a journalistic cliché: 'The Ding-Ding special that spelled love for Sid and Jan Parker will take a trip down memory lane . . . to celebrate their 25th wedding anniversary. The happy couple will kiss and cuddle on the top deck of the No. 44 bus, just like they did when they were courting'. (*Sun*, 15 October 1983.)

It seems to have developed from 'Memory Lane', the title of a popular waltz of the 1920s and 1930s written by Buddy De Sylva, Larry Spier and Con Conrad – not to be confused with 'Down Forget-Me-Not Lane' by Horatio Nicholls, Charlie Chester and Reg Morgan (1941). The *OED Supp.* gives 'Down Memory Lane' as a 'title by Dannet and Rachel'.

down to the (real) nitty-gritty. See LET'S GET DOWN . . .

do you know the Bishop of Norwich? *Catch Phrase.* This is something that is traditionally said to a port drinker who is holding on to the bottle and not passing it round. I have no idea when it started, or why – except that Partridge/*Slang* lists a 'norwicher' as 'one who drinks too much from a shared jug . . . an unfair drinker'. Perhaps this is a subtle way of calling somebody such?

dragged kicking and screaming into the twentieth century. *Catch Phrase* > For-

mat Phrase. For a well-known phrase, this is curiously little documented. The only example I have found in this precise form comes from an article by Kenneth Tynan written in 1959 and collected in *Curtains* (1961): 'A change, slight but unmistakable, has taken place; the English theatre has been dragged, as Adlai Stevenson once said of the Republican Party, kicking and screaming into the twentieth century.'

Tony Benn said during a by-election, fought on his right to renounce a peerage, in May 1961: 'It is given to Bristol in this election to wrench the parliamentary system away from its feudal origins, and pitchfork it kicking and screaming into the twentieth century.'

It is, as I say, an adaptable 'format' phrase. From the *Daily Telegraph*, 11 September 1979: 'Mr Ian McIntyre, whose ambition was to bring Radio 4 kicking and screaming into the 1970s . . .'

Dragnet. The American TV series *Dragnet* was made between 1951 and 1958 and revived 1967–9. It was largely the creation of Jack Webb (1920–82) who produced, directed and starred. As Police Sergeant Joe Friday he had a deadpan style which was much parodied. The show had first appeared on radio in 1949 and was said to draw its stories from actual cases dealt with by the Los Angeles police – hence the famous announcement: 'Ladies and gentlemen, the story you are about to hear is true. Only the names have been changed to protect the innocent.'

The signature tune was almost a catch phrase in itself – 'Dum-de-dum-dum'. Joe Friday had a staccato style of questioning: **just the facts, ma'am** or **all we want is the facts, ma'am**. These were probably the first big phrases to catch on in Britain from the onset of commercial TV in 1955.

And to add to the list of memorable phrases, here is the opening narration from a typical TV episode: 'Ladies and gentlemen, the story you are about to see is true, the names have been changed to protect the innocent . . . **This is the city**. Everything in it is one way or the other. There's no middle ground – narrow alleys, broad highways; mansions on the hill, shacks in the gulleys; people who work for a living and people who steal. These are the ones that cause me trouble. **I'm a cop**. It was Monday April 17. We were working the day-watch on a forgery detail. My partner: Frank Smith. The boss is Captain Welch. **My name's Friday . . .**'

The phrase 'all we want is the facts' is almost a cliché when importunate journalists are represented in sketches. In 'Long-Distance Divorce', a revue sketch from *Nine Sharp* (1938), Herbert Farjeon put it in the mouth of a British reporter interviewing a Hollywood star.

drawers. See ALL KID GLOVES . . .

dreaded lergy, the. See under *GOON SHOW*.

dream. See LIKE A ~ COME TRUE.

dress. See PLEASE ADJUST YOUR ~ BEFORE LEAVING; WHEN ARE YOU GOING TO FINISH OFF THAT ~?

dressed up. See ALL ~ AND NOWHERE TO GO.

dressed up to the nines. *Idiom*. Ie 'very smartly dressed'. This may have come to us via a pronunciation shift. If you were to say dressed up 'to then eyne', that would mean, in Old English, 'dressed up to the eyes' (*eyne* being the old plural of eye). The snag with this is that no examples of the phrase being used occur before the eighteenth century.

I do not accept the *Longman Dictionary of English Idioms* definition which suggests that it refers to the setting of a standard with ten as the highest point one can reach. (If you were up to nine, you were very nearly the best. Compare the catch phrase, 'How would you rate it/her/anything ON A SCALE OF ONE TO TEN?' or 'She's a ten' which was all the rage after the film *10* in 1979.)

Nor do I agree with Ewart that it has anything to do with setting oneself up to match the Nine Muses of Classical Mythology; nor with Partridge/*Slang* that it has to do with the mystic number nine; nor with whoever suggested that as the 99th Regiment of Foot was renowned for smartness of dress, anyone well turned out was 'dressed up [to equal] the nines'.

The origin remains a bit of a mystery.

drink. See ANOTHER LITTLE D . . . ; EAT, ~ AND BE MERRY.

Drinka Pinta Milka Day. *Slogan*. The target was to get everyone drinking one pint of milk a day and the slogan was a piece of bath-tub inspiration that came from the client, namely Bertrand Whitehead, Executive Officer of the National Milk Publicity Council of England and Wales in 1958. The creative department of Mather & Crowther took an instant dislike to it, but Francis Ogilvy, the agency chairman, insisted on it being used despite the protests.

It was the kind of coinage to drive teachers and pedants mad, but eventually 'a pinta' achieved a kind of respectability when accorded an entry in *Chambers' Twentieth Century Dictionary* and others.

drive a coach and horses through something, to. *Idiom > Cliché.* Meaning 'to overturn something wantonly, and to render it useless'. Sir Stephen Rice (1637–1715), a Roman Catholic Chief Baron of the Exchequer used the courts in Dublin to get his own back on the Act of Settlement. 'I will drive a coach and six horses through the Act of Settlement,' he is quoted as saying in 1672.

In 1843, Charles Dickens wrote in *A Christmas Carol*: 'You may talk vaguely about driving a coach-and-six up a good old flight of stairs, or through a bad young Act of Parliament . . .' (which might seem to allude to the first example).

From an editorial in *The Times* concerning the premature police jubilation over the arrest of a man suspected of being the Yorkshire Ripper in January 1981 – jubilation which was 'to drive a number of coaches and horses through the contempt laws: the popular press seems to have decided that this was such a fantastic story that they would publish what they wanted and let the lawyers pick up the pieces later.'

From *The Times* (22 October 1983): 'Labour lawyers argued that Mr Justice Mervyn Davies had "driven a coach and horses" through Conservative legislation designed to limit the scope of trade disputes and outlaw political strikes, by refusing to ban the "blacking" of Mercury'.

drive/ go/ ride/ sail off into the sunset, to. *Idiom > Cliché.* To end happily, and probably romantically. Derived from the visual cliché of the silent film era when a united couple would often do just that at the end of a story. Used inevitably when Ronald Reagan retired from the White House: 'As Reagan rides off into the sunset we offer two opposing verdicts on his eight years in office . . .' (*Observer*, 15 January 1989). *OED Supp.*'s first citation is from 1967.

droit de seigneur. *Idiom.* This phrase is used to suggest that a man has exercised some imagined 'right' in order to force a woman to go to bed with him, as perhaps a boss might do with his secretary. The belief is that this 'right' dates from the days when medieval barons would claim first go at the newly-wedded daughters of their vassals – the so-called *ius primae noctis* (law of the first night).

In March 1988, it was reported that Dr Wilhelm Schmidt-Bleibtreu of Bonn had looked into the matter very thoroughly and discovered there was never any such legal right and that reliable records of it ever happening were rare. He concluded that the whole thing was really a male fantasy – and it was exclusively men who had used the phrase – though he didn't rule out the possibility that sex of the kind *had* taken place between lords and brides in one or two cases, legally or otherwise.

drop. See GOOD TO THE LAST ~; TURN ON, TUNE IN, ~ OUT.

drop a clanger, to. *Idiom*. To say something socially embarrassing, or commit an act of similar kind. According to a photograph caption in the *Sunday Times Magazine* (30 January 1983), 'the nerveless men who worked on the construction of New York's Woolworth Building in 1912 had nightmares of dropping a girder, or "clanger" in the phrase they gave to the language'. I wonder ...

Rather curiously, Partridge/*Slang* calls 'clanger' here a synonym for 'testicle', but derives it from the inoffensive 'drop a brick'. *OED Supp.*'s first citation is from 1958.

drop dead! *Catch Phrase*. Said by (mostly) young persons in almost any situation to someone with whom they are in disagreement. Partridge/*Catch Phrases* correctly notes that it is short for 'Why don't you drop dead!' and dates it from the US in the late 1930s. The earliest *OED Supp.* citation is from a John O'Hara story of 1934.

Leo Rosten in *Hooray for Yiddish* (1982) draws attention to the Yiddish equivalent *Ver derharget!*, meaning 'get yourself killed'. As he also suggests, this is a vigorous version of 'Fuck you!' and the more useful because its component words are perfectly respectable. He points to the enormously impactful use of the phrase as the Act Two curtain line of Garson Kanin's play *Born Yesterday* (1946). Judy Holliday said 'Du-rop du-ead!' – and 'the slow, sweet, studied rendition was stupendous. Waspish ladies have been tossing "Drop dead!" into their phones (to obscene callers) and as retorts (to abusive cabbies) ever since'.

drop the gun, Looey! *Catch Phrase*. Alistair Cooke writing in *Six Men* (1977) remarked of Humphrey Bogart: 'He gave currency to another phrase with which the small fry of the English-speaking world brought the neighbourhood sneak to heel: "Drop the gun, Looey!" '

Quite how Bogart did this, Cooke does not reveal. We have Bogart's word for it: 'I never said, "Drop the gun, Louie" ' (quoted in Ezra Goodman, *Bogey: The Good-Bad Guy*).

It's just another of those lines that people would like to have heard spoken but which never were. At the end of *Casablanca* (1942) what Bogart says to Claude Rains (playing Captain Louis Renault) is: 'Not so fast, Louis.' Ironically, it is *Renault* who says: 'Put that gun down.'

drugs. See SEX'N'~'N'ROCK'N'ROLL.

drum. See PUT A PENNY ON THE ~.

duck. See CAN A ~ SWIM?; IF IT LOOKS LIKE A ~ ...

due to circumstances beyond our control. *Cliché*. Of apology. The 1st Duke of Wellington used the phrase, 'Circumstances over which I have no control' in an 1839 letter. Charles Dickens had Mr Micawber talk of 'circumstances beyond my individual control' in *David Copperfield* (1849–50). The broadcaster Fred W. Friendly entitled a critical survey of American TV, *Due to Circumstances Beyond Our Control* (1967), presumably from the TV announcer's, 'We regret we are unable to proceed with the scheduled programme, due to ...'

dull it isn't. *Slogan.* For the Metropolitan police, 1972. The day after the brief TV and poster campaign using this curiously memorable slogan started, it was apparent that the phrase was catching on. A senior Scotland Yard officer told me that a young policeman went to break up a fight at White Hart Lane football ground. Having seized a young hooligan, the constable emerged, dishevelled but triumphant from the mêlée. A voice from the crowd cried out, 'Dull it effing isn't, eh?'

dumb. See KEEP MUM, SHE'S NOT SO ~ under BE LIKE DAD . . .

dunny, country. See under AS BUSY AS . . .

dynamite. See THESE ARE ~!

E

each and every one of us/you. *Cliché.* Mostly American and especially political periphrastic use – dating from the Nixon era at least. Harold Washington on becoming Mayor of Chicago in May 1983: 'I'm a peacemaker who reaches out to each and every one of you.'

eagle. See LEGAL ~.

ear. See EYES AND ~S OF THE WORLD; IN YOUR SHELL-LIKE ~; WALLS HAVE ~S.

early. See CHRISTMAS HAS COME ~ . . . ; ~ BATH under UP AND UNDER.

earner. See NICE LITTLE ~.

earth. See DID THE ~ MOVE . . . ; GREATEST SHOW ON ~.

eastern. See FULL OF ~ PROMISE.

easy. See under AS BUSY AS . . .

ea-sy, ea-sy! *Catch Phrase.* Crowd chant. I recall it being used by supporters of candidates at the declaration in the Hillhead, Glasgow by-election of 1982. More usually to be heard from football crowds. The Scotland World Cup Squad recorded a song called 'Easy, Easy' in 1974.

eat. See BET YOU CAN'T ~ JUST ONE; YOU ARE WHAT YOU ~.

eat, drink and be merry – for tomorrow we die. *Saying.* Derived from Isaiah 22:13 – 'Let us eat and drink, for tomorrow we shall die.' Brewer comments: 'A traditional saying of the Egyptians who, at their banquets, exhibited a skeleton to the guests to remind them of the brevity of life.'

However, Ecclesiastes 8:15 has the first part: 'A man hath no better thing under the sun, than to eat, and to drink, and to be merry', and Luke 12:19 has: 'Take thine ease, eat, drink and be merry.'

——, eat your heart out! *Catch Phrase*. A minor singer having just finished a powerful ballad might exult defiantly, 'Frank Sinatra, eat your heart out!' Partridge/*Catch Phrases* glosses it as: 'Doesn't *that* make you jealous, fella!' As something said *to* another person, this expression acquired popularity in the mid-twentieth century largely, I would say, through its American show-business use.

As such, it is probably another of those Jewish expressions popularized by showbiz. Originally, 'to eat one's (own) heart out', simply meaning 'to pine', it was current in English by the sixteenth century, and Leo Rosten in *Hooray for Yiddish* (1983) finds it in the Yiddish *Es dir oys s'harts*.

Eccles, shut up. See under GOON SHOW.

economical with the truth. *Idiom*. On 18 November 1986, the British Cabinet Secretary, Sir Robert Armstrong, was being cross-examined in the Supreme Court of New South Wales. The British Government was attempting to prevent publication in Australia of a book about MI5, the British secret service. Defence counsel Malcolm Turnbull asked Sir Robert about the contents of a letter he had written which had been intended to convey a misleading impression. 'What's a "misleading impression"?' inquired Turnbull. 'A sort of bent untruth?'

Sir Robert replied: 'It is perhaps being economical with the truth.' This explanation was greeted with derision not only in the court but in the world beyond, and it looked as though a new euphemism for lying had been coined.

In fact, Sir Robert had prefaced his remark with, 'As one person said . . .' and, when the court apparently found cause for laughter in what he said, added: 'It is not very original, I'm afraid.'

Indeed not. Dr E.H.H. Green, writing to the *Guardian* on 4 February 1987, said he had found a note penned by Sir William Strang, later to become head of the Foreign Office, in February 1942. Describing the character of the exiled Czech president Benes, Strang had written: 'Dr Benes's methods are exasperating; he is a master of misrepresentation and . . . he is apt to be economical with the truth.'

The notion thus appears to have been a familiar one in the civil service for a very long time – and not only there. Mark Twain is reported to have said: 'Truth is a mighty valuable commodity, we need to be economical with it.' And, before him, Edmund Burke remarked: 'We practise an economy of truth, that we may live to tell it the longer.'

In March 1988, (by now) Lord Armstrong said in a TV interview that he had no regrets about using the phrase. And he said, again, it was not his own, but Edmund Burke's.

Two other early citations came to light about the same time: Arnold Bennett in *These Twain* (1915), Chapter 17 has: 'The boy was undoubtedly crafty; he could conceal subtle designs under a simple exterior; he was also undoubtedly secretive. The recent changes in his disposition had put Edwin and Hilda on their guard, and every time young George displayed cunning, or economized the truth, or lied, the fear visited them.' Samuel Pepys used the precise phrase in his evidence before the Brooke House Committee in its examination of the Navy Board in 1669/70.

There is evidence to show that the phrase has been used more post-Armstrong. Longman/*Register* has three citations from 1988, including: 'Whether you're being economical with the truth or just boiling inside, body language can be a terrible giveaway' (*Daily Telegraph*, 25 April 1988).

Eddie. See ARE YOU READY, ~?

Eden must go. See —— MUST GO!

Educating Archie. Bizarre though the idea of a radio ventriloquist is, this show, starring Peter Brough and his wooden dummy Archie Andrews, was first broadcast by the BBC on 6 June 1950 and ran for ten years. The show was a noted breeding ground for young entertainers, and catch phrases abounded.

The 'catch phrase of the year' in 1951, according to Peter Brough, was spoken by Tony Hancock as one of the dummy's long line of 'tutors'. **Flippin' kids!** he would say. Indeed, 'The Lad 'imself' was billed as 'Tony (Flippin' Kids) Hancock' before moving on to his own shows, which more or less eschewed the use of catch phrases.

During his period as Archie's tutor, Max Bygraves made a splash with **I've arrived – and to prove it, I'm here!** (which formed part of his bill matter when he appeared at the London Palladium in 1952) and **a good idea . . . son!** (also

incorporated in a song). Bygraves told me (1980): 'None of them were planned. They just came up in the reading. When Archie read a line, it was so stilted, I would ape him. This happened a couple of times and people sensed I was reading the line rather than saying it. They're still saying it today, a lot of people.'

Robert Moreton (*b* 1922) had a brief taste of fame as another of the tutors and was noted for his *Bumper Fun Book*, out of which he would quote jokes. His catch phrase was **Oh, get in there, Moreton!** Alas, after only a year he was dropped from the show, was unable to get other work and committed suicide (*c* 1952).

For a while, Beryl Reid played Monica – Archie's posh, toothy, schoolgirl friend, who would introduce herself by saying **my name's Monica!** (See also AS THE ART MISTRESS SAID TO THE GARDENER!) Beryl told me in 1979: 'Even though I've done so many other things, straight acting parts and so on, people always remember these little phrases and want me to say them still.'

Above all, Beryl's Monica seems to have given rise to the expression **jolly hockey sticks!** – first used as an exclamation and then adjectivally to describe a type of woman – public school, gushing, games-playing and enthusiastic. Beryl Reid claims to have coined it: 'I can't write comedy material . . . but I know what sort of thing my characters should say!' In this case she seems to have lighted upon a masterly phrase which has entered the language (compare OH, JOLLY D!)

Having established Monica, Beryl wanted to find another character from a different social class. This turned out to be Marlene from Birmingham, complete with Brum accent and girlfriend, Deirdre. She helped establish the American import IT SENDS ME! as the archetypical 1950s phrase for the effect of music on the hearts and minds of the young. She also had a wonderful way of saying **good evening, each!** and **it's terrific!** (pronounced 'turreefeek').

Following his success as the gormless private in TV's *The Army Game*, Bernard Bresslaw was a natural choice as another of Archie's educators. Usually preceded by the sound of heavy footsteps he would arrive and give his 'thicko' greeting, **hello, it's me – Twinkletoes!**

Towards the end of the run, Dick Emery made his mark as more than one character in the show. As Mr Monty, he would say, **we've got a right one 'ere!** – a familiar phrase also employed at one time and another by Tony Hancock, Frankie Howerd and Bruce Forsyth.

ee, ain't it grand to be daft. *Catch Phrase.* Said by Albert Modley (1901–79), the North Country comedian who achieved nationwide fame through radio's *Variety Bandbox* in the late 1940s.

ee, it was agony, Ivy! See under *RAY'S A LAUGH*.

effect is shattering, the. See under I THOUGHT —— UNTIL I DISCOVERED ——.

egg. See DON'T TEACH YOUR GRANDMOTHER ...; GO TO WORK ON AN ~.

eight. See ONE OVER THE ~.

elementary, my dear Watson! *Catch Phrase.* The Sherlock Holmes phrase appears nowhere in the writings of Sir Arthur Conan Doyle (1859–1930), though the great detective does exclaim 'Elementary' to Dr Watson in *The Memoirs of Sherlock Holmes* ('The Crooked Man')(1894).

Conan Doyle brought out his last Holmes book in 1927. His son Adrian (in collaboration with John Dickson Carr) was one of those who used the phrase in follow-up stories – as have adapters of the stories in film and broadcast versions. In the 1929 film *The Return of Sherlock Holmes* – the first with sound – the final lines of dialogue are:

Watson: Amazing, Holmes!

Holmes: Elementary, my dear Watson, elementary.

elephant never forgets, an. *Saying.* What one might say of one's self when complimented on remembering a piece of information forgotten by others. Based on the view that elephants are supposed to remember trainers, keepers and so on, especially those who have showed kindness to them. A song with the title 'The Elephant Never Forgets' was featured in the play *The Golden Toy* by Carl Zuckmayer (London, 1934) and recorded by Lupino Lane. *Stevenson's Book of Proverbs, Maxims and Familiar Phrases* (1949) has that it derives from a Greek proverb, 'The *camel* never forgets *an injury*' (my italics).

eleventh commandment, the. *Catch Phrase.* But which is it? Mencken has 'Mind your own business' as 'borrowed from Cervantes, *Don Quixote*, 1605 ... often called, in the United States, the Eleventh Commandment'. But he also records 'The Eleventh Commandment: Thou shalt not be found out – George

Whyte-Melville, *Holmby House*, 1860', and that is the much more usual meaning.

The 1981 remake of the film *The Postman Always Rings Twice* was promoted with the slogan: 'If there was an 11th Commandment, they would have broken that too.'

Elizabeth. See QUEEN ~ SLEPT HERE.

embarrass. See AW, DON'T ~ ME.

embarrassing moments. See under *HAVE A GO*.

embarrassment. See DEEPLY REGRET ANY ~ . . .

emotional. See TIRED AND ~.

encounter. See CLOSE ~.

end. See AT THE ~ OF THE DAY; LIGHT AT THE ~ OF THE TUNNEL.

end is nigh, the. *Saying*. The traditional slogan of placard-bearing religious fanatics refers to the end of the world and the day of judgement. But, although 'nigh' is a biblical word, this phrase does not occur as such in the Authorized Version: 'The day of the Lord . . . is nigh at hand' (Joel 2:1); 'the kingdom of God is nigh at hand' (Luke 21:31); 'the end of all things is at hand' (1 Peter 4:7).

end of civilization as we know it, the. *Catch Phrase/Cliché*. A supposed Hollywood cliché – the kind of thing said when people are under threat from invaders from Mars, or wherever: 'This could mean the end of civilization as we know it . . .'

I don't have an example from sci-fi films, but the deathless phrase does get uttered in *Citizen Kane* (1941). Orson Welles as the newspaper magnate Kane is shown giving a pre-war press conference: 'I've talked with the responsible leaders of the Great Powers – England, France, Germany, and Italy. They're too intelligent to embark on a project which would mean the end of civilization as we now know it. You can take my word for it: there'll be no war!'

From the *Independent* Magazine (4 February 1989): '[A second Danish television channel] was about to take to the air, with the certain result that culture would be relegated to the dustbin . . . In short, it will be for Danes the end of civilisation as they know it.'

See also AS WE KNOW IT.

enemy. See PUBLIC ~ NO. 1.

enemy within, the. *Idiom > Slogan*. This phrase – used to describe an internal rather than external threat – has been used in an unusual range of situations. In 1980 Julian Mitchell used it as the title of a play about anorexia, though he tells me he considered it 'an old phrase' then. Indeed, *ODCIE*'s entry suggests that it is a shortened version of 'the enemy/traitor within the gate(s)' – 'one who acts, or is thought to act, against the interests of the family, group, society etc of which he is a member'.

On 22 January 1983, *The Economist* wrote of the industrial relations scene in Britain: 'The government may be trusting that public outrage will increasingly be its ally. Fresh from the Falklands, Mrs

Thatcher may even relish a punch-up with the enemy within to enhance her "resolute approach" further.'

Seven months later, Mrs Thatcher was using exactly the same phrase and context regarding the British miners' strike. She 'told Tory MPs that her government had fought the enemy without in the Falklands conflict and now had to face an enemy within . . . she declared that the docks and pit strikers posed as great a threat to democracy as General Galtieri, the deposed Argentine leader' (*Guardian*, 20 July 1984).

The phrase does not appear to have been used, as such, in films and TV – though we have had *The Enemy Below* (1957) and *The Enemy at the Door* (1978). It does not occur in the Bible or Shakespeare.

England. See CLOSE YOUR EYES . . . ; SOMEWHERE IN ~; THINGS I'VE DONE FOR ~.

enjoy. See SHE SHOULD LIE BACK AND ~ IT; YOURS TO ~ IN THE PRIVACY . . .

enough blue to make a pair of sailor's trousers. *Saying.* Meaning that there is a sufficient blue in the sky to make mention of it? But only used in connection with the weather, I think. It is listed in *Nanny Says* (1972) as an example of 'nanny philosophy': 'If there's enough blue sky to make a pair of sailor's trousers then you can go out.'

Epps's Cocoa. See GRATEFUL AND COMFORTING . . .

equal. See ALL ANIMALS ARE ~ . . .

'er indoors. *Catch Phrase.* Meaning 'the wife' (unseen, but domineering), this was popularized by George Cole as 'Arthur Daley' in the ITV series *Minder* (1979–). The series, which was created by Leon Griffiths, had a field-day with (predominantly) South London slang.

'I'm talking about Lodge Hill estate, in Bucks. This lies cheek-by-jowl with Chequers . . . the country seat of Her Indoors [ie Mrs Thatcher], and it's up for sale' – *Guardian*, 25 January 1989.

Eth, yes. See under TAKE IT FROM HERE.

even Homer nods. See HOMER NODS.

evenin' all! *Catch Phrase.* Accompanied by a shaky salute to the helmet, PC George Dixon (Jack Warner) would bid us welcome this way through several decades of *Dixon of Dock Green* on BBC TV (1955–76). His farewell, **mind how you go!**, achieved equal status as the phrase that all real policemen ought to say, even if not all of them do.

even your best friends won't tell you. *Slogan.* A line which may have come from a Listerine mouthwash advertisement (originally in the US), though I think the idea may have been used to promote another such product in the UK – Lifebuoy soap, according to *ODCIE* – in the late 1950s perhaps? Partridge/*Catch Phrases* suggests that it became a catch phrase in the form **your best friend(s) won't tell you** (= 'you stink!').

In the film *Dangerous Moonlight* (UK, 1941), the Anton Walbrook character says to a man putting on hair oil (in New York), 'Even your best friend won't *smell* you'. This helps with the dating, but does not really confirm the American origin as the film was made and scripted in England.

A similar idea was used by Amplex, the breath purifier, in advertisements (current 1957) showing two people reacting to a smelly colleague with the slogan **someone isn't using Amplex**.

ever after. See AND THEY ALL LIVED HAPPILY ~.

ever-open door, the. *Slogan > Catch Phrase.* This was used to describe Dr Barnado's Homes, the orphaned children's charity (by the 1950s). However, I can recall it being applied to the insatiable mouth, representing the appetite of an un-orphaned youth (me), also in the 1950s. But note, from Alexander Pope's translation of the *Iliad* (VI.14) (1715–20):

He held his seat; a friend to human race
Fast by the road, his ever-open door
Obliged the wealthy and relieved the poor.

every. See EACH AND ~ ONE OF US.

everybody has one book in them. *Cliché.* Ex the publishing world – or perhaps not, for it advances a popular belief which publishers might well disagree with. Presumably, the idea behind the saying is that every person has one story that they alone can tell – namely, the story of their life.

everybody out! *Catch Phrase. The Rag Trade* (written by Ronald Wolfe and Ronald Chesney) had the unusual, though not unique, experience of running on BBC TV from 1961–5 and then being revived on London Weekend Television

from 1977. Miriam Karlin in her best flame-thrower voice as Paddy, the Cockney shop steward, would shout the phrase at every opportunity. Now connected in the public mind with all strike-happy trade union leaders.

everybody wants to get into the act! See GOODNIGHT, MRS CALABASH . . .

everyday story of country-folk, an. See ARCHERS.

every —— gets the —— it deserves. *Format Phrase.* Eg 'Every country gets the television/newspapers it deserves.' *ODQ* cites Joseph de Maistre in *Lettres et Opscules Inédits* as saying, 'Every country has the government it deserves' on 15 August 1811.

every home should have one. *Slogan.* All-purpose, deriving from American advertising in the 1920s/30s, I would guess. Used as the title of a British film about an advertising man in 1970.

every man has his price. *Saying.* Mencken has: 'Ascribed to Robert Walpole *c* 1740 in William Coxe, *Memoirs of the Life and Administration of Robert Walpole*, 1798'. Here the form was, 'All those men have their price'. But *CODP* finds W. Wyndham in *The Bee* (1734) saying, 'It is an old Maxim, that every Man has his Price, if you can but come up to it.'

every picture tells a story. *Slogan > Catch Phrase.* Used to promote Doan's Backache and Kidney Pills (not 'Sloane's', as in the *Penguin Dictionary of Modern Quotations*, 1980), and current in 1904. The picture showed a person bent over with pain.

everything. See CHIPS WITH ~; MAN WHO HAS ~.

everything in the garden's lovely. *Catch Phrase.* Meaning 'all is well'. From the title of a song made popular by Marie Lloyd (1870–1922), I believe.

everything you always wanted to know about —— but were afraid to ask. *Format Phrase > Cliché. Everything You Always Wanted To Know About Sex But Were Afraid to Ask* was the self-explanatory title of a book (published in 1970) by David Reuben MD (*b* 1933). It gave to the language a format phrase, compounded by its use as a film title by Woody Allen in 1972 – though, in fact, Allen simply bought the title of the book and none of its contents.

Subsequently, almost any subject you could think of has been inserted into the sentence. An advertisement for the UK *Video Today* magazine (December 1981) promised: 'All you ever wanted to know about video but were afraid to ask.' In 1984, I drew up this short list from the scores of books that bore similar titles: *Everything That Linguists Have Always Wanted to Know About Logic But Were Ashamed To Ask; Everything You Always Wanted to Know About Drinking Problems And Then a Few Things You Didn't Want to Know; Everything You Always Wanted to Know About Elementary Statistics But Were Afraid to Ask; Everything You Always Wanted to Know About Mergers, Acquisitions and Divestitures But Didn't Know Whom to Ask; Everything You Wanted to Know About Stars But Didn't Know Where to Ask; Everything You Wanted to Know About the Catholic Church But Were Too Pious to Ask; Everything You Wanted to Know About the Catholic Church But Were Too Weak to Ask . . .*

In 1988, the publishers of this dictionary brought out a paperback edition of a book by Robert Goldenson and Kenneth Anderson called *Everything You Ever Wanted to Know About Sex – But Never Dared Ask* – which is surely where we came in.

evil. See WE MUST STAMP OUT THIS ~ IN OUR MIDST.

excuse. See IF YOU'LL ~ THE PUN; OUR REPORTER MADE AN ~ . . .

expectation. See DESPERATION . . .

experience. See GROWING ~.

expletive deleted. *Colloquialism.* The American way of indicating that an obscenity or blasphemous remark has been left out of a printed document became famous during Watergate. Upon the release of transcripts of conversations between President Nixon and his aides – published as *The White House Transcripts* (1974) – 'expletive deleted' became known to a wider public. The documents also used 'expletive removed', 'adjective omitted', 'characterization omitted'. British practice had been to rely on **** (asterisks) or . . . (dots) or —— (dashes) for sensitive deletions.

I note this in a 1937 *Time* review of Hemingway's *To Have and Have Not*: 'No matter how a man alone ain't got no bloody (Obscenity deleted) chance.'

For a while after Watergate people even exclaimed 'Expletive Deleted!' instead of swearing.

exterminate, exterminate! *Catch Phrase*. The science fiction TV series *Dr Who* has given rise to numerous beasties since its inception in 1963 but none more successful than the Daleks (who arrived in 1964) – deadly, mobile pepperpots whose metallic voices barked out 'Exterminate, exterminate!' as they set about doing so with ray guns. Much imitated by children.

——— **extraordinaire!** *Format Phrase* > *Cliché*. '[Culture Club's] flexible eight-piece includes Steve Grainger's sax, Terry Bailey's trumpet, Phil Pickett's keyboards, and their secret weapon, Helen Terry, a backing singer extraordinaire' – *The Times*, 27 September 1983.

eyeball to eyeball. *Idiom*. Meaning 'in close confrontation'. Use of this expression is of comparatively recent origin. In the missile crisis of October 1962, the US took a tough line when the Soviet Union placed missiles on Cuban soil. After a tense few days, the Soviets withdrew. Safire records that Secretary of State Dean Rusk (*b* 1909) was speaking to an ABC news correspondent, John Scali, on 24 October and said: 'Remember, when you report this, that, eyeball to eyeball, they blinked first.' Columnists Charles Bartlett and Stewart Alsop then helped to popularize this as, 'We're eyeball to eyeball and the other fellow just blinked.'

Before this, 'eyeball to eyeball' was a Black American serviceman's idiom. Safire quotes a reply given by the all-Black 24th Infantry Regiment to an inquiry from General MacArthur's HQ in Korea (November 1950): 'Do you have contact with the enemy?' 'We is eyeball to eyeball.'

eyes. See CLOSE YOUR ~ . . . ; HERE AND NOW, BEFORE . . . ; MY ~ ARE DIM.

eyes and ears of the world, the. *Slogan*. Promoting the cinema newsreel, Paramount News, from 1927–57. Not Gaumont British News, as in Partridge/*Slang*.

face. See HIS ~ WAS HIS FORTUNE; UNACCEPT-ABLE ~ OF ——.

facts. See JUST THE ~, MA'AM under *DRAGNET*.

fade. See OLD SOLDIERS NEVER DIE . . .

failure. See IT WENT FROM ~ TO CLASSIC . . .

fair. See ALL IS FAIR . . .

fairy-tale. See LIKE A ~ PRINCESS.

faith. See THIS HAS RESTORED MY ~ . . .

fallen in the water. See under *GOON SHOW*.

Family Favourites. A potent memory of Sunday mornings in the 1950s and early 1960s: the smell of roast and gravy wafting out of the kitchen and from the radio: **it's twelve o'clock in London, one o'clock in Cologne – at home and away it's time for** *Two-Way Family Favourites* (or words to that effect) followed by the sweeping strings of the signature tune – the André Kostelanetz version of Rodgers and Hart's 'With a Song in My Heart' . . .

The BBC programme began on 7 October 1945 as a link between home and the British occupying troops in Germany. Cliff Michelmore, who used to introduce the programme from Hamburg, and later met and married the London presenter, Jean Metcalfe, recalls the origin of the phrase **bumper bundle**: 'It was invented by Jean. Her road to Damascus was at the crossroads on Banstead Heath one Sunday morning when driving in to do the programme. It was used to describe a large number of requests all for the same record, especially "Top Ten" hits, *circa* 1952–3.'

The programme took various forms and various presenters before closing in the 1970s. The title change to *Two-Way*

Family Favourites was in 1960 (giving rise to a slang expression for a type of sexual intercourse).

family newspaper, not in a. *Cliché.* Journalistic humbug of the OUR REPORTER MADE AN EXCUSE AND LEFT variety. The reporter sails as close to the wind as he can and then states, 'She committed an act which we cannot describe in a family newspaper', or some such. Now spread to broadcasting – 'This is a family show, so I couldn't possibly tell you what happened . . .'

famous. See RICH AND ~; YOU'RE ~ WHEN . . .

famous for being famous. *Catch Phrase.* Dating, I would guess from the 1960s/70s – used to describe people who are celebrated by the media, although it is difficult to work out precisely what it is they have done to deserve such attention. Nowadays, they appear as guests on TV quiz shows, participate in charity telethons, and – as they have always done – feature on guest-lists for first nights and film premieres. From the *Daily Mail* (4 March 1989): 'With Christine Keeler in person . . . and with the attendant chorus of showbiz froth and nonentities famous for being famous, the film's premiere brazenly upheld all the meretricious values.'

Daniel J. Boorstin in *The Image* (1962) noted: 'The celebrity is a person who is known for his well-knownness.'

fancy. See LITTLE OF WHAT YOU ~ . . .

Fanny Adams. See SWEET ~.

far. See THUS ~ SHALT THOU GO.

farewell. See AND SO WE SAY ~; SO, ~ THEN.

Farnsbarns. See CHARLIE ~.

fart. See HE CAN'T ~ AND CHEW GUM . . .

fart in a wind-storm. See under AS BUSY AS . . .

faster than a speeding bullet! See under SUPERMAN.

fast lane. See LIVING LIFE IN THE ~.

fate. See FLYING FICKLE FINGER OF ~ under LAUGH-IN.

fat, hairy legs. See under MORECAMBE AND WISE SHOW.

father. See AND WHEN DID YOU LAST SEE YOUR ~?; LLOYD GEORGE KNEW MY ~.

favourite airline. See THE WORLD'S ~ under BOAC TAKES GOOD CARE OF YOU.

fear. See FLIGHT FROM ~.

feel. See HOW DID YOU ~?

fellows. See I SAY YOU ~ under YAROOOO!

Fergusons. See FINE SETS THESE ~.

few and far between. *Colloquialism.* 'Our semi-tautological phrase "few and far between" is a corrupt formulation by the nineteenth-century Scottish poet Thomas Campbell of an old folk saying to the effect that the visits of angels to our world are "brief and far between" ' – *Observer*, 26 June 1988.

few vouchers short of a pop-up toaster, a. *Idiom.* One of those phrases used to describe mental shortcomings, or 'a deficiency in the marbles department'. I first noticed this one being used around May 1987. Another version: 'Not quite enough coupons for the coffee percolator and matching set of cups'. More venerable idioms for the same thing would include: that a person is 'eleven pence half-penny' (ie not the full twelve pence of a shilling); 'rowing with one oar in the water'; 'not playing with a full deck'; 'one brick/a few bricks short of a load'; or that 'the light's on, but no one's in'.

Moving a shade to one side, I can but print my favourite description of a TV producer who was not at his best after lunch. Said his assistant, apologetically, 'He transmits, but he doesn't receive'.

fickle finger of fate. See under *LAUGH-IN.*

fiddling and fooling. *Slogan.* This was comedian/violinist Ted Ray's bill matter by the late 1940s. But the alliteration had appealed long before. Swift in *Polite Conversation* has: 'For my Part, I believe the young Gentleman is his Sweet-heart; there's such fooling and fiddling betwixt them.'

57 varieties. See HEINZ ~.

fight his/her way out of a paper bag. See under COULDN'T RUN A WHELK-STALL.

find. See SPEAK AS YOU ~ . . .

fine mess. See HERE'S ANOTHER ~ . . .

fine sets these Fergusons. *Slogan.* Curiously memorable – for Ferguson radio

sets (current in the 1950s), accompanied by what looked like a wood-cut of a man, smoking a pipe, listening to one of them.

fingerlickin'. See IT'S ~ GOOD.

finger of fate. See FLYING FICKLE ~ AWARD under *LAUGH-IN.*

fingers. See LET YOUR ~ DO THE WALKING.

fings. See under THINGS AIN'T WHAT . . .

finish. See I'VE STARTED SO I'LL ~!; NICE GUYS ~ LAST; WHEN ARE YOU GOING TO ~ OFF THAT DRESS?

fire. See C'MON COLMAN'S . . . ; GREAT BALLS OF ~; SET THE THAMES ON ~.

first. See LOVE AT ~ FLIGHT under BOAC TAKES GOOD CARE OF YOU; TODAY IS THE ~ DAY . . . ; WOMEN AND CHILDREN ~.

first —— years are the hardest, the. *Format Phrase.* Usually of marriage, or a job – suggesting, in an ironical way, that the initial stages of anything are the most difficult. Probably derives from the army saying, 'Cheer up – the first seven years are the worst!' (from *circa* the First World War, referring to the term of a regular soldier's service). (Partridge/*Catch Phrases* also finds 'the first hundred years are the hardest/worst' from about the same period.

Compare SEVEN YEAR ITCH.

fish. See CAN A DUCK SWIM?

fit. See ALL THE NEWS THAT'S ~ TO PRINT; LOOKING BRONZED AND ~.

five. See HOW MANY BEANS MAKE ~?; I'LL GIVE IT FOIVE.

5–4–3–2–1. *Stock Phrase*. A case of life imitating art. It is said that the backward countdown to a rocket launch was first thought of by the German film director Fritz Lang (1890–1976). He thought it would make things more suspenseful if the count was reversed – 5–4–3–2–1 – so, in his 1928 film *By Rocket to the Moon*, he established the routine for future real-life space shots. I await challenges to this theory. However, I note that the 1931 American novel with the same title (by Otto Willi Gail) does not appear to include the phrase.

five o'clock shadow. See AVOID ~.

fix. See IF IT AIN'T BROKEN . . .

flag. See FLY THE ~ under BOAC TAKES GOOD CARE OF YOU.

flagpole, run it up the. See under LET'S ── AND SEE IF ──.

flaunt. See WHEN YOU GOT IT, ~ IT.

flavour of the month. *Idiom*. Originally a generic phrase aimed at persuading people to try new varieties of ice cream and not just stick to their customary choice (principally in the US). Latterly, it has become an idiom for any fad, craze or person that is quickly discarded after a period of being in the news or in demand. From the Longman/*Register*: 'The metaphorical possibilities of the word *ambush* are catching on in several areas of activity in the USA, making it the lexical flavour-of-the-month in American English.'

fleet's lit up, the. *Catch Phrase*. The most famous broadcasting boob came from Lt-Cdr Tommy Woodrooffe (1899–1978), a leading BBC radio commentator of the 1930s. On the night of 20 May 1937 he was due to give a fifteen-minute description of the 'illumination' of the Fleet after the Coronation Naval Review at Spithead. What he said, in a commentary that was faded out after less than four minutes, began: 'At the present moment, the whole Fleet's lit up. When I say "lit up", I mean lit up by fairy lamps. We've forgotten the whole Royal Review. We've forgotten the Royal Review. The whole thing is lit up by fairy lamps. It's fantastic. It isn't the Fleet at all. It's just . . . fairy land. The whole fleet is in fairy land . . .'

Eventually the commentary was taken off the air. Naturally, many listeners concluded that Woodrooffe himself had been 'lit up' as the result of enjoying too much hospitality from his former shipmates on board HMS *Nelson* before the broadcast. But he denied this. 'I had a kind of nervous blackout. I had been working too hard and my mind just went blank.' He told the *News Chronicle*: 'I was so overcome by the occasion that I literally burst into tears . . . I found I could say no more.'

The BBC took a kindly view and the incident did not put paid to Woodrooffe's broadcasting career. But the phrase became so famous that it was used as the title of a revue at the London Hippodrome in 1938 and Bud Flanagan recorded a song called 'The Fleet's Lit Up'.

The Second World War song 'I'm Going to Get Lit Up When the Lights Go Up in London' by Hubert Gregg (1943) probably owes something to the Woodrooffe affair, though use of 'lit up' to mean 'tipsy' dates back to 1914, at least.

flight. See LOVE AT FIRST ~ under BOAC TAKES GOOD CARE OF YOU.

flight from fear, a. *Cliché.* Of journalism. The lure of alliteration again. 'TO BRITAIN ON FLIGHT FROM FEAR. A flight from fear ended at Heathrow Airport yesterday for passengers on the first plane to arrive from Poland since martial law was proclaimed at the weekend' (*Daily Mail*, 18 December 1981).

flippin' kids! See under *EDUCATING ARCHIE.*

flog the bishop. See BASH THE BISHOP.

flood, Johnstown. See DON'T SPIT . . .

flowers. See SAY IT WITH ~.

flying fickle finger of fate award, the. See under *LAUGH-IN.*

fly me. See I'M ——.

Flynn. See IN LIKE ~.

fly the flag. See under BOAC TAKES GOOD CARE OF YOU.

folks. See HELLO, FOLKS under *BAND WAGGON;* THAT'S ALL, ~!

follow that taxi/van! *Cliché.* Of the cinema. Said to a taxi driver by the hero/policeman in pursuit of a villain. It is not known whether anyone has ever said it in real life. (It is as much of a cliché as the ability film actors have, on getting *out* of taxis, of tendering exactly the right change to the driver.) The film *Amsterdamned* (1989), a cop thriller set amid the canals of the Dutch capital, included the memorable injunction, 'Follow those bubbles!'

fooling. See FIDDLING AND ~.

foolish things. See THESE ~.

fools. See ONLY ~ AND HORSES WORK.

foot. See ONE ~ IN THE GRAVE; PUT ONE'S BEST ~ FORWARD.

force. See MAY THE ~ BE WITH YOU.

forest. See DOWN IN THE ~ SOMETHING STIRRED.

forever. See DIAMOND IS ~; NOW AND ~.

forget. See DON'T ~ THE DIVER!; DON'T ~ THE FRUIT GUMS, MUM; ELEPHANT NEVER ~S; I'LL ~ MY OWN NAME under *ITMA.*

forgiven. See ALL IS ~ under WHERE ARE YOU NOW?

forgotten. See GONE, BUT NOT ~.

for —— of —— opportunity knocks. See *OPPORTUNITY KNOCKS.*

fort. See HOLD THE ~.

fortifies. See PHYLLOSAN ~ THE OVER-FORTIES.

fortune. See HIS FACE WAS HIS ~.

forty. See LIFE BEGINS AT ~.

forward. See ONE STEP ~ . . . ; PUT ONE'S BEST FOOT ~.

fox. See CRAZY LIKE A ~.

Freddie. See READY FOR ~ under ARE YOU READY, EDDIE?

free. See I'M ~!; I'M NOT A NUMBER . . . ; NO SUCH A THING AS A ~ LUNCH; THIS IS A ~ COUNTRY; WITH ONE BOUND HE WAS ~.

free, gratis and for nothing. *Colloquialism*. A double tautology. Partridge/*Slang* quotes Thomas Bridges as saying in 1770 that 'the common people' always put 'free' and 'gratis' together; and notes that the longer version occurs in an 1841 book. In fact, a touch earlier, *The Pickwick Papers* (1836–7) by Charles Dickens has Sam Weller's father saying 'free gratis for nothin' ' (Chapter 26). In *Usage and Abusage*, Partridge decides that it is a cliché, only excusable as a jocularity.

free the ——. *Slogan/ Format Phrase.* This all-purpose slogan came into its own in the 1960s – usually in conjunction with a place and number. Hence: 'Free the Chicago 7' (charged with creating disorder during the Democratic Convention in 1968), 'Free the Wilmington 10', and so on. Dignifying protesters with a group name incorporating place and number began with the 'Hollywood 10' (protesters against McCarthyite investigations) in 1947.

The form has become a cliché of sloganeering now. Various joke slogans from the late 1970s demanded: 'Free the Beethoven 9/ the Heinz 57/ the Intercity 125/ the Chiltern Hundreds/ the Indianapolis 500/ the Grecian 2000'.

French. See NO MORE LATIN . . . ; THAT'S YOUR ACTUAL ~ under *ROUND THE HORNE*.

Friday. See MY NAME'S ~ under *DRAGNET*.

Friday night is Amami night. *Slogan*. For Amami hair products, current in the 1920s. Presumably this inspired the title of the long-running BBC radio show *Friday Night is Music Night* (from 1953).

friendly. See YOUR ~ NEIGHBOURHOOD ——.

friend of Dorothy? See IS SHE A ~?

friends. See EVEN YOUR BEST ~ . . . ; MY ~; SOME OF MY BEST ~ . . . ; WE ARE JUST GOOD ~; WITH —— LIKE THAT . . .

from your mouth to God's ear. *Saying*. Meaning 'I hope what you say will come true by being acted upon by God'. I first heard this expression used by Joan Collins in a TV interview in 1982. Jewish/American?

frozen mit, to give someone the. *Idiom* Meaning, 'to freeze out/ give the cold shoulder to someone' ('mit' = 'mitten' = 'hand'). Lady Diana Cooper writing to Duff Cooper on 14 September 1925 (in a letter printed in *A Durable Fire*, 1983) said: 'Duffy, don't be deathly proud, my darling . . . you probably dish out the frozen mit to all, and I want all men to love and admire you.' Partridge/*Slang* finds it in *Punch* in 1915.

fruit gums. See DON'T FORGET THE ~, MUM!

F.T.A. (Fuck The Army). *Slogan/Catch Phrase*. Especially as graffiti, much used in the US Army. *DOAS* adds: 'Since *c*

1960, as a counter expression to disliked orders, rules etc.' *F.T.A.* was the title of an anti-Vietnam War film made by Jane Fonda in 1972.

The 'initial' strategy has also been used regarding the Pope ('F.T.P.') and the Queen ('F.T.Q.') especially in Northern Ireland (both types recorded in Belfast, 1971).

fuck. See WHO DO I HAVE TO ~ . . .

full circle. See WHEEL HAS COME ~.

full of Eastern promise. *Slogan.* For Fry's Turkish Delight, current in the late 1950s. One of the longest-running British TV ads, appealing to escapist fantasies. One of the first showed a male slave unrolling a carpet containing a woman captive in front of an eastern potentate.

fully paid-up member of the human race, a. *Catch Phrase.* Complimentary. Of politician Kenneth Clarke, the *Observer* wrote (31 July 1988): 'He is always well-informed (or anyway well-briefed), always reasonable and equable. He seems to be a fully paid-up member of the human race.'

——**fulness is terrific, the.** See under YAROOOO!

fun. See DOUBLE YOUR PLEASURE . . . ; A SPOT OF HOMELY ~ under HAVE A GO; GETTING THERE IS HALF THE ~; MOST ~ I'VE HAD . . . ; MOST ~ YOU CAN HAVE . . .

Funf. See THIS IS ~ SPEAKING.

Funk and Wagnalls. See under *LAUGH-IN.*

funny thing happened (to me) on the way to the theatre tonight . . . , a. *Stock Phrase.* The uninspired comedian's preliminary to telling a joke, and dating presumably from music-hall/vaudeville days. Compare the title of the comedy musical *A Funny Thing Happened on the Way to the Forum* (filmed 1966) set in ancient Rome, based on Plautus (but the phrase can't be *quite* as old as that, surely?).

fur coat. See ALL ~ . . . under ALL KID GLOVES . . .

further. See THUS FAR SHALT THOU GO . . .

future. See YOUR ~ IS IN YOUR HANDS.

G

gag. See MAN THEY COULDN'T ~.

galahs, gumtree full of. See under AS BUSY AS . . .

gallery. See ROGUE'S ~.

gals. See HOW'S ABOUT THAT THEN . . . under AS IT HAPPENS.

game. See ~S FINISHED under THERE'LL NEVER BE ANOTHER; GOOD ~ under *GENERATION GAME*; I DO NOT LIKE THIS ~ under *GOON SHOW*; —— IS THE NAME OF THE ~.

garden. See EVERYTHING IN THE ~'S LOVELY; I NEVER PROMISED YOU A ROSE ~.

gardener. See AS THE ART MISTRESS SAID . . .

——gate. *Format Phrase > Cliché.* In the wake of the 'Watergate' affair in US politics (1972–4) – a name derived, lest it be forgot, from an apartment block in Washington DC where a bungled burglary led to the scandal – it has become standard practice to apply the suffix '——gate' to any political scandal: Koreagate, Lancegate, Billygate, Liffeygate, Westlandgate, Contragate, Irangate, Thatchergate, and so on. Debategate and Briefingate were applied to the flap in 1983 over how Ronald Reagan's campaign team got hold of President Carter's briefing books before a 1980 debate on TV. The usage shows no sign of ending. The *Independent* (3 March 1989) even managed to coin a 'prequel' version for the 1963 Profumo Affair – 'Profumogate'.

geddit? *Catch Phrase.* Meaning 'Do you get it?' and said after a poor joke. Popularized from the early 1980s onwards by the 'Glenda Slag' column in *Private Eye*.

generation. See BIG CHILL ~; COME ALIVE . . .

Generation Game, The. As host of BBC TV's hugely popular silly games show of the mid-1970s, Bruce Forsyth soon had the nation once more parroting his catch phrases. **Didn't he do well?** first arose when a contestant recalled almost all the items that had passed before him on a conveyor belt (in a version of Kim's Game). However, it is also said to have originated *c* 1973 with what a studio attendant used to shout down from the lighting grid during rehearsals. **Good game . . . good game!** was encouragement to contestants. **Nice to see you, to see you . . . /Nice!** (with the audience supplying the last word) was the opening exchange of greetings with the studio audience.

Genghis Khan. See SOMEWHERE TO THE RIGHT OF ~.

gentle giant, a. *Nickname > Cliché.* The alliteration is important and the application to any tall, strong person has become a journalistic cliché. A policeman killed by an IRA bomb outside Harrods store in London (December 1983) was so dubbed. Terry Wogan used the expression allusively to describe the BBC's Radio 2 network (compare the BIG ONE, beloved of advertising folk). Larry Holmes (*b* 1950), world heavyweight boxing champion, is another to whom the label has been affixed, as also James Randel Matson (*b* 1945), the US track and field champion.

In 1967, there was an American film entitled *The Gentle Giant.* This was about a small boy in Florida who befriends a bear which later saves the life of the boy's disapproving father. Going back even further, the journalist William Howard Russell wrote of Dr Thomas Alexander, a surgeon who served in the Crimean War, as a 'gentle giant of a Scotchman'.

gentleman and a scholar, a. *Catch Phrase.* In *c* 1964, when I was an undergraduate at Oxford, I was approached by an Irish 'gentleman of the road' who asked, 'May I shake the hand of a scholar and a gentleman?' In fact, what he was after was 'sixpence for a cup of tea' but I was intrigued by his complimentary/complementary combination of 'scholar' and 'gentleman' (though more usually the words are placed in reverse order).

Paul Beale notes in Partridge/*Catch Phrases* that he was familiar (in *c* 1960) with the use of the phrase, 'Sir, you are a Christian, a scholar and a gentleman' in the British army. It was 'often used as jocular, fulsome, though quite genuine, thanks for services rendered'.

Partridge, earlier, had been tracking down a longer version – 'A gentleman, a scholar, and a fine judge of whiskey' – but had only been able to find the 'gentleman and scholar' in Robert Burns (1786):

His locked, lettered, braw brass collar
Shew'd him the gentleman an' the scholar.

It looks, however, as though the conjunction goes back even further. The *OED* has a citation from 1621: 'As becommed a Gentleman and a Scholer'. I suspect the phrase was born out of a very real respect for anyone who could claim to have both these highest of attributes. However, equally as old, is the combination 'a gentleman and a soldier'.

gentlemen. See I ALWAYS DO MY BEST . . . under *ITMA*.

gently, Bentley! See under TAKE IT FROM HERE.

George. See LLOYD ~ KNEW MY FATHER.

George Washington slept here. See QUEEN ELIZABETH SLEPT HERE.

get away from it all, to. *Idiom* > *Cliché*. Of travel journalism/advertising, and meaning 'to have a rest, holiday'. From an advertisement for the Moroccan National Tourist Office (February 1989): 'In 1943 where did Churchill go to get away from it all?'

get away with something scot-free, to. *Colloquialism*. 'If we could do that, she might go scot-free for aught I cared' - Charles Dickens, *The Old Curiosity Shop* (1840–1). But why 'scot-free'? It is not 'scot', as in Scotland, but *sceot*, a medieval municipal tax paid to the local bailiff or sheriff. So it means, in a sense, 'tax-free', without penalty.

get back on your jam jar. *Catch Phrase*. Said dismissively to someone who is behaving objectionably. This appears to be rhyming slang for 'get back on your tram-car' (ie go away). And so, it is not in origin a racist slur alluding to the golliwog figure who appears on jars of Robertson's Jam.

get out of one's pram, to. *Idiom*. Meaning, 'to get angry, over-excited.' Learned debate over this phrase followed in the wake of Labour leader Neil Kinnock's use of 'Schultz got out of his pram' to describe US Secretary of State George Schultz during the Labour leader's visit to Washington in February 1984. Mr Kinnock said: 'It's a colloquialism. I believe it is becoming more common in its usage. It means Mr Schultz was departing from his normal diplomatic calm. Nothing so undiplomatic as losing his temper.'

Nevertheless, other forms are more widely known. London East End and Glasgow slang both have, 'Don't get out of your pram about it', when someone is 'off his head' about something. A touch of OFF ONE'S TROLLEY seems to be involved, too.

getting. See WE'RE ~ THERE.

getting there is half the fun. *Slogan*. This expression sloganizes Robert Louis Stevenson's views: 'I travel not to go anywhere, but to go' and 'to travel hopefully is a better thing than to arrive'. It also reflects 'the journey not the arrival matters' (an expression used as the title of an autobiographical volume by Leonard Woolf, 1969). I believe that, as a slogan, it may have been used to advertise Cunard steamships in the 1920s/30s. It was definitely used to promote the Peter Sellers film *Being There* (1980) in the form, 'Getting there is half the fun. Being there is all of it.'

get up them stairs! *Catch Phrase*. A reference to the prospect of sexual intercourse. Partridge/*Catch Phrases* finds it in 1942 with 'Blossom' added. Denis Gifford in *The Golden Age of Radio* gives it as comedian Hal Monty's catch phrase (noting that it seems to have escaped the BBC's BLUE PENCIL).

giant. See GENTLE ~; HE WAS A BIG MAN; ONE SMALL STEP . . .

gift. See MAN WHO HAS EVERYTHING.

gifted. See YOUNG, ~ AND BLACK.

girl. See COULD MAKE ANY ORDINARY ~ . . . ; NEVER CHASE ~S OR BUSES; WHAT'S A NICE ~ LIKE YOU . . .

gi'us a job, I could do that. *Catch Phrase* > *Slogan* – almost. A rare example of a catch phrase coming out of a TV drama series. Alan Bleasdale's *The Boys from the Blackstuff* (about unemployment in Liverpool) was first shown in 1982 and introduced the character of Yosser Hughes. His plea became a nationally repeated catch phrase, not least because of the political ramifications. It was chanted by football crowds in Liverpool and printed on T-shirts with Yosser confronting Prime Minister Margaret Thatcher. From the *Observer* (30 January 1983): 'At Anfield nowadays whenever the Liverpool goalkeeper makes a save, the Kop affectionately chants at him the catch-phrase of Yosser Hughes: "We could do that." It's a slogan which might usefully rise to the lips of the chairbound viewer just as often.'

give 'im the money, Barney/ Mabel! See under HAVE A GO.

gloves. See ALL KID GLOVES . . .

glow. See HORSES SWEAT . . .

go. See ALL DRESSED UP AND NOWHERE TO ~; AND AWA-A-AAY WE ~!; DO NOT PASS ~; HERE WE ~ . . . ; I ~, I COME BACK under *ITMA*; —— MUST

~; MUST YOU ~?; TO BOLDLY ~ under BEAM ME UP, SCOTTY; WHERE DO WE ~ FROM HERE?

go ahead, make my day. *Catch Phrase*. In March 1985, President Ronald Reagan told the American Business Conference, 'I have my veto pen drawn and ready for any tax increase that Congress might even think of sending up. And I have only one thing to say to the tax increasers. Go ahead – make my day.'

For once, he was not quoting from one of his own film roles, or old Hollywood. The laconicism was originally spoken by Clint Eastwood, himself brandishing a .44 Magnum, to a gunman he was holding at bay in *Sudden Impact* (1983). At the end of the film he says (to another villain, similarly armed), 'Come on, make my day'. In neither case does he add 'punk', as is sometimes supposed.

The phrase may have been eased into Reagan's speech by having appeared in a parody of the New York *Post* put together by editors, many of them anti-Reagan, in the autumn of 1984. Reagan was shown starting a nuclear war by throwing down this dare to the Kremlin (information from *Time*, 25 March 1985).

goal. See OWN ~.

goalposts. See MOVE THE ~.

god. See FROM YOUR MOUTH TO ~'S EAR; IN ~ WE TRUST . . . ; PREPARE TO MEET THY ~.

God's own country. *Catch Phrase*. There can be few countries which have not elected to call themselves this. It is certainly not exclusive.

Of the United States: the *OED Supp.* provides an example from 1865, and tags the phrase as being of US origin. Flexner says that in the Civil War the shorter 'God's country' was the Union troops' term for the North, 'especially when battling heat, humidity, and mosquitoes in the South. Not until the 1880s did the term mean any section of the country one loved or the open spaces of the West.' A 1937 US film had the title *God's Country and the Woman*.

Of Australia: Dr Richard Arthur (1865–1932), a State politician and President of the Immigration League of Australasia, was quoted in *Australia Today* (1 November 1911) as saying, 'This Australia is "God's Own Country" for the brave.' The *Dictionary of Australian Quotations* (1984) notes that at the time, 'Australia was frequently referred to as "God's Own Country", the phrase drawing satirical comments from the foreign unenlightened.'

Of South Africa/Ireland: I have heard both these countries so dubbed informally (in the 1970s), with varying degrees of appropriateness and irony.

I have also heard Yorkshiremen describe their homeland as 'God's own *county*'. 'Yorkshire's natural reluctance to play second fiddle to London has faced some difficulty in the matter of house prices . . . God's own county is at the centre of things yet again' – *Guardian*, 23 January 1989.

Compare the expression, 'God's Acre' – which means a cemetery or churchyard, and is a borrowing from the German – although Longfellow called it 'an ancient Saxon phrase' (Brewer).

go for gold. *Slogan.* Meaning, literally, 'aim for a gold medal'. As far as I can tell, this slogan was first used by the US Olym-

pic team at the Lake Placid Winter Olympics in 1980. (*Going for Gold* became the title of an Emma Lathen thriller set in Lake Placid (1983), and there was a TV movie *Going for the Gold* in 1985.) Other teams, including the British, had taken it up by the time of the 1984 Olympics. A BBC TV quiz called *Going for Gold* began in 1987.

Just to show, as always, that there is nothing new under the sun: in 1832, there was a political slogan 'To Stop the Duke, Go for Gold' – which was somehow intended, through its alliterative force, to prevent the Duke of Wellington from forming a government in the run up to the Reform Bill.

The slogan was coined by a radical politician, Francis Place, for a poster, on 12 May 1832. (I think it was intended to cause a run on the Bank of England.)

go for it! *Slogan > Cliché.* This was a popular expression from the early 1980s, mostly in America – though any number of Sales Managers have encouraged their teams to strive this way in the UK, too.

In June 1985, President Reagan's call on tax reform was, 'America, go for it!' Victor Kiam, an American razor entrepreneur, entitled his 1986 memoirs *Going For it!*; and 'Go for it, America' was the slogan used by British Airways in the same year to get more US tourists to ignore the terrorist threat and travel to Europe.

Lisa Bernbach in *The Official Preppy Handbook* (1981) points to a possible US campus origin, giving the phrase as a general exhortation to act crazily. At about the same time, the phrase was used in aerobics. Jane Fonda in a work-out book (1981) and video (c 1983), cried, 'Go for it, go for the burn!' (where the burn was a sensation felt during exercise). There was also a US slogan (current 1981) for beer, 'Go for it! Schlitz makes it great'.

Partridge/*Slang* has 'to go for it' as Australian for being 'extremely eager for sexual intercourse' (*c* 1925).

going. See WHEN THE ~ GETS TOUGH . . .

gold. See GO FOR ~; THERE'S ~ IN THEM THAR HILLS; STREETS PAVED WITH ~.

go, man, go! *Catch Phrase.* This was a phrase of encouragement originally shouted at jazz musicians in the 1940s. Then it took on wider use. At the beginning of the number 'It's Too Darn Hot' in Cole Porter's *Kiss Me Kate* (film version, 1953) a dancer cried, 'Go, girl, go!'

TV newscaster Walter Cronkite reverted famously to 'Go, baby, go!' when describing the launch of Apollo XI in 1969 and this form became a fairly standard cry at rocket and missile departures thereafter. *Time* magazine reported it being shouted at a test firing of a Pershing missile (29 November 1982).

Crazy, man, crazy! originated at about the same time as 'Go, man, go!' but was, perhaps, better suited to rock'n'roll usage than the earlier bop.

One wonders whether T.S. Eliot's 'Go go go said the bird' ('Burnt Norton', *Four Quartets*, 1935) or Hamlet's 'Come, bird, come' (the cry of a falconer recalling his hawk) relate to these cries in any way!

gone. See WHERE HAVE ALL THE —— ~?

gone, but not forgotten. *Stock Phrase.* On tombstones, memorial notices and such, and used as the title of a Victorian print showing children at a grave or similar, I think. I recall in the 1950s, the GOON SHOW adopting 'Goon, but not forgotten' somewhere along the line.

gone for a Burton. *Idiom.* Early in the Second World War, an RAF expression arose to describe what had happened to a missing person, presumed dead. He had 'gone for a Burton', meaning that he had gone for a drink (*in* the drink = the sea) or, as another phrase put it, 'he'd bought it'.

Folk memory has it that 'Gone for a Burton' had been used in advertisements to promote a Bass beer known in the trade as 'a Burton' (though, in fact, several ales are produced at Burton-on-Trent). More positive proof is lacking. An advert for Carlsberg in the 1987 Egon Ronay *Good Food in Pubs and Bars* described Burton thus: 'A strong ale, dark in colour, made with a proportion of highly dried or roasted malts. It is not necessarily brewed in Burton and a variety of strong or old ales were given the term.'

Another fanciful theory is that RAF casualty records were kept in an office above or near a branch of Burton Menswear in Blackpool, but I think we may discount this one.

go now, pay later. *Slogan > Format Phrase.* Daniel Boorstin in *The Image* (1962) makes oblique reference to travel advertisements using the line 'Go now, pay later'. Was hire purchase ever promoted with 'Buy now, pay later'? It seems likely. These lines – in the US and UK – seem to be the starting point for a construction much used and adapted since.

Live Now Pay Later was the title of Jack Trevor Story's 1962 screenplay based on the novel *All on the Never Never* by Jack Lindsay. As a simple graffito, the same line was recorded in Los Angeles (1970), according to *The Encyclopedia of Graffiti* (1974). The same book records a New York subway graffito on a funeral parlour ad: 'Our layaway plan – die now, pay later.' 'Book now, pay later' was used in an ad in the programme of the Royal Opera House, Covent Garden, in 1977.

good. See ALL PUBLICITY IS ~ PUBLICITY; ~ GAME under *GENERATION GAME*; GUINNESS IS ~ FOR YOU; HE'S VERY ~, YOU KNOW under *GOON SHOW*; IF YOU CAN'T BE ~ . . . ; TWELVE ~ MEN AND TRUE; WAS IT ~ FOR YOU, TOO?; WE ARE JUST ~ FRIENDS; YOU'VE NEVER HAD IT SO ~.

good evening. See HELLO, ~, AND WELCOME.

good evening, each! See under *EDUCATING ARCHIE*.

good idea. See ~, SON under *EDUCATING ARCHIE*; IT SEEMED LIKE A ~ AT THE TIME.

good man is hard to find, a. *Saying.* Is this the same as the proverb 'Good men are scarce' found by *CODP* in 1609? In this form, it was the title of a song by Eddie Green (1919).

Nowadays, it is most frequently encountered in reverse. 'A hard man is good to find' was used, nudgingly, as the slogan for Soloflex body-building equipment in the US (1985). Ads showed a woman's hand touching the bodies of well-known brawny athletes. In this form the saying is sometimes attributed to Mae West.

good morning . . . nice day! See under *ITMA*.

good morning, sir! Was there something? See under *MUCH BINDING IN THE MARSH*.

goodness gracious me! *Catch Phrase.* This was the key phrase in Peter Sellers's Indian doctor impersonation which all citizens of the subcontinent subsequently rushed to emulate. It occurred in a song called 'Goodness Gracious Me' (written by Herbert Kretzmer and Dave Lee) recorded by Sellers and Sophia Loren in 1960 and based on their characters in the film of Shaw's *The Millionairess*.

goodnight. See AND A SPECIAL ~; IT'S ~ FROM ME . . . ; SAY ~ DICK under *LAUGH-IN*.

goodnight, children . . . everywhere! *Stock Phrase.* Derek McCulloch (Uncle Mac) was one of the original Uncles and Aunts who introduced BBC radio *Children's Hour* from the 1920s. He developed this special farewell during the Second World War when many of the programme's listeners were evacuees. Vera Lynn recorded a song with the title (1939). J.B. Priestley wrote a war-time play with the title, also.

goodnight, Mrs Calabash . . . wherever you are! *Catch Phrase.* Jimmy 'Schnozzle' Durante (1893–1980), the big-nosed American comedian had a gaggle of phrases – including an exasperated **everybody wants to get into the act!** and (after a successful joke), **I've got a million of 'em!** (also used in the UK by Max Miller and others). But he used to sign off his radio and TV shows in the 1940s and 1950s with the Calabash phrase. It was a pet name for his first wife, Maud, who died in 1943. The word comes from an American idiom for 'empty head', taken from the calabash or gourd. For a long time, Durante resisted explaining the phrase. His biographer, Gene Fowler, writing in 1952, could only note: 'When he says that line his manner changes to one of great seriousness, and his voice takes on a tender, emotional depth . . . when asked to explain the Calabash farewells, Jim replied, "That's my secret – I want it to rest where it is." '

good to the last drop. *Slogan.* For Maxwell House coffee, in the US, from 1907. President Theodore Roosevelt was visiting Joel Cheek, perfector of the Maxwell House blend. After the President had had a cup, he said of it that it was 'Good . . . to the last drop'. It has been used as a slogan ever since, despite those who have inquired what was wrong with the last drop. Professors of English have been called in to consider the problem and ruled that 'to' can be inclusive and not just mean 'up to but not including'.

good war, a. *Colloquialism.* I don't know who first started talking about having had 'a good war' – I think it has *usually* been said by survivors of the Second World War – but I can give one example from fiction. In Henry Reed's radio play of 1959, *Not a Drum Was Heard: the War Memoirs of General Gland*, Gland says: 'It was, I think a *good* war, one of the best there have so far been. I've often advanced the view that it was a war deserving of better generalship than it received on either side.'

From Julian Critchley MP in the *Guardian* (3 May 1989): 'I well remember some years ago at the Savoy a colleague who had had a good war leaping to his feet (before the Loyal Toast) in order to pull back the curtains which separated the party from the outside world . . .' From the *Independent* (13 July 1989): 'British Rail has not had a good war. The public relations battle in the industrial dispute seems to have been all but lost.'

goody, goody gumdrops! *Catch Phrase* – used by Humphrey Lestocq, host of BBC TV's children's show *Whirligig* in the 1950s, though I rather suspect he did not originate it.

Goon Show, The. The Goons – Peter Sellers, Harry Secombe and Spike Milligan – first appeared in a BBC radio show called *Crazy People* in May 1951. At that time, Michael Bentine was also of their number. *The Goon Show* proper (later known simply as *The Goons*) ran from 1952–60, with one extra programme in 1972, and numerous re-runs.

The humour was zany, often taking basic music-hall jokes and giving them further infusions of surrealism. The cast of three did all the funny voices, though Harry Secombe concentrated on the main character, Neddie Seagoon. *Catch Phrases* included:

and this is where the story really begins . . .

brandy-y-y-y! Accompanied by the sound of rushing footsteps, this was the show's beloved way of getting anybody out of a situation that was proving too much for him.

damn(ed) clever these Chinese! A Second World War phrase taken up from time to time by the Goons. (Or 'dead clever chaps/devils these Chinese!') Referring to a reputation for wiliness rather than skill.

dreaded lergy, the. Pronounced 'lurgy' (hard 'g'), and = allergy (soft 'g').

have a gorilla! Neddie Seagoon's way of offering a cigarette, to which the reply might be 'No, thank you, I'm trying to give them up' or 'No, thanks, I only smoke baboons!'

he's fallen in the water! Said by Little Jim (Milligan):
Voice: Oh, dear, children – look what's happened to Uncle Harry!
Little Jim (helpfully, in simple sing-song voice): He's fallen in the water!

he's very good, you know! Ironic commendation, spoken by various characters.

I do not like this game! Said by Bluebottle (Sellers):
Seagoon: Now, Bluebottle, take this stick of dynamite.
Bluebottle: No, I do not like this game!

it's all in the mind, you know. Convincing explanation of anything heard in the show – often said as a final word by Wallace Greenslade, the announcer.

I've been sponned! Oddly, this phrase does not actually occur in the episode called 'The Spon Plague' broadcast in March 1958, but I clearly remember running around saying it at school. The symptoms of sponning included bare knees – of which we had quite a few in those days. In 'Tales of Men's Shirts', however, Sellers's 'Mate' character gets clobbered and says,

'Ow! I've been sponned from the film of the same name' and proceeds to write his memoirs, 'How I was sponned in action'.

needle, nardle, noo! Nonsense phrase, spoken by various characters.

only in the mating season. The Goons' response to the traditional chatting up line, 'Do you come here often?'

sapristi!(as in 'sapristi nuckoes!' etc). Count Jim Moriarty (Milligan) used this fairly traditional exclamation of surprise – a corruption of the French *'sacristi'*. Some will remember it being said, also, by Corporal Trenet, friend of 'Luck of the Legion' in the boys' paper *Eagle*, also in the 1950s.

shut up, Eccles! Said by Seagoon, repeated by Eccles (Milligan), and then taken up by everyone.

ying-tong-iddle-i-po! All-purpose nonsense phrase, notably incorporated in 'The Ying Tong Song'.

you can't get the wood, you know! Said by Minnie Bannister or Henry Crun.

you dirty rotten swine you! Bluebottle on being visited by some punishment or disaster.

See also AND THERE'S MORE . . . ; BY JOVE, I NEEDED THAT!; I DON'T WISH TO KNOW THAT . . . ; 2–4–6–8 . . .

Gordon Bennett! *Catch Phrase.* My inquiries into this odd expletive began in about 1982. The first person I consulted – a cheery Londoner with the absolute confidence of the amateur etymologist – assured me that it was short for 'Gawd and St Benet!' Quite who St Benet was, and why people invoked his name, I never found out. Except that in Shakespeare's

Twelfth Night, 'the bells of Saint Bennet' (= Saint Benedict, or possibly St Bennet Hithe, Paul's Wharf, opposite the Globe Theatre) is alluded to at V.i.37.

Then, shortly afterwards, on a visit to Paris, I found myself staring up in amazement at a street sign which bore the legend 'Avenue Gordon-Bennett'. I felt like exclaiming, *'Mon Dieu et St Benet!'*

Reading Churchill's *History of the Second World War*, I came across one Lt Gen. Gordon Bennett. Knowing how many slang expressions have come out of the services, I wondered whether he had done something to impress himself upon the language.

Next, I talked to a man at the annual convention of the Institute of Concrete Technology. He told me he thought the expression was current in the 1930s. Hadn't Gordon Bennett been a comedian? Indeed, there were comedians called Billy Bennett, Wheeler and Bennett, Bennett and Moreny, Bennett and Williams, though why any of *them* should have been commemorated by having a street named after then in Paris (even had their first names been Gordon) is anybody's guess.

'Ah,' said the concrete man, 'the *French* Gordon Bennett was probably the man who gave his name to a motor race in the early 1900s.'

In fact, he wasn't French at all, but American, and there were two of him. James Gordon Bennett I (1795–1872) was a Scot who went to the US and became a megalomaniac newspaper proprietor. James Gordon Bennett II (1841–1918) was the even more noted editor-in-chief of the *New York Herald* and the man who sent Henry Morton Stanley to find Dr Livingstone in Africa.

But why should either of these gentlemen have a street named after him in Paris, not to mention a motor race, as well as bequeath his moniker as a British expletive?

James Gordon Bennett II (for we must concentrate on him) was quite a character. He was exiled to Paris after a scandal but somehow managed to run his New York newspaper from there (the cable bills ran up and up, so he bought the cable company). He disposed of some $40 million in his lifetime. He offered numerous trophies to stimulate French sport and, when the motor car was in its infancy, presented the Gordon Bennett cup to be competed for.

On one occasion, he tipped a train guard $14,000 and, on another, drew a wad of 1000 franc notes from his back pocket (where they had been causing him discomfort) and threw them on the fire. He became, as the *Dictionary of American Biography* puts it, 'one of the most picturesque figures of two continents'.

This, if anything does, probably explains why it was *his* name that ended up on people's lips and why they did not go around exclaiming, 'Gordon of Khartoum!' or 'Gordon Selfridge!' or anything else. Gordon Bennett was a man with an amazing reputation.

I don't take very seriously the suggestion that stunned members of the public shouted 'Gordon Bennett!' when Stanley found Livingstone. Nor that there were cartoons of Stanley phoning his editor (from the jungle?) and shouting, 'Gordon Bennett, I've found him!' The truth of the matter seems to be that people found some peculiar appeal in the name Gordon Bennett – but the important thing is that the first name was 'Gordon'.

Understandably, people shrink from blaspheming. 'Oh Gawd!' is felt to be less offensive than 'Oh God!' At the turn of the century it was natural for people facetiously to water down the exclamation 'God!' by saying 'Gordon!' The name Gordon Bennett was to hand. The initial letters of the name also had the explosive quality found in '*Gor*blimey! [God blind me!]'

A decade or two later, in similar fashion – and with a view to circumventing the strict Hollywood Hay's Code – W.C. Fields would exclaim 'Godfrey Daniel!' in place of 'God, damn you!'

But who was Godfrey Daniel . . . ?

gorilla. See HAVE A ~ under *GOON SHOW*.

got. See THAT ALMOST ~ AWAY; WHEN YOU ~ IT, FLAUNT IT.

go to it! *Slogan*. In the summer of 1940, the Minister of Supply, Herbert Morrison, called for a voluntary labour force in words that echoed the public mood after Dunkirk. The quotation was used in a campaign run by the S.H. Benson agency (which later indulged in self-parody on behalf of Bovril, with 'Glow to it' in 1951/ 2). 'Go to it', meaning 'to act vigorously, set to with a will' dates at least from the early nineteenth century.

In Shakespeare, it means something else, of course:

Die for adultery! No:
The wren goes to't, and the small gilded fly
Does lecher in my sight.
(*King Lear*, IV.vi.112)

go to work on an egg. *Slogan*. In 1957, Fay Weldon (*b* 1932), later known as a novelist and TV playwright, was a copywriter on the British Egg Marketing Board account at the Mather & Crowther agency. In 1981 she poured a little cold water on the frequent linking of her name with the slogan: 'I was certainly in charge of copy at the time "Go to work on an egg" was first used as a slogan as the main theme for an advertising campaign. The phrase itself had been in existence for some time and hung about in the middle of paragraphs and was sometimes promoted to base lines. Who invented it, it would be hard to say. It is perfectly possible, indeed probable, that I put those particular six words together in that particular order but I would not swear to it.'

gotta. See I ~ HORSE; MAN'S ~ DO . . . ; MILK'S ~ LOTTA BOTTLE.

gottle o' geer. *Stock Phrase*. The standard showbiz way of mocking the inadequacies of many ventriloquist acts. It represents 'bottle of beer', said with teeth tightly-clenched.

government health warning. *Idiom*. Any warning which suggests that a person, thing or activity should be avoided – as, for example, 'Mind yourself with him; he ought to carry a government health warning.'

The phrase came originally from cigarette advertising and packets which, in the UK from 1971, have carried a message to this effect: 'DANGER. H.M. GOVERNMENT HEALTH DEPARTMENT'S WARNING: CIGARETTES CAN SERIOUSLY DAMAGE YOUR HEALTH.' The 'seriously' was added in 1977; the 'danger' in 1980.

In the US, from 1965, packs carried the message: 'CAUTION: CIGARETTE SMOKING MAY BE HAZARDOUS TO YOUR HEALTH.' Five years later, this was strengthened to read: 'WARNING; THE SURGEON-GENERAL HAS DETERMINED THAT CIGARETTE SMOKING IS DANGEROUS TO YOUR HEALTH.'

gracious. See GOODNESS, ~ ME!

grand. See EE, AIN'T IT ~ TO BE DAFT; SERIOUSLY, THOUGH, HE'S DOING A ~ JOB.

grandmother. See DON'T TEACH YOUR ~; I HAVEN'T BEEN SO HAPPY SINCE . . .

grape. See BEULAH, PEEL ME A ~.

grateful and comforting like Epps's Cocoa. *Slogan.* In Noël Coward's play *Peace In Our Time* (1947) one character says, 'One quick brandy, like Epps's Cocoa, would be both grateful and comforting.' When asked, 'Who is Epps?' he replies, 'Epps's cocoa – it's an advertisement I remember when I was a little boy.' The slogan has, indeed, been used since *c* 1900.

gratis. See FREE, ~ AND FOR NOTHING.

grave. See ONE FOOT IN THE ~; TURN OVER IN ONE'S ~.

greasepaint. See DOCTOR ~ WILL CURE ME.

great. See AH, WOODBINE . . . ; LATE ~ ——; THIS ~ MOVEMENT OF OURS.

great balls of fire! *Catch Phrase.* To those who are most familiar with this exclamation from the Jerry Lee Lewis hit song of 1957 (written by Jack Hammer and Otis

Blackwell), it should be pointed out that, of course, it didn't begin there.

In fact, it occurs in the script of the film *Gone With the Wind* (1939), confirming what I would suspect are its distinctly southern US origins. While the *OED Supp.* and other dictionaries content themselves with the slang meaning of 'ball of fire' (glass of brandy/a person of great liveliness of spirit), even Partridge/*Slang* and American slang dictionaries avoid recording the phrase.

I mean, goodness gracious . . .

greatest. See I AM THE ~.

greatest show on earth, the. *Slogan.* Name given by P.T. Barnum (1810–91) to the circus formed by the merger with his rival, Bailey's, in the US, from 1881. It is still the slogan of what is now Ringling Bros. and Barnum & Bailey Circus. It was used as the title of a Cecil B. de Mille circus film in 1952.

greatest thing since sliced bread, the (sometimes **hottest**). *Idiom.* A 1981 ad in the UK: 'Sainsbury's bring you the greatest thing since sliced bread. Unsliced bread' – neatly turning an old formula on its head. Quite when the idea that pre-sliced bread was one of the landmark inventions arose, I am not sure. Sliced bread had first appeared on the market by the 1920s – so a suitable period of time after that, I suppose.

great Scott! *Catch Phrase.* As with GORDON BENNETT!, one is dealing here with a watered-down expletive. 'Great Scott!' is clearly NOT A MILLION MILES FROM sounding like 'Great God!' and yet is not blasphemous. Can one be precise about which particular Scott is having his name taken in vain?

The Morrises say the expression became popular in the mid-nineteenth century when US General Winfield Scott (1786–1866) was the hero of the Mexican War (1847) and 'probably our most admired general between Washington and Lee'.

No rival candidate seems to have been proposed and the origination is almost certainly American. The *OED*'s earliest British English example dates from 1885.

Great War. See DADDY, WHAT DID YOU DO IN THE ~?

ground. See HIT THE ~ RUNNING.

growing experience, a. *Idiom > Cliché.* Meaning 'an experience which leads to the positive development of your character'. The American film people David and Talia Shire experienced 'a very loving separation'. Said she, 'We're going to rotate the house and we even rotate the car. We've been separated for four months and it's a growing experience' (quoted in William Safire, *On Language*, 1980).

grub. See LOVELY ~ under *ITMA*.

guilty. See WE NAME THE ~ MEN.

Guinness is good for you. *Slogan.* After 170 years without advertising, Arthur Guinness, Son & Company, decided to call in the image-makers for their beer in 1929. So, Oswald Greene at the S.H. Benson agency initiated some consumer research (unusual in those days) into why people did drink Guinness. It transpired that they thought it did them good.

Today, ask any British person to give you an example of an advertising slogan and the chances are they are likely to quote 'Guinness is Good for You'. It is etched on the national consciousness although the slogan was discontinued *c* 1941 and has not been revived since 1963.

gumdrops. See GOODY, GOODY, ~.

gumtree full of galahs. See under AS BUSY AS . . .

gun. See DROP THE ~, LOOEY; HAVE ~ WILL TRAVEL.

guys. See HOW'S ABOUT THEN . . . under AS IT HAPPENS; NICE ~ FINISH LAST.

Hades. See NO MORE CHANCE THAN . . .

Haig. See DON'T BE VAGUE . . .

hairdresser. See ONLY HER ~ . . . under DOES SHE . . . OR DOESN'T SHE?

hairy legs. See under *MORECAMBE AND WISE SHOW.*

half. See BELIEVE ONLY ~ . . . ; GETTING THERE IS ~ THE FUN.; HOW THE OTHER ~ LIVES.

Hancock's Half-Hour. Co-scriptwriter Ray Galton has said of this BBC radio show's start in 1954: 'Alan Simpson and I wanted a show without breaks, guest singers and catch phrases – something that hadn't been done before. After the first week with Kenneth Williams in the show, bang went out the idea of no funny voices and no catch phrases!'

Although Williams's cameos occupied a very tiny part of the show, they were enough to start him on an outrageous career (see also *BEYOND OUR KEN* and *ROUND THE HORNE.*) His **stop messin' abaht!** began with the Hancock show and was later used as the title of a radio show of which Williams, by that time, was the star.

Hancock himself had not so much catch phrases as distinctive phraseology, on radio and in the TV series (from 1956): **a man of my calibre** (pronounced 'cal-aye-ber'), **are you looking for a punch up the bracket?** and **stone me!**

See also *EDUCATING ARCHIE.*

hand. See CLAP ~S, HERE COMES CHARLEY; CLOUD NO BIGGER THAN A MAN'S ~; LEFT ~ DOWN A BIT; YOUR FUTURE IS IN YOUR ~S.

handsome. See TALL, DARK AND ~.

hangs. See AND THEREBY ~ A TALE.

hang the Kaiser. *Slogan.* Given the role played in the First World War by Kaiser Wilhelm II, there was pressure for retribution at the war's end during the 1918 British General Election. It was largely fuelled by the press. The Treaty of Versailles (1919) committed the Allies to trying the Kaiser (who was forced to abdicate), but the government of the Netherlands refused to hand him over. He lived until 1941.

happen. See ACCIDENT WAITING TO ~; ANYTHING CAN ~ . . . under *TAKE IT FROM HERE.*

happened. See WHATEVER ~ TO ——?

happiest days of your life, the. *Catch Phrase > Cliché.* The traditional platitude intoned by the old buffer who gives away prizes at school speech days is that his listeners will agree that schooldays are 'the happiest days of your life'. I'm sure the expression of this sentiment predates its use as the title of a famous play by John Dighton (produced in London in 1948, filmed 1950.) However, the schoolchildren in that work may have had special cause to believe the catch phrase as the plot hinges on war-time confusion in which a boys' school and a girls' school are lodged under the same roof.

The Best Years of Our Lives is the title of an American film (1946) about what happens to a group of ex-servicemen when they return from the war – presumably having 'given the best years of their lives' to their country. 'The best *days* of our lives' is also an expression used in this kind of context.

I tend to remark that I have spent the best years of my life waiting for lifts.

happily. See AND THEY ALL LIVED ~ . . .

happiness is ——. *Format Phrase.* Samuel Johnson declared in 1766, 'Happiness consists in the multiplicity of agreeable consciousness', but he wasn't the first to have a go at defining happiness, nor the last. In 1942, along came E.Y. Harburg with the lyrics to his song 'Happiness is a Thing Called Joe'. However, it was Charles M. Schultz (*b* 1922) creator of the Peanuts comic strip, who really launched the 'Happiness is ——' format.

In *c* 1957 he had drawn a strip 'centring around some kid hugging Snoopy and saying in the fourth panel that "Happiness is a warm puppy".' This became the title of a best-selling book in 1962 and let loose a stream of promotional phrases using the format, including: 'Happiness is egg-shaped', 'Happiness is a cigar called Hamlet', 'Happiness is a warm earpiece' (UK ad slogans); 'Happiness is being elected team captain – and getting a Bulova watch', 'Happiness is a $49 table' (both US ad slogans); 'Happiness is seeing Lubbock, Texas, in the rear view mirror' (line from a Country and Western song); 'Happiness is a Warm Gun' (song title); 'Happiness is Wren-shaped', and many, many more.

By which time one might conclude that 'Happiness is . . . a worn cliché'.

happy. See DON'T WORRY, BE ~; I HAVEN'T BEEN SO ~ SINCE . . . ; YOU'VE MADE AN OLD MAN VERY ~.

happy as a sandboy, as. *Idiom.* The *OED* has 'jolly as a sandboy' as the original nineteenth-century expression, referring to the boys who hawked sand from door to door. The *OED Supp.* finds a quotation from Pierce Egan (1821): 'As happy as a sandboy who had unexpectedly met with good luck in disposing of his hampers full of the above-household commodity.'

Dickens in *The Old Curiosity Shop* (1840–1) has 'The Jolly Sandboys' as the name of a pub, with a sign, 'representing three Sandboys increasing their jollity with as many jugs of ale and bags of gold'. Angus Easson in his Penguin edition, notes: 'Sand was sold for scouring, as a floor cover to absorb liquids, and for bird cages. Sandboys were proverbially happy people, as indeed they might be in 1840 when they could buy a load of about 2½ tons for 3s. 6d. (17½p), and take £6 or £7 in a morning . . . .During the century, sawdust tended to replace sand for floors . . . and, by 1851, those in the trade were much less happy.'

happy as Larry, as. *Idiom.* Meaning, 'extremely happy.' Brewer has it as an Australian expression and supposedly referring to the boxer Larry Foley (1847–1917). The first *OED Supp.* citation (indeed Australian) is from 1905.

happy days! See under *BAND WAGGON*.

hardest. See FIRST —— YEARS ARE THE ~.

hard knocks. See SCHOOL OF ~.

hard man is good to find, a. See GOOD MAN IS HARD TO FIND.

harm. See ANOTHER LITTLE DRINK . . .

harp. See I TOOK MY ~ TO A PARTY.

hat. See IF YOU WANT TO GET AHEAD . . . ; KEEP IT UNDER YOUR ~.

hate. See MAN YOU LOVE TO ~.

hat-trick, to perform a. *Idiom.* Meaning, in cricket, three wickets taken with successive balls – which *OED* finds in 1882. The player so doing is entitled to be awarded a new hat – 'or equivalent' – by the club. The expression went on to mean any three-in-a-row achievement.

Another origin: the Barons of Kingsale – in the Irish peerage – have long maintained that they can remain covered in the presence of the Sovereign. Almericus, the 18th Baron Kingsale, 'walked to and fro with his hat on his head' in the presence chamber of William III, claiming he was asserting an ancient privilege. He did it three times, the original hat-trick (Simon Winchester, *Their Noble Lordships*, 1981). (I rather doubt this explanation.)

have a banana! *Catch Phrase.* Britain became 'banana conscious' in the early years of the twentieth century following the appointment of Roger Ackerley as chief salesman of Elders & Fyffes, banana importers, in 1898. The phrase 'have a banana!' – never a slogan as such – was popularly interpolated at the end of the first line of the song 'Let's All Go Down the Strand', which was published in 1904. It had not been put there by the composer, but was so successful that later printings of the song always included it. Every time it was sung, the phrase reinforced the sales campaign free of charge. A slight sexual implication, of course, as in the song 'Burlington Bertie from Bow' (1914) – 'I've had a banana with Lady Diana'.

Have a Go. 'Ladies and gentlemen of Bingley, 'ow do, 'ow are yer?' – that was how Wilfred Pickles introduced the first edition of this folksy, travelling radio show in 1946. Within twelve months, it had an audience of twenty million and ran for twenty-one years in all. It was to the 1940s and 50s what TV's GENERATION GAME was to the 1970s – a simple quiz which enabled the host, accompanied by his wife, to indulge in folksy chatting-up of contestants.

Indeed, Pickles (1904–78) spent most of the programme chatting to the quiz contestants and fishing for laughs with questions like **have you ever had any embarrassing moments?** One reply he received was from a woman who had been out with a very shy young man. Getting desperate for conversation with him she had said, 'If there's one thing I can't stand, it's people who sit on you and use you as a convenience.'

Chatting up spinsters, of any age from NINETEEN TO NINETY, Pickles would ask, **are yer courtin'?** But, after all, this was what the programme set out to provide: **a spot of homely fun, presenting the people to the people.**

Winners of the quiz took away, not cars or consumer goods or holidays abroad, but pots of jam and the odd shilling or two. **Give 'im/'er the money, Barney!** was the cry when a winner was established (sometimes with a good deal of help from Pickles). The Barney in question was Barney Colehan, a BBC producer. Later, wife

Mabel Pickles supervised the prizes – hence the alternative **give 'im/'er the money, Mabel!** and the references to **Mabel at the table** and the query **what's on the table, Mabel?**

The original phrase 'have a go' – meaning 'make an attempt' (dating from the nineteenth century, at least), was used in a rather different context when, in 1964, Sir Ranulph Bacon, then Assistant Commissioner at Scotland Yard, urged members of the public to 'have a go' if they saw an armed robbery. His advice caused a storm of protest, and was labelled 'madness' and 'suicidal' by the British Safety Council, but the phrase is still used in this sense.

have a gorilla. See under GOON SHOW.

have a nice day. *Catch Phrase*. William Safire traced the origins of this pervasive American greeting in his book *On Language* (1980). Beginning with an early flourish in Chaucer's 'The Knight's Tale' ('Fare well, have good day') it then jumped to 1956 and the Carson/Roberts advertising agency in Los Angeles. 'Our phone was answered "Good morning, Carson/Roberts. Have a happy day",' recalled Ralph Carson. 'We used the salutation on all letters, tie tacks, cuff buttons, beach towels, blazer crests, the works.' Shortly after this, WCBS-TV weather-girl Carol Reed would wave goodbye with 'Have a happy'.

In the 1960s, 'Have a good day' was still going strong. Then, the early 1970s saw 'Have a nice day' push its insidious way in, although Kirk Douglas had got his tongue round it in the 1948 film *A Letter to Three Wives*. 'Have a nice city' was a slogan in the 1970 Los Angeles mayoral election.

From all this, it may be understood that the usage seems likely to have been a Californian imposition upon the rest of the USA.

have gun will travel. *Catch Phrase > Format Phrase.* Best known as the title of a Western TV series (made in the US, 1957–64), this led to a format phrase capable of much variation. Originally it was what might have been on the calling card of a hired gun – eg 'Have gun, will travel . . . wire Paladin, San Francisco'. Later, the phrase turned up in many ways – as joke slogans ('Have pill, will'; 'Have wife, must travel') and even as the UK title of another TV series (1981) *Have Girls, Will Travel* (but known as *The American Girls* in the US).

haves and the have-nots, the. *Nickname > Cliché.* A way of distinguishing between the advantaged and disadvantaged of society. Safire points to Sancho Panza's saying in *Don Quixote*, 'There are only two families in the world, the Haves and the Have-Nots' (Spanish *el tener* and *el no tener*). Edward Bulwer-Lytton in *Athens*, 1836, wrote: 'The division . . . of the Rich and the Poor – the havenots and the haves.'

R.A. Butler, at a Conservative Political Centre Summer School, 8 July 1960: 'We have developed an affluent, open and democratic society . . . in which people are divided not so much between "haves" and "have-nots" as between "haves" and "have mores".'

have you ever had any embarrassing moments? See under *HAVE A GO.*

have you met my niece? *Catch Phrase > Cliché.* A well-known British political figure arriving at some function with a nubile young girl on his arm tends to introduce her by asking, 'Have you met my niece?' He is not alone. According to the *Independent*'s obituary of film producer Nat Cohen (11 February 1988), 'He was much loved – not least by the young ladies usually introduced as "Have you met my niece?" ' And according to *Soho* by Judith Summers (1989), the first Lord Beaverbrook habitually dined upstairs at the French (restaurant) with sundry 'nieces' – 'He had more nieces than any man I've known', one Gaston confides to the author.

(The lines 'Moreover, if you please, a niece of mine/ Shall there attend you' – Shakespeare, *Pericles*, III.iv.14 – are unfortunately not connected.)

having a wonderful time. See under WISH YOU WERE HERE.

hay. See AND THAT AIN'T ~.

he. See WHO ~?

heals. See HOLE ~ UP . . .

health. See WHAT ME, IN MY STATE OF ~? under *YTMA*; GOVERNMENT ~ WARNING.

hear. See BELIEVE ONLY HALF . . . ; CAN YOU ~ ME, MOTHER?

heard. See YOU AIN'T SEEN NOTHIN' YET.

heart. See EAT YOUR ~ OUT!; IN YOUR ~ YOU KNOW . . .

heartbeat away from the presidency, a. *Saying.* The traditional description of the position of the US vice-president and, as Safire puts it, 'a reminder to voters to examine the shortcomings of a vice-presidential candidate'. The earliest use of the phrase Safire finds is Adlai Stevenson beginning an attack on Richard Nixon in 1952 with, 'The Republican Vice-Presidential candidate, who asks you to place him a heartbeat from the Presidency . . .'

Jules Witcover entitled a book on Vice-President Spiro Agnew's enforced resignation, *A Heartbeat Away*. The phrase was much in evidence again when George Bush selected Dan Quayle as his running-mate in 1988.

hearts and minds. *Slogan* – or, rather, a description of what had to be won in the Vietnam War by the US Government. Its origins go back to Theodore Roosevelt's day when Douglas MacArthur, as a young aide, asked him (in 1906) to what he attributed his popularity. The President replied: '[My ability] to put into words what is in their hearts and minds but not in their mouths.'

Safire also points out that, in 1954, Earl Warren ruled in the case of Brown *v* Board of Education of Topeka: 'To separate [Negro children] from others of similar age and qualifications solely because of their race generates a feeling of inferiority as to their status in the community that may affect their hearts and minds in a way unlikely ever to be undone.'

The Blessing in the Holy Communion service of the Prayer Book is: 'The peace of God, which passeth all understanding, keep your hearts and minds in the knowl-edge and love of God, and of his Son Jesus Christ Our Lord.' This is drawn from the Epistle of Paul the Apostle to the Philippians 4:7.

heat. See IF YOU CAN'T STAND THE ~ . . .

he can't fart and chew gum at the same time. *Saying.* Meaning 'he's stupid'. This is the correct version – advanced on the authority of John Kenneth Galbraith, no less – of what President Lyndon Johnson once said about Gerald Ford. Ie rather more colourful than **he can't *walk* and chew gum at the same time,** the version usually quoted when Ford became president in 1974. Like much of Johnson's earthy speech, I think it might have been a Texan expression rather than of his own invention.

Heineken refreshes the parts other beers cannot reach. *Slogan.* 'I wrote the slogan,' said Terry Lovelock, 'during December 1974 at 3 am at the Hotel Marmounia in Marakesh. After eight weeks of incubation with the agency [Collett, Dickenson, Pearce], it was really a brainstorm. No other lines were written. The trip was to refresh the brain, but it worked.'

The resulting sentence – though not tripping easily off the tongue – became one of the most popular slogans ever used in Britain and is still running (1989). The merits of the lager were always demonstrated with amusing visuals: the 'droop-snoot' of Concorde raised by an infusion of the brew; a piano tuner's ears sharpened; a policeman's toes refreshed. There was also a strong topical element. When Chia-Chia, a panda from London Zoo, was sent off in

1981 to mate with Ling-Ling in Washington, a full-page press ad merely said 'Good Luck Chia-Chia from Heineken', the slogan being understood.

Much parodied – in graffiti: 'Courage reaches the parts other beers don't bother with', 'Joe Jordan [Scottish footballer] kicks the parts other beers don't reach', 'Hook Norton ale reaches the parts Heineken daren't mention', 'Mavis Brown reaches parts most beers can't reach', 'Vindaloo purges the parts other curries can't reach'; in political speeches: 'When I think of our much-travelled Foreign Secretary [Lord Carrington] I am reminded of . . . the peer that reaches those foreign parts other peers cannot reach' (Margaret Thatcher, Conservative Party Conference, 1980).

Heinz 57 Varieties. *Slogan* – or brand name as slogan. The name has been used for Heinz canned foods since 1896. In that year, Henry Heinz was travelling through New York City on the overhead railway. He saw a street-car window advertising twenty-one styles of shoe; the idea appealed to him and, although he could list fifty-eight or fifty-nine Heinz products, he settled on 57 because it sounded right. Heinz commented later: 'I myself did not realize how successful a slogan it was going to be.' In housey-housey or bingo, 'all the beans' is now the cry for '57'.

Partridge/*Slang* has 'Heinz' and '57 Varieties' as expressions for a 'mongrel dog'.

See also BEANZ MEANZ HEINZ.

heir. See SON AND ~.

hell. See COME ~ AND HIGH WATER; NO MORE CHANCE THAN . . .

hello, folks! See under *BAND WAGGON*.

hello, good evening, and welcome! *Stock Phrase* > *Catch Phrase*. A greeting well-known on TV on both sides of the Atlantic. It derives from the period when David Frost (*b* 1939) was commuting back and forth to host TV chat shows in London and New York. It may have been contrived to say three things where only one is needed but it became an essential part of the Frost impersonator's kit (not to mention the Frost self-impersonator's kit). He was certainly saying it by 1970 and he was still staying it in 1983 when, with a small alteration, it became 'Hello, good *morning*, and welcome!' at the debut of TV-am, the breakfast-TV station.

hello, I'm Julian . . . See under *ROUND THE HORNE*.

hello, it's me – Twinkletoes! See under *EDUCATING ARCHIE*.

hello, my darlings! *Catch Phrase*. From the early 1950s, this has been the greeting of comedian Charlie Drake (*b* 1925). Perhaps rendered curiously memorable because of the husky, baby-voiced way in which it is spoken.

hello, playmates! See under *BAND WAGGON*.

hello, Rodney!/ hello, Charles! See under *BEYOND OUR KEN*.

hello, sailor! *Catch Phrase*. This phrase must long have been around – with varying degrees of homosexual and heterosexual emphasis – but as a camp catch phrase it had quite a vogue in the early 1970s, reaching a peak in 1975/6, promoted by various branches of the media.

The first appearance of the phrase that I have come across is in Spike Milligan's script for 'Tales of Men's Shirts' in the GOON SHOW (31 December 1959). 'Hello, sailor!' is spoken, for no very good reason, by Minnie Bannister.

However, perhaps originally it *was* something that would have been called out by a female prostitute to a potential customer in somewhere like Portsmouth (along the lines of, 'Like a nice time, dearie?')

Milligan told me (1978) he thought he had started the 'seventies revival in one of his *Q* TV shows. To fill up time, he had just sat and said it a number of times. However, Dudley Moore also used it, and the cast of radio's *I'm Sorry I'll Read That Again* promoted it heavily – perhaps influenced by there being a number of newsworthy sailors about in the early 1970s, including Prince Philip, Prince Charles and the Prime Minister, Edward Heath.

In the end, it was usually used by a speaker to indicate that the person he was addressing was homosexual.

helping the police with their inquiries. *Stock Phrase > Cliché*. When a suspect is being interviewed by the police but has not yet been charged with any offence, this rather quaint euphemism is trotted out and eagerly passed on by the media. It is quite possible, of course, that the suspect in question is, in fact, being quite unhelpful to the police in their inquiries

and that they are being impolite to him in equal measure.

here. See I'M ONLY ~ FOR THE BEER; QUEEN ELIZABETH SLEPT ~; WISH YOU WERE ~!

here and now, before your very eyes! *Stock Phrase*. When Arthur Askey moved to TV in the early 1950s, his first series was called *Before Your Very Eyes*. Indeed, he was one of the first comedians to address the viewer through the camera in an intimate way rather than just do a variety act as if to a theatre audience. Arthur registered the title in conversation with the BBC's Ronnie Waldman, even before he had been given the series – although, in the end, it was made by ITV. He would say the phrase to emphasize that the show was, indeed, done live. (I take it that 'before your very eyes' predates the Askey use – perhaps it comes from the patter of magicians, showmen, etc?)

here come de judge. See under *LAUGH-IN*.

here's another fine mess you've gotten me into! *Catch Phrase*. With several variations. The anguished cry of Oliver Hardy after some ineptitude on Stan Laurel's part managed to instate itself as one of the few film catch phrases because there was a sufficient number of Laurel and Hardy features for it to register with audiences. One of their thirty-minute features (released in 1930) was actually called *Another Fine Mess*. A graffito from the Falklands war of 1982 declared: 'There's another fine mess you got me into, [Port] Stanley.'

here's a pretty kettle of fish! *Idiom.* That Queen Mary did indeed exclaim 'Here's a pretty kettle of fish' to Prime Minister Stanley Baldwin at the time of the Abdication crisis, there is no doubt. A differently-worded version has turned up with, however, the precise date. Nancy Dugdale (*d* 1969) wrote a diary from data supplied by her husband, Thomas, Parliamentary Private Secretary to Baldwin from 1935 to 1937.

On Tuesday 17 November 1936 she wrote: 'Mr Baldwin went today to see the Queen, who enchanted him by the sentence with which she greeted him: "This is a nice kettle of fish, isn't it?" She was naturally very upset . . .'

On the broader question of why we use the expression 'kettle of fish' in this way: in the 1740s, Henry Fielding uses 'pretty kettle of fish' in both *Joseph Andrews* and *Tom Jones*, so it was obviously well-established by then. Brewer has a plausible explanation, saying that 'kettle of fish' is an old Border country name for a kind of *fête champêtre*, or riverside picnic, where a newly caught salmon is boiled and eaten. 'The discomfort of this sort of party may have led to the phrase, "A pretty kettle of fish", meaning an awkward state of affairs, a mess, a muddle.'

A 'fish kettle' as the name of a cauldron for cooking fish has been a term in use since the seventeenth century, though this appears not to have much to do with this expression.

I rather prefer the explanation given in *English Idioms* published by Nelson (*c* 1912) that kettle comes from 'kiddle' = a net. So all one is saying is, 'here is a nice net of fish', as one might on drawing it out of the sea, not being totally sure what it contains.

here's Johnny! *Stock Phrase.* Said with a drawn-out, rising inflection on the first word, this has been Ed McMahon's introduction to Johnny Carson on NBC's *Tonight* show since 1961: '[*Drum roll*] And now . . . heeeeere's Johnny!' It was emulated during Simon Dee's brief reign as a chat-show host in Britain during the 1960s. The studio audience joined in the rising inflection of the announcer's **it's Siiimon Dee!** Jack Nicholson playing a psychopath chopped through a door with an axe and cried 'Here's Johnny!' in the film *The Shining* (1981).

here's looking at you, kid! *Catch Phrase.* From the film *Casablanca* (1942), a line based on existing drinking phrases and turned into a catch phrase by Humphrey Bogart impersonators. 'Here's Looking At You' had been the title of one of the first revues transmitted by the BBC from Alexandra Palace in the early days of television (*c* 1936).

here we are again! *Catch Phrase.* Perhaps the oldest it is possible to attach to a particular performer. Joseph Grimaldi (1779–1837) used it as Joey the Clown in pantomime and it has subsequently been used by almost all clowns on entering the circus ring or theatre stage . . . for example, by Harry Paine in the 1870s and 1880s. He would turn a somersault on entering and declare it.

here we go, here we go, here we go! *Catch Phrase.* This chant, sung to the tune of Sousa's 'Stars and Stripes for Ever', is one beloved of British football supporters, though it has other applications. It suddenly became very noticeable at the time of the Mexico World Cup in

June 1986. The previous year, the Everton football team had made a record of the chant, arranged and adapted by Tony Hiller and Harold Spiro. This version included an excursion into Offenbach's famous Can-Can tune.

he's fallen in the water! See under GOON SHOW.

hesitation. See WITHOUT ~ . . .

he's loo-vely, Mrs Hardcastle . . . See under RAY'S A LAUGH.

he's very good, you know! See under GOON SHOW.

he was a big man in every sense of the word/a giant among men. *Cliché*. In obituaries. From *Money-Brief* (from stockbrokers Gerrard Vivian Gray, April 1989): 'Roddy was an excellent stockbroker and wonderful friend. His memorial service . . . was a marvellous tribute to a man who was larger than life in every way.'

hide. See YOU CAN RUN BUT YOU CAN'T ~.

hi-de-hi! *Catch Phrase*. For several years from 1980 onwards, BBC Television had a long-running situation comedy series set in a 1950s holiday camp called *Hi-de-hi*. The title probably came to be used in this way from a camper's song special to Butlin's:

Tramp, tramp, tramp, tramp,
Here we come, to jolly old Butlin's every year.
All come down to Butlin's, all by the sea.
Never mind the weather, we're as happy as can be.

Hi-de-hi! Ho-de-ho!
(quoted in the *Observer* magazine, 12 June 1983)
This possibly dates from the late 1930s. The origin of the phrase seems to lie in the dance band vocals of the 1920s/30s – the 'Hi-de-ho, vo-de-o-do' sort of thing. However, according to Denis Gifford's *The Golden Age of Radio*, 'Hi-de-hi! Ho-de-ho!' was the catch phrase of Christopher Stone, the BBC's first 'disc-jockey', when he went off and presented *Post Toasties Radio Corner*, a children's programme for Radio Normandy in 1937.

The catch phrase achieved notoriety when a commanding officer in the army faced a court of inquiry or court-martial for making his troops answer 'Ho-de-ho' when he (or his fellow officers) yelled 'Hi-de-hi'. I don't know when this case was, but it was well in the past when *Notes and Queries* got around to it in 1943–4, and there was a revue with the title at the Palace Theatre, London, in 1943. Gerald Kersh referred to army use of the exchange (though not to the specific case) in *They Die with their Boots Clean* in 1941.

high. See PILE IT ~; COME HELL AND ~ WATER.

hills. See THERE'S GOLD IN THEM THAR ~.

him bad man, kemo sabe! See HI-YO, SILVER!

his death diminishes us all. *Cliché*. In obituaries, possibly deriving originally from John Donne's *Devotions*, XVII (1624): 'Any man's death diminishes me, because I am involved in Mankind: and therefore never send to know for whom the bell tolls; it tolls for thee.'

his/her face was his/her fortune. *Cliché.* 'My face is my fortune' occurs, for example, in the (laundered) sea shanty 'Rio Grande' (trad./anon.) to be found in various students' song-books.

history. See REST IS ~.

hit. See YOU DON'T REWRITE A ~.

hit the ground running, to. *Idiom.* From the *Independent* (29 March 1989): '*The Late Show* has so far generated an overwhelmingly favourable response . . . "To hit the ground running with four shows a week", said Alex Graham, editor of *The Media Show* on Channel 4, "that's really impressive."' I think this comes from military use – leaping from assault craft, even from parachutes, and, without preamble, successfully getting straight on with the business in hand, is probably what is being alluded to.

hi-yo, Silver (away)! *Stock Phrase.* 'Who *was* that masked man? . . . A fiery horse with the speed of light, a cloud of dust, and a hearty "Hi-yo, Silver!" The Lone Ranger! With his faithful Indian companion Tonto, the daring and resourceful masked rider of the plains led the fight for law and order in the early western United States. Nowhere in the pages of history can one find a greater champion of justice. **Return with us now to those thrilling days of yesteryear** . . . From out of the past come the thundering hoofbeats of the great horse Silver. **The Lone Ranger rides again!**

' "Come on, Silver! Let's go, big fellow! Hi-yo, Silver, away!" '

The above was more or less the introduction to the masked Lone Ranger and his horse, Silver, in the various American radio and cinema accounts of their exploits – accompanied, of course, by Rossini's 'William Tell' overture.

Groucho Marx used to say that George Seaton (the first Lone Ranger on radio from 1933) invented the call 'Hi-yo, Silver!' because he was unable to whistle for his horse. It seems that the phrase was minted by Seaton and not by Fran Striker, the chief scriptwriter in the early days.

The Lone Ranger's Indian friend, Tonto, wrestled meanwhile with such lines as, **him bad man, kemo sabe!** ('kemos sabe' – whichever way you spell it – is supposed to mean 'trusty scout' and was derived from the name of a boys' camp at Mullet Lake, Michigan, in 1911).

hockey-sticks. See JOLLY ~.

ho-ho, *very* satirical. *Catch Phrase.* Expressing ironical appreciation of a satirical joke. Probably a reaction to the 'satire boom' of the early 1960s. But still alive. A 'Mini-Trog' cartoon in the *Observer* of 17 July 1988, at a time of long delays at British airports, showed a little man looking at an advertisement jokily promoting Gatwick as 'Gatqwick'. He is saying to himself, '*Very* satirical'.

hold it against me. See IF I SAID YOU HAD A BEAUTIFUL BODY . . .

hold it up to the light, not a stain, and shining bright. *Slogan.* For Surf washing powder, current in the late 1950s.

This was a line from the 'Mrs Bradshaw' series of TV ads in which the eponymous lady never appeared but her male lodger did. (From an edition of the GOON SHOW of the same period: 'The BBC – hold it up to the light – not a brain in sight!')

hold the fort, to. *Idiom.* One might say 'Hold the fort' to mean 'Look after this place while I'm away', but in the sense of 'Hang on, relief is at hand' there is a specific origin. In the American Civil War, General William T. Sherman signalled words to this effect to General John M. Corse at the Battle of Allatoona, Georgia, 5 October 1864. What he actually semaphored from Keneshaw Mountain was: 'Sherman says hold fast. We are coming' (Mencken) or 'Hold out. Relief is coming' (Bartlett).

The phrase became popularized in its present form as the first line of a hymn/gospel song written by Philip Paul Bliss in c 1870 ('Ho, My Comrades, See the Signal!' in *The Charm*). This was introduced to Britain by Moody and Sankey during their evangelical tour of the British Isles in 1873 (and not written by them, as is sometimes supposed):

'Hold the fort, for I am coming,'
　Jesus signals still;
Wave the answer back to heaven,
　'By thy grace we will.'
More recently, perhaps thanks to a pun on 'union' (as in the American Civil War and trade union), the song has been adapted as a trade union song in Britain:
Hold the fort, for we are coming
Union men be strong
Side by side keep pressing onward.
Victory will come.

hole heals up as soon as you leave the car park, the. *Saying.* Meaning 'you will not be missed, no one is irreplaceable'. Michael Grade said it on leaving the BBC for Channel 4 in November 1987 and called it a 'BBC saying'.

holy —— ! See under BATMAN.

home. See ARE THERE ANY MORE AT ~ LIKE YOU?; AT ~ AND AWAY . . . under FAMILY FAVOURITES; EVERY ~ SHOULD HAVE ONE; I THINK I GO ~; YOURS TO ENJOY IN THE PRIVACY . . .

homely fun. See A SPOT OF . . . under HAVE A GO.

Homer nods, even. *Idiom.* Meaning 'even the greatest, best and wisest of us can't be perfect all the time, and can make mistakes'. Mencken has 'Even Homer sometimes nods' as an English proverb derived from Horace, *De Arte Poetica*, c 8 BC ['I am indignant when worthy Homer nods'], and familiar since the seventeenth century.

hook. See BY ~ OR BY CROOK.

hoots mon! *Catch Phrase.* The 1958 British hit instrumental record 'Hoots Mon', performed by Lord Rockingham's XI, was punctuated at strategic points by the speaking of the cod Scotticisms, 'Hoots Mon, there's a moose loose aboot this hoose' and **it's a braw brecht moonlicht nicht**.

The last phrase also occurs in the song 'Just a wee deoch-an-duoris' that Sir Harry Lauder performed and which he wrote in 1912 in collaboration with G. Grafton, R.F. Morrison and Whit Cunliffe.

As for 'hoots mon' (ie 'man') on its own, the *Collins English Dictionary* describes 'hoot/s' as 'an exclamation of impatience or dissatisfaction; a supposed Scotticism – C17: of unknown origin'.

The *OED* weighs in with the word being 'of Scottish and Northern England use', comparing the Swedish *hut*, 'begone', the Welsh *hwt*, 'away', and the Irish *ut*, 'out', all used in a similar sense.

In 1982, I put the phrase to a panel including such noted Scottish word-persons as John Byrne, Cliff Hanley and Jimmy Reid. One thought it was a greeting with the meaning, 'How's it going, man?' Another thought it might mean 'Have a big dram, man' – a 'hoot' being a drink. Finally, Jimmy Reid dismissed it as 'stage Scots . . . bastardized Scots, for the placation of Sassenachs'.

Horlicks. See THINKS . . . THANKS TO ~.

horrible. See YOU 'ORRIBLE LITTLE MAN.

horror. See SHOCK, ~!

horse. See I GOTTA ~; IF YOU CAN'T RIDE TWO ~S . . . ; ONLY FOOLS AND ~S WORK.

horses sweat, men perspire, and women merely glow. *Saying.* In the form, 'Here's a little proverb that you surely ought to know:/ Horses sweat and men perspire, but ladies only glow', J.M. Cohen includes it in *Comic and Curious Verse* (1952–9) as merely by Anon.

Used to reprove someone who talks of 'sweating'. It is listed as a nanny's reprimand in *Nanny Says* (1972) in the form, 'Horses sweat, gentlemen perspire, but ladies only gently glow.'

hot. See LONG ~ SUMMER.

house. See IS THERE A DOCTOR IN THE ~?

Hovis. See DON'T SAY BROWN . . .

how did you feel when ——? *Cliché.* From TV news, chiefly. 'How did you feel when your daughter was raped before your eyes/ your house was blown up/ you'd forgotten to post the pools coupon and lost your next-door neighbour a million pounds?' It may be necessary for the question to be asked in order to elicit a response but the nearest any of the news-gatherers has come to doing anything about it is to suggest that, while asking the question is a legitimate activity, it shouldn't actually be broadcast – only the answer.

how do? See 'OW DO under *HAVE A GO*.

how many beans make five? *Catch Phrase.* Or 'catch question', rather. A joke riddle, but also uttered as an answer to an impossible question (along the lines of **how long is a piece of string?** etc). Miss Alice Lloyd was singing a music-hall song in November 1898 which contained these lines:

You say you've never heard
    How many beans make five?
It's time you knew a thing or two -
    You don't know you're alive!

how now, brown cow? *Catch Phrase.* I suppose this has long been an elocution exercise, though it was not included along with 'The rain in Spain stays mainly in the plain' and 'In Hertford, Hereford and Hampshire hurricanes hardly ever happen' in the elocution song in *My Fair Lady*.

The earliest trace I have found of it is in a reminiscence of the Oxford University Dramatic Society in the 1920s by Osbert Lancaster in *With an Eye to the Future* (1967). Of an OUDS Last Night party, he writes: 'The principal entertainment was provided by musical members past and present repeating the numbers which they had composed for OUDS smokers, many of which – such as "How now brown cow" – had, after some slight modification of the lyrics at the request of the Lord Chamberlain, reappeared in West End revues.'

Indeed, 'How Now Brown Cow' with words by Rowland Leigh and music by Richard Addinsell was sung by Joyce Barbour in the revue *RSVP* at the Vaudeville Theatre on 23 February 1926 and was recorded by her on Columbia 4072. (Incidentally, the *OED* has an example of the simple interjection 'How now?', meaning 'How goes it?', dating from 1480.)

The rhyming of 'rain' and 'Spain' seems a venerable activity, too. In *Polite Conversation* (1738), Swift has this exchange:

I see 'tis raining again.
Why then, Madam, we must do as they do in Spain.
Pray, my Lord, how is that?
Why, Madam, we must let it rain.

Yet another speaking exercise appears in *Little Dorrit* by Charles Dickens (1857). Mrs General opines, 'Papa, potatoes, poultry, prunes and prism, are all very good words for the lips: especially prunes and prism.'

Two undated speaking exercises from the schooldays of the actress Eleanor Bron (shall we say 1950s?) went: 'Lippy

and Loppy were two little rabbits – lippity, lippity, lippity, lop', and, 'They put the lady in the tar. They said that she was in their power. They left her there for half-an-hour'.

how's about that then, guys and gals? See under AS IT HAPPENS.

how sweet it is! See under AND AWA-A-AAY WE GO!

how the other half lives. *Saying*. Ie how people live who belong to different social groups, especially the rich. The *Longman Dictionary of English Idioms* (1979) suggests that this phrase was launched through the title of a book (1890) by Jacob Riis (1849–1914), an American newspaper reporter. He described the conditions in which poor people lived in New York City. Indeed, the expression seems basically to have referred to the poor but has since been used about any 'other half'.

Maybe, but even Riis alludes to the core-saying in these words: 'Long ago it was said that "one half of the world does not know how the other half lives".' The *OED Supp.* finds this proverb in 1607, in English, and, in French, in *Pantagruel* by Rabelais (1532).

Alan Ayckbourn entitled one of his plays *How the Other Half Loves* (1970).

human. See ALL ~ LIFE IS THERE; FULLY PAID-UP MEMBER OF THE ~ RACE.

husband. See MY ~ AND I.

hush, hush, hush, here comes the bogey man. *Catch Phrase*. Compton Mackenzie recalled going to pantomimes in the

1890s and, in particular, hearing the Demon King sing:

Hush, hush, hush!
Here comes the bogey man,
Be on your best behaviour,
For he'll catch you if he can.

He adds (in *Echoes*, 1925): 'At these words children were fain to clutch parent or nurse or governess in panic, and I remember hearing it debated whether a theatre management was justified in ter-rifying children with such songs.'

I first encountered the song on the B-side of the famous Henry Hall recording of 'The Teddy Bears' Picnic' (1932).

The golf term 'bogey' apparently was derived from 'bogey-man' (as recounted in *OED Supp.*) on an occasion in 1890. 'Bogey' meaning 'goblin, phantom or sprite' is very old indeed.

hush, keep it dark! See KEEP IT DARK.

I. See MY HUSBAND AND ~.

I always do my best for all my gentlemen. See *ITMA*.

I am the greatest. *Catch Phrase*. Muhammad Ali, formerly Cassius Clay (*b* 1942), became world heavyweight boxing champion in 1964. He admitted that he copied his 'I am the greatest . . . I am the prettiest' routine from a wrestler called Gorgeous George he once saw in Las Vegas: 'I noticed they all paid to get in – and I said, this is a good idea!' In a moment of unusual modesty, Ali added: 'I'm not really the greatest. I only say I'm the greatest because it sells tickets.'

I could do that. See GI'US A JOB.

idea. See A GOOD ~, SON under *EDUCATING ARCHIE*; IT SEEMED LIKE A GOOD ~ AT THE TIME.

I didn't get where I am today . . . *Catch Phrase*. In BBC TV's The Fall and Rise of Reginald Perrin (1976–80), 'C.J.', the boss (John Barron) would thus frequently muse. This popularized a characteristic phrase of the pompous.

I do not like this game. See under *GOON SHOW*.

I don't mind if I do! See under *ITMA*.

I don't wish to know that, kindly leave the stage. *Stock Phrase*. The traditional response to a corny joke, usually said by a person who has been interrupted while engaged in some other activity on stage. Impossible to say when, and with whom, it started, but in the 1950s the phrase was given a new lease of life by the *GOON SHOW* on radio and by other British entertainers who still owe much to the routines and spirit of music-hall. Rowan used to say to Martin on *LAUGH-IN*, 'I don't want to hear about it', in similar circumstances. See also I SAY, I SAY, I SAY!

I dreamed I —— in my Maidenform bra. *Slogan.* A classic ad from the days when bras were not for burning but for dreaming about. The series, devised by the Norman Craig & Kummel agency in the US, ran for twenty years from 1949. Maidenform offered prizes up to $10,000 for dream situations that could be used in the advertising, in addition to: 'I dreamed I took the bull by the horns/ Went walking/ Stopped the traffic/ Was a social butterfly/ Rode in a gondola/ Was Cleopatra . . . in my Maidenform bra.' 'I dreamed I went to blazes . . .' was illustrated by a girl in bra, fireman's helmet and boots, swinging from a fire engine.

if anything can go wrong, it will. *Saying.* Most commonly known as **Murphy's Law** (and indistinguishable from **Sod's Law** or **Spode's Law**), this saying dates back to the 1940s. *The Macquarie Dictionary* (1981) suggests that it was named after a character who always made mistakes, in a series of educational cartoons published by the US Navy.

CODP suggests that it was invented by George Nichols, a project manager for Northrop, the Californian aviation firm, in 1949. He developed the idea from a remark by a colleague, Captain E. Murphy of the Wright Field-Aircraft Laboratory.

The most notable demonstration of Murphy's Law is that a piece of bread when dropped on the floor will always fall with its buttered side facing down (otherwise known as the Law of Universal Cus-sedness). This, however, pre-dates the promulgation of the Law. In 1867, A.D. Eichardson wrote in *Beyond Mississippi*: 'His bread never fell on the buttered side.' In 1884, James Payn composed the lines:

I never had a piece of toast
Particularly long and wide,
But fell upon the sanded floor
And always on the buttered side.

The corollary of this aspect of the Law is that bread always falls buttered side down *except when demonstrating the Law*!

Some have argued that the point of Murphy's Law is constructive rather than defeatist – that it was a prescription for avoiding mistakes in the design of a valve for an aircraft's hydraulic system. If the valve could be fitted in more than one way, then sooner or later someone would fit it the wrong way. The idea was to design it so that the valve could only be fitted the right way.

if in doubt, strike it out. *Saying.* A piece of (I would say) journalist's lore is, 'If in doubt, strike it out' – meaning, if you're not sure of a fact or about the wisdom of including an item of information or opinion, leave it out. It may be that the advice was more specific, originally. Mark Twain in *Pudd'nhead Wilson* (1894) says: 'As to the adjective, when in doubt strike it out.' Ernest Hemingway recommended striking out adverbs, I believe.

Compare this with the advice Samuel Johnson quoted from a college tutor (30 April 1773): 'Read over your compositions, and where ever you meet with a passage which you think is particularly fine, strike it out.' Which might be recommended to journalists also.

The precise phrase appears in the notorious 'Green Book' issued c 1949 to guide BBC Light Entertainment producers as to which jokes were, or were not, then permissible on the radio: 'Material about which a producer has any doubts should, if it cannot be submitted to someone in higher authority, be deleted, and an artist's assurance that it has been previously broadcast is no justification for repeating it. "When in doubt, take it out" is the wisest maxim.'

Partridge/*Slang* has 'when/if in doubt, toss it out' as, curiously, a 'pharmaceutical catch phrase C20'. 'When in doubt, do nowt' is a North Country (I would say) proverb which *CODP* first finds in 1884.

if I said you had a beautiful body, would you hold it against me? *Saying*. A simple punning question became the title of a hit song by the American duo, the Bellamy Brothers, in 1979 (though they sang 'have' instead of 'had'). *The Naff Sex Guide* (1984) listed it among 'Naff Pick-Up Lines'.

The British comedian Max Miller ('The Cheeky Chappie') (1895–1963), not unexpectedly, had got there first. In a selection of his jokes once published by the *Sunday Dispatch* (and reprinted in *The Last Empires*, ed. Benny Green, 1986) we find: 'I saw a girl who was proud of her figure. Just to make conversation I asked her, "What would you do if a chap criticised your figure?" "Well," she said, "I wouldn't hold it against him." '

if it ain't broke(n), why fix it? *Saying*. This seems to be a very modern proverb indeed. I came across it several times in late 1988, without having registered it before. In the *Independent* (3 November 1988), a TV reviewer asked it of the Government's plans to deregulate broadcasting. On the 12 November, in the same paper, this appeared about changes made in the musical *Chess* once it had opened: 'Tim Rice [the writer, said], "The notices were very good and people liked it, so we could have said, 'If it ain't broken, don't fix it.' But we felt that certain aspects weren't quite right." '

Safire, however, attributes it to Bert Lance, President Carter's Director of the Office of Management and Budget (1977), speaking on the subject of governmental reorganization.

if it looks like a duck, walks like a duck and quacks like a duck, it's a duck. *Saying*. Usually ascribed to Walter Reuther, the American labour leader during the McCarthyite witch-hunts of the 1950s. He came up with it as a test of whether someone was a Communist: 'If it walks like a duck, and quacks like a duck, then it just may be a duck.'

Then applied elsewhere – but usually in politics: 'Mr Richard Darman, the new [US] Budget director, explained the other day what "no new taxes" means. He will apply the **duck test**. "If it looks like a duck, walks like a duck and quacks like a duck, it's a duck." ' – *Guardian*, 25 January 1989.

if it's ——, this must be ——. *Format Phrase. If It's Tuesday, This Must be Belgium* was the title of a 1969 film about a group of American tourists rushing around Europe. It popularized a format phrase which people could use when they were in the midst of some hectic activity, whilst also reflecting on the confused state of many tourists superficially 'doing' the sights without really knowing where they are. A *Guardian* headline (7 April 1989) on a brief visit to London by Mikhail Gorbachev: 'If It's Thursday, Then It Must Be Thatcherland'.

if you can't beat 'em, join 'em. *Saying.* A familiar proverb, probably American in origin in the alternative form, 'If you can't lick 'em, join 'em'. The earliest citation in the *CODP* is from Quentin Reynolds, the American writer, in 1941. Mencken had it in his dictionary, however, by 1942.

Safire calls it 'a frequent bit of advice, origin obscure, given in areas dominated by one (political) party . . . The phrase, akin to the Scottish proverb "Better bend than break", carries no connotation of surrender; it is used to indicate that the way to take over the opposition's strength is to adopt their positions and platform.'

ODCIE (1985) takes in a broader view of the phrase's use: 'If a rival faction, political party, business firm, foreign power, etc. continues to be more successful than one's own, it is better to go over to their side and get what advantages one can from the alliance.'

if you can't be good, be careful! *Catch Phrase.* Mencken calls it an American proverb, though *CODP*'s pedigree is mostly British, finding its first proper citation here in 1903 (from A.M. Binstead, *Pitcher in Paradise*.) But in 1907, there was an American song called 'Be Good! If You Can't Be Good, be Careful!'

It is a nudging farewell, sometimes completed with 'and if you can't be careful, name it after me' – or 'buy a pram'.

The same sort of farewell remark as **don't do anything I wouldn't do!**

if you can't ride two horses at once, you shouldn't be in the circus. *Saying.* Jimmy Maxton (1855–1946) was an Independent Labour Party MP. At a Scottish Conference of the Party in 1931, a motion was moved that the ILP should disaffiliate from the Labour Party. Maxton made a brief statement to the effect that he was against such a move. In the debate, he had been told that he could not be in two parties – or ride two horses – at the same time. 'My reply to that,' he said, 'is . . . that if my friend cannot ride two horses – what's he doing in the bloody circus?'

This expression went on to have limited further use, not only in the political field.

if you can't stand the heat, get out of the kitchen. *Saying.* In 1960, former US President Harry S Truman said: 'Some men can make decisions and some cannot. Some men fret and delay under criticism. I used to have a saying that applies here, and I note that some people have picked it up.'

When Truman announced that he would not stand again as President, *Time* (28 April 1952) had him give a 'down-to-earth reason for his retirement, quoting a favourite expression of his military jester Major General Harry Vaughan', namely, 'If you can't stand the heat, get out of the kitchen.'

The attribution is usually given to Truman himself but it may not be what he said at all. 'Down-to-earth' is not quite how I would describe this remark, whereas 'If you can't stand the stink, get out of the shit-house' would be. I have only hearsay evidence for this, but given Truman's reputation for salty expressions, it is not improbable.

Bartlett quotes Philip D. Lagerquist of the Harry S Truman Library as saying, 'President Truman has used variations of the aphorism . . . for many years, both orally and in his writings' (1966). Note the 'variations'.

if you'll excuse the pun! *Catch Phrase*. Of the kind used by the humourless, when having sunk to one. So ghastly, I feel like calling it a cliché, which it isn't really.

if you've never been to Manchester, you've never lived! See under *RAY'S A LAUGH*.

if you want anything, just whistle. *Saying > Catch Phrase*. This is not a direct quotation, but is derived, from lines in the film *To Have and Have Not* (1945). What Lauren Bacall says to Humphrey Bogart (and not the other way round) is: 'You know you don't have to act with me, Steve. You don't have to say anything, and you don't have to do anything. Not a thing. Oh, maybe just whistle. You know how to whistle, don't you, Steve? You just put your lips together and blow.'

if you want to get ahead, get a hat. *Slogan*. For the Hat Council – and curiously memorable. Quoted in 1965, but also remembered from the early 1950s, and perhaps even dating from the 1930s.

I go – I come back! See under *ITMA*.

I gotta horse! *Catch Phrase*. 'Ras Prince Monolulu' was a racing tipster who flourished – perhaps the only nationally famous one of his kind – from the 1930s to the 1950s. His real name was Peter Carl McKay, he was black, and he used to wander around dressed up like a Masai warrior, or similar.

Partridge/*Catch Phrases* renders his cry as 'I got an 'orse!' or 'I gotta norse!' and finds that it was coined when Monolulu was trying to outdo a race-track evangelist who carried the placard 'I got Heaven'.

There seem to be many ways of reproducing the cry. However, there is a record on which he sings it – Regal MR 812 – but I've not been able to trace a copy – and there the title is given as 'I got a 'orse'.

I've Got a Horse appears to have been the title of a Noël Gay revue (London, 1938) and definitely of a British film, featuring the singer Billy Fury, in 1965. A black version of Cinderella, originally entitled *I Gotta Shoe*, was presented in London in 1976 and may distantly allude to this phrase.

I hate J.R. See WHO SHOT J.R.?

I haven't been so happy since my grandmother caught her tit in a mangle. *Saying*. Daley Thompson, the British athlete, actually had the nerve to say it on winning a gold medal in the decathlon at the 1984 Los Angeles Olympics.

More commonly, it would go, 'I haven't *laughed* so much since . . .' The rest can vary. It might be 'mother/aunt' and 'left tit/tits'. There is a version in Nicholas Monsarrat's *The Cruel Sea* (1951), which hints at a probable origin in the services. Alan Bennett in *Forty Years On* (1968) has a victorious rugby team sing:

I haven't laughed so much since Grandma died
And Aunty Mabel caught her left titty in
the mangle
And whitewashed the ceiling.

I like Ike. *Slogan.* These words began appearing on buttons in 1947 as the Second
World War US general, Dwight David
Eisenhower, began to be spoken of as a
possible presidential nominee (initially
as a Democrat). By 1950, Irving Berlin
was including one of his least memorable
songs, 'They Like Ike', in *Call Me Madam,*
and 15,000 people at a rally in Madison
Square Gardens were urging Eisenhower
to return from a military posting in Paris
and run as a Republican in 1952, with the
chant 'We like Ike'. It worked. The three
sharp monosyllables, and the effectiveness of the repeated 'i' sound in 'I like
Ike', made it an enduring slogan
throughout the 1950s.

I like the backing. See under I'LL GIVE IT
FOIVE.

I'll 'ave to ask me Dad. See under *ITMA.*

I'll be leaving you now, sir . . . *Stock
Phrase.* A phrase anticipating a tip –
given new life by Claud Snudge (Bill
Fraser) in Granada TV's Bootsie and
Snudge (1960–2). He played a doorman
at a London club.

illegitimi non carborundum. *Catch
Phrase.* This cod-Latin phrase – supposed to mean 'Don't let the bastards
grind you down' – was used by US
General 'Vinegar Joe' Stilwell as his
motto during the Second World War,
though it is not suggested he devised it.

Partridge/*Catch Phrases* gives it as *'illegitimis'* and its origins in British army
intelligence very early on in the same
war.
'Carborundum' is the trade-name of a
very hard substance composed of silicon
carbide, used in grinding.
The same meaning is also conveyed by
the phrase *nil carborundum . . .* (as in the
title of a play by Henry Livings, 1962) – a
pun upon the genuine Latin *nil desperandum* ('never say die' – lit.: 'there is
nought to be despaired of'.)
Perhaps because it is a made-up one,
the phrase takes many forms, eg: *'nil
illegitimis . . .'*, *'nil bastardo illegitimi . . .'*, *'nil bastardo carborundum . . .'*
etc. When the Rt Rev. David Jenkins, the
Bishop of Durham, was unwise enough
to make use of the phrase at a private
meeting in March 1985, a cloth-eared
journalist reported him as having said,
'Nil desperandum illegitimi . . .'

I'll forget my own name in a minute. See
under *ITMA.*

I'll give it foive. *Stock Phrase > Catch
Phrase.* That rarity – a catch phrase launched by a member of the public. Not that
Janice Nicholls, a Brum girl conscripted
on to the 'Spin-a-Disc' panel of ABC TV's
pop show *Thank Your Lucky Stars* in c
1963 could avoid a type of celebrity for
long. Awarding points to newly-released
records in her local dialect and declaring
(as if in mitigation for some awful performance) 'But **I like the backing . . .**' she
became a minor celebrity herself. She
even made a record called 'I'll Give it
Five' (coupled with 'The Wednesbury Madison') – which later she was prepared to
admit was worth about *minus* five.

She was only sixteen, had just left school and was working as a junior clerk/telephonist at a local factory. She was soon meeting 'all the stars except Elvis' and became the pin-up of three ships, a submarine and a fire station. Janice told me in 1980: 'I think it was just the accent really. It's a broad Black Country accent, y'know. I think it must have took the fancy of a lot of people. So they just kept asking me to go back and it ended up being three years before I finished.'

I'll give you the results in reverse order. *Stock Phrase.* Eric Morley founded the Miss World beauty contest in 1951. He assured himself a small measure of fame each year by appearing in the TV show and announcing the winners in the order No. 3, No. 2, No. 1. In consequence, whenever anyone has to give similar results in this way, it is said they are being given **in Miss World order**.

I'll try anything once. *Catch Phrase.* Meaning 'there's always a first time'. Mencken has 'I am always glad to try anything once' as an 'American saying not recorded before the nineteenth century'.

I Love/♥ ——. *Slogan > Format Phrase.* In June 1977, the New York State Department of Commerce launched a campaign to attract tourists. The first commercial showed people enjoying themselves in outdoor activities – fishing, horseback riding, camping, and so forth. Each one said something like, 'I'm from New Hampshire, but I love New York', 'I'm from Cape Cod, but I love New York', and ended with a man in a camping scene saying, 'I'm from Brooklyn, but I loooove New York.'

Since then 'I Love New York' has become one of the best-known advertising slogans in the world but has been swamped by the use of the 'I Love ——' formula on stickers and T-shirts to promote almost every other place in the world (and much else), particularly with the word 'love' replaced by a heart shape.

Charlie Moss at the Wells, Rich, Greene agency is credited with having coined the phrase – though maybe he had heard the song 'How About You?' (lyrics by Ralph Freed, music by Burton Lane) which includes the line 'I like New York in June' and was written for the Garland/Rooney film *Babes on Broadway* (1941). Earlier, Cole Porter had written 'I Happen to Like New York' for his show *The New Yorkers* (1930).

I love it but it doesn't love me. *Cliché.* Of conversation. What people say to soften the refusal of what they have been offered – usually food or drink. And they have been using it for many a year. Swift lists it in *Polite Conversation:*

> *Lady Smart:* Madam, do you love bohea tea?
> *Lady Answerall:* Why, madam, I must confess I do love it; but it does not love me . . .

I'm a cop. See under DRAGNET.

I'm all behind – like the cow's tail. *Catch Phrase.* What people say when they are behind with their tasks. One of a number of ritual additions (like AS THE ART MISTRESS SAID . . . , but without the innuendo). Another is: 'What's the time?' – 'Half past nine . . . knickers on the line.'

I'm/I'll be a monkey's uncle, well. *Catch Phrase*. Expressing astonishment, surprise. *OED Supp*. finds it established in a 1926 'wise-crack' dictionary, which rather rules out one origin I have been given for it – that it had something to do with the famous 'Scopes' or 'Monkey Trial' (of a teacher who taught evolutionary theory in Tennessee). But as the trial was only the year before, the connection is unlikely. As, too, is anything to do with the fact that in London East End slang a 'monkey' = £500 and an 'uncle' = pawnbroker. Partridge/*Slang* has it of American origin.

I meanter say! *Catch Phrase*. This was one of the phrases used by the comedian, Sir George Robey (1869–1954). Neville Cardus recalled him arriving on a stage filled with girls posing as nude Greek statues: 'I can see now his eyebrows going up and him saying, "Well, I mean to say, I mean to say".'
   But it is quite a common expression, as a kind of slightly exasperated apology or exclamation. I have come across it in a Frank Richards 'Billy Bunter' story in a 1915 edition of *The Magnet*.

I'm ——, fly me. *Slogan*. Eg 'I'm Margie', referring to (supposedly actual) air hostesses with National Airlines in the US. Current *c* 1971. The campaign aroused the ire of feminist groups (another suggestive line used was, 'I'm going to fly you like you've never been flown before'). The group 10 cc had a hit with 'I'm Mandy Fly Me', obviously inspired by the slogan, in 1976. Wall's Sausages later parodied it with, 'I'm meaty, fry me' (current 1976).

I'm free! *Catch Phrase*. From the BBC TV comedy series *Are You Being Served?* (first broadcast 1974). The lilting cry of Mr Humphries (John Inman), the lighter-than-air menswear salesman of Grace Bros. store.

I'm going down now, sir! See under DON'T FORGET THE DIVER!

I'm going to make him an offer he can't refuse. *Catch Phrase*. In 1969, Mario Puzo (*b* 1920) published his novel about the Mafia called *The Godfather*. It gave to the language a new expression which, as far as one can tell, was Mr Puzo's invention. Johnny Fontane, a singer, desperately wants a part in a movie and goes to see his godfather, Don Corleone, for help. All the contracts have been signed and there is no chance of the studio chief changing his mind. Still, the godfather promises Fontane he will get him the part. As he says of the studio chief, 'He's a businessman. I'll make him an offer he can't refuse.'
   In the 1971 film, this was turned into the following dialogue: 'In a month from now this Hollywood big shot's going to give you what you want.' 'Too late, they start shooting in a week.' 'I'm going to make him an offer he can't refuse.'
   In 1973, Jimmy Helms had a hit with the song 'Gonna Make You An Offer You Can't Refuse'.

I'm in charge! *Catch Phrase*. Bruce Forsyth (*b* 1928) first achieved fame as an entertainer when host of the ATV show *Sunday Night at the London Palladium* (from 1958). One night he was surpervising 'Beat the Clock', a game involving members of the audience. A young couple was in a muddle, throwing plates at a see-saw table. Bruce Forsyth recalled (1980): 'We had a particularly stroppy contestant. In the end I just turned round and told him, "Hold on a minute . . . I'm in charge!" It just happened, but the audience loved it and it caught on.' Lapel badges began appearing with the slogan, foremen had it painted on their hardhats. The phrase suited Forsyth's mockbossy manner to a tee.

I'm looking for someone to love. See under *BEYOND OUR KEN*.

I'm not a number, I'm a free man. *Stock Phrase*. First shown on British TV in 1967, *The Prisoner*, Patrick McGoohan's unusual series about a man at odds with a '1984'-type world, acquired a new cult following in the late 1970s. The McGoohan character was 'Political Prisoner Number Six'. **Six of one** was another phrase from the series. The Six of One Appreciation Society had 2000 members in 1982.

I'm only here for the beer. *Slogan* > *Catch Phrase* > *Idiom*. In 1971, a visiting American copywriter, Ros Levenstein, contributed this phrase to a British campaign for Double Diamond. It passed into the language as an inconsequential catch phrase, though – from the advertiser's point of view – it was not a good slogan because it came detached from the particular brand of beer.

ODCIE glosses it thus: 'We don't pretend to be present in order to help, show goodwill, etc. but just to get the drink, or other hospitality.' Indeed, in September 1971, Prince Philip attended a champagne reception at Burghley. 'Don't look at me,' he was quoted as saying, 'I'm only here for the beer.'

See also DOUBLE DIAMOND WORKS WONDERS, A.

impossible. See MISSION ~.

I'm sorry, I'll read that again. *Stock Phrase* > *Cliché*. The BBC radio newsreader's traditional apology for a stumble was registered as a cliché when the phrase was taken as the title of a longrunning radio comedy show (1964–73) featuring ex-Cambridge Footlights performers.

I'm worried about Jim. *Stock Phrase*. Ellis Powell played the eponymous heroine of BBC radio's *Mrs Dale's Diary* (1948–69) and this is what she always seemed to be confiding to it about her doctor husband. Although she may not have spoken the phrase very often, it was essential in parodies of the programme. Her successor in the part, Jessie Matthews, once had the line, 'I'm afraid one thing's never going to change: I shall always worry about you, Jim.'

inconspicuous. See under AS BUSY AS . . .

inconvenience. See DEEPLY REGRET ANY ~ . . .

India. See WHEN PEOPLE ARE STARVING IN ~.

indoors. See 'ER ~.

indubitably! See under OH, CALAMITY!

industrial action. *Cliché*. Used in journalism for a strike or stoppage, and thus denoting 'inaction'. An odd coinage, from the 1960s? Certainly established by

1971. There even used to be the occasional 'Day of Action' on which no-one did any work!

I never promised you a rose garden. *Saying.* I'm not sure about this one. Used by Joanne Greenberg as the title of a best-selling (American) novel in 1964, and as a line in the song 'Rose Garden' in 1971, I take it to mean: 'It wasn't going to be roses, roses all the way between us' or 'a bed of roses'. But did Greenberg coin it?

in God we trust – all others pay cash. *Saying.* After the Washington summit between Mikhail Gorbachev and Ronald Reagan in December 1987, the US Secretary of State George Schultz commented on a Russian slogan that Reagan had made much of: ' "Trust but verify" is really an ancient saying in the United States, but in a different guise. Remember the storekeeper who was a little leery of credit, and he had a sign in his store that said, IN GOD WE TRUST – ALL OTHERS CASH.' Referring to the verification procedures over arms reductions signed by the leaders in Washington, Shultz said, 'This is the cash.'

Mencken in 1942 was listing 'In God we trust; all others must pay cash' as an 'American saying'. 'In God we trust' has been the official national motto of the United States since 1956, when it superseded 'E Pluribus Unum', but had been known since 1864 when it was first put on a 2-cent bronze coin.

There is a similar joke on this side of the Atlantic – of the type printed on small cards and sold for display in pubs and shops. It made an appearance as a quote in the early 1940s in Flann O'Brien's column for the *Irish Times*: 'We have come to an arrangement with our bankers. They have agreed not to sell drink. We, on our part, have agreed not to cash cheques.'

A parallel saying to 'In God we trust etc.' is that attributed to the American striptease artiste, Gypsy Rose Lee (1914–70): 'God is love, but get it in writing.'

in like Flynn. *Idiom.* Someone who is 'in like Flynn' is a quick seducer – at least, according to the Australian use of the phrase. Appropriately, it is derived from the name of Errol Flynn (1909–59), the Australian-born film actor. It alludes to his legendary bedroom prowess, though the phrase can also mean that a person simply seizes an offered opportunity (of any kind).

According to *The Intimate Sex Lives of Famous People* (Irving Wallace *et al*, 1981), Flynn frowned on the expression when it became popular, especially among servicemen, in the Second World War. It 'implied he was a fun-loving rapist', though 'in fact, Flynn's reputation stemmed partly from his having been charged with statutory rape'. After a celebrated trial, he was acquitted. Nevertheless, he 'boasted that he had spent between 12,000 and 14,000 nights making love'.

Rather weakly, a US film of 1967 was entitled *In Like Flint*.

Partridge/*Catch Phrases* turns up an American version which refers to Ed Flynn, a Democratic machine politician in the Bronx, New York City, in the 1940s. Here the meaning is simply 'to be in automatically' – as his candidates would have been.

in Miss World order. See I'LL GIVE YOU THE RESULTS . . .

innocent. See ONLY THE NAMES HAVE BEEN CHANGED . . . under DRAGNET.

inquiries. See HELPING THE POLICE WITH THEIR ~.

instinctively. See ONE ~ KNOWS . . .

integrity. See IT'S ABSOLUTELY VITAL . . .

interesting. See VERY ~ . . . BUT STUPID! under LAUGH-IN.

in the pipeline. *Idiom > Cliché*. Meaning 'in train, on the way'. The *OED Supp.* finds it in used in 1955. 'We have several more [test-tube] babies in the pipeline' – said a doctor on the radio in 1985.

In Town Tonight. From 1933 to 1960 this was the nearest BBC Radio came to a chat show. It was introduced by what now sounds a very quaint montage of 'The Knightsbridge March' by Eric Coates, traffic noises, the voice of a woman selling violets in Piccadilly Circus, and then a stentorian voice – which I always believed (wrongly) to be that of Lord Reith – shouting '**Stopppp!**' Then an announcer would intone: '**Once again we stop the mighty roar of London's traffic and from the great crowds we bring you some of the interesting people who have come by land, sea and air to be "In Town Tonight."** '

At the end of the programme, to get the traffic moving again, the stentorian voice would bellow, '**Carry on, London!**' Various people were 'The Voice' but I am told that Freddie Grisewood was the first to be it.

in your heart you know I'm/he's right. *Slogan.* This was Barry Goldwater's much-parodied slogan when he attempted to unseat President Lyndon Johnson in the 1964 US presidential election. Come-backs included: 'In your gut, you know he's nuts' and 'You know in your heart he's right – far right.'

in your shell-like (ear). *Colloquialism.* Used when asking to have a 'quiet word' with someone. '(Let me have a word) in your ear', is all the phrase means, but it makes gentle fun of a poetic simile. Longman/*Register* finds the full form in Thomas Hood's *Bianca's Dream* (1827) – 'Her small and shell-like ear' and wonders whether the elliptical use of the adjective as noun was popularized by the TV series *Minder* (1979–). *The Complete Naff Guide* (1983) has 'a word in your shell-like ear' among 'naff things schoolmasters say'.

I only arsked! *Catch Phrase.* Quite the most popular one of the late 1950s. Bernard Bresslaw played a large, gormless army private – 'Popeye' Popplewell – in Granada TV's *The Army Game* from 1957 to 1962. This was his response when anyone put him down and the phrase occurred in the very first episode. A feature film for the cinema called *I Only Arsked* was made in 1958.

—— **is** ——. *Slogan > Format Phrase > Cliché.* The film *You Only Live Twice* (1967) was promoted with the slogan, 'Sean Connery *is* James Bond' – surely, a debatable proposition at the best of times and only likely to encourage a regrettable tendency, particularly among journalists, to confuse actors with their roles. Other examples: 'Paul Hogan *is* Crocodile Dundee' (1987); 'Phil Collins *is* Buster' (title of a video about the making of the film *Buster*, 1988); 'Domingo *is* Otello' [*sic*], ad in *Los Angeles Magazine*, March 1989; 'Jessye Norman *is* Carmen'. ad on LBC radio, August 1989.

—— **is a long time in** ——. *Format Phrase*. When I asked Harold Wilson (*b* 1916), later Lord Wilson, when he first uttered the much-quoted dictum, 'A week is a long time in politics', he was uncharacteristically unable to remember. For someone who, as Labour Prime Minister 1964–70, 1974–6, used to be able to cite the columns of *Hansard* in which his speeches appeared, this was a curious lapse. When I approached him on the matter in 1977, he also challenged the accepted interpretation of the words – which most people would think was along the lines of 'What a difference a day makes', 'Wait and see', and 'Don't panic, it'll all blow over.'

'It does not mean I'm living from day to day,' he said, but was intended as 'a prescription for long-term strategic thinking and planning, ignoring the day-to-day issues and pressures which may hit the headlines but which must not be allowed to get out of focus while longer-term policies are taking effect.'

Inquiries among political journalists led to the conclusion that in its present form the phrase was probably first used at a meeting between Wilson and the Parliamentary lobby correspondents in the wake of the Sterling crisis shortly after he first took office as Prime Minister

in 1964. However, Robert Carvel of the London *Evening Standard* recalled Wilson at a Labour Party conference in 1960 having said, 'Forty-eight hours is a long time in politics.'

In the late 1980s, Channel 4 carried a weekly review with the title *A Week in Politics*, clearly alluding to Wilson's phrase – which provides an easily-variable format. From the *Independent* (19 May 1989), on the outgoing editor of the TV programme *Forty Minutes*: 'His successor will have to work hard, though, to keep the formula fresh. 2,400 seconds is a long time in television.'

I say, I say, I say! *Stock Phrase*. Hard to know whether Murray and Mooney, the variety duo, invented this interruption, but they perfected the routine in their act during the 1930s. Mooney would interrupt with 'I say, I say, I say!' To whatever he had to impart, Murray would reply with the traditional I DON'T WISH TO KNOW THAT, KINDLY LEAVE THE STAGE. Harry Murray died in 1967; Harry Mooney in 1972.

I say, what a smasher! *Catch Phrase*. From a post-war BBC radio programme called *Stand Easy* (1946–51) featuring Charlie Chester (*b* 1914). The origin of the line lay in an occasion when his wife was sitting in the studio audience with a broken arm. Iona and Peter Opie in *The Lore and Language of Schoolchildren* (1959) show how this phrase had penetrated, firstly, to 'Girls, 13, Swansea, 1952' who recited: 'I say, what a smasher,/ Betty Grable's getting fatter,/ Pick a brick and throw it at her./ If you wish to steal a kiss,/ I say, what a smasher.' And, secondly, to 'Boy, 11, Birmingham': 'I say what a smasher/ Pick it up and slosh it at her./

If you miss/ Give her a kiss/ I say what a smasher.'

Partridge/*Catch Phrases* finds someone, however, who thinks the phrase originally came out of a toothpaste ad in the Second World War.

I say you fellows! See under YAROOOO!

I see what you mean. See under ARCHERS.

is he one of us? *Catch Phrase.* Asked concerning anyone being considered for membership of a select group, but specifically said to have been a frequent test of her colleagues' loyalty by Margaret Thatcher (after 1979). I don't know whether this has spread much beyond No. 10 Downing Street where it became known quite early on in the Thatcher years. From the *Independent* (28 January 1989): 'Mr [Kenneth] Clarke also failed the is-he-one-of-us? test applied by Mrs Thatcher to favoured colleagues.' Hugo Young's biography of Mrs Thatcher (1989) had the title *One of Us*.

I should cocoa! *Catch Phrase.* A slightly dated British English exclamation meaning 'certainly not!' Longman's *English Idioms* adds a word of caution: 'This phrase is not recommended for use by the foreign student.'

But why 'cocoa'? As always when in difficulty with a phrase origin, turn to rhyming slang. 'Cocoa' is from 'coffee and cocoa', almost rhyming slang for 'I should say/think so!' Often used ironically. Current by 1936.

I should of stood in bed. See under WE WUZ ROBBED!

is she a friend of Dorothy? *Catch Phrase.* Ie 'Is he [*sic*] a homosexual?' Probably this originated among American homosexuals. It was current by 1984. 'Dorothy' was the put-upon heroine of *The Wizard of Oz* and was played in the film by Judy Garland, a woman much revered in male homosexual circles.

is she . . . or isn't she? *Slogan.* For Harmony hair-spray, in the UK, current in 1980. Nothing to do with DOES SHE . . . OR DOESN'T SHE? but a deliberate echo – as, presumably, was the line 'Is she or isn't she a phoney?', spoken in the film *Breakfast at Tiffany's* (1961).

The ad went on: 'Harmony has an ultra-fine spray to leave hair softer and more natural. She *is* wearing a hairspray but with Harmony it's so fine you're the only one that knows for sure.'

is that a chicken joke? See under LAUGH-IN.

—— is the name of the game. *Format Phrase > Cliché.* An over-used phrase from the mid-1960s, meaning '. . . is what it's really about'. Partridge/*Catch Phrases* finds an example in 1961. US National Security Adviser McGeorge Bundy talking about foreign policy goals in Europe in 1966 said: 'Settlement is the name of the game.' In time, almost everything was, following the title of an American TV movie called *Fame Is the Name of the Game* (1966). Then followed several series of TV's *The Name of the Game* (1968–71). The expression was replaced for a while by '. . . is where it's at'.

is there a doctor in the house? *Stock Phrase.* The traditional cry, usually in a theatre or at some other large gathering of people, when a member of the audience is taken ill. One suspects it dates from the nineteenth century, if not before. The *Daily Mirror* (10 October 1984) reports a member of the audience passing out during the film *1984*: 'There was a kerfuffle as people rallied round and an excited rustle as the traditional call went out: "Is there a doctor in the house?" ' ... Dr David Owen, a few rows away, continued to be transfixed by the activities on the screen.'

Sir Ralph Richardson used to tell of taking part in a very bad play. Half-way through, he said, he turned to the audience and asked, 'Is there a doctor in the house?' When one stood up, Richardson said, 'Doctor, isn't this show *terrible!*'

is there life after ——? *Cliché.* Presumably derived from the age-old question, 'Is there life after death?' There seems no end to the variations on this theme. On a single Sunday – 14 October 1984 – the *Sunday Times* Magazine had, 'Is there life after redundancy?' and the *Sunday People*, 'Can there be life after Wogan?' I have just noticed an American book with the title *Is There Life After Housework?* by Don A. Aslett (1981).

is your journey really necessary? *Slogan.* First coined in 1939 to discourage evacuated civil servants from going home for Christmas. 'From 1941, the question was constantly addressed to all civilians, for, after considering a scheme for rationing on the "points" principle, or to ban all travel without a permit over more than fifty miles, the government had finally decided to rely on voluntary appeals, and on making travel uncomfortable by re-

ducing the number of trains' (Norman Longmate, *How We Lived Then*, 1973).

it all depends what you mean by . . . *Stock Phrase > Catch Phrase. The Brains Trust* was a discussion programme first broadcast by the BBC in 1941, taking its title from President Roosevelt's name for his circle of advisers (in America, more usually, '*brain* trust'). A regular participant, who became a national figure, was C.E.M. Joad (1891–1953) – often called 'Professor', though not entitled to be. His discussion technique was to jump in first and leave the other speakers with little else to say. Alternatively, he would try and undermine arguments by using the phrase with which he became famous. When the chairman once read out a question from a listener, Mr W.E. Jack of Keynsham – 'Are thoughts things or about things?' – Joad inevitably began his answer with 'It all depends what you mean by a "thing".'

His broadcasting career ended rather abruptly when he was found travelling by rail using a ticket that was not valid. The BBC banished him.

it beats as it sweeps as it cleans. *Slogan.* For Hoover carpet sweepers, in the US, from 1919. Still current in the UK in the 1980s. Coined by Gerald Page-Wood of the Erwin Wasey agency in Cleveland, Ohio. The exclusive feature of Hoovers was that they gently beat or tapped the carpet to loosen dirt and grit embedded in it. An agitator bar performed this function, together with strong suction with revolving brushes – giving the Hoover the 'triple action' enshrined in the slogan. The words 'Hoover' and 'to hoover' became generic terms for vacuum cleaners and for vacuuming.

itch. See AS BUSY AS . . . ; SEVEN YEAR ~.

I thank you! See under BAND WAGGON.

I think I go home. *Saying > Catch Phrase.* At one time, 'I tink I go home', spoken in a would-be Swedish accent, was as much part of the impressionist's view of Greta Garbo as 'I want to be alone'. One version of how the line came to be spoken is told by Norman Zierold in *Moguls* (1969): 'After such films as *The Torrent* and *Flesh and the Devil*, Garbo decided to exploit her box-office power and asked Louis B. Mayer for a raise – from three hundred and fifty to five thousand dollars a week. Mayer offered her twenty-five hundred. "I tink I go home," said Garbo. She went back to her hotel and stayed there for a full seven months until Mayer finally gave way.'

Alexander Walker in *Garbo* (1980) recalls, rather, what Sven-Hugo Borg, the actress's interpreter, said of the time in 1926 when Mauritz Stiller, who had come with her from Sweden, was fired from directing *The Temptress*: 'She was tired, terrified and lost . . . as she returned to my side after a trying scene, she sank down beside me and said so low it was almost a whisper, "Borg, I think I shall go home now. It isn't worth it, is it?" '

Walker comments: 'That catch-phrase, shortened into "I think I go home", soon passed into the repertoire of a legion of Garbo-imitators and helped publicize her strong-willed temperament.'

A caricatured Garbo was shown hugging Mickey Mouse in a cartoon film in the 1930s. 'Ah tahnk ah kees you now' and 'ah tink ah go home,' she said. This cartoon was, incidentally, the last item to be shown on British television before the transmitters were closed down on the brink of war on 1 September 1939.

I think that shows we're getting it about right. *Cliché.* Of argument. For example, when defending itself, the BBC points out that half the letters of complaint it receives about a programme are critical, the other half supportive. 'I think that shows we're getting it about right . . .'

I think the answer lies in the soil. See under BEYOND OUR KEN.

I think we should be told. *Stock Phrase.* In the mid-1980s, *Private Eye* ran a parody of the opinion column written by John Junor for the *Sunday Express*. It frequently included the would-be campaigning journalist's line, 'I think we should be told'. In 1985, Sir John – as he was by then – told me that he had never once used the phrase in his column. He did, however, admit to having used the *Eye* parody's other stock phrase – **pass the sick-bag, Alice** – though only once.

I thought —— until I discovered ——. *Format Phrase.* The common advertising notion of a way of life or a belief being swept away by some sudden revelation was given memorable form from 1970 to 1975 in a series of slogans for Smirnoff vodka. The variations included:

I thought . . .

St Tropez was a Spanish monk . . .
accountancy was my life . . .
I was the mainstay of the public library . . .

the Kama Sutra was an Indian restaurant . . .

. . . until I discovered Smirnoff. David Tree, an art director at the Young & Rubicam agency, recalled how he and John Bacon, the copywriter, had struggled for weeks to get the right idea. One day, after a fruitless session, he was leaving for lunch when he happened to glance at a magazine pin-up adorning the wall of their office. 'If we really get stuck,' he said, 'we can always say, "I was a boring housewife in Southgate until . . ." ' (Southgate was where he was living at the time.)

The tag-line to the ads was **the effect is shattering**.

it'll be all right on the night. *Catch Phrase > Cliché.* Theatrical, and dating from the late nineteenth century, at least. Curiously, when it has to be invoked, things quite often *are* better on the subsequent (first) night. In the same way, a disastrous dress rehearsal is said to betoken a successful first night.

ITV hi-jacked the phrase for a long-running series of TV 'blooper' programmes in the 1980s, though witlessly spelt it 'alright'.

it'll be all right with a bit of doing up. See under BAND WAGGON.

it'll play in Peoria. *Idiom.* In about 1968, during the Nixon election campaign, John Ehrlichman is credited with having devised a yardstick for judging whether policies would appeal to voters in 'Middle America'. They had to be judged on whether they would 'play in Peoria'. He later told William Safire, 'Onomatopoeia was the only reason for Peoria, I suppose.

And it . . . exemplified a place, far removed from the media centres of the coasts where the national verdict is cast.' Peoria is in Illinois and was earlier the hometown of one of Sgt Bilko's merry men in the 1950s TV series – so good for a laugh even then.

it looks like something out of *Quatermass. Catch Phrase.* This alludes to *The Quatermass Experiment* (BBC TV, 1953) – the first in a series of science-fiction drama series involving a certain Professor Quatermass. In this one, viewers were held enthralled by the tale of a British astronaut who returned from a space trip and started turning into a plant. Eventually, he holed up in Poets' Corner at Westminster Abbey, by which time he was a mass of waving fronds. Although the phrase was not used in the programme, it gave to an expression still to be heard in the 1980s, used to describe any peculiar – but especially rambling and leafy – specimen.

ITMA. It is appropriate that *ITMA*, the radio programme incorporating more catch phrases per square minute than any other, before or since, should have had as its title an acronym based on a catch phrase. **It's that man again!** was a late 1930s expression, often used in newspaper headlines, for Adolf Hitler, who was always bursting into the news with some territorial claim or other. Winston Churchill was to speak often of Hitler as 'that man'.

ITMA was first broadcast in July 1939 and ran until January 1949, when its star, Tommy Handley, died. What did the show consist of? There would be a knock on the famous *ITMA* door, a character would engage in a little banter with Tommy Handley, the catch phrase would be delivered (usually receiving a gigantic ovation), and then the next one would be wheeled in. Given this format, it is not easy now to appreciate why the show was so popular. But the laughter undoubtedly took people's minds off the war and the programmes brought together the whole country, fostering a family feeling and a sense of sharing which in turn encouraged the spread of catch phrases. The writing is not to everyone's taste nowadays (it relied heavily on feeble rather than atrocious puns) but Handley's brisk, cheerful personality was the magic ingredient that held the proceedings together.

Characters came and went over the years, the cast fluctuated, and catch phrases changed. But here are some of the more than fifty I have pinned down:

ain't it a shame, eh? ain't it a shame? Spoken by Carleton Hobbs as the nameless man who told banal tales ('I waited for hours in the fish queue . . . and a man took my plaice') – always prefaced and concluded with, 'Ain't it a shame?'

boss, boss, sumpin' terrible's happened! Spoken in a gangster drawl by Sam Scram (Sydney Keith), Handley's henchman.

but I'm all right now. Sophie Tuckshop (Hattie Jacques) was always stuffing herself and giggling and pretending to suffer. Then, with a squeal, she would say this.

good morning . . . nice day! Said by Clarence Wright as a commercial traveller who never seemed to sell anything.

I always do my best for all my gentlemen. Mrs Lola Tickle (Maurice Denham) appeared within six weeks of the start of the show in 1939. As office charlady to Mr ITMA (Handley), she was the precursor by a full year of Mrs Mopp.

I don't mind if I do! The immortal reply of Colonel Chinstrap (Jack Train) whenever a drink was even so much as hinted at. The idea first appeared in 1940/1 in the form, 'Thanks, I will!' The Colonel was based on an elderly friend of John Snagge's – a typical ex-Indian Army type, well-pleased with himself. The phrase had existed before, of course. *Punch* carried a cartoon in 1880 with the following caption:

Porter: Virginia Water!

Bibulous old gentleman (seated in railway carriage): Gin and water! I don't mind if I do!

ITMA, however, secured the phrase a place in the language, as the Colonel doggedly turned every hint of liquid refreshment into an offer:

Handley: Hello, what's this group? King John signing the Magna Carta at Runnymede?

Chinstrap: Rum and mead, sir? I don't mind if I do!

I go – I come back! Said in a hoarse whisper by Ali Oop (Horace Percival), the saucy postcard vendor. First used in the summer of 1940.

I'll 'ave to ask me Dad. The point of this phrase was that it was spoken by a character who sounded about a hundred. He was called the Ancient Mark Time. Randolph Churchill, speaking at a general election meeting in 1945, was heckled with the remark, 'He'll have to ask *his* Dad!'

I'll forget my own name in a minute. The nameless man from the ministry (Horace Percival). An old phrase to show the limits of one's forgetfulness. It occurs in Charles Dickens, *The Chimes* (First Quarter)(1844) as 'I'll forget my own name next.'

it's being so cheerful as keeps me going. Said by Mona Lott (Joan Harben), the gloomy laundrywoman. When told to keep her pecker up by Handley, she would reply, 'I always do, sir, it's being so cheerful . . .' Her family was always running into bad luck, so she had plenty upon which to exercise her particular form of fortitude.

it's me noives! Lefty (Jack Train), friend of Sam Scram. An unexpected complaint for a gangster to have.

lovely grub, lovely grub! Said by George Gorge (Fred Yule), the 'greediest man ever to have two ration books'. He used to say it smacking his lips.

nobody tells me nothing! (or, 'nobody tells no one nothing') – Dan Dungeon, the gloomy Liverpudlian (Deryck Guyler).

no likey? oh, crikey! Usually said by Ali Oop (Horace Percival), the show's saucy postcard vendor who frequently rhymed English idioms like 'very jolly – oh golly!' or 'Your hands are grimy/Grimy? Oh, blimey!' Peter Black, the TV critic, once wrote: 'This lunatic exchange sank so deeply into the minds of the girl I was to marry and myself that we still use it thirty years later.'

open the door, Richard! A line from the popular American song (1947), first sung in Britain on *ITMA*.

T.T.F.N. ('Ta-ta for now') The farewell of Mrs Mopp (Dorothy Summers) after having presented her weekly gift to Mayor Handley. It is said that during the War, quite a few people died with the phrase on their lips. Still quite widely in use today.

what me – in my state of health? Charles Atlas (Fred Yule).

See also AFTER YOU, CLAUDE/NO, AFTER YOU, CECIL!; AS IF I CARED . . . ; CAN I DO YOU NOW, SIR?; DON'T FORGET THE DIVER!; THIS IS FUNF SPEAKING!

it never rains, but it pours. *Saying.* John Arbuthnot, the pamphleteer, entitled a piece thus in 1726, and since then the phrase has gained proverbial status, meaning 'misfortunes never come singly'.

A famous American *Slogan* was **when it rains, it pours** which was used from 1911 by Morton salt. The logo showed a girl in the rain, sheltering the salt under her umbrella, and capitalized on the fact that the Morton grade ran freely from salt cellars even when the atmosphere was damp. The film *Cocktail* (US, 1989), about a barman, was promoted with the line 'When he pours, he reigns'.

I took my harp to a party (but nobody asked me to play). *Catch Phrase.* Meaning 'I went prepared to do something, but wasn't given the opportunity.' From a song by Desmond Carter & Noël Gay, popularized by Gracie Fields and Phyllis Robins, 1933/4.

it pays to advertise. *Saying/Slogan*. This is a proverbial saying which almost certainly originated in the US. Indeed, Mencken in 1942 lists it simply as an 'American proverb'.

Bartlett quotes the anonymous rhyme:
The codfish lays ten thousand eggs,
The homely hen lays one.
The codfish never cackles
To tell you what she's done.
And so we scorn the codfish,
While the humble hen we prize,
Which only goes to show you
That it pays to advertise.

I feel sure, though, that this rhyme came after the proverb or slogan was established.

It is possible to push back the dating of the phrase rather more positively. There was a play co-written by Walter Hackett (1876–1944) which had it for a title in 1914, and this was turned into a film in 1931. Back even earlier, Cole Porter entitled one of his earliest songs 'It Pays to Advertise'. The song alludes to a number of advertising lines that were current when he was a student at Yale (*c* 1912):
I'd walk a mile for that schoolgirl complexion,
Palmolive soap will do it every time.
Oh cream, oh best cigar!
Maxwell Motor Car!
Do you have a baby vacuum in your home?
Gum is good for you,
Try our new shampoo,
Flit will always free your home of flies.
If you travel, travel, travel at all,
You know, it pays to advertise.
(included in *The Complete Lyrics of Cole Porter*, ed. Robert Kimball, 1983).

This suggests to me that the phrase, though not Porter's own, was not too much a of cliché by 1912. Ezra Pound wrote in a letter to his father in 1908 about the launch of his poems: 'Sound trumpet. Let rip the drum & swatt the big bassoon. It pays to advertise.'

We are probably looking for an origin in the 1870s to 1890s when advertising really took off in America (as in Britain). Indeed, *Benham's Book of Quotations* (1960 revision) lists an 'American saying *c* 1870' – 'The man who on his trade relies must either bust or advertise' – and notes that 'Sir Thomas Lipton [*d* 1931] is said to have derived inspiration and success through seeing this couplet in New York about 1875.'

it's a bird . . . it's a plane . . . See under *SUPERMAN*.

it's a braw bricht moonlicht nicht. See HOOTS MON.

it's absolutely vital both to the character and to the integrity of the script. *Cliché*. Actresses (and, I suppose, occasionally actors) invariably answer something to this effect when asked whether there is any nudity in the play or film they are about to appear in or whether they take their clothes off. When I consulted Glenda Jackson about this in 1983, she suggested that the remark was usually made in reply to a reporter's question, 'Is there any nudity in this film?' – 'Yes, but it is absolutely vital to the character and the part.' The Naff Sex Guide (1984) gave as one of the 'naff things starlets say': 'Yes, I would appear nude, as long as I trusted the director and the integrity of the script demanded it.'

Alternative responses to the nudity question include, 'I don't mind if it's *rele-*

vant to the script' or '. . . .if it's done in a meaningful way'. Lord Delfont, the impresario, is quoted by Hunter Davies in *The Grades* (1981) as saying: 'I do allow four-letter words and nudity in my films, if they are in the right context, if it has integrity.'

Compare the following entry:

it's all done in the best possible taste. *Catch Phrase.* This was spoken by Kenny Everett (*b* 1944), with beard, playing a large-breasted Hollywood actress, Cupid Stunt, being 'interviewed' by a cardboard cut-out Michael Parkinson in *The Kenny Everett Television Show* (after 1981). 'She' was explaining how she justified playing in some forthcoming film of less than award-winning potential [see IT'S ABSOLUTELY VITAL . . .].

According to the co-scriptwriter Barry Cryer, this was never intended to be Dolly Parton. He had heard these very words said in an interview by an American actress whose name he has since, fortunately, forgotten. (In *Time* magazine, 20 July 1981, I did, however, come across John Derek, director of *Tarzan the Ape Man*, declaring almost the same thing: 'The sacrifice scene was done in the finest of taste – taste the Pope would applaud.')

As an illustration of how a good catch phrase is seized upon by the media, I noted that in the *Scottish Daily Express* of 28 April 1982, there were two separate stories making use of this one: 'Pia [Zadora] . . . in the best possible taste' and 'Spicy Geraldine . . . in the best possible taste.'

Understandably, too, Wills Tobacco began to promote Three Castles brand with the slogan 'In the best possible taste'.

it's all in the mind, you know. See GOON SHOW.

it's all part of life's rich pageant. *Catch Phrase.* Peter Sellers as Inspector Clouseau has just fallen into a fountain in *A Shot in the Dark* (1964) when Elke Sommer commiserates with him: 'You'll catch your death of pneumonia.' Playing it phlegmatically, Clouseau replies, 'It's all part of life's rich pageant.'

The origin of this happy phrase – sometimes 'pattern' or 'tapestry' is substituted for 'pageant' – was the subject of an inquiry by Michael Watts of the *Sunday Express* in 1982. The earliest he came up with was from a record called 'The Games Mistress', written and performed by Arthur Marshall (1910–89) in *c* 1935. The monologue concludes, 'Never mind, dear – laugh it off, laugh it off. It's all part of life's rich pageant.' Consequently, Arthur called his autobiography, *Life's Rich Pageant* (1984).

it's being so cheerful as keeps me going. See under ITMA.

it seemed like a good idea at the time, well. *Catch Phrase.* Partridge/*Catch Phrases* has this limp excuse for something that has gone awry as dating back to the 1950s. But Halliwell found it in a 1931 film called *The Last Flight.* It is the story of a group of American airmen who remain in Europe after the First World War. One of them is gored to death when he leaps into the arena during a bullfight. Journalists outside the hospital ask his friend why the man should have done such a thing. The friend (played by Richard Barthelmess) replies: 'Because it seemed like a good idea at the time.'

it sends me! *Catch Phrase*. The 1950s way for young people to describe the effect of popular music on their souls. However, in a letter to *The Times* in 1945 (18 December), Evelyn Waugh was writing: 'He [Picasso] can only be treated as crooners are treated by their devotees. In the United States the adolescents, speaking of music, do not ask: "What do you think of So-and-so?" They say: "Does So-and-so *send* you?" '

Indeed, *OED Supp.* finds this use in the early 1930s.

See also *EDUCATING ARCHIE*.

it's fingerlickin' good! *Slogan*. For Kentucky Fried Chicken, current by 1958. Several songs/instrumental numbers with the title 'Fingerlickin' Good' appear to have been derived from this advertising use in the 1970s, though I am not sure whether the slogan was in use by 1968 when Lonnie Smith had a record album called 'Fingerlickin' Good Soul Organ'. In 1966, 'Finger Lickin' ', on its own, was the title of a (guitar) instrumental by Barbara Clark. This makes me think that 'fingerlickin' ' was an established southern US/possibly black/ musicians' phrase before being made famous by the slogan.

it's for yoo-hoo! *Slogan > Catch Phrase*. In c 1985, British Telecom made advertising use of the familiar phrase of someone answering the phone, 'It's for you'. But it was pronounced in a distinctive way which no doubt led to it 'catching on'.

According to the *Guardian* (24 October 1985), detectives seeking a man on assault charges – a man known to be a keen Chelsea supporter – put an 'urgent message for Graham Montagu' sign on the electronic scoreboard at Stamford Bridge football ground. Thousands of fans spontaneously sang out, 'Montagu, it's for yoo-hoo!', the man fell for the ruse, and was arrested.

it's goodnight from me/ and it's goodnight from him! *Stock Phrase*. In their long-running comedy series *The Two Ronnies* (1970s/80s), Ronnie Corbett and Ronnie Barker always ended editions with a gentle poke at a cliché of TV presentation. Ronnie C. would feed Ronnie B. with, 'It's goodnight from me . . .' And Ronnie B. would sabotage this with, 'And it's goodnight from him.'

it's me noives. See under *ITMA*.

it's not for me, it's for my daughter. *Cliché*. What people almost invariably say when asking famous people for an autograph. From the *Guardian*'s obituary of Arthur Marshall (28 January 1989): 'One of his favourite stories was about how, on coming out of the BBC TV centre, he was once accosted and asked for an autograph. The woman making the request explained that she wanted it for her daughter . . .'

it's only rock'n'roll. *Catch Phrase*. Meaning 'It doesn't matter; the importance should not be exaggerated'. The title of a Mick Jagger/Keith Richard composition of 1974 has entered the language to a certain extent. In a 1983 *Sunday Express* interview, Tim Rice was quoted as saying, 'It would be nice if [the musical *Blondel*] is a success but I won't be upset if it isn't. It is only rock'n'roll after all and it doesn't really matter a hoot.'

it's Siiimon Dee! See HERE'S JOHNNY!

it's/Skegness is so bracing! *Slogan.* Skegness, the seaside resort in Lincolnshire, was promoted along with the London & North Eastern Railway company in advertisements current from 1909. The slogan is inseparable from the accompanying jolly fisherman drawn by John Hassall (1868–1948). Actually, Hassall did not visit Skegness until twenty-eight years after he drew the poster. His first visit was when he was made a freeman of the town.

it's terrific! See under *EDUCATING ARCHIE*.

it's that man again! See under *ITMA*.

it's the real thing. See under COME ALIVE . . . ; REAL THING.

it's the way I tell 'em! *Catch Phrase.* Almost any comedian could say this of a joke that has just gone down well (and no doubt most of them would agree with the observation) but Frank Carson, the Ulster comedian (*b* 1926) managed to make it his own (from the mid-70s.) In full, the line is: 'You've heard them all before, but . . . it's the way I tell 'em.'

it's turned out nice again! *Stock Phrase.* The comedian George Formby (1904–61) disclaimed any credit for originating the phrase with which he always opened his act. 'It's simply a familiar Lancashire expression,' he once said. 'People use it naturally up there. I used it as part of a gag and have been doing so ever since' – particularly in his films when emerging from some disaster or other. It was used as the title of a film in 1941 (as well as being the punchline of it) and as the title of a song.

it's twelve o'clock in London . . . See under *FAMILY FAVOURITES*.

it's what your right arm's for. *Slogan >* *Catch Phrase.* For Courage Tavern (ale), current in 1972. Although this line became a popular catch phrase, it risks being applied to rival products. Possibly of earlier origin.

it was going to be a long night. *Cliché.* 'He was doing the crossword from *The Washington Star*. He had finished three clues; it was going to be a long night' – Jeffrey Archer, *Shall We Tell the President* (1977), but much earlier in origin than this.

it was like an Aladdin's cave in there! *Cliché.* What – according to the press – ordinary members of the public invariably say when they stumble upon a burglar's horde, or similar.

it was worse than the Blitz. *Cliché.* What – according to the press – ordinary members of the public invariably say when involved in bomb incidents, train crashes, etc. Note, however, this interesting variation apropos an incident in which police rained shots on an innocent man: 'Mr David Steele . . . in a Volkswagen van which was behind the Mini carrying Mr Waldorf [when asked about the number of police officers he saw, said]: "I saw one, then two, then it was World War Two all over again." ' (*Daily Telegraph*, 14 October 1983.)

it went from failure to classic without ever passing through success. *Saying.* Mostly arts, showbiz use. For example, George Axelrod, writer of the film *The Manchurian Candidate*, said it to *Time* magazine (21 March 1988). The film was a flop when first launched in 1962, languished in a vault for twenty-five years, and then became something of a cult.

I've arrived – and to prove it – I'm here! See under *EDUCATING ARCHIE*.

I've been sponned! See under *GOON SHOW*.

I've got a million of 'em! See GOODNIGHT, MRS CALABASH . . .

I've got his pecker in my pocket. *Catch Phrase.* Meaning 'he is under obligation to me', this was one of Lyndon Johnson's earthy phrases from his time as Senate Majority leader in Washington. 'Pecker' means 'penis' in North America (rather less so in Britain) – though this should not inhibit people from using the old British expression 'keep your pecker up', where the word has been derived from 'peck' meaning appetite. In other words, this phrase is merely a way of wishing someone good health, though *OED* has 'pecker' meaning 'courage, resolution' in 1855.

I've never believed in anything so much in all my life. *Cliché.* Of film scriptwriting, though perhaps not too painful as clichés go. An example occurs in *Dangerous Moonlight* (UK, 1941).

I've started so I'll finish! *Stock Phrase > Catch Phrase.* In BBC TV's *Mastermind* quiz, the chairman, Magnus Magnusson, would say this if one of his questions was interrupted when the time ran out. It became a figure of speech – sometimes also given a double meaning.

From the same programme has come **Pass!** Noted *The Times* (8 November 1977): 'For proof of how . . . *Mastermind* is catching on, I would refer you to this story sent in by a reader from London NW6. He was accosted by a small lad, asking for a penny for the guy. On being asked if he knew who Guy Fawkes was, the lad replied with engaging honesty, "Pass".'

The word is used by participants in the quiz when they do not know the answer to a question and wish to move on to the next, so as not to waste valuable time. It is not the most obvious of things to say. 'Next question' or 'I dunno' would spring more readily to mind but, so deep has this phrase penetrated the public consciousness that when I was chairing a quiz called *Challenge of the South* for TVS in 1987/8, I found that contestants automatically reached for 'Pass'.

In 1981, London Transport advertisements showed an empty studio chair, of the type used in the programme, with the query, 'How can you save money on bus fares?' The answer was, 'Correct. The London Bus pass.'

I wanna tell you a story! *Catch Phrase.* Launched on a sea of catch phrases in *EDUCATING ARCHIE*, Max Bygraves (*b* 1922) later became associated with a phrase wished upon him by an impersonator. It is possible that he may have said of his own accord, 'I wanna tell you a story' (with the appropriate hand-gestures – as if shaking water off them) but it was Mike Yarwood who capitalized on it in his impersonation. Bygraves then used the phrase himself in self-parody and chose it as the title of his autobiography (1976). Still, as he says, he once went into a competition for Max Bygraves impressionists – and came fifth.

Of having successful catch phrases in general, Bygraves told me (1980): 'It's like having a hit record!'

I want me tea! *Stock Phrase. The Grove Family* was the first British TV soap opera – or something approaching one – and ran for three years from 1953. It told of a suburban family that included a wonderfully irritable Grandma Grove (Nancy Roberts) who used to make this demand.

I want to be alone. *Catch Phrase.* Greta Garbo (*b* 1905) claimed that what she said was 'I want to be *let* alone' – ie she wanted privacy rather than solitude. Oddly, as Alexander Walker observed in *Sex in the Movies* (1968): 'Nowhere in anything she said, either in the lengthy interviews she gave in her Hollywood days when she was perfectly approachable, or in the statements on-the-run from the publicity-shy fugitive she later became, has it been possible to find the famous phrase, "I want to be alone". What one can find, in abundance, later on, is "Why don't you let me alone?" and even "I want to be left alone", but neither is redolent of any more exotic order of being than a harassed celebrity. Yet the world prefers to believe the mythical and much more mysterious catch phrase utterance.'

What complicates the issue is that Garbo herself *did* use the line several times on the screen. For example, in the 1929 silent film *The Single Standard* she gives the brush-off to a stranger and the subtitle declares: 'I am walking alone because I want to be alone.' And, as the ageing ballerina who loses her nerve and flees back to her suite in *Grand Hotel* (1932), she actually *speaks* it. Walker calls this 'an excellent example of art borrowing its effects from a myth that was reality for millions of people'.

The phrase was obviously well-established by 1935 when Groucho Marx uttered it in *A Night at the Opera*. Garbo herself says, 'Go to bed, little father. We want to be alone' in *Ninotchka* (1939). So it is not surprising that the myth has taken such a firm hold, and particularly since Garbo became a virtual recluse for the second half of her life.

I want to make it perfectly clear. *Cliché.* Of politics. Often said when doing quite the opposite. Much used by William Whitelaw, Conservative politician – especially when Home Secretary.

I was a seven stone weakling. See YOU, TOO, CAN HAVE A BODY LIKE MINE.

I wasn't born yesterday. *Saying > Catch Phrase.* The *OED Supp.* has it as an established saying by 1757. But I can't help feeling its modern use must have been encouraged by the play/film title *Born Yesterday*, Garson Kanin's excellent vehicle for Judy Holliday (1946), about an ignorant girl who wins out in the end.

I was only obeying orders. *Saying > Catch Phrase.* The Charter of the International Military Tribunal at Nuremberg (1945–6) specifically excluded the traditional German defence of 'superior order'. But the plea was, nevertheless, much advanced.

This approach was summed up in the catch phrase 'I was only obeying orders', often used grotesquely in parody of such buck-passing. Not that everyone seemed aware of this. From the *New York Times* (6 July 1983): 'Herbert Bechtold, a German-born officer in the [US] counter-intelligence who became [the "handler" of Klaus Barbie, the Nazi war criminal] was asked if he questioned the morality of hiring a man like Barbie by the United States. "I am not in a position to pass judgement on that," Mr Bechtold replied, "I was just following orders".'

I went to New Zealand but it was closed.
Saying. This is a joke which gets rediscovered every so often. The Beatles found it in the 1960s; slightly before, Anna Russell, the musical comedienne, said it on one of her records. It has also been attributed to Clement Freud. But William Franklyn, son of the Antipodean actor, Leo Franklyn, tells me that his father was saying it in the 1920s.

I expect W.C. Fields began saying 'I went to Philadelphia and found that it was closed' about the same time (if indeed he did).

I wonder if they are by any chance related? *Stock Phrase.* It is an obsession with some to make assumptions about people being related to one another on the basis that they look similar or have names in common. For many years from the 1970s, *Private Eye* ran a feature in which people would write in, under a pseudonym, drawing attention to facial similarities – almost always ending up with the line, 'I wonder if they are by any chance related?' [eg Lyndon Johnson/ Mrs Golda Meir; Alfred Brendel/Roy Hudd.] The US magazine *Spy* has run a similar feature headed 'Separated at Birth?'

I won't take me coat off – I'm not stopping. *Catch Phrase.* Ken Platt (*b* 1922), the nasal-voiced, somewhat lugubrious northern comedian, was handed this catch phrase on a plate by Ronnie Taylor, producer of radio's *Variety Fanfare* in January 1951. Platt told me (1979): 'I told him rather grudgingly that I thought it was "as good as anything" . . . and I've been stuck with it ever since. People are disappointed if I don't say it.'

See also DAFT AS A BRUSH.

J

Jack Robinson. See BEFORE ONE CAN SAY ~.

jam jar. See GET BACK ON YOUR . . .

Jane. See ME, TARZAN . . .

Jennifer! See under *RAY'S A LAUGH*.

Jesus wept! *Catch Phrase*. John 11:35 is the shortest verse in the Bible (the shortest sentence would be 'Amen.'). It occurs in the story of the raising of Lazarus. Jesus is moved by the plight of Mary and Martha, the sisters of Lazarus, who break down and weep when Lazarus is sick. When Jesus sees the dying man he, too, weeps.

Like it or not, the phrase has become an expletive to express exasperation. The most notable uttering was by Richard Dimbleby, the TV commentator, on 27 May 1965. In a broadcast in which everything went wrong during a Royal visit to West Germany, Dimbleby let slip this oath when he thought his words were not being broadcast.

A graffito from the 1970s, from the advertising agency which lost the Schweppes account, was: 'Jesus wepped'.

jewel in the crown, the/a. *Idiom > Cliché*. In the space of a single day – 2 March 1988 – I read in the *Guardian*, 'Poor David Steel. He's bound for Southport on Saturday for a regional conference in what ought to be one of the precious few jewels in the Liberals' dented crown'; in *Harpers & Queen* I read, 'Annecy is considered to be the jewel in the Savoyard crown'; and in Michael Powell's book *A Life in Movies* (published two years before), 'Sir Thomas Beecham, Bart., conducting the "Ballet of the Red Shoes" would be the final jewel in our crown.'

It would be reasonable to suppose that the 1984 television adaptation of Paul Scott's 'Raj Quartet' of novels had something to do with the popularity of this phrase. The first of Scott's novels (published in 1966) is called *The Jewel in the Crown* and gave its name to the TV series. 'The Jewel in *Her* Crown' [my italics] is the title of a 'semi-historical, semi-allegorical' picture referred to early on in the book. It showed Queen Victoria, 'surrounded by representative figures of her Indian Empire: Princes, landowners, merchants, money-lenders, sepoys, farmers, servants, children, mothers, and remarkably clean and tidy beggars . . . An Indian prince, attended by native servants, was approaching the throne bearing a velvet cushion on which he offered a large and sparkling gem.' (In fact, Victoria, like Disraeli, who is also portrayed, never set foot in India.)

Children at the school where the picture was displayed had to be told that, 'the gem was simply representative of tribute, and that the jewel of the title was India herself.' The picture must have been painted *after* 1877, the year in which Victoria became Empress of India. I imagine it was an actual picture, no doubt much reproduced, but I have no idea who painted it.

The *OED Supp.* refers only to the 'jewels of the crown', as a rhetorical phrase for the colonies of the British Empire, and has a citation from 1901. The specifying of India as *the* jewel is understandable. The Kohinoor, a very large oval diamond of 108.8 carats, from India, had been part of the British crown jewels since 1849. In *Dombey and Son* (1844–6)(Chapter 39), Charles Dickens writes: 'Clemency is the brightest jewel in the crown of a Briton's head.' Earlier, in *The Pickwick Papers* (1836–7)(Chapter 24), he has (of Magna Carta): 'One of the brightest jewels in the British crown'.

Jewish. See YOU DON'T HAVE TO BE ~.

Jim. See I'M WORRIED ABOUT ~; SUNNY ~.

jingo. See BY ~.

job. See GI'US A ~; SERIOUSLY, THOUGH, HE'S DOING A GRAND . . .

Johnnie Walker. See BORN 1820 . . .

Johnny. See HERE'S ~.

Johnstown flood. See DON'T SPIT . . .

join. See IF YOU CAN'T BEAT 'EM . . . ; YOU CAN'T SEE THE ~ under *MORECAMBE AND WISE SHOW*.

joint. See WHAT'S A NICE GIRL LIKE YOU . . .

join the army/navy and see the world. *Slogan.* The army version seems to have been used in both Britain and the US in the 1920s and 30s. Partridge/*Slang* dates the riposte '. . . the next one' as *c* 1948.

In the film *Duck Soup* (1933), Harpo Marx holds up a placard which says, 'Join the Army and See the Navy'. Irving Berlin's song 'We Saw the Sea' from *Follow the Fleet* (US, 1936) goes 'I joined the Navy to see the world. And what did I see? I saw the sea.'

'I joined the navy to see the world' is quoted ironically, by a sailor in the film *In Which We Serve* (UK, 1942).

jolly D. See OH, ~! under *MUCH BINDING IN THE MARSH*.

jolly hockey sticks! See under *EDUCATING ARCHIE*.

Josephine. See NOT TONIGHT, ~.

journey. See IS YOUR ~ REALLY NECESSARY?

journey into the unknown, a. *Cliché.* Usually journalistic. At the beginning of the Falklands War, for example: 'To the strains of "We are Sailing", the ropes were slipped and *Canberra* was off into the unknown' (J. Hands & R. McGowan, *Don't Cry for Me, Sergeant-Major*, 1983).

Jove. See BY ~, I NEEDED THAT!

joy of ——, the. *Cliché.* Usually in book titling. First on the scene were I.S. Rombauer and M.R. Becker, American cookery experts, with *The Joy of Cooking* (1931). Then, in 1972, along came Alex Comfort with *The Joy of Sex* and even *More Joy of Sex*. Then everyone joined in, so that we have had books about the 'joys' of Computers, Chickens, Cheesecake, Breastfeeding and Geraniums, among many others.

In 1984, I published *The Joy of Clichés* – which I thought would be seen to be ironical – though Fritz Spiegl seems to have had no compunction in naming a book *The Joy of Words* (1986) or Gyles Brandreth *The Joy of Lex* (1980).

J.R. See WHO SHOT ~?

judge. See HERE COME DE ~ under *LAUGH-IN*.

juggling with soot. See under AS BUSY AS . . .

Julian. See OH, HELLO, I'M ~ under *ROUND THE HORNE*.

jumpy. See under AS BUSY AS . . .

just and lasting settlement, a. *Cliché.* Used in politics, and usually with regard to the Middle East. However, it does come with the Abraham Lincoln seal of approval. He talked of a 'just and lasting peace' in his Second Inaugural address, referring to the end of the American Civil War.

just how serious . . . ? *Cliché.* Usually in broadcast journalism, the invariable start to a thrusting, probing question. In the mid-1970s, Michael Leapman, as diarist on *The Times*, invented a character called 'Justow Serious'.

justice. See THIS HAS RESTORED MY FAITH . . . ; TRUTH, ~ AND THE AMERICAN WAY under *SUPERMAN*.

just like a fairy-tale. See LIKE A FAIRY-TALE PRINCESS.

just one of those things. *Catch Phrase.* Meaning 'something inexplicable or inevitable'. The *OED Supp.* finds this first in John O'Hara's story *Appointment in Samarra* (1934), and in the following year as the title of the Cole Porter song which undoubtedly ensured its enduring place in the language. Five years earlier, however, Porter had used the title for a completely different song which was published, though dropped from the show it was supposed to be in.

just the facts, ma'am. See ALL I WANT IS THE FACTS . . . under *DRAGNET*.

**just when you thought it was safe to
——.** *Format Phrase.* The film *Jaws 2*
(US, 1978) – a sequel to the successful
shark saga – was promoted with the line,
'Just when you thought it was safe to go
back in the water . . .' A graffito reported
to me in 1979 was 'Jaws 3 – just when you
thought it was safe to go to the toilet'.
Headline from the *Observer* (16 July
1989): 'Just when you thought it was safe
to get back in a bikini . . .'

K

Kaiser. See ARF A MO, ~; HANG THE ~.

Karachi. See SNOWSTORM IN ~ under AS BUSY AS; YOU'RE FAMOUS WHEN . . .

keep Britain tidy. *Slogan.* The simplest of messages and one of the most enduring. Promoted through the Central Office of Information, it first appeared in their records as a sticker produced for the Ministry of Housing and Local Government in 1952. However, it was probably coined about 1949.

keep death off the road (carelessness kills). *Slogan.* Nobody knows who created this message – the best known of any used in government-sponsored advertising campaigns through the Central Office of Information. It was used in the memorable poster by W. Little featuring the so-called 'Black Widow' in 1946.

Discussing the pointlessness of the campaign in *Tribune* (8 November 1946), George Orwell referred to 'Keep Death off the *Roads*', though the poster version I have seen uses the singular.

keep it dark! *Slogan.* A security slogan from the Second World War, appearing in more than one formulation, and also in verse:

If you've news of our munitions
                KEEP IT DARK
Ships or plans or troop positions
                KEEP IT DARK
Lives are lost through conversation
Here's a tip for the duration
When you've private information.
                KEEP IT DARK.

Shush, Keep It Dark was the title of a variety show running in London during September 1940. Later, the naval version of the radio show *Merry Go Round* (1943–8) featured a character called Commander High-Price (Jon Pertwee) whose catch phrase was, 'Hush, keep it dark!'

None of this had been forgotten by 1983, apparently, when Anthony Beaumont-Dark, a Tory candidate in the General Election, campaigned successfully for re-election with the slogan, 'Keep it Dark'.

keep it under your hat/ stetson. *Slogan.* Security slogans from the Second World War for the UK and US, respectively. *Under Your Hat* had been the title of a Cicely Courtneidge/Jack Hulbert musical comedy in the West End (1938).

keep mum, she's not so dumb. See BE LIKE DAD, KEEP MUM.

keep on muddling through. See MUDDLING THROUGH.

keep on truckin'. *Catch Phrase.* This expression, meaning that you've got to 'persevere' or 'keep on keeping on' is described in Bartlett as the 'slogan of a cartoon character' created by Robert Crumb (b 1943).' Crumb drew 'dirty' cartoons for a number of underground periodicals like *Snatch* and created 'Fritz the Cat', later the subject of a full-length cartoon film. There were a number of records with the title by 1970, and there was certainly a vogue for the phrase in the 1960s and 70s.

I notice, however, that there was a song called simply 'Truckin'' in 1935 (words by Ted Koehler and music by Rube Bloom) and that the *OED Supp.* finds 'the truck' or 'trucking' was a jerky dance that came out of Harlem in the summer of 1934. Partridge/*Catch Phrases* plumps for a suggestion that the phrase, while of Negro dance origin, came out of the great American dance marathons of the 1930s, though one of its contributors hotly disputes this.

Stuart Berg Flexner discussing 'hoboes, tramps and bums' on the American railroad in *Listening to America* (1982) probably gets nearest to the source. He defines 'trucking it' thus: 'riding or clinging to the trucking hardware between the wheels. This may have contributed to the jitterbug's use of *trucking* (also meaning to leave or move on in the 1930s) and to the 1960 students' phrase *keep on trucking*, keep moving, keep trying, keep "doing one's (own) thing" with good cheer.'

keep that schoolgirl complexion. *Slogan.* Used to promote Palmolive soap, in the US, from 1917. Coined by Charles S. Pearce, a Palmolive executive. Beverley Nichols wrote in *The Star-Spangled Manner* (1928) that in his 'riotous youth' he had been comforted through 'numberless orgies' only by the conviction that if he used a certain soap he would retain his schoolboy complexion: 'It did not matter how much I drank or smoked, how many nameless and exquisite sins I enjoyed – they would all be washed out in the morning by that magical soap . . . I bought it merely because years ago a bright young American sat down in an office on the other side of the Atlantic and thought of a slogan to sell soap. And he certainly sold it.'

During the Second World War, Palmolive was still plugging the old line in the UK: 'Driving through blitzes won't spoil that schoolgirl complexion'.

Kemo Sabe. See HI-YO, SILVER.

kettle. See CHOCOLATE ~ under AS BUSY AS . . . ; HERE'S A PRETTY ~ OF FISH.

Keynsham – that's K-E-Y-N-S-H-A-M . . . *Stock Phrase.* Listeners to Radio Luxembourg in the 1950s and 60s will remember the rolling, West Country accent of Horace Batchelor (1898–1977) who appeared in commercials for his own method of winning the football pools. At his death it was said he had netted £12 million for his clients. His usual message was something like: 'Good evening, friends. This is Horace Batchelor at the microphone – the inventor of the Infra-Draw Method for the Treble Chance. I have myself, with my own coupon entries, won 1012 first Treble Chance top dividends. And my ingenious method can help you to win also. Don't send any money – just your name and address.'

Then came the high-spot of his ads: 'Send now to Horace Batchelor, Department One, Keynsham – spelt K-E-Y-N-S-H-A-M, Bristol.'

kicking. See DRAGGED ~ AND SCREAMING . . .

kid. See ALL ~ GLOVES . . . ; HERE'S LOOKING AT YOU, ~!

kindly leave the stage. See I DON'T WISH TO KNOW THAT . . .

king. See TRUE, O ~!; SPORT OF ~S.

kiss of death/life, the. *Idiom.* 'Kiss of death' derives from the kiss of betrayal given by Judas to Christ which foreshadowed the latter's death. In the Mafia, too, a kiss from the boss is an indication that your time is up. Safire defines the political use of the phrase as 'unwelcome support from an unpopular source, occasionally engineered by the opposition'. He suggests that Governor Al Smith popularized the phrase in 1926, when he called William Randolph Hearst's support for Smith's opponent, Ogden Mills, 'the kiss of death'.

In Britain, Winston Churchill used the phrase in the House of Commons on 16 November 1948. Nationalization and all its methods were a 'murderous theme'; the remarks of Government spokesmen about the control of raw materials, 'about as refreshing to the minor firms as the kiss of death'.

'Kiss of life' as the name of a method of mouth-to-mouth artificial respiration was current by the beginning of the 1960s. On one unfortunate occasion I heard a Radio 4 newsreader confuse the two. 'Having been pulled out of the river,' he said, 'the boy did not survive, despite being given the kiss of death by a passing policeman.'

kitchen. See IF YOU CAN'T STAND THE HEAT . . .

knickers. See ALL FUR COAT under ALL KID GLOVES . . .

knives. See NIGHT OF THE LONG ~.

knocks. See OPPORTUNITY K; SCHOOL OF HARD ~.

know. See AS EVERY SCHOOLBOY ~S; AS WE ~ IT; END OF CIVILIZATION AS WE ~ IT; EVERYTHING YOU ALWAYS WANTED TO ~; I DON'T WISH TO ~ THAT . . . ; NOT MANY PEOPLE ~ THAT; ONE INSTINCTIVELY ~S; SHE ~S, YOU KNOW.

kosher nostra. See under TAFFIA.

lady. See AND ALL BECAUSE . . .

lady bountiful. *Idiom.* Applied (now only ironically) to a woman who is conspicuously generous to others less fortunate than herself. The term comes from the name of a character in George Farquhar's *The Beaux' Stratagem*, 1707.

lager. See PROBABLY THE BEST ~ IN THE WORLD.

lager lout. *Nickname.* For a young person in the UK, noted for lager consumption and a tendency to violence, particularly when attending football matches. The species was identified in 1988, the name clearly owing much to alliteration. According to Simon Walters, Political Correspondent of the *Sun*, in a letter to the *Independent* (13 April 1989): 'It dates back to last August when the Home Office referred to the "lager culture" among young troublemakers . . . from that I coined the term "lager lout" to give it more meaning.'

land. See BACK TO THE ~.

——land. *Format Phrase.* As in 'radioland', 'listenerland' 'viewerland', a suffix construction originating, I would say, in the US. 'Hi there, all you folks out their in radioland!' a presenter might well have said in the 1930s/40s. In the late 1950s/early 1960s, Granada TV in the UK was promoted via a series of print ads giving facts about 'Granadaland', the area covered by the company and then comprising Lancashire and Yorkshire. From the American *Spy* magazine (February 1989): 'And from the *Spy* mailroom floor: The Unsoliciteds out in Returnenvelopeland continue to ply us with free verse and promises of loose fiction.'

Larry. See HAPPY AS ~.

last. See AND WHEN DID YOU ~ SEE YOUR FATHER?; NICE GUYS FINISH ~.

last drop. See GOOD TO THE ~.

lasting. See JUST AND ~ SETTLEMENT.

late. See TOO LITTLE, TOO ~.

late great ——, the. *Cliché.* Mostly pop and DJ use. That death can confer status on a pop star, and do wonders for record sales, is certainly true – however, one feels that the use of 'great' here has often rather more to do with the demands of rhyme than truth.

Latin. See NO MORE ~ . . .

laugh. See MEET THE WIFE . . . under 'AS 'E BIN IN, WHACK?

laugh and the world laughs with you;/ weep, and you weep alone. *Saying.* These lines are from a poem called 'Solitude' (1883) by Ella Wheeler Wilcox (1855–1919) and, as *CODP* points out, are an alteration of the sentiment expressed by Horace in his *Ars Poetica*: 'Men's faces laugh on those who laugh, and correspondingly weep on those who weep.'

Another alteration is: '. . . weep, and you sleep alone'. In this form it was said to the architectural historian James Lees-Milne and recorded by him in his diary on 6 June 1945 (published in *Prophesying Peace*, 1977).

laughed. See THEY ~ WHEN I SAT DOWN . . .

Laugh-In. A quintessential late 1960s sound was announcer Gary Owens, with hand cupped to ear, intoning, **This is beautiful downtown Burbank** – an ironic compliment to the area of Los Angeles where NBC TV's studios are located and where *Rowan and Martin's Laugh-In* was recorded. An enormous hit on US television from its inception in 1967, *Laugh-In* lasted until 1973 and was briefly revived, without Rowan and Martin, and with little success, in 1977. The original was a brightly-coloured, fast-moving series of sketches and gags, with a wide range of stock characters, linked together by the relaxed charm of Dan Rowan (1922–87) and Dick Martin (*b* 1923).

For a while, the whole of America was ringing to the programme's catch phrases. The most famous of these was **sock it to me!** spoken by the English actress, Judy Carne (*b* 1939) who became known as the Sock-It-To-Me Girl. She would appear and chant the phrase until – ever unsuspecting – something dreadful happened to her. She would be drenched with a bucket of water, fall through a trap door, get blown up, or find herself shot from a cannon.

The phrase 'to sock it to someone' originally meant 'to put something bluntly' (and was used as such by Mark Twain). Negro jazz musicians gave it a sexual meaning, as in 'I'd like to sock it to *her*.'

The precise way in which this old phrase came to be adopted by *Laugh-In* was described to me by Judy Carne in 1980: 'George Schlatter, the producer, had had great success in America with a show starring Ernie Kovacs in the 1950s. The wife on that show used to get a pie in the face every week and got enormous sympathy mail as a result. So George wanted a spot where an actress would have *horrendous* things done to her each week – a sort of "Perils of Pauline" thing – and then find a catch phrase to fit it.'

In the summer of 1967, Aretha Franklin had a hit record with 'Respect' which featured a chorus repeating 'Sock it to me' quite rapidly in the background. The previous year there had been a disc called 'Sock it to 'em, J.B.' by Rex Garvin with Mighty Craven, and in February 1967 an LP entitled 'Sock it to me, baby' had come from Mitch Ryder and the Detroit Wheels. But Aretha Franklin's record was where the *Laugh-In* catch phrase came from. 'George came up with the idea of making it literal. I said, "Well it should be Cockney." He said, "How far are you prepared to go?" And I said, "I'll do anything for a laugh. If I'm safe, I don't mind what you do to me."

'It all happened very fast . . . in about three weeks we were No. 1 with fifty million people watching. The sayings caught on at exactly the same time the show did . . . It had a dirty connotation and it was also very clean and was great for the kids. That's why I think that it took off the way it did – because it appealed to everyone at one level or another.'

On being known as the Sock-It-To-Me Girl: 'It got in the way for a while. You have to go through a period of living a tag like that down, and proving that you are not just a saying. The main thing is not to identify with it, not to sit about worrying that people think of you as a saying. But better they think of you as a saying than not at all.'

Among the guests on the show who spoke the line were John Wayne, Mae West, Jack Lemmon, Jimmy Durante, Marcel Marceau (even) and Richard Nixon. The latter, running for the US presidency, said it on the show broadcast 16 September 1968. He pronounced it in a perplexed manner: 'Sock it to *me*?' And, lo, they finally did.

The next most famous phrase from the show was probably, **very interesting . . . but stupid!** ('but it stinks', or some other variant). This was spoken in a thick accent by Arte Johnson as a bespectacled German soldier wearing a helmet and peering through a potted plant.

The third notable phrase was **you bet your sweet bippy!** – usually spoken by Dick Martin.

Other phrases from the show included:
here come de judge! The old vaudeville phrase had a revival when Dewey 'Pigmeat' Markham, a black vaudeville veteran, was brought back to take part in a series of blackout sketches to which the build-up was the chant, 'Here comes de judge!'
Judge: Have you ever been up before me?
Defendant: I don't know – what time do you get up?
In July 1968, Pigmeat and an American vocalist called Shorty Long both had records of a song called 'Here Come(s) the Judge' in the US and UK charts.
is that a chicken joke? Asked by Jo Ann Worley (presumably alluding to the age-old variety, Q. Why did the chicken cross the road? A. To get to the other side/ For some foul reason, etc).
look that up in your Funk and Wagnalls! Referring to the American dictionary.
say goodnight, Dick/ goodnight, Dick! Rowan and Martin's concluding

exchange was a straight lift from the old George Burns and Gracie Allen sign-off on *The Burns and Allen Show*:

Burns: Say goodnight, Gracie.
Allen: Goodnight, Gracie!

Compare IT'S GOODNIGHT FROM ME/AND IT'S GOODNIGHT FROM HIM!

the Flying Fickle Finger of Fate Award. This was the name of the prize in a mock talent contest segment of the show ('who knows when the Fickle Finger of Fate may beckon *you* to stardom?'). According to Partridge/*Slang*, 'fucked by the Fickle Finger of Fate' was a Canadian armed forces' expression in the 1930s.

laughing. See MOST FUN I'VE HAD WITHOUT ~; MUM, MUM, THEY ARE ~ AT ME.

law. See LONG ARM OF THE ~.

lay it on with a trowel, to. *Idiom.* Disraeli is said to have told Matthew Arnold: 'Everyone likes flattery; and when you come to Royalty you should lay it on with a trowel.' But the figure of speech was an old one even then. 'That was laid on with a trowel' appears in Shakespeare's *As You Like It* (I.ii.98) which the Arden edition glosses as 'slapped on thick and without nicety, like mortar'.

The trowel in question is not a garden one, but of the kind used by painters for spreading paint thickly.

leading. See WHERE IS ALL THIS ~ US . . . ? under MORNING ALL!

lead on Macduff. *Idiom.* Strictly speaking, it should be: '*Lay on*, Macduff;/And damn'd be he that first cries, "Hold enough!" ' [my italic] (Shakespeare, *Macbeth*, V.iii.33).

It would be interesting to know at what stage people started saying 'Lead on, Macduff' to mean, 'You lead the way, let's get started . . .' Partridge/*Catch Phrases* has an example from 1912, but I suspect it started long before then.

There has been a change of meaning along the way. Macbeth uses the words 'lay on' as defined by *OED*: 'to deal blows with vigour, to make vigorous attack, assail.' The shape of the phrase was clearly so appealing that it was adapted to a different purpose.

leaks. See under LET'S —— AND SEE IF ——.

leap. See ONE SMALL STEP . . .

leave. See LOVE ME, OR ~ ME.

leave no stone unturned, to. *Idiom.* Meaning 'to search for something with complete thoroughness'. It was used by President Johnson in 1963 when announcing the terms of the Warren Commission's investigations into the cause of President Kennedy's assassination. An example from an anonymously published attack on dice-playing, c 1550: 'He will refuse no labour nor leave no stone unturned, to pick up a penny.'

Diana Rigg neatly twisted the phrase for her book of bad theatrical reviews – *No Turn Unstoned* (1982).

leaving. See I'LL BE ~ YOU NOW, SIR . . . ; PLEASE ADJUST YOUR DRESS BEFORE ~.

left a bit . . . under BERNIE, THE BOLT!

left hand down a bit. *Stock Phrase*. From the standard instruction to someone with their hands on the steering wheel of a vehicle. Meaning to turn it in an anticlockwise direction. Applied to navigation in many editions of *The Navy Lark* on BBC Radio (1960s/70s). Leslie Phillips would say it as a naval officer steering a boat. Jon Pertwee would reply, 'Left hand down it is, sir!'

leg. See BREAK A ~; SHORT, FAT, HAIRY ~S. under *MORECAMBE AND WISE SHOW*.

legal eagle. *Colloquialism > Stock Phrase*. For many years in the 1980s, Jimmy Young (see MORNING ALL) referred to his visiting legal expert thus (also 'legal beagle', I believe). Obviously, the rhyme dictates the 'eagle' bit, though this might be an appropriate epithet for one playing a look-out role. Partridge/*Slang* dates it from 'late 1940s, ex US.'

legend in one's own lifetime, a./living legend, a. *Idioms > Clichés*. Both of these phrases are now clichés of tribute. In a speech marking the retirement of George Thomas, Speaker of the House of Commons, in May 1983, Mrs Margaret Thatcher said: 'A great many have occupied your chair but it is a measure of your Speakership that you have become a legend in your own lifetime.'

On 25 August 1984, the *Guardian* reported that Tony Blackburn, a disc jockey, was writing his autobiography: ' "It's called The Living Legend – The Tony Blackburn Story," he explains more or less tongue-in-cheek. "They call me the Living Legend at Radio One . . . I'm known as the Survivor around there." '

The Oxford Companion to English Literature (1985) has this: 'In 1888 [Robert Louis] Stevenson had set out with his family entourage for the South Seas, becoming a legend in his lifetime.'

Where did it all begin? A possibility exists that the first person to whom both versions of the epithet were applied (and within a couple of pages of each other), actually deserved them. Lytton Strachey in *Eminent Victorians* (1918) wrote of Florence Nightingale: 'She was a legend in her lifetime, and she knew it . . . Once or twice a year, perhaps, but nobody could be quite certain, in deadly secrecy, she went for a drive in the park. Unrecognised, the living legend flitted for a moment before the common gaze.'

I recall that in about 1976, Christopher Wordsworth, reviewing a novel by Clifford Makins, a sporting journalist, described the author as having been, 'a legend in his own lunchtime'. A joke reported to me in 1981 wondered, 'Is Michael Foot a leg-end in his own lifetime?'

lergy, dreaded. See under *GOON SHOW*.

let's —— and see if ——. *Format Phrase*. Particularly in business and advertising, this construction is much used to indicate how an idea should be researched and tested, or rather, simply put to the public to see what reaction will be. Some of the versions:

Let's . . .

. . . run it up the flagpole and see if anyone salutes it.

. . . put it on the porch and see if the cat will eat it.

. . . put it on the train and see if it gets off at Westchester.

. . . leave it in the water overnight and see if it springs any leaks.

Not forgetting: 'Let me just pull something out of the hat here and see if it hops for us.'

let's do the show (right here in the barn)! *Stock Phrase*. This is taken to be a staple line in the films featuring the young Mickey Rooney and Judy Garland from 1939 onwards. It had several forms: 'Hey! I've got it! Why don't we **put on a show**?'/ 'Hey kids! We can put on the show in the backyard!'/ 'Let's do the show right here in the barn!'

In *Babes in Arms* (1939) – the only one of the genre I have looked at – Rooney and Garland play the teenage children of retired vaudeville players who decide to put on a big show of their own. Alas, they do not actually say any of the above lines, though they do express their determination to 'put on a show'.

In whatever form, the line became a film cliché, now used only with amused affection.

let's get America moving again. *Slogan* – also *Format Phrase*, as **let's get —— moving again**. A recurring theme in election slogans is that of promising to move forward after a period of inertia. John F. Kennedy used this one in 1960 – Walt Rostow is credited with suggesting it (sometimes it was '. . . this country moving again').

The Irish politician Jack Lynch ran in 1980 under the banner 'Get our country moving'.

It is a short step from these to Ronald Reagan's 'Let's make America great again' in 1980. All of them are inter-changeable slogans that could be applied to any politician, party or country.

let's get down to the (real) nitty-gritty. *Idiom*. Meaning, 'let's get down to the real basics of a problem or situation' (like getting down to brass tacks). Sheilah Graham, the Hollywood columnist, in her book *Scratch an Actor* (1969) says of Steve McQueen: 'Without a formal education – Steve left school when he was fifteen – he has invented his own vocabulary to express what he means . . . His "Let's get down to the nitty-gritty" has gone into the American language.'

All she meant, I feel, is that McQueen popularized the term, for it is generally held to be a Negro phrase and was talked about before the film star came on the scene. It seems to have had a particular vogue among Black Power campaigners *c* 1963, and the first *OED Supp.* citation is from that year. In 1963, Shirley Ellis recorded a song 'The Nitty Gritty' to launch a new dance (like 'The Locomotion' before it). The opening line of the record is, 'Now let's get down to the real nitty-gritty'.

Stuart Berg Flexner (*Listening to America*, 1982) comments: 'It may have originally referred to the grit-like nits or small lice that are hard to get out of one's hair or scalp or to a Black English term for the anus.'

let's get outta here! *Stock Phrase*. A survey of 150 feature films made in the US between 1938 and 1974, and shown on British TV, revealed that the cry 'Let's get outta here!' was used once in 84% of them and more than once in 17%.

let's put on a show! See LET'S DO THE SHOW . . .

letter. See SOMEONE, SOMEWHERE . . .

let your fingers do the walking. *Slogan.* For Yellow Pages (classified phone directories) from American Telephone & Telegraph Co., current from the 1960s. Also in the UK.

Liberace at a wharfies' picnic. See under AS BUSY AS . . .

lie. See LIVING A ~; SHE SHOULD ~ BACK AND ENJOY IT.

lie down, I think I love you. *Saying.* This was considered a sufficiently well-established, smart, jokey remark to be listed by the *Sun* (10 October 1984) as one of 'ten top chat-up lines'. I have a feeling it may also have been used in a song or cartoon just a little before that. Indeed, there was a song entitled 'Lie Down (A Modern Love Song)' written and performed by the British group Whitesnake in 1978.

And then again, there was the Marx Brothers' line from *The Cocoanuts* (1929), 'Ah, Mrs Rittenhouse, won't you . . . lie down?'

As ever, there is nothing new under the sun. Horace Walpole, in a letter to H.S. Conway on 23 October 1778, wrote: 'This sublime age reduces everything to its quintessence; all periphrases and expletives are so much in disuse, that I suppose soon the only way to making love will be to say "Lie down".'

life. See ALL HUMAN ~ IS THERE; ANOTHER PAGE TURNED IN THE BOOK OF ~; HAPPIEST DAYS OF YOUR ~; IS THERE ~ AFTER ——; KISS OF DEATH; IT'S ALL PART OF ~'S RICH PAGEANT; LIVING ~ IN THE FAST LANE; PRIVATE ~ OF ——; YOUR MONEY OR YOUR ~!

life begins at forty. *Saying/Catch Phrase.* In 1932, William B. Pitkin (1878–1953), Professor of Journalism at Columbia University, published a book called *Life Begins at Forty* in which he dealt with 'adult reorientation' at a time when the problems of extended life and leisure were beginning to be recognized. Based on lectures Pitkin had given, the book was a hearty bit of uplift: 'Every day brings forth some new thing that adds to the joy of life after forty. Work becomes easy and brief. Play grows richer and longer. Leisure lengthens. Life's afternoon is brighter, warmer, fuller of song; and long before shadows stretch, every fruit grows ripe . . . Life begins at forty. This is the revolutionary outcome of our new era . . . TODAY it is half a truth. TOMORROW it will be an axiom.' It is certainly a well-established catch phrase. Helping it along was a song with the title by Jack Yellen and Ted Shapiro (recorded by Sophie Tucker in 1937).

life. Be in it. See under BEWDY NEWK!

life of Reilly/ Riley, to live the. *Idiom.* Meaning, 'to have a high old time, wallow in luxury, live it up, without much effort – have an easy life'. *The Life of Riley* was used as the title of an American TV sitcom with Jackie Gleason (1949–50), but I have not come across an earlier citation. Partridge/*Catch Phrases* guesses *c* 1935 and suggests an Anglo-Irish origin – but, surely, it is not necessary to assume that? In 1919 (in the US) there was a song by

Harry Pease with the title 'My Name Is Kelly' which went, 'Faith and my name is Kelly, Michael Kelly,/ But I'm living the life of Reilly just the same.' But that seems to be using an established phrase – for the origins of which, the hunt continues.

Morris thinks the name was 'O'Reilly' and that the association arose from a US vaudeville song about such a character, from the 1880s – though it doesn't appear to incorporate the line as we know it. Bartlett, however, quotes from the chorus of an 1882 song with the title 'Is That Mr Reilly [*sic*]' and adds that this is the 'assumed origin of "the life of Riley" '.

lifetime. See LEGEND IN ONE'S OWN ~.

light. See HOLD IT UP TO THE ~ . . . ; C'MON COLMAN'S . . . ; ~ THE BLUE TOUCHPAPER . . . under *BAND WAGGON*; THOUSAND POINTS OF ~; WHERE WERE YOU WHEN THE ~S WENT OUT?

light at the end of the tunnel. *Idiom > Cliché.* Usually in politics. The *OED Supp.*'s earliest citation is from 1922, in a non-political context. In June 1983, the diarist of *The Times* tried to find the first Tory politician to have spotted this phenomenon. Stanley Baldwin in 1929 was the first, it seems, and Neville Chamberlain spotted it again at a Lord Mayor's banquet in 1937.

As for Churchill – well, John Colville, his private secretary, seems to quote a French source in his diary for 13 June 1940 ('some gleam of light at the far end of the tunnel'), quotes Paul Reynaud, the French PM on 16 June ('the ray of light at the end of the tunnel'), and himself uses it on 31 May 1952, 'I think it is more that he [Churchill] cannot see the light

at the end of the tunnel.' But I have been unable to locate the source of Churchill's reported use of the cliché on 3 May 1941.

The old expression was later dusted down and invoked with regard to the Vietnam War. In 1967, New Year's Eve invitations at the American Embassy in Saigon bore the legend: 'Come and see the light at the end of the tunnel.' President Kennedy nearly employed the expression apropos something else at a press conference on 12 December 1962: 'We don't see the end of the tunnel, but I must say I don't think it is darker than it was a year ago, and in some ways lighter.'

Somewhere about this time, a joke was added: 'If we see the light at the end of the tunnel, it's the light of the oncoming train.' Though not original to him, the line appears in Robert Lowell's poem 'Day by Day' (1977). In 1988, I heard of a graffito in Dublin which ran: 'Because of the present economic situation, the light at the end of the tunnel will be switched off at weekends.'

like. See I ~ IKE; SOMEONE UP THERE ~S ME; WE SHALL NOT SEE HIS ~ AGAIN.

like a dream come true. *Idiom > Cliché.* What any stroke of luck is to an ordinary member of the public, when reported by journalists. Examples: 'British radio hams are to be able to talk to an astronaut on board the latest US space shuttle . . . Dr Garriott said: "This will be a dream come true. I have had this project on my mind since I first became an astronaut" ' (*The Times*, October 1983); 'A club cricket enthusiast has inherited a fortune and his own village cricket club from an elderly widow who was a distant relative he never knew . . . Mr Hews, aged

68, a retired company representative, lives in a semi-detached house in Arnold Avenue, Coventry. "It's like a dream come true", he said' (*The Times*, 22 October 1983).

like a fairy-tale (princess). *Format Phrase > Cliché.* The urge to say that everything in sight was 'like a fairy-tale' was, of course, rampant at the nuptials of the Prince of Wales and Lady Diana Spencer in July 1981. Tom Fleming, the BBC TV commentator for the fixture, said the bride was 'like a fairy-tale princess'. Even Robert Runcie, Archbishop of Canterbury, began his address at St Paul's: 'Here is the stuff of which fairy-tales are made.'

'It was just like a fairy-tale' is also a cliché put into the mouths of unsuspecting members of the public by popular journalists when they are trying to describe some rather pleasant thing that has happened to them. As Iona and Peter Opie point out, however, in *The Classic Fairy Tales* (1974), this is a very partial way of looking at such matters: 'When the wonderful happens, when a holiday abroad is a splendid success or an unlikely romance ends happily, we commonly exclaim it was "just like a fairy tale", overlooking that most events in fairy tales are remarkable for their unpleasantness, and that in some of the tales there is no happy ending, not even the hero or heroine escaping with their life.'

like a red rag to a bull. *Idiom.* Meaning 'obviously provocative'. No example before 1873, but John Lyly in *Euphues and His England* (1580) has: 'He that cometh before [a bull] will not wear . . . red', based on the belief that bulls are aggra-vated by the colour. In fact, they are colour blind. In all probability, if they do react, it is simply the *movement* of material in a bright colour that causes the animal to charge.

The *Longman Dictionary of English Idioms* says the expression refers to 'the large piece of red cloth waved by bull-fighters in Spain to make the bull attack'. I don't think this is the origin of the phrase, however.

'Red rag', from the sixteenth century, was also a term for the tongue – though I do not see how this is connected.

like a vicarage tea-party, makes ——— look. *Format Phrase.* Such critical similes may verge on the cliché but can still be fun. One which lingers in my memory is from a *Daily Telegraph* review of Alan Sillitoe's novel *Saturday Night and Sunday Morning* (1958): 'A novel of today, with a freshness and raw fury that makes *Room at the Top* look like a vicar-age tea-party.' The quote was used on the cover of the paperback of Sillitoe's novel.

When Jacqueline Suzann's *Valley of the Dolls* came out in 1966, a publication called *This Week* noted that it made '*Peyton Place* look like a Bobbsey Twins escapade' [the Bobbsey Twins were nice, clean-cut Americans who got into and out of scrapes in juvenile fiction].

The *Sunday Times* (21 August 1988), quoting an earlier *Sun* profile, said of Charles Saatchi that his advertisements, 'Made previous campaigns look like Mary Poppins'. From the *Sun* (16 March 1989), quoting the reported words of Pamella Bordes during a political/sexual scandal: 'The City would grind to a standstill if I spoke out. What I could reveal would make the film *Scandal* look like a teddy bears' picnic.'

likely. See under AS BUSY AS . . .

like mother makes/used to make, just. *Slogan.* Ie like home cooking and very acceptable. This expression seems to have acquired figurative quotation marks around it by the early years of this century. As such, it is of American origin and was soon used by advertisers as a form of slogan (compare the US pop song of the Second World War, 'Ma, I Miss Your Apple Pie'.)

Vance Packard in *The Hidden Persuaders* (1957) records an example of its effectiveness when slightly altered: 'When the Mogen David wine people were seeking some way to add magic to their wine's sales appeal, they turned to motivation research via their agency. Psychiatrists and other probers listening to people talk at random about wine found that many related it to old family-centred or festive occasions. The campaign tied home and mother into the selling themes. One line was: "the good old days – the home sweet home wine – the wine that grandma used to make." As a result of these carefully "motivated" slogans, the sales of Mogen David doubled within a year.'

Which reminds me of the advertisement which proclaimed:
BUCK WHEAT CAKES
Like mother used to bake – $1.25
Like mother thought she made – $2.25.

like rats deserting/leaving a sinking ship. *Idiom.* Ie hurriedly, desperately. This comes from the English proverb to the effect that 'rats desert/forsake/leave a

falling house/sinking ship.' *ODP* finds an example of the 'house' version in 1579 and of the 'ship' (in Shakespeare) in 1611. Brewer adds: 'It was an old superstition that rats deserted a ship before she set out on a voyage that was to end in her loss.'

'Rat' to mean 'a politician who deserts his party' was used by the 1st Earl of Malmesbury in 1792 (*OED*). In the US it made its first appearance in the saying 'like a rat deserting a sinking ship' around 1800 (Safire).

A number of good jokes have grown from this usage. In Malcolm Muggeridge's diary for 14 February 1948 (published 1981), he notes: 'Remark of Churchill's was quoted to me about the Liberal candidature of Air Vice-Marshal Bennett in Croydon. "It was the first time," Churchill said, "that he had heard of a rat actually swimming out to join a sinking ship".'

In his diary for 26 January 1941, John Colville noted that Churchill had reflected on the difficulty of 'crossing the floor' (changing parties) in the House of Commons: 'He had done it and he knew. Indeed he had re-done it, which everybody said was impossible. They had said you could rat but you couldn't re-rat.'

(When TV-am, the breakfast-television company, had a disastrous start in 1983 and was pulled round, in part, by the introduction of a puppet called Roland Rat, an unnamed spokesman from the rival BBC said, 'This must be the first time a rat has come to the aid of a sinking ship.')

like taking money from blind beggars. *Idiom.* Meaning 'achieving something effortlessly, by taking advantage.'

Compare, 'as easy as taking/stealing pennies from a blind man' or 'sweets/candy/money from a child'. I first heard this form in *c* 1962 – said by my English teacher who had just given a talk to a (wildly-impressed) Women's Institute or some such. But it is an old idea. Charles Dickens in *Nicholas Nickleby* (1838–9) has Newman Noggs say: 'If I would sell my soul for drink, why wasn't I a thief, swindler, housebreaker, area sneak, robber of pence out of the trays of blind men's dogs . . .' (Chapter 59.)

likey. See NO, ~ under *ITMA*.

lips. See READ MY ~.

listening. See COME AND TALK TO THE . . .

lit. See FLEET'S ~ UP.

little. See TOO ~, TOO LATE.

little of what you fancy does you good, a. *Catch Phrase/Saying.* A nudging point of view from a song by Fred W. Leigh and George Arthurs. It was popularized, with a wink, by Marie Lloyd (1870–1922) in the 1890s.

lived. See AND THEY ALL ~ HAPPILY . . .

live now, pay later. See GO NOW, PAY LATER.

living. See ALIVE AND WELL AND ~ IN . . . ; LEGEND IN ONE'S OWN . . . ; WORLD OWES ONE A ~.

living a lie. *Cliché.* Of journalism. 'Zany Kenny Everett's wife kept her love secret from the outside world for four years – to save hurting his feelings. Cuddly Ken knew of the affair. But Lee Everett and her lover, Sweeney actor John Atkin, lived a lie to avoid publicity.' (*News of the World*, 2 October 1983.)

living life in the fast lane. *Idiom > Cliché* – of journalism. Meaning 'living expensively, indulgently and dangerously'. From the association of such a lifestyle with 'fast cars' and such. Used with plodding literalness in these two examples: 'Controversial racing car genius Colin Chapman lived life in the fast lane' – *Daily Star*, 11 October 1984; 'Jackie Stewart lives life in the fast lane. Like any businessman, really' – ad for Toshiba computer, February 1989.

Lloyd George knew my father. *Saying.* Even before David Lloyd George's death in 1945, Welsh people away from home liked to claim some affinity with the Great Man. In time, this inclination was encapsulated in the singing of the words 'Lloyd George knew my father, my father knew Lloyd George' to the strains of 'Onward Christian Soldiers', which they neatly fit.

In Welsh legal and Liberal circles the credit for this happy coinage has been given to Tommy Rhys Roberts QC (1910–75) whose father did indeed know Lloyd George. Arthur Rhys Roberts was a Newport solicitor who set up a London practice with Lloyd George in 1897. The partnership continued for many years, although on two occasions Lloyd George's political activities caused them to lose practically all their clients.

The junior Rhys Roberts was a gourmet, a wine-bibber and of enormous girth. Martin Thomas QC, a prominent Welsh liberal of the next generation, recalls: 'It was, and is a tradition of the Welsh circuit that there should be, following the after-dinner speeches, a full-blooded sing-song. For as long as anyone can remember, Rhys Roberts's set-piece was to sing the phrase to the tune of "Onward Christian Soldiers" – it is widely believed that he started the practice . . . By the 'fifties it had certainly entered the repertoire of Welsh Rugby Clubs. In the 'sixties, it became customary for Welsh Liberals to hold a Noson Lawen, or sing-song, on the Friday night of the Liberal Assemblies. It became thoroughly adopted in the party. I recall it as being strikingly daring and new in the late 'sixties for Young Liberals to sing the so-called second verse, "Lloyd George knew my mother". William Douglas-Home's play *Lloyd George Knew My Father* was produced in London in 1972. One of the leading Welsh Silks recalls persuading Rhys Roberts to see it with him.'

loadsamoney! *Catch Phrase.* 'Loadsamoney' was the name of a character portrayed by Harry Enfield, chiefly in the Channel 4 TV series *Friday Night Live* in 1987–8. A 'monster son of the enterprise culture', as he was described, he waved wads of tenners about and proclaimed his belief in what he referred to as 'dosh' (money).

A *Guardian* editorial on 30 April 1988 noted that, 'to his horror (for in private life Mr Enfield is a politics graduate of impeccable left-wing persuasions) a creation intended to be a satire of the money-worshipping philistinism of Thatcher's Britain appears to be savoured and loved. Real yobs all over the City, according to eye-witness reports, have begun appearing in pubs brandishing bundles of genuine bank notes and screaming "loadsamoney, loadsamoney".'

As sometimes happens, a satirical invention threatened to become a role model instead, and Mr Enfield took steps to abandon the character. The following month, Neil Kinnock, the Labour Party leader, was telling a conference at Tenby, 'We've got the loadsamoney economy – and behind it comes loadsatrouble.' And there were signs of a *Format Phrase* in the making: 'Loadsa-sermons won't stop the Thatcherite rot' – *Sunday Times* headline, 29 May 1988; 'Loadsateachers' – *Daily Mail* headline, 25 July 1989.

Earlier constructions on the same theme have included **big money!** (said by Max Bygraves of what contestants stood to win on ITV's *Family Fortunes*, current 1985) and *Tons of Money*, the title of a long-running stage farce (and film) of the 1920s.

loaf. See SERVE THAT LADY WITH A CRUSTY ~ under *BAND WAGGON*.

local. See SUPPORT YOUR ~ ——.

lonely. See under AS BUSY AS . . .

Lone Ranger. See THE ~ RIDES AGAIN under HI-YO, SILVER!

long. See HOW ~ IS A PIECE . . . under HOW MANY BEANS . . . ; —— IS A ~ TIME IN ——; IT WAS GOING TO BE A ~ NIGHT; NIGHT OF THE ~ KNIVES.

long arm of the law, the. *Idiom.* Signifying that justice cannot be escaped by attempting to hide away from it at a distance. *The Long Arm* was the title of an

Ealing film (GB, 1956) about a Scotland Yard superintendent solving a series of robberies. But the idea is an old one. Charles Dickens in *The Pickwick Papers* (1836/7) has, 'Here was the strong arm of the law, coming down with twenty gold-beater force', and in *The Mystery of Edwin Drood* (1870), 'The arm of the law is a strong arm, and a long arm.'

In Shakespeare's *King Richard II*, Aumerle is quoted as saying (IV.i.11):

Is not my arm of length,
That reacheth from the restful English court
As far as Callice, to mine uncle's head?

This – and 'the long arm of the law' – may be a development of the proverb 'Kings have long arms/hands/many ears and many eyes', found by *ODP* in Ovid, and in English by 1539.

long hot summer, a/the. *Saying* > *Cliché*. Of journalism. 'It looks as if it will be a long hot summer for the dons of Christ's College, Cambridge, who are once again faced with the tricky business of electing a Master.' (Lady Olga Maitland, *Sunday Express*, 11 July 1982.)

This once-bright phrase rapidly turned into a journalist's cliché following the 1967 riots in the black ghettos of eighteen US cities, notably Detroit and Newark. In June of that year, the Rev. Dr Martin Luther King Jr warned: 'Everyone is worrying about the long hot summer with its threat of riots. We had a long cold winter when little was done about the conditions that create riots.'

The Long Hot Summer was the title of a 1958 film based on the stories of William Faulkner (using a phrase formulated by him in 1928) and also a spin-off TV series (1965–6).

looking. See HERE'S ~ AT YOU.

looking bronzed and fit. *Cliché*. Of journalism. An inevitable pairing when someone (probably a politician) 'returns to the fray' having acquired a suntan, perhaps after earlier being ill, and having enjoyed the inevitable 'well-earned rest.' A variation: 'Eric Burdon: Tan, fit and living in the desert' (*San Diego Union*, 25 March 1989).

look that up in your Funk and Wagnalls! See under *LAUGH-IN*.

lot. See AYE, AYE, THAT'S YER ~!; NOT A ~.

loudest noise. See AT 60 MILES AN HOUR . . .

Louis. See DROP THE GUN, LOOEY!

lout. See LAGER ~.

love. See ALL IS FAIR IN ~ . . . ; I ~ IT, BUT . . . ; I ~ ——; LIE DOWN, I THINK I ~ YOU; I'M LOOKING FOR SOMEONE TO ~ under *BEYOND OUR KEN*; MAKE ~ NOT WAR; MAN YOU ~ TO HATE.

love at first flight. See under BOAC TAKES GOOD CARE OF YOU.

love in a ——. *Format Phrase*. Partridge/*Slang* finds 'love in a punt' as a 1950s naval expression for very weak beer (because it's 'fucking-near-water'). But much earlier we have *The Comical Revenge, or Love in a Tub* by George Etherege, 1664, *Love in a Village* (the comic opera by Isaac Bickerstaffe, 1762). Charles Dickens refers to 'love in a cottage' in *Little Dorrit* (1855). And then we have **love in a mist**, the popular name for the misty-blue plant *Nigella*. This was the title of a silent film (1916) with two popular British stars, Stewart Rome and Alma Taylor, and of several popular songs, especially one in the musical comedy *Dear Love* (London, 1929). It was also the title of a play by Kenneth Horne (the writer not the comedian), presented in London, 1942. This last is a light comedy about two couples who find themselves fog-bound in a duck farm on Exmoor.

Love in a Cold Climate, the novel by Nancy Mitford (1949), caused Evelyn Waugh to write to her (10 October): '[It] has become a phrase. I mean when people want to be witty they say I've caught a cold in a cold climate and everyone understands.' The film *Love in a Goldfish Bowl* followed in the US (1961).

lovelier. See YOU'LL LOOK A LITTLE ~ EACH DAY . . .

lovely. See HE'S LOO-VELY, MRS HARDCASTLE . . . under *RAY'S A LAUGH*.

lovely grub, lovely grub! See under *ITMA*.

love me, love my dog. *Saying*. Meaning 'if you are inclined to take my side in matters generally, you must put up with one or two things you don't like at the same time'.

Of all people, St Bernard wrote in a sermon '*Qui me amat, amat et canem meum*' [Who loves me, also loves my dog]. Alas, to spoil a good story, this was a different St Bernard to the one after whom the breed of Alpine dog is named. It was said (or quoted) by St Bernard of Clairvaux (1090–1153) rather than St Bernard of Menthon (923–1008).

love me, or leave me. *Saying*. During the Vietnam War, one of the few memorable patriotic slogans, current from 1969, was 'America, Love It or Leave It'. This was perhaps inspired by the song 'Love Me or Leave Me' (1928, hit version 1955), although since the nineteenth century there has been the semi-proverbial, semi-jocular farewell, 'I must love you and leave you'.

lovers. See PARIS IS FOR ~.

loves ya. See WHO ~, BABY?

love you madly. *Stock Phrase*. Duke Ellington (1899–1974), the composer, pianist and band-leader, used to say, 'We'd like you to know that the boys in the band all *love you madly!*' Also the title of one of his songs.

loving. See TENDER ~ CARE.

LS/MFT. *Slogan*. For Lucky Strike cigarettes, in the US, current in the 1940s. The initials, spoken in radio ads, meant 'Lucky Strike Means Finer Tobacco'. A graffito collected in my *Graffiti 4* (1982) translated the initials as 'Let's Screw, My Finger's Tired', though this merely reproduces 'oral tradition'.

luck. See AND THE BEST OF ~!

Lulu. See BUY SOME FOR ~ under WOTALOTIGOT.

lunch. See NO SUCH THING AS A FREE ~.

lust. See SAVAGE STORY OF ~ AND AMBITION.

Luton Airport. See under NICE 'ERE, INNIT?

M

ma'am. See JUST THE FACTS, ~ under DRAG-NET.

Mabel. See ~ AT THE TABLE, GIVE 'IM THE MONEY, ~!, WHAT'S ON THE TABLE, ~? under HAVE A GO.

Macduff. See LEAD ON ~.

mad. See under AS BUSY AS . . . ; DON'T GET ME, ~, SEE!

madly. See LOVE YOU ~.

maestro. See MUSIC, ~, PLEASE!

magical mystery tour, a. *Idiom.* Name given to a winding journey, caused by the driver not knowing where he is going. A 'Mystery Tour' is a journey undertaken in a coach from a holiday resort when the passengers are not told of the intended destination (and known as such, I should think, from the 1920s onwards). The 'magical' derives from the Beatles' title for a largely unsuccessful attempt at making their own film in 1967. In *Next Horizon* (1973), Chris Bonington wrote: 'Climbing with Tom Patey was a kind of Magical Mystery Tour, in which no one, except perhaps himself, knew what was coming next.' From the *Daily Express* (12 April 1989): 'On and on went the city bus driver's magical mystery tour. Passengers point out their way home – and get a lift to the door.'

magnificent. See MEAN! MOODY! ~!

Maidenform bra. See I DREAMED I . . .

make. See GO AHEAD, ~ MY DAY; LIKE MOTHER . . . ; THEY DON'T ~ —— LIKE THAT . . .

make love, not war. *Slogan.* A 'peacenik' and 'flower power' sentiment from the mid-1960s onwards. It was not just applied to the Vietnam War but was used to express the attitude of a whole generation of protest. It was written up (in English) at the University of Nanterre during the French student revolution of 1968.

In the 1970s/80s, it was still current, as part of a well-known car-sticker joke: 'Make love not war – see driver for details'.

makes —— look like a ——. See LIKE A VICARAGE TEA-PARTY.

makes you feel like a queen. *Slogan.* For Summer County margarine, current in the 1960s. Barry Day, vice-chairman of McCann-Erickson Worldwide, pointed out to me in 1985 that this slogan was originally used in the US for Imperial Margarine (also a Unilever product.) 'The sudden magical appearance of the crown on the mother clever enough to use the brand made more sense. It was considered to be a successful brand property and used on several brands in other markets, irrespective of brand name. In none of the other cases was it markedly successful. The device seems to have been a piece of Americana that did not travel well.'

The idea is not new. In November 1864, Tolstoy's wife Sonya wrote to him, 'Without you, I am nothing. With you, I feel like a queen' – though this is from a translation for an American edition of a French biography (1967).

man. See EVERY ~ HAS HIS PRICE; GO, ~, GO!; IT'S THAT ~ AGAIN under *ITMA*; MOUNTIES AL-WAYS GET THEIR ~; RENAISSANCE ~; YOU 'OR-RIBLE LITTLE ~!

Manchester. See IF YOU'VE NEVER BEEN . . . under *RAY'S A LAUGH*.

man for all seasons, a. *Idiom > Cliché.* Robert Bolt's title for his 1960 play about Sir Thomas More (filmed 1967) has provided a popular phrase for an accomplished, adaptable, appealing person – also a *Format Phrase*, more than verging on the cliché, whereby almost anything can be described as 'a —— for all seasons'. From Laurence Olivier, *On Acting* (1986): '[Ralph Richardson] was warm and what the public might call ordinary and, therefore, quite exceptional. That was his ability, that was his talent; he really was a man for all seasons.' Jean Rook wrote of Margaret Thatcher in the *Daily Express* (in 1982/3): 'She has proved herself not the "best man in Britain" but "the Woman For All Seasons".'

Robert Bolt found his play-title in a description of More (1478–1535) by a contemporary, Robert Whittington: 'More is a man of angel's wit and singular learning; I know not his fellow. For where is the man of that gentleness, lowliness and affability? And as time requireth, a man of marvellous mirth and pastimes; and sometimes of as sad a gravity: as who say a man for all seasons.'

Whittington (*c* 1480 – *c* 1530) wrote the passage for schoolboys to put into Latin in his book *Vulgaria* (*c* 1521). It translates a comment on More by Erasmus – who wrote in his preface to *In Praise of Folly* (1509) that More was '*omnium horarum hominem*'.

man from the Pru, the. See ASK ~.

mangle. See I HAVEN'T BEEN SO HAPPY SINCE . . .

man in the street, the. *Idiom > Cliché.* Of journalism. As in, 'Let's find out what the man in the street wants to know/ really thinks.' Patronizing. Greville was using the phrase in his memoirs by 1831.
Compare MAN ON THE CLAPHAM OMNIBUS.

manners, please – tits first. *Stock Phrase.* Used by the seducer's victim, when she considers that foreplay has started in the wrong place. Current in the 1960s and probably a bit earlier.

man of my calibre, a. See under HANCOCK'S HALF-HOUR.

man on the Clapham omnibus, the. *Idiom.* Ie the ordinary or average person, the MAN IN THE STREET, particularly when his/her point of view is instanced by the Courts, newspaper editorials, etc. This person was first evoked in 1903 by Lord Bowen when hearing a case of negligence: 'We must ask ourselves what the man on the Clapham omnibus would think.'
Quite why he singled out that particular route we shall never know. It sounds suitably prosaic, of course, and the present 77A to Clapham Junction (1989) does pass though Whitehall and Westminster, thus providing a link between governors and governed.
There is evidence to suggest that the 'Clapham omnibus' in itself had already become a figure of speech by the mid-nineteenth century. In 1857, there was talk of the 'occupant of the knife-board of a Clapham omnibus'.

man's gotta do what a man's gotta do, a. *Catch Phrase.* Partridge/*Catch Phrases* dates this from *c* 1945. Donald Hickling tells me he recalls hearing it in a war-time concert party, and suggests it came out of some late 1930s Western (*Hopalong Cassidy?*) or from an American strip cartoon.
The only printed reference to a definite source I have found is to the Alan Ladd film *Shane* (1953), which was based on a novel by Jack Shaeffer, though – on checking – neither book nor film contains the exact line. Ladd says: 'A man has to be what he is, Joey.' Another male character in the film says: 'I couldn't do what I gotta do if . . .' And a woman notes: 'Shane did what he had to do.' In the novel, we find only: 'A man is what he is, Bob, and there's no breaking the mould.'
Perhaps the phrase was used in promotional material for the film? Other suggested residing places of the phrase include *High Noon*, *The Sheepman* and *Stagecoach*. In the latter, John Wayne gets to say something like, 'There are some things a man just has to do.' By the 1970s, several songs had been recorded with the title.

man they couldn't gag, the. *Nickname.* Now only a joke name for an outspoken journalist. However, it was the (reasonably serious) by-line of Peter Wilson (*d* 1981), sports writer on the *Daily Mirror*. He was famous for his hard-hitting style and outspoken opinions.

manure, rocking-horse. See under AS BUSY AS . . .

man/woman who has everything, (the gift) for the. *Slogan.* Ex-America in the

1920s/30s? Promoting some odd luxury item, inessential and over-priced – like a gold remover of fluff from belly-buttons, or the like. A salesman at the eponymous jewellery store in *Breakfast at Tiffany's* (film, 1961) produces something, 'For the lady and gentleman who has everything'.

In *Sunday Today* (4 January 1987), Alana Stewart was quoted as saying of her ex-husband Rod: 'What do you give to the man who's had everyone?'

many, many times! See under ROUND THE HORNE.

man you love to hate, the. *Catch Phrase/Idiom.* Coming across a 1979 film with this title, made as tribute to the Hollywood director Erich von Stroheim (1885–1957), I was curious to know where the phrase came from. In fact, it was a billing phrase applied to von Stroheim himself when he appeared as an actor in the 1918 propaganda film *The Heart of Humanity*. In it, he played an obnoxious German officer who not only attempted to violate the leading lady but nonchalantly tossed a baby out of the window. At the film's premiere in Los Angeles, von Stroheim was hooted and jeered at when he walked on stage. He had to explain that he was only an actor – and was himself an Austrian.

marches. See TIME ~ ON.

Marples must go. See —— MUST GO!

marrying. See NOT THE ~ SORT.

Martini – shaken not stirred, a. *Catch Phrase.* This example of would-be soph-istication became a running-joke in the immensely popular James Bond films of the 1960s and 70s. I think the line was an invention of the screenwriters and does not occur as such in Ian Fleming's novels.

However, the idea stems from the very first book in the series, *Casino Royale* (1953), in which Bond orders a cocktail of his own devising. It consists of one dry Martini 'in a deep champagne goblet', three measures of Gordon's gin, one of vodka – 'made with grain instead of potatoes' – and half a measure of Kina Lillet. 'Shake it very well until it's ice-cold.' Bond justifies this fussiness a page or two later: 'I take a ridiculous pleasure in what I eat and drink. It comes partly from being a bachelor, but mostly from a habit of taking a lot of trouble over details. It's very pernickety and old-maidish really, but when I'm working I generally have to eat all my meals alone and it makes them more interesting when one takes trouble.'

This characteristic was aped by the writers of the first Bond story to be filmed – *Dr No* (1962). A West Indian servant brings Bond a vodka and Martini and says: 'Martini like you said, sir, and not stirred'. Dr No also mentions the fad, though the words are not spoken by Bond. In the third film, *Goldfinger* (1964), Bond (played by Sean Connery) does get to say 'a Martini, shaken not stirred' – he needs a drink after just escaping a laser death-ray – and there are references to it in *You Only Live Twice* (1967) and *On Her Majesty's Secret Service* (1969), among others.

The phrase was taken up in all the numerous parodies of the Bond phenomenon on film, TV and radio, though

– curiously enough – it may be a piece of absolute nonsense. According to one expert, shaking a dry Martini 'turns it from something crystal-clear into a dreary frosted drink. It should be stirred quickly with ice in a jug.'

mating. See ONLY IN THE ~ SEASON under *GOON SHOW*.

maybe. See AND I DON'T MEAN ~.

may the Force be with you! *Catch Phrase*. A delicious piece of hokum from the film *Star Wars* (1977) was this benediction/valediction. At one point, Alec Guinness explains what it means: 'The Force is what gives the Jedi its power. It's an energy field created by all living things. It surrounds us, it penetrates us, it binds the galaxy together.'

The phrase turned up in Cornwall a short while after the film was released in Britain – as a police-recruiting slogan. Later, President Reagan, promoting his 'Star Wars' weapon system, said: 'It isn't about fear, it's about hope, and in that struggle, if you'll pardon my stealing a film line, "The force is with us".'

mean. See I MEANTER SAY!; I SEE WHAT YOU ~ under *ARCHERS*; IT ALL DEPENDS WHAT YOU ~ BY . . . ; WE HAVE WAYS AND ~S OF MAKING YOU TALK.

mean! moody! magnificent! *Slogan*. From the most notorious of all film advertising campaigns – for the Howard Hughes production of *The Outlaw* in 1943. As if 'The Two Great Reasons for Jane Russell's Rise to Stardom' (skilfully supported by the Hughes-designed cantilever bra) were not enough, there were various pictures of the skimpily clad new star. One version had her reclining with a long whip. It's a very tame film, but the campaign has to be an early example of promotional hype.

meanwhile back at the ranch . . . *Stock Phrase > Catch Phrase*. One of the captions/subtitles from the days of the silent cinema which has endured and still has some currency. I think it may also have been used in US radio 'horse operas', when recapping the story after a commercial break.

meet. See ~ THE WIFE under 'AS 'E BIN IN, WHACK?; PREPARE TO ~ THY GOD.

member of the human race. See FULLY PAID-UP MEMBER . . .

memory. See DOWN ~ LANE.

men. See YESTERDAY'S ~.

Meredith, we're in! *Catch Phrase*. A shout of triumph which originated in a music-hall sketch called 'The Bailiff' (or 'Moses and Son'), performed by Fred Kitchen (1872–1950), the leading comedian with Fred Karno's company. The sketch was first seen in 1907. The phrase was used each time a bailiff and his assistant looked like gaining entrance to a house. Fred Kitchen even had it put on his gravestone.

merry. See ALWAYS ~ AND BRIGHT; EAT, DRINK AND BE ~.

mess. See HERE'S ANOTHER FINE ~ . . .

message of ——, the. *Cliché.* Of politics. ' "The SDP bubble has burst," crowed Fallon. "That is the message of Darlington" ' (*Time*, 4 April 1983).

messing. See STOP MESSIN' ABAHT! under HANCOCK'S HALF-HOUR.

Me, Tarzan – you, Jane. *Catch Phrase.* A box-office sensation of 1932 was the first sound Tarzan film – *Tarzan the Ape Man.* It spawned a long-running series and starred Johnny Weismuller, an ex-US swimming champion, as Tarzan, and Maureen O'Sullivan as Jane. At one point the ape man whisks Jane away to his tree-top abode and indulges in some elementary conversation with her. Thumping his chest, he says, 'Tarzan!', pointing at her, he says, 'Jane!'. So, in fact, he does not say the catch phrase commonly associated with him – though I suppose he might have done in one of the later movies. Interestingly, this great moment of movie dialogue appears to have been 'written' by the British playwright and actor Ivor Novello. In the original novel, *Tarzan of the Apes* (1914), by Edgar Rice Burroughs, the line does not occur – not least because, in the jungle, Tarzan and Jane are only able to communicate by writing notes to each other.

mickey. See TAKE THE ~.

midstream. See NEVER SWAP HORSES IN ~.

mighty roar. See STOP THE ~ under *IN TOWN TONIGHT.*

miles. See NOT A MILLION ~ FROM ——.

milk. See DRINKA PINTA MILKA DAY.

milk's gotta lotta bottle. *Slogan.* Thus was milk promoted in 1982. Milk comes in bottles, of course, but why was the word 'bottle' used to denote courage or guts in this major attempt to get rid of milk's wimpish image?

Actually, the word 'bottle' has been used in this sense since the late 1940s at least. To 'bottle out' consequently means to shrink from, eg in *Private Eye* (17 December 1982): 'Cowed by the thought of six-figure legal bills and years in the courts, the Dirty Digger has "bottled out" of a confrontation with Sir Jams.'

One suggestion is that 'bottle' acquired the meaning through rhyming slang: either 'bottle and glass' = 'class' (said to date from the 1920s, this one); 'bottle and glass' = 'arse'; or, 'bottle of beer' = fear. But the reason for the leap from 'class/arse' to 'courage', and from 'fear' to 'guts', is not terribly clear. Though it has been explained that 'arse' is what you would void your bowels through in an alarming situation. And 'class' is what a boxer has. If he loses it, he has 'lost his bottle'.

Other clues? Much earlier, in *Swell's Night Guide* (1846), there had occurred the line: 'She thought it would be no bottle 'cos her rival could go in a buster', where 'no bottle' = 'no good'. In a play by Frank Norman (1958), there occurs the line: 'What's the matter, Frank? Your bottle fallen out?'

There is an old-established brewers, Courage Ltd, whose products can, of course, be had in bottles.

Milk Tray. See AND ALL BECAUSE . . .

million. See I'VE GOT A ~ OF 'EM! under GOODNIGHT, MRS CALABASH . . . ; NOT A ~ MILES FROM ——.

mind. See HEARTS AND ~S; I DON'T ~ IF I DO under *ITMA*; IT'S ALL IN THE ~ under *GOON SHOW*; OUT OF YOUR TINY CHINESE ~S.

mind how you go! See under EVENIN' ALL!

mind my bike! *Catch Phrase.* Jack Warner (1895–1981) wrote in his autobiography, *Jack of All Trades* (1975): 'When I dropped the phrase for two weeks, I had 3,000 letters from listeners asking why . . . the only other complaint came from a father who wrote, "I am very keen on your *Garrison Theatre* show, but I have spent several hundreds of pounds on my son's education and all he can do is shout 'Mind my bike!' in a very raucous Cockney voice. I'm trying to break him of the habit, so will you please stop saying it?" '
See also BLUE PENCIL.

mineral. See ANIMAL, VEGETABLE OR ~.

Minnie(s). See MOANING ~.

misrule. THIRTEEN YEARS OF TORY ~.

mission impossible. *Catch Phrase.* The title of this TV series has achieved Catch Phrase status. The series was first broadcast in the US, 1966–72. The show had something to do with government agents in the Impossible Missions Force.

Miss World order. See under I'LL GIVE YOU THE RESULTS . . .

mist. See under LOVE IN A ——.

mistake. See DID YOU SPOT . . . ?; SHOME ~, SHURELY?

mit. See FROZEN ~.

mo. See ARF A ~, KAISER.

Moaning Minnie(s). *Nickname.* On 11 September 1985, Margaret Thatcher paid a visit to Tyneside and was reported as accusing those who complained about the effects of unemployment of being 'Moaning Minnies'. In the ensuing uproar, a Downing Street spokesman had to point out that it was the reporters attempting to question her, rather than the unemployed, on whom Mrs Thatcher bestowed the title.
As a nickname, it was not an original alliterative coinage. Anyone who complains is a 'moaner' and a 'minnie' can mean a lost lamb which finds itself an adoptive mother. From the *Observer* (20 May 1989): 'Broadcasters are right to complain about the restrictions placed on them for the broadcasting of the House of Commons . . . But the Moaning Minnies have only themselves to blame.'
The original 'Moaning Minnie' was something quite different. In the First World War, a 'Minnie' was the slang name for a German *Minenwerfer*, a trench mortar or the shell that came from it, making a distinctive moaning noise. In the Second World War, the name was also applied to air-raid sirens which were also that way inclined.

moment. See AT THIS ~ IN TIME.

moment of truth, the. *Idiom* – verging on the *Cliché* – for a turning point or other significant moment. Originally it comes from '*El momento de la verdad*' in Spanish bullfighting – the final sword-thrust which kills the animal.

money. See GIVE 'IM THE MONEY under *HAVE A GO*; LIKE TAKING ~ FROM BLIND BEGGARS; SERIOUS ~; TAKE THE ~ AND RUN; YOUR ~ OR YOUR LIFE.

money makes the world go (a)round. *Saying.* With this phrase, as with TOMORROW BELONGS TO ME, we may have to thank the writers of the musical *Cabaret* (1966) for either creating an instant 'saying' or, perhaps in this instance, for introducing to the English language something that has been known in others. 'Money makes the world go round' is clearly built on the well-established proverb ''Tis love, that makes the world go round', but is not recorded in either the *ODP* or the *CODP* (the nearest they get is, 'Money makes the mare to go').

I see that it appears in the English language key to the Flemish Proverbs picture by David Teniers the Younger (1610–90), at Belvoir Castle. The painting shows an obviously wealthy man holding a globe. How odd that it should, apparently, have taken a song in a 1960s musical to get this expression into English.

Monica. See MY NAME'S ~! under *EDUCATING ARCHIE*.

monkey. See RIGHT ~!; I'M A ~'S UNCLE.

month. See FLAVOUR OF THE ~.

Monty Python's Flying Circus. Like most graduate comedy shows of the 1960s and 70s, *Monty Python* rather frowned upon

the use of catch phrases as something belonging to another type of show business. However, **naughty bits!**, from a lecture on parts of the body, caught on as a euphemism for the genitals, as also **nudge-nudge, wink-wink, say no more!** following Eric Idle's use of the words as the prurient character who accosted people with remarks like, 'Is your wife a goer, then? Eh, eh?' The show was first aired 1969–74.

See also AND NOW FOR SOMETHING COMPLETELY DIFFERENT . . . ; DEAD PARROT.

moo. See SILLY (OLD) ~.

moody. See MEAN! ~! MAGNIFICENT!

moon. See OVER THE ~.

more. See ALL ANIMALS ARE EQUAL . . . ; AND THERE'S ~; ARE THERE ANY ~ AT HOME LIKE YOU?

Morecambe and Wise Show, The. The long-running double-act of comedians Eric Morecambe (1926–84) and Ernie Wise (*b* 1925) began on the variety stage, went through a period on ITV, and finally achieved the status of a national institution on BBC TV from the late 1960s to the late 1970s. Then, once more, they returned to ITV. The essence of their crosstalk was the inconsequentiality of Eric's interruptions of the relatively 'straight' Ernie's posturings. Their many phrases included:

short, fat, hairy legs. Applied by Eric to Ernie's, in contrast with his own long, elegant legs. Ernie says that this emerged, like most of their phrases, during rehearsals – particularly during their spell at ATV. I have heard of people who refer to short trousers that reveal hairy legs as 'Morecambes'.

there's no answer to that! Eric's standard innuendo-laden response to such comments as: '*Casanova (Frank Finlay)* "I'll be perfectly frank with you – I have a long felt want." '

this play what I have wrote. From the long-running joke that Ernie was capable of writing plays (in which guest stars could perform on the show).

what do you think of it [the show] so far?/Rubbish! Eric's customary inquiry of audiences animate or inanimate. He said he got the idea from his family and it was first put into a famous sketch between Antony and Cleopatra (featuring Glenda Jackson) in 1971. Eric recalled (1980): 'I said it during rehearsals in a sketch with a ventriloquist's dummy. It got such a laugh that we kept it in . . . but it's bounced back on me more than once. When I was a director of Luton Town, I dreaded going to see away games. If we were down at half time, home fans would shout up to me, "What do you think of it so far?" '

you can't see the join. Eric to Ernie, concerning his (presumed) hairpiece. Ernie recalled (1979) the origin of this: 'We shared digs in Chiswick with an American acrobat who had a toupee which – like all toupees – was perfectly obvious as such. We would whisper to each other, out of the side of our mouths, "You can hardly see the join!" '

See also BOOM, BOOM! and WHAT ABOUT THE WORKERS?

Moreton. See OH, GET IN THERE, ~ under *EDUCATING ARCHIE*.

morning. See GOOD ~ . . . NICE DAY under *ITMA*.

morning all! *Stock Phrase.* Jimmy Young (*b* 1923), one-time crooner, became an unlikely recruit to BBC Radio 1 as a disc-jockey in the late 1960s, and became hugely popular with the mainly female morning audience. He would begin with a routine like this: 'Morning all! I hope you're all leaping about to your entire satisfaction, especially those **sur le continong**[1] . . . and **orft we jolly well go!**' He would frequently wonder **where is it all leading us, I ask myself?** before concluding with **B.F.N. – 'bye for now!** (perhaps harking back to 'T.T.F.N.' in *ITMA*.).

His recipe spot was heralded by a chipmunk-voiced 'Raymondo' who asked **what's the recipe today, Jim?** Jim would then recite the ingredients, after which Raymondo would intone **and this is what you do!** Jim would also chat to listeners on the phone, which he would refer to in curious Euro-lingo as being done **sur le telephoneo**.

In the mid-1970s, Young transferred to Radio 2 and became more involved with current affairs subjects, and virtually dropped all his stock phrases (but see LEGAL EAGLE).

most fun I've had without laughing, the. *Saying.* This is how the Woody Allen character compliments the Diane Keaton character in the film *Annie Hall* (1977). As a description of sex it clearly complements the next entry. However, Mencken was recording, 'Love [he prob-

---

1 The pronunciation 'continong', approximating to the French, was established by the turn of the century. Marie Lloyd had a song called 'The Naughty Continong'.

ably meant sex] is the most fun you can have without laughing' in 1942. And I have seen 'Nothing beats making love – it's the most fun you can have without laughing' attributed to Humphrey Bogart.

most fun you can have with your clothes on, the. *Saying.* Of something other than sex (naturally). I feel this probably predates the above, though the earliest example I have is from Jerry Della Femina in *From Those Wonderful Folks Who Gave You Pearl Harbor* (1970): 'Advertising is the most fun you can have with your clothes on'. People are still drawn to play with the phrase: 'Touch Dancing is the closest you can get to making love with a stranger without actually taking your clothes off' (*London Evening Standard*, 20 October 1987).

mother. See CAN YOU HEAR ME, ~?; DON'T SOME ~S HAVE 'EM; LIKE ~ MAKES; YOUR ~ WOULDN'T LIKE IT.

motley. See ON WITH THE ~.

motto. See SPEAK AS YOU FIND . . .

mountain stream. See COOL AS A ~.

Mounties always get their man, the. *Slogan.* In fact, this is the *unofficial* motto of the Royal Canadian Mounted Police. John J. Healy, editor of the Fort Benton (Montana) *Record*, wrote on 13 April 1877 that the Mounties, 'Fetch their man every time'. The official motto since 1873 has been 'Maintain the right/*Maintiens le droit*'.

mouth. See FROM YOUR ~ TO GOD'S EAR.

move. See DID THE EARTH ~ FOR YOU?

moved. See WE SHALL NOT BE ~.

movement. See THIS GREAT ~ OF OURS.

move/shift the goalposts, to. *Idiom* – verging on the *Cliché*. Meaning 'to change the rules or conditions after something has been started, in order to upset the "players" '.

'Barenboim had been appointed under the *ancien régime* of Chirac. Now that Michel Rocard is Prime Minister, the goalposts have been moved and Barenboim has found himself the target of the new order's distrust of the Bastille [Paris opera house] edifice' (*Independent*, 21 January 1989).

'The people of Kent vote solidly for the Conservative Party . . . Why are these people, therefore, trying to attempt to move the goalposts after the football match has started? [by imposing a new rail line through the county]' (*Guardian*, 1 March 1989).

movie. See ——: THE MOVIE.

moving. See LET'S GET AMERICA ~ AGAIN.

Mr ——. *Format Phrase > Cliché.* Of journalism. Any 'supremo' automatically gets dubbed one of these. *Private Eye* jokingly pointed to the trend by inventing 'Soccer's Mr Football'. Actual examples: 'London's new Mr Railway, David Kirby, likes messing about in boats and singing in the choir' (*The Times*, 8 December 1981); 'Last week it was disclosed that Mewmarch is to be the new chief executive of the Prudential – or, put another way, Mr Insurance UK' (*Observer*, 9 April 1989).

Mr Big. *Nickname.* As a name for the supposed mastermind behind substantial crimes (for example, the Great Train Robbery of 1963), I believe this phrase originated in Ian Fleming's second novel *Live and Let Die* (1954). 'Mr Big', a negro gangster, lives in Harlem: 'Because of the initial letters of his fanciful name, Buonaparte Ignace Gallia, and because of his huge height and bulk, he came to be called, even as a youth "Big Boy" or just "Big". Later this became "The Big Man" or "Mr Big".'

The phrase is also used to denote any major criminal. From the *Observer* (6 August 1989): ' "MR BIG" HELD. Customs officers have arrested a man they believe to be one of London's top criminals.'

Mr Clean. *Nickname.* 'The Secretary of State, James Baker, always regarded as Mr Clean among several highly-placed roguish officials in Ronald Reagan's administration . . .' (*Independent*, 15 February 1989). Originally the name of an American household cleaner, this is a fairly generally applied nickname. Others to whom it has been applied are: Pat Boone (*b* 1934), the US pop singer and actor noted for his clean image and habits (he would never agree to kiss in films); John Lindsay (*b* 1921), Mayor of New York (1965–73); Elliot Richardson (*b* 1920), US Attorney-General who resigned in 1973 rather than agree to the restrictions President Nixon was then placing on investigations into the Watergate affair.

Mr Nice Guy. See NO MORE ~.

Mrs Calabash. See GOODNIGHT, ~ . . .

Mrs Hardcastle. See HE'S LOO-VERLY, ~ under *RAY'S A LAUGH*.

Much Binding in the Marsh. This radio programme grew out of the air-force edition of *Merry-Go-Round* in 1947 and ran until 1953. The programme starred the urbane Kenneth Horne and Richard Murdoch and incorporated the following examples of regular phraseology, among much else:

did I ever tell you about the time I was in Sidi Barrani? Horne to Murdoch, by way of introduction to a boring anecdote.

good morning, sir! Was there something? Sam Costa's entry line. He played a kind of batman to Horne and Murdoch.

oh, jolly D! (short for 'jolly decent') was said by Maurice Denham as 'Dudley Davenport'. Probably taken from earlier public school or RAF usage, though from not much earlier than the Second World War.

read any good books lately? Murdoch's way of changing the subject. An old phrase, of course. It is also what you might say to someone who, for no obvious reason, is staring at you.

muddling through, to keep on. *Colloquialism.* Supposedly what the British have a great talent for. Mencken has 'The English always manage to muddle through' – 'author unidentified; first heard *c* 1885'. Ira Gershwin celebrated the trait in the song 'Stiff Upper Lip' from *A Damsel in Distress* (1937). He remembered the phrase 'Keep muddling through' from much use at the time of the First World War, but knew that it had first been noted in a speech by John Bright MP in *c* 1864 (though, ironically, Bright was talking about the Northern States in the American Civil War).

mum. See BE LIKE DAD . . .

mum, mum, they are laughing at me! *Catch Phrase.* Comedian Arthur English (*b* 1919) was famous in the late 1940s for his spiv character with pencil moustache and big tie. Arthur told me (1979) that this line was ad-libbed in his first broadcast: 'I had my big tie rolled up and proceeded to unfurl it. There was a great laugh and, to cover it, I said, "Mum, mum, they are laughing at me".'

Before this, at the Windmill Theatre, he had been stuck for a finish to his act. 'So I started rambling on with the senseless chatter I became known for . . . [but] I suddenly realised I had no finish to the chatter. I don't know what made me say it, but I said, "I don't know what the devil I'm talking about. **Play the music and open the cage!**" and ran off.' The phrase stuck.

Murphia, the. See under TAFFIA.

Murphy's Law. See IF ANYTHING CAN GO WRONG, IT WILL.

music. See AND WHEN THE ~ STOPS . . . under ARE YOU SITTING COMFORTABLY?; PLAY THE ~ . . . under MUM, MUM, THEY ARE LAUGHING AT ME!

music-lovers. See THANK YOU, ~.

music, maestro, please! *Stock Phrase.* Of 1950s band leader Harry Leader (*d* 1987). It appears to have come from a song by Herb Magidson and Allie Wrubel, featured by Flanagan and Allen in the revue *These Foolish Things* (1938).

—— **must go!** *Slogan.* A slogan incorporating the cry that he or she 'must go' is liable to pursue any prominent politician who falls seriously out of favour. To date, A.J. Balfour, Prime Minister 1902–6, is the first British example I have found. In his case, the cry was sometimes abbreviated to 'B.M.G.'. After losing the 1906 election, Balfour lingered on as leader of his party. Leo Maxse, editor of the *National Review*, wrote an article in the September 1911 edition in the course of which, demonstrating that the Conservative Party needed a new leader, he invented the slogan, 'Balfour must go'. And he went in November.

'Eden Must Go' arose during Sir Anthony Eden's inept premiership (1955–7) when he instigated the disastrous landings in Egypt to 'protect' the Suez canal. On the evening of 4 November 1956, while he met with his cabinet ministers in 10 Downing Street, he could hear roars of 'Eden Must Go!' from an angry mass meeting in Trafalgar Square. He went under the guise of illness early the following year.

The most notable such campaign in British politics was directed at Ernest Marples, an energetic Minister of Transport (1959–64). The slogan arose in October 1962 when he intervened in the build-up of opposition to sweeping cuts in the railway service (announced the following year in the Beeching Report). However, it was because of motoring matters that the slogan was taken up at a more popular level. He introduced various unpopular measures including, in the summer of 1963, a 50 mph speed limit at peak summer weekends in an effort to reduce the number of road accidents. It was this measure that produced a rash of car stickers bearing the cry. It appeared daubed on a bridge over the M1 motorway in August (and remained visible for many years).

'The Saloon Must Go' was the slogan of the Anti-Saloon League in the United States – a temperance movement, organized 18 December 1895, and a precursor of Prohibition.

must you go, can't you stay? *Catch Phrase*. First recorded, I think, by G.W.E. Russell in his *Collections and Recollections* (1898), this was a helpful remark of Dr Vaughan, Head Master of Harrow, designed to get rid of boys he had entertained at breakfast. 'When the muffins and sausages had been devoured . . . and all possible school-topics discussed, there used to ensue a horrid silence . . . Then the Doctor would approach with cat-like softness, and, extending his hand to the shyest and most loutish boy, would say, "Must you go? Can't you stay?" and the party broke up with magical celerity.'

It was later twisted to, 'Must you stay? Can't you go?'

my eyes are dim – I cannot see . . . *Saying*. '. . . I have not got my specs with me'. From the anonymous song, 'In the Quartermaster's Stores', published I know not when, although a version was copyrighted in 1940.

my friends . . . *Cliché*. Of politics. It always presumes rather a lot when politicians make use of this phrase. Safire asserts that the first American to do so – noticeably, at any rate – was Franklin D. Roosevelt who acquired the salutation in 1910 from Richard Connell who was running for Congress at the same time. But Abraham Lincoln had used this form of address on occasions.

During a party political broadcast on 4 June 1945, Winston Churchill said, 'My friends, I must tell you that a Socialist policy is abhorrent to the British idea of freedom.' (This was the occasion on which he made the notorious suggestion that a Labour government would require 'some form of Gestapo' to put down criticism.)

Anthony Eden, in his pained TV broadcast during the Suez crisis (3 November 1956) used the phrase, ingratiatingly, too. But I don't think any British prime minister has done so since. It is hard to imagine Mrs Thatcher getting away with it. Nor has anyone tried to find an equivalent of the standard 'My fellow Americans', beloved of US presidents.

my husband and I. *Stock Phrase*. The Queen's father had quite naturally spoken the words 'The Queen and I' but something in the Queen's drawling delivery turned her version into a joke. It first appeared during her second Christmas broadcast (made from New Zealand) in 1953 – 'My husband and I left London a month ago' – and still survived in 1962: 'My husband and I are greatly looking forward to visiting New Zealand and Australia in the New Year.' By 1967, the phrase had become 'Prince Philip and I'. At a Silver Wedding banquet in 1972, the Queen did allow herself a little joke: 'I think on this occasion I may be forgiven for saying "My husband and I".'

In 1988, the phrase was used as the title of an ITV comedy series with Mollie Sugden.

my name's Monica! See under *EDUCATING ARCHIE*.

my name's Friday. See under *DRAGNET*.

mystery tour. See MAGICAL ~.

N

nah . . . Luton airport! See under NICE
'ERE, INNIT?

name. See I'LL FORGET MY OWN ~ . . . under
ITMA; IS THE ~ OF THE GAME; MY ~'S FRIDAY and
ONLY THE ~S HAVE BEEN CHANGED under
DRAGNET ; WE ~ THE GUILTY MEN.

**nature's way of telling you to slow
down.** *Slogan.* Death is ~ according to
the joke (current by 1978). I wonder if
this had its origins in actual medical
advertising, or similar? The same year,
the American cartoonist Garfield produced a bumper-sticker with the slogan,
'My car is God's way of telling you to slow
down'.

naughty bits. See under *MONTY PYTHON'S
FLYING CIRCUS.*

naughty but nice. *Catch Phrase > Slogan.* Alliteration rules. The phrase was
used in British advertisements for fresh
cream cakes in 1981–4, originated by
Ogilvy and Mather, but has been much
used elsewhere. A 1939 US film had the
title. It was about a professor of classical
music who accidentally wrote a popular
song.

The catch phrase in full is 'It's naughty
but it's nice'. Partridge/*Slang* glosses it
as 'a reference to copulation since *c* 1900
ex a song that Minnie Schult sang and
popularized in the USA, 1890s'.

There have since been various songs
with the title, notably one by Johnny
Mercer and Harry Warren, 'Naughty but
Nice', in *The Belle of New York* (film,
1952). Compare also, 'It's Foolish But It's
Fun' (Gus Kahn/Robert Stolz) sung by
Deanna Durbin in *Spring Parade* (1940).

navy. See JOIN THE ARMY . . .

necessary. See IS YOUR JOURNEY REALLY ~?

needle, nardle, noo! See under GOON SHOW.

needs. See WITH —— LIKE THAT, WHO ~ ——?

neighbourhood. See YOUR FRIENDLY ~ ——.

nerves. See IT'S ME NOIVES under ITMA.

nervous. See NOT SUITABLE FOR THOSE . . .

never. See THERE'LL ~ BE ANOTHER!; WILL ~ BE THE SAME AGAIN; YOU'VE ~ HAD IT SO GOOD.

never again! *Slogan.* Was used during and after the First World War. Winston Churchill in his *The Second World War* (Vol. 1) says of the French: 'with one passionate spasm [they cried] never again'. Later, in the mid-1960s, it became the slogan of the militant Jewish Defence League – referring to the Holocaust. A stone monument erected near the birthplace of Adolf Hitler at Branau, Austria, in 1989 (the centenary of his birth) bore the lines 'For Peace, Freedom and Democracy – Never Again Fascism [*Nie wieder Faschismus*] – Millions of Dead are a warning'. Compare NO MORE WAR.

never chase girls or buses (there will always be another one coming along soon). *Saying.* Turn of the century. Partridge/*Catch Phrases* dates it to the 1920s and derives it from the early US version with 'streetcars' instead of 'buses'.

never darken my door again. *Idiom.* Meaning 'never cross the threshold of my house again'. In James Boswell's journal for 5 December 1786 (included in *Boswell: The English Experiment*) he

writes: 'Satterthwaite used the expression "Never darkened his door". Lonsdale said he had never heard it before, and he durst say it was not in print. I said, "It is in an Irish song" (see it also in Shadwell's *Hasty Wedding*, Act III).'
Shadwell died in 1692, so that takes us back to the seventeenth century. Shakespeare does not use the phrase. Nearer to Boswell's time, the *OED* finds 'Franklin' (I assume Benjamin, in the US) using it in 1729, and Samuel Richardson using it in his 1749 novel *Clarissa*.

never-ending battle. See under SUPERMAN.

never knowingly undersold. *Slogan.* This was a line formulated by the founder of the John Lewis Partnership, John Spedan Lewis, in about 1920, to express a pricing policy which originated with his father, who first opened a small shop in Oxford Street, London, in 1864. The slogan is believed to have been used within the firm before it was given public expression in the 1930s, in the form: 'If you can buy more cheaply elsewhere anything you have just bought from us we will refund the difference.' The firm does not regard the undertaking as an advertising device in the generally accepted sense, although it is displayed on its vans and on sales bills. As John Lewis merchandise is not advertised, the phrase has an almost mystical significance to the Partnership.

never mind the quality, feel the width. *Catch Phrase.* This was used as the title of a multi-ethnic ITV comedy series (1967–9) about 'Manny Cohen' and 'Patrick Kelly' running a tailoring business in the East End of London. Supposedly what a street-tradesman (or Jewish tailor) might say. Paul Beale in Partridge/*Catch Phrases* suggests that this 'mid-C20' saying had, by the later twentieth century come to be used in more serious contexts – 'e.g. the necessity of eking out meagre resources of government aid to cover an impossibly large and neglected field.' Indeed. Headline from *Observer* editorial (29 January 1989) on a National Health Service where 'the pressure will be on to cut overheads and generally sacrifice quality for price' – 'NEVER MIND THE QUALITY'. From the *Independent* (1 March 1989): 'England's senior chief inspector of schools warned . . . "Nor must there be attempts, in trying to reduce shortages, to dilute standards by taking a 'never mind the quality, feel the width' approach." '

never say die! *Catch Phrase*. Meaning 'never give in'. This is used by Charles Dickens in *The Pickwick Papers* (1836/7), the earliest citation in *OED* and *ODP*, but is, notably, the catch phrase of Grip, the raven, in *Barnaby Rudge* (1841). Later, it occurs in the song 'One of the Deathless Army', words by T.W. Thurban, performed by Little Tich (so, late nineteenth century):

If I ever go to war, I'd drive the enemy barmy,

Hi! Hi! Never say die!

I'm one of the deathless army.

never swap/change horses in midstream. *Idiom*. Mencken has 'Never swap horses crossing a stream' as an 'American proverb, traced to *c* 1840'. *CODP*'s earliest citation is Abraham Lincoln saying in 1864: 'I am reminded . . . of a story of an old Dutch farmer, who remarked to a companion once that "it was best not to swap horses when crossing streams".' This would seem to confirm the likely American origin.

'Don't change barrels going over Niagara' was a slogan attributed (satirically) to the Republicans during the presidential campaign of 1932, and is clearly derived from the above.

never work with children or animals. *Saying*. This is a well-known piece of show-business lore, from American vaudeville originally, I should think – and, occasionally, adapted: ' "Never work with children, dogs, or Denholm Elliott", British actors are said to advise one another' (*Guardian*, 29 April 1989).

Phyllis Hartnoll in *Plays and Players* (1985) has: 'W.C. Fields is quoted as saying, "Never act with animals or children".' Although this line reflects his known views, I suspect the attribution may result from confusion with 'Any man who hates dogs and babies can't be all bad' (which he didn't say either: it was said by Leo Rosten *about* him at a dinner in 1939).

Similar sentiment is contained in Noël Coward's remark about the child actress Bonnie Langford, who appeared along with a horse in a West End musical version of *Gone With the Wind* in 1972. Inevitably, there came the moment when the horse messed up the stage. Coward said: 'If they'd stuffed the child's head up the horse's arse, they would have solved two problems at once.'

Sarah Bernhardt had a pronounced aversion to performing with animals (as to children, I know not). When she received an offer to appear in music-hall in a scene from *L'Aiglon*, she replied, 'Between monkeys, *non!*'

new. See WHAT'S ~, PUSSYCAT?

Newk. See BEWDY ~!

news. See ALL THE ~ THAT'S FIT TO PRINT.

newspaper. See FAMILY ~.

newt. See PISSED AS A ~.

New York. See I LOVE ——.

New Zealand. See I WENT TO ~ BUT . . .

next. See AND THE ~ OBJECT . . . ; AND THE NEXT *TONIGHT* . . .

nice. See GOOD MORNING . . . ~ DAY under *ITMA*; HAVE A ~ DAY; IT'S TURNED OUT ~ AGAIN!; NAUGHTY BUT ~; NO MORE MR ~ GUY; WHAT'S A ~ GIRL LIKE YOU . . .

nice 'ere, innit? *Catch Phrase*. From a TV ad in 1976: on a balcony in Venice, an elegant-looking girl sips Campari and then shatters the atmosphere by saying in a rough Cockney voice, 'Nice 'ere, innit?' In the follow-up ad, a smooth type asks the same girl, 'Were you truly wafted here from Paradise?' She: 'Nah . . . Luton Airport.' These nothing phrases were crafted by copywriter Terry Howard and let fall by Lorraine Chase. Campari sales rose by a record 35% in a single year. Lorraine went on to record a song called 'It's Nice 'ere, Innit?' (1979) and Cats UK recorded 'Luton Airport' the same year. Next step was for the personality to be written into a TV sitcom called *The Other 'Arf* (from 1980).

nice guys finish last. *Saying*. During his time as manager of the Brooklyn Dodgers baseball team (1951–4), Leo Durocher (*b* 1906) became known for this view – also in the form, 'Nice guys don't finish first' or '. . . don't play ball games'. Partridge/*Catch Phrases* dates the popular use of the phrase from July 1946. Used as the title of a book by Paul Gardner, subtitled 'Sport and American Life', in 1974.

nice little earner, a. *Stock Phrase*. Much used by George Cole in the character of 'Arthur Daley' in TV's *Minder* (from the late 1970s on). 'Earner' on its own, for 'money earned' (often shadily), may go back to the 1930s.

From the *Independent* (27 April 1989): '[On a large number of claims for tripping over broken paving stones in Northern Ireland] That, said Michael Latham, Tory MP for Rutland, meant that either the state of local pavements was "exceptionally disgraceful . . . ", or the locals saw a "nice little earner there and are trying it on".'

nicely. See THAT'LL DO ~, SIR.

nice one, Cyril! *Slogan > Catch Phrase*. The story of this phrase is a classic instance of a line from an advertisement being taken up by the public, turned into a catch phrase, and then as suddenly discarded. Its origins were quite soon obscured, and then forgotten. The line caught the imagination of TV viewers in a 1972 advertisement for Wonderloaf. Two bakers were shown wearing T-shirts labelled 'Nottingham' and 'Liverpool' respectively. 'All our local bakers reckon they can taste a Wonderloaf and tell you who baked it,' purred a voice-over commentary. 'It was oven-baked at one of our local bakeries.' The following exchange then took place between the bakers:

Liverpool: Leeds? High Wycombe? It's one of Cyril's. Mmm. Good texture, nice colour, very fresh . . .

Nottingham: Cyril . . . I think it's one of Frank's down at Luton . . . it's definitely saying Newcastle to me . . .

The voice-over then intervened: 'The truth is, they can't say for sure. But we can say . . .': *Nottingham:* 'Nice one, Cyril!'

As a phrase, why did 'Nice one, Cyril!' catch on? It has a sibilant ease; it was fun to say. More importantly it could be used in any number of situations, not least sexual ones. In 1973, the phrase was taken up by Tottenham Hotspur football supporters who were fans of the player Cyril Knowles. They even recorded a song about him which went:

Nice one, Cyril
Nice one, son.
Nice one, Cyril,
Let's have another one.

Comedian Cyril Fletcher inevitably used it as the title of his 1978 autobiography. The following year the word 'Cyril' was observed scrawled on the first kilometre sign outside a certain seaside resort in the South of France. Shortly afterwards the phrase disappeared almost completely from use, although in February 1989 posters appeared for a credit card company which showed Sir Cyril Smith, the obese politician, attempting to touch his toes. The slogan was: 'Nice one, Sir Cyril . . . but Access is more flexible.'

nice place you got here. *Catch Phrase >
Cliché.* Dick Vosburgh and Trevor Lyttle-

ton included this film phrase in their delightful catalogue song 'I Love a Film Cliché', which was included in the Broadway hit, *A Day in Hollywood, A Night in the Ukraine* (1980). In it, they gave the longer version – the one uttered by a gangster with a lump in his jacket, viz: 'Nice place you got here, blue eyes. Be too bad if something was to . . . happen to it!' At this point, the heavy usually knocks over an ornament, as a warning.

Often, one hears the version 'nice *little* place you've got here' – used with equal amounts of irony about a dump or somewhere impressively grand. However, in the film *Breakfast at Tiffany's* (1961), it is said almost straight. Partridge/*Catch Phrases* seems to think it all started in Britain in the 1940s, but I feel sure the film use must have started in the US in the 1930s.

From the *Independent* (13 May 1989): 'To this day [Stevie] Wonder habitually talks about "seeing" and catches out sighted friends by walking into unfamiliar rooms, taking a "look" around and saying: "Hey, nice place you've got here".'

nice ——, shame about the ——. *Format Phrase/Slogan.* 'Nice Legs, Shame About Her Face' was the title of a briefly popular song recorded by The Monks in 1979. The title launched a format phrase which appeared, for example, in a take-off by TV's *Not the Nine O'Clock News* team – 'Nice video, shame about the song' and in a slogan for Hofmeister lager, 'Great lager, shame about the . . .' (both in 1982). Just before this, I think Listerine ran an ad with the slogan 'Nice Face, Shame About the Breath'.

Headline to an *Independent* piece on the hundredth birthday of the 'The Flag':

'Good tune, shame about the words' (9 February 1989). Headline from the *Observer* (9 April 1989): 'Nice prints, shame about the books'. Also used loosely: 'Victoria Wood is almost perfect. Lovely lady, pity about the voice' (*Cosmopolitan*, February 1987); headline to an *Observer* report on puny car horns (January 1989): 'NICE CAR, BUT WHAT A VOICE!'

nice to see you . . . to see you . . . / Nice! See under *GENERATION GAME*.

niece. See HAVE YOU MET MY ~?

nigger in the woodpile, the. *Idiom*. Meaning 'something surprising hidden, a concealed factor'. Mencken has: 'There's a nigger in the woodpile – American saying, traced by Thornton to 1864, and probably older.' The *OED Supp.* finds it in Kansas in 1852. Nowadays considered an unacceptable usage.

nigh. See END IS ~.

night. See FRIDAY ~ IS . . . ; IT'LL BE ALL RIGHT ON THE ~; IT WAS GOING TO BE A LONG ~.

night of the long knives, a/the. *Idiom*. During the weekend of 29 June/2 July 1934, there occurred in Nazi Germany '*Die Nacht der Langen Messer* – the Night of the Long Knives', a phrase that has passed into common use for any kind of surprise purge in which no actual blood is spilt. It was applied, for example, to Harold Macmillan's wholesale reorganization of his Cabinet in 1962. When Norman St John Stevas was dropped from his Cabinet post in a 1981 reshuffle, one wit described the changes as Mrs Thatcher's 'night of the long hatpin'.

On the original occasion, Hitler, aided by Himmler's black-shirted SS, liquidated the leadership of the brown-shirted SA. These latter undisciplined stormtroopers had helped Hitler gain power but were now getting in the way of his dealings with the German army. Some eighty-three were murdered on the pretext that they were plotting another revolution.

'It was no secret that this time the revolution would have to be bloody,' Hitler explained to the Reichstag on 13 July. 'When we spoke of it, we called it "The Night of the Long Knives" . . . in every time and place, rebels have been killed . . . I ordered the leaders of the guilty shot. I also ordered the abscesses caused by our internal and external poisons cauterised until the living flesh was burned.' It seems that in using the phrase Hitler was quoting from an early Nazi marching song.

nil carborundum. See under *ILLEGITIMI NON CARBORUNDUM*.

nine days' wonder, a. *Idiom*. Ie something that has short-lived appeal and is soon forgotten. Brewer cites an old proverb: 'A wonder lasts nine days, and then the puppy's eyes are open' – alluding to the fact that dogs (like cats) are born blind. After nine days, in other words, their eyes are open to see clearly.

Another etymologist finds a link with the old religious practice of selling indulgences, one of which – guaranteeing the purchaser nine day's worth of prayers – was called a *novem*. The indulgence was held to be a bit suspect – rather like this explanation.

Chaucer expressed the old proverb thus: 'For wonder last but nine night never in town.' Surely, we need look no further for the origin of an expression of which the truth is self-evident: wonder dies in time.

Incidentally, there is an Italian proverb: 'No wonder can last more than three days.'

nine out of ten ——. *Format Phrase*. Beloved of advertisers. 'Nine out of ten screen stars use Lux Toilet Soap for their priceless smooth skins' – so ran a famous campaign that lasted for twenty years from 1927. Among the stars who were listed as Lux users were Fay Wray, Clara Bow and Joan Crawford. Compare '4 out of 5 people say Big John's Beans taste better' (US ad, quoted 1977). More recently (1987), a graffito – 'Bestiality – nine out of every ten cats said their owners preferred it' – alerts me to the use of the format to promote a cat-food.

nines. See DRESSED UP TO THE ~.

nine/ nineteen to ninety. *Cliché.* 'This show will appeal to everyone from nine to ninety.' Sometimes 'nineteen . . .', if the entertainment in question is a touch more adult.

99 ⁴⁴/₁₀₀ per cent pure. *Slogan.* For Ivory Soap, in the US, from c 1882. One of the clumsiest but most enduring slogans of all. (In 1974, an American gangster film with Richard Harris was entitled *99 And ⁴⁴/₁₀₀ Per Cent Dead*. For the benefit of non-Americans who would not understand the allusion, the film was tardily retitled *Call Harry Crown*. But *Variety*

opined crisply that even the original version was 'As clumsy as its title'.)

nitty-gritty. See LET'S GET DOWN TO THE ~.

nobody tells me nothing! See under *ITMA*.

no comment. *Catch Phrase.* This useful phrase, when people in the news are being hounded by journalists, has not quite been condemned as a cliché. After all, why should people in such a position be required to find something original to say? Nevertheless, it has come to be used as a consciously inadequate form of evasion, often in an obviously jokey way (compare WE ARE JUST GOOD FRIENDS).

From the *Guardian* (25 January 1989): 'Mr [Norman] Willis [TUC General Secretary at book award ceremony] is not going to rock the boat by descending to literary chat. "No comment," he says vigorously when asked if he has read any of the short-listed books.'

I suppose the phrase arose by way of reaction to the ferretings of Hollywood gossip columnists in the 1920s and 30s, though perhaps it was simply a general reaction to the rise of the popular press in the first half of the century.

Winston Churchill appears not to have known it until 1946, so perhaps it was not generally known until then, at least not outside the US? After a meeting with President Truman, Churchill said, 'I think "No Comment" is a splendid expression. I got it from Sumner Welles.'

A good example of its use can be found in a terse broadcast interview conducted with Kim Philby on 10 November 1955 after the diplomat had been cleared of being the 'third man' in the Burgess/Maclean spy case. He later defected to Moscow in 1963 and was shown to have been a liar and a spy all along:

Interviewer: Mr Philby, Mr Macmillan, the Foreign Secretary, said there was no evidence that you were the so-called 'third man' who allegedly tipped off Burgess and Maclean. Are you satisfied with that clearance that he gave you?

Philby: Yes, I am.

Interviewer: Well, if there was a 'third man', were you in fact the 'third man'?

Philby: No, I was not.

Interviewer: Do you think there was one?

Philby: No comment.

Martha 'The Mouth' Mitchell, the blabber who helped get the Watergate investigations under way and who was the wife of President Nixon's disgraced Attorney-General, once declared: 'I don't believe in that "no comment" business. I always have a comment.'

Desmond Wilcox, a TV executive, came up with a variant for the TV age in 1980. When ducking a question, he said, 'Sorry, your camera's run out of film.'

The Financial Times for many years has used the slogan 'No FT . . . no comment' (current 1982).

nods. See HOMER ~.

no good deed goes unpunished. Saying. This is a consciously ironic re-writing of the older expression 'No bad deed goes unpunished' – (surely proverbial but unrecorded in ODP or CODP.)

Joe Orton recorded it in his diary for 13 June 1967: 'Very good line George [Greeves] came out with at dinner: "No good deed ever goes unpunished".' But I have recently seen this ascribed to Oscar

Wilde and, whether or not it is one of his, it is a perfect example of the inversion technique used in so many of his witticisms.

noise, loudest. See AT 60 MILES AN HOUR . . .

no likey? oh, crikey! See under ITMA.

no more chance than (or as much chance as) a snowball/snowflake in Hell/Hades. Idiom. Mencken had this listed as an 'American saying' by 1943. In the form 'Gloom hasn't got a snowball's chance in Hades' the line occurs in Stephen Graham, London Nights (1925). Partridge/Catch Phrases thinks it turn of the century.

no more Latin, no more French,/ no more sitting on a hard board bench (or the old school bench). Saying. I learnt this rhyme at school – the sort of thing you said before the holidays began. It turns out to be the second half of a verse which – in the US – begins, 'No more lessons, no more books./ No more teacher's sassy looks' – at least in the 'schoolboy's song, c 1850' quoted by Mencken.

In the Lore and Language of Schoolchildren (1959), Iona & Peter Opie print two lengthy 'breaking up' rhymes current in Britain this century. Both include these two lines.

no more Mr Nice Guy. Saying. 'Mr Nice Guy' is a nickname applied to 'straight' figures (especially politicians) who may possibly be following someone who is palpably not 'nice' (Gerald Ford after Richard Nixon, for example). They then sometimes feel the need to throw off some of their virtuous image, as presidential challenger Senator Ed Muskie did in 1972 – and his aides declared, 'No more Mr Nice Guy'. In April 1973, Alice Cooper had a song entitled 'No More Mr Nice Guy' in the British charts.

Safire dates to the 'mid-1950s' the joke about Hitler agreeing to make a comeback with the words, 'But this time – no more Mr Nice Guy'.

no more war. *Slogan.* A recurring slogan, limited to the twentieth century, I would suggest. At the UN in 1965, Pope Paul VI quoted President Kennedy 'four years ago' to the effect that 'mankind must put an end to war, or war will put an end to mankind . . . No more war, never again war.' (He said this in Italian.)

Earlier, the phrase was used by Winston Churchill at the end of a letter to Lord Beaverbrook in 1928 (quoted in Martin Gilbert's biography of Churchill, Vol. 5). A.J.P. Taylor in his *English History 1914–45* suggests that the slogan was 'irresistible' at the end of the First World War.

In *Goodbye to Berlin* (1939), Christopher Isherwood describes a Nazi book-burning. The books are from a 'small liberal pacifist publisher'. One of the Nazis holds up a book called *'Nie Wieder Krieg'* as though it were 'a nasty kind of reptile'. 'No More War!' a fat, well-dressed woman laughs scornfully and savagely, 'What an idea!'

Compare NEVER AGAIN.

No.1. See PUBLIC ENEMY ~.

normal service will be resumed as soon as possible. See under DO NOT ADJUST YOUR SET.

Norwich, Bishop of. See DO YOU KNOW THE BISHOP OF NORWICH?

nose. See POWDER ONE'S ~.

no such thing as a free lunch, there is. *Saying.* This old American expression meaning, 'There's no getting something for nothing' dates back to the mid-nineteenth century. Flexner puts an 1840s date on the supply of 'free lunch' – even if no more than thirst-arousing snacks like pretzels – in saloon bars. This was not strictly speaking 'free' because you had to buy beer to obtain it.

The notion was given a new lease of life in the 1970s by the economist Milton Friedman. Indeed, the saying was sometimes ascribed to him by virtue of the fact that he published a book with the title and wrote articles and gave lectures incorporating the phrase. When Margaret Thatcher and Ronald Reagan attempted to embrace, up to a point, Friedman's monetarist thinking, the phrase was trotted out by their acolytes (in Thatcher's case, according to press reports, specific instructions were given for ministers to drop it into their speeches).

In July 1989, US Representative Richard Gephardt, commenting on the announcement of a new American goal in space, commented: 'We don't have the economic strength we need to make it a reality . . . there is no such thing as a free launch.'

no surrender! *Slogan.* According to the BBC's *The Story of English* (1986), 'the never-to-be-forgotten siege of Derry in 1689 gave the language a new phrase: No Surrender'. Certainly, 'Long Live Ulster. No surrender' is a Loyalist slogan. *No*

Surrender was the title of a 1985 film written by Alan Bleasdale about warring Protestant and Roman Catholic factions in Liverpool.

not ——. *Format Phrase.* This construction might seem to have been launched by *Not the Nine O'Clock News* (1979–82) which was broadcast on BBC2 opposite the *Nine O'Clock News* on BBC1. Accordingly, there were any number of derivatives, eg *Not Private Eye* (1986), a spoof of the satirical magazine brought out by some of its supposed victims, and *Not Yet the Times* – when the actual newspaper *The Times* was not being published in 1978–9.

In fact, the model for all these titles was *Not the New York Times*, a spoof on the newspaper, published in 1978.

not a lot. *Catch Phrase.* The Yorkshire magician and comedian Paul Daniels (*b* 1938) says he found his catch phrase early in his career. He was being heckled by someone who didn't like his act. 'A pity,' he said, 'because I like your suit. Not a lot, but I like it.'

not a million miles from ——. *Catch Phrase.* Much used in *Private Eye* since the 1960s, this is, however, a venerable form of ironic exaggeration meaning 'very close to'. Nelson's *English Idioms* (referring to about 1890) explains 'not a hundred miles off/from' thus: 'A phrase often used to avoid a direct reference to any place. The place itself or its immediate neighbourhood is always intended... the phrase is also used of events not far distant in time.' And the example given is from H. Rider Haggard: 'From all of which wise reflections the reader will

gather that our friend Arthur was not a hundred miles off an awkward situation.'

Another, almost facetious variant, appears in the *Eye* phrase, 'a sum not un-adjacent to ...'

No. 10. See BEER AND SANDWICHES AT ~.

nothing venture, nothing win. *Saying.* The first recorded use of the proverb in this precise form is in Sir Charles Sedley's comedy *The Mulberry Garden* (1668). However, the variants 'nothing venture, nothing gain' and 'nothing venture, nothing have' go back further, and may derive from a Latin original.

W.S. Gilbert used this form in the 'proverb' song in Act II of *Iolanthe* (1882). Sir Edmund Hillary, the mountaineer, used it as the title of his autobiography in 1975.

not many people know that. *Catch Phrase.* It is pretty rare for a personal catch phrase to catch on (as opposed to phrases in entertainment, films, advertising that are engineered to do so). But this has certainly been the case with the one that will always be associated with the film actor Michael Caine (*b* 1933) His expression 'Not many people know that ...' was first identified by Peter Sellers. It was delivered in Caine's Cockney mumble – rather as a London taxi-driver might have done if he, too, had been privileged to wander amid the great and glittering of Hollywood.

I first registered that people were using it (and imitating Caine's delivery) in about 1981/2. He was then given the line to say (in the character of an inebriated university lecturer) in the film *Educating Rita* (1983), and he put his name to a book of trivial facts for charity with the slight variant *Not a Lot of People Know That* in 1984.

not so much a ——, more a ——. *Format Phrase.* Use was encouraged by the title of BBC TV's late-night-satire-plus-chat show (from 13 November 1964), *Not So Much a Programme, More a Way of Life.*

However, earlier that year, I find in my personal diary for 20 February that an actress at Oxford who was taking part in an undergraduate show, *Hang Down Your Head and Die*, told me that it was going to Stratford and then on to the West End: 'She concluded, "Not just a show, a way of life".'

This would suggest that the 'more a way of life' part of the construction was in the air at that time, before the TV show took it up. (In 1965, Peter Cook and Dudley Moore chose the loosely similar title *Not Only . . . But Also* for their BBC2 series.)

not suitable for those of a nervous disposition. *Stock Phrase.* This was used in the 1950s on British television – the announcer would say: 'The programme that follows is not suitable . . .' Curiously, the phrase lingers. A 1982 ad for the video of *Macabre* has 'WARNING. UNSUITABLE FOR THOSE OF A NERVOUS DISPOSITION'. Such phraseology, acting as a come-on, almost amounts to a slogan.

not the marrying sort. *Colloquialism.* In Vol. 1 of Anthony Powell's autobiography (1976), he writes of an entertainer called Varda that she 'had been married for a short time to a Greek surrealist painter, Jean Varda, a lively figure . . . but not the marrying sort'. It is not quite clear what is to be inferred from this. However,

when Hugh Montefiore, an Anglican clergyman and later a bishop, wondered at a conference in Oxford (26 July 1967), 'Why did He not marry? Could the answer be that Jesus was not by nature the marrying sort?' – people were outraged at the suggestion that Christ might have been a homosexual.

not tonight, Josephine. *Catch Phrase.* Napoleon Bonaparte did not, so far as we know, ever say the words which have become linked with him. The idea that he had had better things to do than satisfy the Empress Josephine's famous appetite, or was not inclined or able to, must have grown up during the nineteenth century. There was a saying, attributed to Josephine, *'Bon-a-parte est Bon-à-rien'* ('Bonaparte is good for nothing').

The catch phrase probably arose through music-hall in Victorian times. A knockabout sketch filmed for the Pathé Library in *c* 1932 has Lupino Lane as Napoleon and Beatrice Lillie as Josephine. After signing a document of divorce (which Napoleon crumples up), Josephine says, 'When you are refreshed, come as usual to my apartment.' Napoleon says (as the tag to the sketch), 'Not tonight, Josephine,' and she throws a custard pie in his face.

now and forever. *Slogan. Cats*, the longest-running musical in the West End, has used this promotional line since at least 1987. Three films have been made with this title: 1934, with Gary Cooper; 1956, with Janette Scott; and 1983, with Cheryl Ladd. Not having seen them, I take it that it was 'love' which was 'now and forever' in each case. Vera Lynn had a hit in 1954 with a song called this, translated from the German. Indeed, the phrase enshrines an idea common to other languages. Basques demanding that Eta should not keep up its terror campaign (March 1989) bore a banner with the words; *'Paz ahora y para'* ('Peace now and forever').

nowhere to go. See ALL DRESSED UP . . .

nudge-nudge. See under *MONTY PYTHON'S FLYING CIRCUS*.

number. See I'M NOT A ~ . . .

O

obeyed. See SHE WHO MUST BE ~.

obeying. See I WAS ONLY ~ ORDERS.

object. See AND THE NEXT ~.

odour. See BODY ~.

offer. See I'M GOING TO MAKE HIM AN ~ . . .

off one's trolley, to be. *Idiom.* Meaning to be mad. *DOAS* finds it (in the US) by 1909 and calls it 'probably the oldest of the "off [one's] ———" = crazy terms'. Not quite true. 'Off one's head' and 'rocker' are a little older.

An entertaining but probably coincidental derivation of the phrase comes from the days of the Acoustic Recording Machine (*c* 1910). The best effects were obtained not by the use of a volume control, but by physically adjusting the distance between the singer and the machine according to the noise the singer was making. A trolley was employed to effect this. If a singer flounced off from the arrangement, she was said to be 'off her trolley'. Well, it's a thought.

often a bridesmaid, but never a bride. *Slogan.* For Listerine mouthwash, in the US, from *c* 1923. One of the best known lines in advertising, written by Milton Feasley, though there is an echo of the British music-hall song 'Why Am I Always a Bridesmaid?' made famous by Lily Morris (1917).

——— of the century. *Format Phrase >* *Cliché.* When did this begin? Lately, there has been a TV quiz called *Sale of the Century* (1970s/80s). The 1981 Royal nuptials were dubbed by *Time* 'the wedding of the century'. I even wrote a book called *Sayings of the Century* (1984).

But, going back, one finds two films, both called *Crime of the Century*, in 1933 and 1946. The Empire Hotel, Bath (opened 1901) had lavatory bowls with the slogan 'The Closet of the Century' written round the rim. And, in the previous century, the *San Francisco Examiner* (13 April 1895) described the murder of two pretty girls by a Sunday school superintendent as 'THE CRIME OF A CENTURY'. This last points to a likely American origin for the format.

oggi, oggi, oggi/oi, oi, oi! *Catch Phrase.* I first encountered this as a chant at Rugby Union matches in the late 1970s. It was also featured in the routines of the Welsh comedian (and rugby enthusiast) Max Boyce about the same time.

Its use may be much broader than this, especially among children. In 1986, I heard of a Thames River police inspector who believed that the shout (as used by children) was similar to that used by watermen to warn their thieving mates of approaching police.

A correspondent suggests that it could also be related to the Cornish 'oggy' or 'oggie' or 'tiddy-oggie', nicknames for a pasty. Partridge/*Slang* has this nickname and adds that 'Oggy-land' is a name for Cornwall itself. Another correspondent, also from Cornwall, states that 'oggi-oggi-oggi' was long a rallying cry in those parts before being taken up in Wales and elsewhere.

The chant familiar from demos against the Thatcher Government, 'Maggie-Maggie-Maggie, Out-Out-Out!', clearly derives from it.

oh, calamity! *Catch Phrase.* The comic actor Robertson Hare (1891–1979) used to exclaim this. It came from an Aldwych farce of long ago – perhaps one in which the put-upon little man had to lose his trousers – but even he was unable to recall which. His other characteristic utterance was **indubitably!** He called his autobiography *Yours Indubitably*.

oh, get in there, Moreton! See under *EDUCATING ARCHIE*.

oh, hello, I'm Julian . . . See under *ROUND THE HORNE*.

oh, jolly D! See under *MUCH BINDING IN THE MARSH*.

oh no, there isn't! *Stock Phrase.* In pantomime, there is always a scene in which an actor speaks to the audience with his back to someone or something which he denies exists. The following kind of ritual exchange then takes place: 'There isn't a bear behind me, is there, children?' *Audience*: '**oh yes, there is!'** There will also be cries of '**behind you!'** (the phrase 'Oh, no there isn't!' was also used as bill matter by the Two Pirates variety act).

There is the story of a curtain speech by the manager of a provincial theatre halfway through a panto: 'I'm very sorry, ladies and gentlemen, but we cannot continue the performance as our leading lady has just died.' Children in the audience: 'Oh, no, she hasn't!'

oh, Ron/ Yes, Eth? See under *TAKE IT FROM HERE*.

oh yes, there is! See OH NO, THERE ISN'T!

oi, oi, oi. See OGGI . . .

OK. See —— RULES ~.

old as my tongue and a little older than my teeth, as. *Saying.* What nannies (and other older folk) traditionally reply when asked how old they are by young nosey-parkers. Swift has it in *Polite Conversation* (1738).

older. See YOU KNOW YOU'RE GETTING ~ . . .

old man. See YOU'VE MADE AN ~ VERY HAPPY.

old soldiers never die, they simply fade away. *Saying.* A notable use of this was made by General Douglas MacArthur when, following his dismissal by President Truman, he was allowed to address Congress on 19 April 1951. He ended: 'I still remember the refrain of one of the most popular barrack ballads of that day [turn of the century], which proclaimed, most proudly, that "Old soldiers never die. They just fade away." And like the old soldier of that ballad, I now close my military career and just fade away . . .'

The origins of the ballad he quoted lie in a British army parody of the gospel hymn 'Kind Words Can Never Die' which (never mind MacArthur's dating) came out of the First World War. J. Foley copyrighted a version of the parody in 1920.

The format has appealed to many jokers over the years. From the early 1980s come these examples: 'Old soldiers never die, just their privates'; 'Old professors . . . just lose their faculties'; 'Old golfers . . . just lose their balls'; 'Old fishermen never die, they just smell that way'.

on a scale of one to ten. *Catch Phrase.* Usually used in allusively, eg 'a ten', 'a two'. In a West Coast party scene in the film *Annie Hall* (1977), a character says of a woman, 'She's a ten', indicating that she is his ideal. This usage was further popularized by the film *10* (1979) in which the sexual allure or performance of the hero's girl-friends was so rated. Some people still use it. *The Naff Sex Guide* (1984) quoted an unidentified celebrity as having said: 'On a scale of one to ten I'd give him a two, but that's only because I've never met a one.'

An ad in the *New York Times* (26 March 1989) quoted Gary Franklin of KABC-TV as rating the film *Heathers*, 'A 10! Absolutely brilliant, a remarkable film.'

Perhaps the usage derives from the Richter scale of measuring the severity of earthquakes (1 to 10), named after Charles F. Richter who began devising the scale in 1932, or simply from the old school habit of marking things out of ten. 'Ten' also equals intercourse on the schoolboy/girl petting scale.

on behalf of the working classes . . . *Stock Phrase.* Also bill matter, of the music-hall comedian Billy Russell (1893–1971).

once. See I'LL TRY ANYTHING ~.

once a —— always a ——. *Format Phrase.* This derives from a series of proverbs, 'Once a knave/ whore/ captain, always a . . .' Partridge/*Slang* finds more recently, 'Once a teacher/ policeman . . .' To which I would add, from the US, 'Once a Marine, always a Marine' (current in 1987) and the joke (which I first noted in 1967): 'Once a knight, always a knight –

and twice a night, you're doing all right!' Partridge/*Catch Phrases*, however, finishes the joke off: '. . . twice a night, dead at forty' and dates it *c* 1950 'but probably from at least fifty years earlier'.

once again we stop the mighty roar . . . See under *IN TOWN TONIGHT*.

once upon a time. *Catch Phrase > Cliché.* 'Never, in all my childhood, did any one address to me the affecting preamble, "Once upon a time!" ' wrote Edmund Gosse in *Father and Son*, 1907. Poor deprived thing. The traditional start to 'fairy' stories has existed as a phrase for a very long time. George Peele has the line in his play *The Old Wives' Tale* (1595). The Old Woman begins a story she is telling with, 'Once upon a time there was a King, or a Lord, or a Duke . . .' – which suggests that it was a 'formula' phrase even then. No less than thirteen of the twenty-four *Classic Fairy Tales* collected in their earliest English versions by Iona & Peter Opie (1974) begin with the words. Mostly the versions are translations from the French of Charles Perrault's collected *Histories, or Tales of Past Times* (1697). The ready-made English phrase is used to translate his almost invariable, '*Il estoit une fois*'. 'There was once upon a time a King and a Queen . . .'; 'Once upon a time, and be sure 'twas a long time ago . . .'; 'Once upon a time, and twice upon a time . . .'; 'Once upon a time, and a very good time it was . . .' – all these variants hark back to a mythical past. The Opies comment that fairy stories, 'are the space fiction of the past. They describe events that took place when a different range of possibilities operated in the unidentified long

ago; and this is part of their attraction . . . The stories would, curiously, not be so believable if the period in which they took place was specified.'

The Nelson *English Idioms* (*c* 1912) calls it 'a somewhat old-fashioned and pedantic phrase used to introduce an incident or story which took place at some indefinite time in the past.'

one. See BIG ~; JUST ~ OF THOSE THINGS; IS HE ~ OF US?

one and only, the. *Slogan.* Might be used as a promotional phrase about anything or anyone, but Phyllis Dixey, the noted striptease artist of the 1940s, was billed as 'The One and Only', as was Max Miller, the comedian. The Gershwins wrote a song 'My One and Only' for *Funny Face* (1927).

one-armed paperhanger. See AS BUSY AS . . .

one day all this will be yours, my son. *Catch Phrase > Cliché.* I'm not sure where this cliché began. It is, of course, spoken by a proud father gesturing proprietorially over his property. The only examples I have are very recent playings with the formula: 'One day my son all this might *not* be yours' (headline to Albany life assurance advertisement, December 1981); 'One day, my boy, all this *won't* be yours' (headline to National Provident life assurance ad, the same month); 'One day, my son, all this will be yours – but not just yet' (Glenmorangie whisky ad, December 1982).

one door closes and another door closes. *Saying.* This is a cynical variant (which I first heard in 1969) on the old 'Irish proverb' (according to Mencken), 'God never shuts one door but He opens another.' Whether Irish or not, *CODP* has it as already proverbial by 1586.

one foot in the grave, to have. *Idiom*. To have one foot in the grave means to be near death. The earliest citation in the *OED* is from 1621. Swift in *Gulliver's Travels* (1726) uses the phrase in connection with the immortal Struldbruggs of Laputa. Mencken quotes William George Smith as tracing 'One of his feet is already in the grave' to 1566. Bartlett provides a translation of Plutarch's *Morals: Of the Training of Children* which goes, 'An old doting fool, with one foot already in the grave.'

Proof that the phrase was well-known by the eighteenth century can be found in a punning inscription upon the grave of one Samuel Foote in Westminster Abbey. Foote (1720–77) was an actor and dramatist, famous for his mimicry and for making Samuel Johnson laugh against his will. He was buried by torchlight in an unmarked grave but his inscription reads:

Here lies one Foote, whose death may thousands save,

For death has now one foot within the grave.

one instinctively knows when something is right. *Slogan > Catch Phrase*. A line from advertisements (current 1982) for Croft Original Port. It has had some after-life elsewhere.

one-legged cat. See under AS BUSY AS . . .

one over the eight. *Idiom*. Ie drunk. For some reason, eight beers was considered to be a reasonable and safe amount for an average man to drink. One more and you were incapable. From services' slang, but not before the twentieth century.

one small step for ——, one giant leap for ——. *Format Phrase*. What Neil Armstrong claimed he said when stepping on to the moon's surface for the first time on 20 July 1969 was 'That's one small step for a man, one giant leap for mankind'. The indefinite article before 'man' was, however, completely inaudible, thus ruining the sense.

Many reference books have been thrown into confusion since. Several follow the version – 'One small step for (. . .) man, one big step for mankind' [*sic*] – which appeared in the magazine *Nature* in 1974.

The *Observer* 'Sayings of the Week' column in the week after the landing had, 'That's one small step for [. . .] man, one giant leap for all [*sic*] mankind' [my brackets].

Either way, Armstrong launched an imperishable format: 'SMALL STEP FOR NON-WHITE MANKIND' (*The Times*, 29 October 1983); 'Up to 10.75% – ONE SMALL STEP FOR YOUR MONEY, ONE GIANT LEAP FOR YOUR INTEREST RATE. You'll be over the moon to discover you only need £1,000 to open a Capital Choice account at the Alliance & Leicester' (advertisement, July 1989).

The correct version has even been set to music. I have heard the Great Mormon Tabernacle Choir sing: 'One small step for a man, one giant leap for mankind -/It shows what a man can do, if he has the will.'

one step forwards, two steps back. *Idiom*. In 1904, Lenin wrote a book about 'the crisis within our party' under this title. I once regularly used to interview an expert on Portugal (in the early 1970s) who invariably made use of this phrase to describe the Caetano regime and its moves, such as they were, towards any form of liberalization. And from Russell Grant, the astrologer, in the *Chiswick and Brent Gazette* (22 September 1983): 'GEMINI. It's been a one-step-forward-two-steps-backwards time.'

Variations occur, of course: 'Alternatively, try retro-dressing. It's here again. One step forward, thirty years back. The 'Fifties look is determined to make a comeback . . .' (*Cosmopolitan*, February 1987).

only. See ONE AND ~.

only fools and horses work. *Saying*. The BBC Television comedy with the title *Only Fools and Horses*, written by John Sullivan, has been on the air since 1981 and concerns itself with a pair of wide boy brothers sparring together in London. The title must have puzzled many people. Although unrecorded in reference books, it apparently comes from an old Cockney expression, 'Only fools and horses *work*.'

only her hairdresser knows for sure. See under DOES SHE . . . OR DOESN'T SHE?

only in America . . . ! *Catch Phrase*. Used as the title of a TV series in 1980, this exclamation means 'Only in America is this possible.' Leo Rosten in *Hooray for Yiddish!* (1982) wrote: 'Not a week passed during my boyhood (or two weeks, since then) without my hearing this exclama-

tion. It is the immigrants' testament, an affirmation of the opportunities imbedded in that Promised Land . . . America. Scarcely a new shop, new product, a new journal or school or fad could appear without ecstatic *Only in Americas!*.'

only in the mating season. See under *GOON SHOW*.

only the names have been changed . . . See under DRAGNET.

only time will tell. *Cliché*. Used particularly by reporters to round off a story when they can't think of anything. *Time* (March 1984) quoted Edwin Newman, a former NBC-TV correspondent, on a continuing weakness of TV news: 'There are too many correspondents standing outside buildings and saying, "Time will tell".'

onwards and upwards! *Catch Phrase*. Now, a humorously uplifting phrase designed to encourage those around one. Perhaps it derives from a religious notion of striving onwards and upwards through the everlasting night? Perhaps it occurs in a hymn? In James Russell Lowell's *The Present Crisis* (1844) we find: 'They must upward still, and onward, who would keep abreast of truth.' That might be the source. The phrase was used light-heartedly in Stewart Parker's TV play *Radio Pictures* (BBC TV, repeated 1989).

on with the motley! *Catch Phrase*. An ironic use of the Clown's cry – '*vesti la giubba*' – from Leoncavallo's opera *I Pagliacci* (1892). The Clown has to 'carry on with the show' despite having a broken heart. It might be said jokingly nowadays by anyone who is having to proceed with something in spite of difficulties – though Laurence Olivier used the phrase in its original sense when describing a sudden return dash from Ceylon during a crisis in his marriage to Vivien Leigh: 'I got myself on to a plane . . . and was in Paris on the Saturday afternoon. I went straight on home the next day as I had music sessions for *The Beggar's Opera* from the Monday; and so, on with the motley' (*Confessions of an Actor*, 1982).

'*Giubba*', in Italian, means simply 'jacket' (in the sense of costume). 'The motley' is the old English word for an actor or clown's clothes, originally the many-coloured coat worn by a jester or fool (as mentioned several times in Shakespeare's *As You Like It*.)

on your bike! *Catch Phrase.* Newly-appointed as Employment Secretary, Norman Tebbit (*b* 1931) addressed the Conservative Party conference on 15 October 1981. He related how he had grown up in the 1930s when unemployment was all around. '[My father] did not riot. He got on his bike and looked for work. And he kept on looking till he found it.'

This gave rise to the pejorative catch phrase 'on your bike' or 'get on your bike' from the lips of Mr Tebbit's opponents, and gave a new twist to a saying which Partridge/*Slang* dates from *c* 1960, meaning 'go away' or 'be off with you'.

Tebbit later pointed out that he had not actually been suggesting that the unemployed should literally get on their bikes, but claimed to find the catch phrase 'fun'.

ooh, Betty! *Catch Phrase.* Became a key phrase for impersonators of the accident-prone Frank Spencer (Michael Crawford)

in the BBC TV series which ran from 1974 to 1979.

ooh, bold! very bold! See under *ROUND THE HORNE*.

oooh, you are awful . . . but I like you! *Catch Phrase.* In TV series of the 1970s, one of the characters played by the comedian Dick Emery (1917–83) was Mandy, a man-hungry spinster. The last word of the phrase was followed by a quick bash with her handbag. Also the title of a song and of a feature film (1980).

oooo arr, me ol' pal, me ol' beauty! See under *ARCHERS*.

open sesame! *Catch Phrase.* Used meaning 'open up (the door)!' or as a mock password, this comes from the tale of 'The Forty Thieves' in the ancient Oriental *Tales of the Arabian Nights*.

Sesame seed is also famous for its other opening qualities – as a laxative.

open the box! *Stock Phrase.* Contestants in the old ITV quiz *Take Your Pick* – which ran for almost twenty years from 1955 – were given the option of opening a numbered box (which might contain anything from air-tickets to Ena Sharples's hairnet) or accepting a sum of money which might turn out to be worth more – or less – than what was in the box. The studio audience would chant its advice – 'take the money' or, more usually, 'open the box!'

When the host, Michael Miles ('Your Quiz Inquisitor'), died, it was said that his funeral was interrupted by the congregation shouting, 'Open the box! Open the box! . . .'

open the door, Richard! See under *ITMA*.

Opportunity Knocks. A talent contest with this title ran on British ITV from 1956 to 1977. Introducing contestants, the host, Hughie Green, would say: **For —— of ——, opportunity knocks!** and so characteristic was the pronunciation that the phrase became his.

It derives, of course, from the rather more restrictive proverbial expression, 'Opportunity knocks *but once*'. As *CODP* notes, 'fortune' occurs instead of 'opportunity' in earlier forms of the proverb and slightly different ideas are expressed – 'opportunity is said to knock once or more, but in other quotations, once only'.

From Sir Geoffrey Fenton's *Bandello* (1567) comes the example: 'Fortune once in the course of our life, doth put into our hands the offer of a good turn.'

orange. See QUEER AS A CLOCKWORK ~.

orders. See I WAS ONLY OBEYING ~.

orft we jolly well go! See under MORNING ALL!

O.T.T. See OVER THE TOP.

our reporter made an excuse and left. *Stock Phrase.* With the rise of the mass-circulation newspaper came the rise of a two-faced mode of reporting which sought to depict vice and crime in a titilating way while covering itself with righteous condemnation and crusading zeal. The *People,* which was founded in 1881 as a weekly (and became the *Sunday People* in 1971), was one of those muck-raking papers that developed a method of reporting sexual scandals which sometimes involved a reporter setting up a compromising situation – eg provoking prostitutes and pimps to reveal their game – and then making it clear that, of course, the journalist had taken no part in what was on offer. Having found out all that was needed, 'our reporter made an excuse and left' – a classic exit line, probably from the 1920s onwards. It was still going strong, more or less, in the *News of the World* (12 March 1989): 'Our investigator declined her [Pamella Bordes's] services and she put her clothes back on.'

out of ——. *Format Phrase.* A small epidemic of 'out of's' broke out with the release of the film *Out of Africa* (US/UK, 1985) based on Isak Dinesen's 1938 book. In 1986, the *Independent* launched a series of weekly columns entitled 'Out of Europe/Asia/etc'. The same year, both Ruth Prawer Jhabvala and Tim Piggot-Smith brought out books called *Out of India.*

Perhaps the original had something to do with Pliny's version of a Greek proverb, '*Ex Africa semper aliquid novi*' ('there is always something new out of Africa'), in his *Natural History*, VIII.17?

out of the closet(s and into the streets). *Slogan.* For the US homosexual rights organization known as the Gay Liberation Front, *c* 1969. The starting point was the term 'closet homosexual' or 'closet queen' for one who hid his inclinations away in a closet ('cupboard' in American usage rather than 'lavatory' or 'small room').

out of your tiny Chinese mind, you must be. *Colloquialism.* Meaning 'mad'. Gratuitously offensive but I suspect that the only reason for 'Chinese' is because it rhymes with 'tiny'. The older expression is simply 'out of your tiny mind'. Compare DAMN CLEVER THESE CHINESE! under GOON SHOW.

It caused inevitable offence when used by Labour Chancellor of the Exchequer, Denis Healey, in February 1976 of left-wing opponents of his public expenditure cuts. The Chinese community complained.

Probably no earlier than the second half of the twentieth century.

outta. See LET'S GET ~ HERE!

over. See WAR'S ~, YOU KNOW.

over-forties. See PHYLLOSAN FORTIFIES THE ~.

over the moon. *Idiom > Cliché.* In about 1978, two cliché expressions became notorious if one wished to express either pleasure or dismay at the outcome of anything, but especially a football match. The speaker was either 'over the moon' or **sick as a parrot.**

It probably all began because of the remorseless post-game analysis by TV football commentators and the consequent need for players and managers to provide pithy comments. Liverpool footballer Phil Thompson said he felt 'sick as a parrot' after his team's defeat in the 1978 Football League Cup Final.

Ironically, *Private Eye* fuelled the cliché by constant mockery, to such an extent that by 1980 an 'instant' BBC radio play about the European Cup Final (written on the spot by Neville Smith according to the outcome) was given the alternative titles *Over the Moon/ Sick as a Parrot.*

Some failed to note the cliché. *The Times* (21 January 1982) reported the reaction of M. Albert Roux, the London restaurateur, on gaining three stars in the *Michelin Guide*: ' "I am over the moon," M. Roux said yesterday . . . he quickly denied, however, that his brother [another celebrated restaurateur] would be "sick as a parrot".'

'Over the moon' is probably the older of the two phrases. Indeed, in the diaries of May, Lady Cavendish (published 1927), there is an entry for 7 February 1857 saying how she broke the news of her youngest brother's birth to the rest of her siblings: 'I had told the little ones who were first utterly incredulous and then over the moon.' The family of Catherine Gladstone (*née* Gwynne), wife of the Prime Minister, is said to have had its own idiomatic language and originated the phrase. However, the nursery rhyme 'Hey diddle diddle/ The cat and the fiddle,/ The cow jumped over the moon' dates back to 1765 at least and surely conveys the same meaning.

The specific application to football was already in evidence in 1962, when Alf Ramsey (a team manager) was quoted as saying, on one occasion, 'I feel like jumping over the moon.'

What may be an early version of 'sick as a parrot' appears in Robert Southey's Cumbrian dialect poem *The Terrible Knitters e' Dent* (1834). There, 'sick as a peeate' (pronounced 'pee-at') means a feeling like a heavy lump of peat in the stomach – the equivalent of having a heart feeling 'as heavy as lead' perhaps?

A more likely origin is in connection with psittacosis or parrot disease/fever. In about 1973, there were a number of cases of people dying of this in West Africa. It is basically a viral disease of parrots (and other birds) but can be transmitted to humans. Even so, there may be an older source. In the seventeenth and eighteenth centuries, there was an expression 'melancholy as a (sick) parrot' (in the plays of Aphra Behn, for example). And Desmond Morris in *Cat-watching* (1986) claims that the original expression was 'as sick as a parrot with a rubber beak', meaning that the animal was incapacitated without a sharp weapon, as in the expression, 'no more chance than a cat in hell with no claws'.

over the top. *Idiom.* Ie exaggerated in manner of performance, 'too much'. The expression 'to go over the top' originated in the trenches of the First World War. It was used to describe the method of charging over the parapet and out of the trenches on the attack.

In a curious transition, the phrase was later adopted for use by show-business people when describing a performance that has gone beyond the bounds of restraint. In 1982, a near-the-bone TV series reflected this by calling itself *O.T.T.* After which, you heard people saying that something was 'a bit O.T.T.' instead of the full expression. On 15 February 1989, the *Independent* quoted from a play called *State of Play* at the Soho Poly theatre: 'Look at sport – I'm sure you'll agree:/ It's much more fun when it's OTT.'

'ow do, 'ow are yer? See under HAVE A GO.

owes. See WORLD ~ ONE A LIVING.

own. See YOUR ~, YOUR VERY ~.

own goal, to score an. *Idiom.* Meaning to bring harm upon oneself ('Ozal risks own goal in move to kick life into slack election' [by attending a Turkish football team's foray into European soccer – when it might have lost the game] – *Guardian*, 20 March 1989).

The phrase (based on football) came originally from the security forces in Northern Ireland in the 1980s and was used to describe what happened when a terrorist blew himself up with his own bomb. It is a very similar coinage to 'shooting oneself in the foot' or 'being hoist with one's own petard' (as in Shakespeare's *Hamlet*, III.iv.209, where the reference is to the operator of a device used for blowing up walls, etc with gunpowder, being blown up himself).

pacification. See DESPERATION . . .

page. See ANOTHER ~ TURNED . . .

pageant. See IT'S ALL PART OF LIFE'S RICH ~.

paid-up member. See FULLY ~ . . .

pal. See ME OL' ~ under ARCHERS.

paperbag. See under COULDN'T RUN A WHELK-STALL.

paperhanger. See under AS BUSY AS . . .

Paris by Night. *Slogan.* The title of David Hare's film (1989) is a promotional tag for tourism in the French capital, in use since the 1950s at least. A London West End revue used the somewhat nudging phrase as its title in 1955. From the 1930s onwards there had been a cheap perfume, available from Woolworth and manufac-tured by Bourjois *(sic)*, called 'Evening in Paris' – which also traded on the city's reputation for sophisticated pleasures.

Paris is for lovers. *Slogan?* This phrase is spoken in Billy Wilder's film *Sabrina* [*Sabrina Fair* in the UK] (1954). It almost has the ring of an official slogan, though this was long before the days of 'I Love New York' (1977) and 'Virginia is for Lovers' (1981).

Nor have I found a song including the phrase or using it as a title, though Cole Porter's musical *Silk Stockings* (Broadway, 1955) has a song called 'Paris Loves Lovers'.

parrot. See DEAD ~; SICK AS A ~ under OVER THE MOON.

part. See IT'S ALL ~ OF LIFE'S RICH PAGEANT; HEINEKEN REFRESHES THE ~S . . .

pass. See under I'VE STARTED SO I'LL FINISH; CUT OFF AT THE ~; DO NOT ~ GO; ~ THE SICKBAG, ALICE under I THINK WE SHOULD BE TOLD.

passed. See TIME HAS ~ BY ——.

Patagonia. See WHEN I WAS IN ~.

paved. See STREETS ~ WITH GOLD.

pay. See GO NOW, ~ LATER; IT ~S TO ADVERTISE.

pecker. See I'VE GOT HIS ~ IN MY POCKET.

peel. See BEULAH, ~ ME A GRAPE!

peg. See SQUARE ~ IN A ROUND HOLE.

pencil. See BLUE ~.

penny. See PUT A ~ ON THE DRUM; SPEND A ~.

penny plain, twopence (or **tuppence**) **coloured.** *Idiom.* But what does it mean? *ODCIE* has 'in cheap or more expensive (attractive or merely showy) form (from, formerly, paper cut-outs of characters and scenery for toy theatres)'. It gives a citation from *Radio Times*: 'Adapter Ian Cotterell describes the eight-part serialisation of *Hard Times* as part reading, part dramatisation; a radio way, as he puts it, of presenting Dickens "penny plain and tuppence coloured".'

On the other hand, the *Longman Dictionary of English Idioms* (1979) takes things a little further: '*rather old-fash*.: although one of two similar things may be more attractive or bright in appearance than the other, they both basically have the same use or value.'

There is no question that, meaning 'plain or fancy', the saying was princi-

pally connected with toy theatres of the last century and referred to the prices of characters and scenery you could buy already coloured or in black and white to colour yourself.

'A Penny Plain and Twopence Coloured' was the title of a noted essay (in *The Magazine of Art*, 1884) by Robert Louis Stevenson on the toy theatres or 'juvenile drama' of his youth. He began with Skelt's Juvenile Drama: 'The world was plain before I knew him [Skelt], a poor penny world; but soon it was all coloured with romance.'

The Longman dictionary also finds a (questionable) different origin: 'Probably . . . referring to cheap magazines and books. Those with a plain cover costing a penny, while those with a coloured cover cost twopence.' (Could there be confusion here with 'penny dreadful' as applied to vulgar comics?)

Tuppence Coloured was the title of a theatrical novel by Patrick Hamilton (1927) and of a revue that toured (with Joyce Grenfell and others) in 1947. Some of the original cut-outs are still available from Pollock's Toy Theatres Ltd, London. So, as Stevenson wrote, 'If you love art, folly, or the bright eyes of children, speed to Pollock's' – though things cost rather more than penny plain and twopence coloured now.

people. See BEAUTIFUL ~; NOT MANY ~ KNOW THAT; TOP ~ TAKE *THE TIMES*; WHEN ~ ARE STARVING IN INDIA.

Peoria. See IT'LL PLAY IN ~.

Pepsi. See COME ALIVE . . .

perfectly. See I WANT TO MAKE IT ~ CLEAR; SMALL, BUT ~ FORMED.

perspire. See HORSES SWEAT . . .

phew, what a scorcher! *Catch Phrase*. *Private Eye*'s joke headline (since the 1960s) for hot-weather reports from tabloid newspapers. Presumably it did once appear in an actual newspaper. A 'scorcher' was common usage in the 1930s. In Patrick Hamilton's radio play *Money with Menaces* (1937) the events take place in a heatwave: 'Weather hot enough for you, sir?' – 'Yes, it's a scorcher, isn't it?' In fact, *OED Supp.* finds 'scorcher' in 1874.

Phyllosan fortifies the over-forties. *Slogan*. For Phyllosan tonic, current from the 1940s. (This gave rise to the BBC saying of the 1970s, 'Radio 4 over-fortifies the over-forties'.)

piano. See THEY LAUGHED WHEN I SAT DOWN . . .

picnic, wharfies. See under AS BUSY AS . . .

picture. See EVERY ~ TELLS A STORY.

picture is worth a thousand words, a. *Saying*. This famous saying – which occurs for example in the David Gates song 'If' (*c* 1975) – is sometimes said to be a Chinese proverb. Bartlett lists it as such in the form, 'One picture is worth more than ten thousand words' and compares what Turgenev says in *Fathers and Sons*, 'A picture shows me at a glance what it takes dozens of pages of a book to expound.'

But *CODP* points out that it originated in an American paper *Printers' Ink* (8 December 1921) in the form 'One look is worth a thousand words' and was there ascribed by its actual author, Frederick R. Barnard, to a Chinese source (to give it instant proverbial status, I suppose).

piece of string. See under HOW MANY BEANS . . . ?

pile it high, sell it cheap. *Slogan*. Sir John Cohen (1898–1979), founder of Tesco supermarkets, built his fortune upon this golden rule.

Pink Camay. See YOU'LL LOOK A LITTLE LOVELIER . . .

pinta. See DRINKA ~ MILKA DAY.

pipeline. See IN THE ~.

pissed as a newt. *Idiom*. Ie 'very drunk'. Partridge/*Slang* gives various metaphors for drunkenness from the animal kingdom – 'pissed as a coot/rat/parrot' among them. None seems particularly apposite. And why 'newt'? Could it be that the newt, being an amphibious reptile, can submerge itself in liquid as a drunk might do? Or is it because its tight-fitting skin reflects the state of being 'tight'?

We may never know, though the alternative (and, according to Partridge, original) expression 'tight as a newt' has a pleasing sound to it. Folk expressions have been coined with less reason. (Partridge's reviser Paul Beale wrote to me in December 1987: 'The great thing about newts is the characteristic they share with fishes' arse'oles: they are watertight. And you can't get tighter than that!')

piss off. See P.O.E.T.S.' DAY.

piss-up in a brewery. See under COULDN'T RUN A WHELK-STALL.

place. See ANY TIME . . . ; NICE ~ YOU GOT HERE.

plague. See AVOID —— LIKE THE ~.

plane. See IT'S A ~ under *SUPERMAN*.

play. See IT'LL ~ IN PEORIA; THIS ~ WHAT I HAVE WROTE under *MORECAMBE AND WISE SHOW*; SCOTTISH ~ under BREAK A LEG; THEY LAUGHED WHEN I SAT DOWN . . .

playing our tune. See THEY'RE ~, DARLING.

play it again, Sam. *Catch Phrase.* AS EVERY SCHOOLBOY KNOWS by now, neither Humphrey Bogart nor Ingrid Bergman actually used this phrase in the film *Casablanca* (1942). All one should say now is that the saying was utterly well-established by the time Woody Allen thus entitled his play (1969, filmed 1972) about a film critic who is abandoned by his wife and obtains the help of Bogart's 'shade'. By listing it under Allen's name, Bartlett might be thought to suggest that Allen coined the phrase. It would be interesting to know by which year it had really become established.

playmates. See HELLO, ~ under *BAND WAGGON*.

play the music and open the cage! See under MUM, MUM, THEY ARE LAUGHING AT ME.

please adjust your dress before leaving. *Stock Phrase.* From notices in public lavatories (nineteenth century onwards, presumably, because of the particular use in railway loos?). 'Adjust' is a perfectly normal word for 'arranging' one's clothes (and has been since the early eighteenth century), but here it is euphemistic. Churchill denied having said of a long-winded memorandum from Sir Anthony Eden that, 'as far as I can see, you have used every cliché except "God is love" and "Please adjust your dress before leaving".' A graffito (reported 1980): 'Please adjust your dress before leaving – as a refusal often offends'.

pleased. See AS ~ AS PUNCH.

please do not ask for credit as a refusal often offends. *Stock Phrase.* In shops since 1920s/30s? A more recent variant, spotted by Bernard Levin in the 1980s, and deplored, was taken from a photocopying shop in London W1: 'We do *NOT* give facilities for change, telephone calls, or anything not pertaining to this business.' From the same decade – a 'Bureau de Change' at Waverley Station, Edinburgh, had a notice in the window, 'We do not give change'.

pleasure. See DOUBLE YOUR ~ . . .

plonker. See YER ~!

plume de ma tante, la. *Catch Phrase.* As 'the cat sat on the mat' is to learning the English language, so *'je n'ai pas la plume de ma tante'* is to learning French. I don't know why this should be (unless there is some frightful *double entendre* itching to get out), but I suspect it must have occurred in some widely used French grammar in British schools – from some time just prior to the First World War, I should think. A revue with this title played at the Garrick Theatre in 1955.

pocket. See I'VE GOT HIS PECKER IN MY ~.

P.O.E.T.S.' Day. *Colloquialism.* Acronym for 'Piss/Push Off Early Tomorrow's Saturday' – indicating a frequent inclination of workers on Friday afternoons. Perhaps quite recent – say 1960s.
Compare T.G.I.F.

poet though I didn't know it, I am a. *Catch Phrase.* Said by a person accidentally making a rhyme. An old one this: Swift's *Polite Conversation* has this exchange:
Neverout: Well, miss . . .
Miss Notable: Ay, ay; many a one says well, that thinks ill.
Neverout: Well, miss; I'll think of this.
Miss Notable: That's rhyme, if you take it in time.
Neverout: What! I see you are a poet.
Miss Notable: Yes, if I had but the wit to show it.

point. See AT THIS MOMENT IN TIME; BROWNIE ~S; THOUSAND ~S OF LIGHT.

police. See HELPING THE ~ WITH THEIR INQUIRIES.

policeman. See RAIN IS THE BEST ~ . . .

policemen. See YOU KNOW YOU'RE GETTING OLDER . . . ; YOUR ~ ARE WONDERFUL.

pop. See SNAP! CRACKLE! ~!

pop goes the weasel. *Saying > Catch Phrase.* At some time in the nineteenth century, possibly in 1853, a Mr W.R. Mandale may have written the celebrated words:
Up and down the City Road,
In and out of the Eagle,
That's the way the money goes –
Pop goes the weasel!
Mandale may have put these words to a tune or dance which already existed, but what did he mean by them? His song 'Pop goes the weasel' is still the subject of debate. What is plain is that 'the Eagle' refers to the Eagle Tavern, then a theatre and pub in the City Road, London (the present tavern was built at the turn of the century).
Those who went 'in and out', spent plenty of money and were forced to 'pop', or pawn, something. But what was the 'weasel' they pawned? That is what is most in question. The word has been said to mean a kind of tool used by a carpenter or a hatter, also for a tailor's flat iron, but why anyone should wish to pawn a tool of the trade is a puzzle. Perhaps a 'weasel' was no more than just an item of value.
Vernon Noble suggested to Partridge/ *Catch Phrases* that a weasel was a flat iron in a domestic situation and therefore was an item that could easily be spared. No one seems to have suggested that the weasel might be from rhyming slang 'weasel and stoat' = coat. What could be more straightforward than having to pawn your coat if you ran out of money? As for 'pop goes the weasel' meaning an orgasm, I feel this is probably a later play on an established phrase.
According to Morris, there is an American version of the song which goes:
Every night when I come home,
The Monkey's on the table.
I take a stick and knock him off
And pop goes the weasel!

pop one's clogs, to. *Idiom.* To die. Judging from its absence from Partridge/*Slang* and *OED Supp.*, I think this must be a fairly recent blending of 'to pop off' and 'to die with one's boots on/off'.

pop-up toaster. See FEW VOUCHERS SHORT OF A ~.

porch, put it on the. See under LET'S —— AND SEE IF ——.

pours. See IT NEVER RAINS, BUT IT ~.

powder one's nose, to. *Idiom.* Euphemism for a woman's going to the lavatory. *OED Supp.* doesn't find it before 1921 when Somerset Maugham daringly put it in his play *The Circle*. Cole Porter put it in *The New Yorkers, 1930* – though there is some doubt whether it was actually used in the show: 'The girls today/ Have but one thing to say, / "Where can one powder one's nose?" '

power. See BLACK ~.

pram. See GET OUT OF ONE'S ~.

prepared. See BE ~.

prepare to meet thy God. *Slogan.* Unlike the END IS NIGH, this favourite of placard-bearing religious fanatics does actually come from the Bible: Amos 4:12.

presidency. See HEARTBEAT AWAY FROM THE ~.

pretty. See HERE'S A ~ KETTLE OF FISH!

price. See EVERY MAN HAS HIS ~.

princess. See COULD MAKE ANY ORDINARY GIRL . . . ; LIKE A FAIRY-TALE ~.

print. See ALL THE NEWS THAT'S FIT TO ~.

privacy. See YOURS TO ENJOY IN THE ~ . . .

private life/lives of ——, the. *Format Phrase.* Although Alexander Korda had directed a film called *The Private Life of Helen of Troy* (1927), the original of all the 'Private Life of . . .' books and films was surely his immensely successful *The Private Life of Henry VIII* (1933). The following year, Julian Huxley with R.M. Lockley produced a natural history film called *The Private Life of Gannets* (which won an Oscar).

Since then, in the cinema, we have had private lives of Don Juan (1934), Elizabeth and Essex (1939), Sherlock Holmes (1970), and so on. And, on TV, there have been numerous natural history films since the mid-1960s, eg the BBC's *The Private Life of the Kingfisher*.

There is, of course, a nudging note to the use of the phrase – as though we are not just being promised a glimpse of domestic happenings, but probably sex life, too.

probably the best lager in the world. *Slogan.* For Carlsberg, from 1973. Even if it had not been intoned by Orson Welles in the TV ads, the 'probably' inserted into this hyperbole would still have fascinated. However, it is by no means the first product to be advertised with such caution. Zephyr, imported by A. Gale & Co. Ltd of Glasgow, was called 'Possibly the finest tobacco in the world' in ads current in 1961.

promised. See I NEVER ~ YOU A ROSE GARDEN.

proper Charlie, a. *Idiom.* The phrase a **right Charlie** probably grew out of rhyming slang 'Charlie Hunt', used to describe a fool or simpleton. I think it probably arose during the Second World War – it may have been a simultaneous British and American coinage, too. 'Proper Charlie' presumably developed from the same source. It was commandeered by the comedian Charlie Chester (*b* 1914) on radio immediately after the war and later used by him as the title of a radio show.

From the *Guardian* (1 December 1988) concerning a judge, Sir Harold Cassel QC: 'He once gave a robber an hour's bail, warning: "If you do not turn up you will make me look a proper Charlie." The man never returned.'

(Charlie Chester was billed as '**cheerful Charlie** Chester'. The alliteration is all important and I think the phrase has found use elsewhere.)

Pru. See ASK THE MAN FROM THE ~.

public enemy No. 1. *Idiom.* John Dillinger (1903–34) was the first officially designated 'Public Enemy No. 1'. He robbed banks and killed people in Illinois, Indiana and Ohio during 1933–4 to such an extent that the Attorney General, Homer Cummings, called him this. In fact, he was the only person ever so-named. The FBI's 'Ten Most Wanted Men' list did not give a ranking. Dillinger's exploits and his escape from captivity aroused great public interest. He was eventually shot dead by FBI agents outside a cinema in Chicago.

The coining of the term 'Public Enemy' in this context has been attributed to Frank Loesch, president of the Chicago Crime Commission, who had to try to deal with Al Capone's hold over the city in 1923. The idea was to try and dispel the romantic aura such gangsters had been invested with by the popular press. James Cagney starred in a gangster film called *The Public Enemy* in 1931.

The phrase soon passed into general usage. In June 1934, P.G. Wodehouse, referring in a letter to difficulties with US income-tax officials, said: 'I got an offer from Paramount to go to Hollywood at $1,500 a week and had to refuse as I am Public Enemy No. 1 in America, and can't go there.'

The words have since been applied to any form of supposed undesirable, while Raymond Postgate, founder of the *Good Food Guide*, was dubbed 'Public Stomach No. 1', and Beverley Nichols, the author and journalist, called himself 'Public Anemone No. 1'.

publicity. See ALL ~ IS GOOD ~.

public speaking. See UNACCUSTOMED AS I AM . . .

pun. See IF YOU'LL EXCUSE THE ~!

Punch. See AS PLEASED AS ~.

punch up the bracket. See under HANCOCK'S HALF-HOUR.

pure. See 99 44/100 PER CENT ~.

pussycat. See WHAT'S NEW, ~?

put a penny on the drum. *Stock Phrase.* Said by Clay Keyes (who pretended to be an American) in a BBC radio show called *The Old Town Hall* in 1941. Members of the studio orchestra had to guess musical riddles sent in by listeners, failing which they paid a forfeit to charity, eg: 'Where did the salt and vinegar go?' Musical answer: 'All over the pla(i)ce'.

put a smile on your face. See under COME ALIVE . . .

put a sock in it! *Catch Phrase.* 'Shut up!' 'Shut your mouth!' addressed to a noisy person. Ewart confidently asserts that this dates from the days of the wind-up, 'acoustic' gramophones where the sound emerged from a horn. With no electronic controls to raise or lower the volume, the only way to regulate the sound was to put in or take out an article of clothing, which deadened it. (Presumably, mutes as stuck in the horns of brass instruments were not supplied.)

The *OED Supp.* has a citation from 1919 – an explanation of the term from the *Athenaeum* journal – which suggests the phrase was not widely known even then.

I am not totally convinced by the gramophone explanation. Partridge/*Slang* compares the earlier expression '(to) put a bung in it' – as in a bath or leak. So I reserve judgement. Why shouldn't a sock inserted in the human mouth be the origin? After all, a sock in the jaw would be the next best thing.

put a tiger in your tank. *Slogan.* The Esso Tiger had been around in the US for a long time before 1964 when a cartoon version was introduced for the first time (a year later in the UK) to promote Esso petroleum. It became a national craze, with countless tiger tails adorning the petrol caps of the nation's cars. Sub-

sequently, with the slogan 'Put a Tiger in Your Tank', the idea spread even further afield. *'Mettez un tigre dans votre moteur'* appeared in France; in Germany, *'Pack den Tiger in den Tank'*.

In the US, especially, the slogan gave rise to numerous tiger derivatives: 'If you feel like a tiger is in your throat, reach for Guardets Lozenges . . .' A hamburger stand advertised, 'Put a tiger in your tummy'. Tiger Beer in the Japanese *Times* sloganned, 'Put a tiger in your tankard'. Standard Rochester Beer countered with, 'Put a tankard in your tiger'. The UK campaign ran for two years before it flagged.

Perhaps the slogan owed something to the Muddy Waters song '(I Want to Put a) Tiger in Your Tank' (by W. Dixon) which he was performing by 1960 and which gave double meanings to a number of motoring phrases (not least in the title).

put a woman on top for a change. *Slogan.* Promoting the idea of Margaret Thatcher as Prime Minister prior to the Conservative election win in 1979. Rob Hayward MP told me in 1984 that the idea first came up when he was National Vice-Chairman of the Young Conservatives. Originally, 'Have a Woman on Top' (or 'Fuck Me, I'm a Tory'), it was devised by Young Conservatives in 1976 and distributed as a sticker at the Tory Party Conference. It was taken up as an official slogan by the party.

put one's best foot forward, to. *Idiom.* Ie to walk as fast as possible, make a good impression. This derives from the earlier form 'to put one's best foot/leg foremost'. In Shakespeare, *King John* (IV.ii.170), we find: 'Nay, but make haste; the better foot before.'

The *right foot* has, from ancient times, been regarded as the best foot – the right side being associated with reason, the left with emotion. To put your right foot forward was thus to guard against ill-luck.

quality. See NEVER MIND THE ~ . . .

Quatermass. See IT LOOKS LIKE SOMETHING OUT OF ~.

¿qué? Catch Phrase. In the BBC TV comedy series *Fawlty Towers*, Manuel the Spanish waiter (Andrew Sachs) seemed to do very little else than ask 'What?' in Spanish. But then, as Basil Fawlty (John Cleese) would explain, 'You'll have to excuse him – he comes from Barcelona.' (The show was first aired 1975–9).

queen. See MAKES YOU FEEL LIKE A ~.

Queen Anne's dead. *Catch Phrase*. This is a phrase used to put down someone who has just told you some very old news or what you knew already. Mencken glosses it slightly differently: 'Reply to an inquiry for news, signifying that there is none not stale.' He also supplies the al-ternative 'Queen Elizabeth is dead' (which I have never heard used) and says that both forms appear to date from *c* 1720. In George Colman the Younger's play *The Heir-at-Law* (1797), there occurs the line, 'Tell 'em Queen Anne's dead.'

She actually died in 1714. Partridge/*Slang* dates 'Queen Anne is dead' to 1722, in a ballad cited by Apperson, 'He's as dead as Queen Anne the day after she dy'd' (which doesn't seem to convey the modern meaning of the expression); 'Queen Elizabeth is dead' to 1738 in Swift's *Polite Conversation* – 'What news, Mr Neverout?' *Neverout*: 'Why, Madam, Queen Elizabeth's dead'; and puts 'My Lord Baldwin is dead' to *c* 1670–1710.

An American equivalent is, 'Bryan has carried Texas' – which I take to refer to William Jennings Bryan (1860–1925) who stood thrice for the US presidency and was thrice unsuccessful.

Queen Elizabeth slept here. *Slogan.* A line that has been used to promote visits to English stately homes – and some inns – probably since such tourism began in the eighteenth century. Elizabeth I was an inveterate traveller and guest. By 1888, Jerome K. Jerome was writing in *Three Men in a Boat*: 'She was nuts on public houses, was England's Virgin Queen. There's scarcely a pub of any attractions within ten miles of London that she does not seem to have looked in at, stopped at, or slept at, some time or other.'

In the US, the equivalent slogan is 'George Washington slept here' (as in the title of Kauffman and Hart's play, 1940, filmed 1942, which, when adapted by Talbot Rothwell for the Strand Theatre, London, later in the 1940s, was called *Queen Elizabeth Slept Here*).

queen for a day. *Catch Phrase.* Used for a woman who is given a special treat. It derives from an American radio programme of *c* 1940. According to an informant, 'being a queen for a day didn't mean they gave you a country; you only got your wish, that's what. No one complained.'

I note that when Radio Luxembourg adopted the format (from 1955, introduced by Richard Attenborough, sponsored by Phensic!) they changed the title to *Princess for a Day*. Was this because the wishes fulfilled were more modest, the participants younger, or had the word 'queen' become too tainted by that time?

queer as a clockwork orange, to be as. *Idiom.* Meaning 'homosexual'. Since the mid-1950s, says Paul Beale. Although Anthony Burgess entitled his novel (and thus the film) *A Clockwork Orange* (1962, 1971) I don't recall there being an overt homosexual theme to the story.

question. See SIXTY-FOUR DOLLAR ~.

Question of ——, A. *Format Phrase >* *Cliché.* Of broadcast programme titles. As in *A Question of Sport/ Confidence/ Stars/ Politics/ Degree* etc. Also in the form *The Body/ Week In Question*.

quick. See BEFORE ONE CAN SAY 'JACK ROBINSON'; SLOW, SLOW, ~, ~, SLOW.

quick thinking, Batman! See under BATMAN.

R

rabbit, rabbit . . . *Catch Phrase*. The singers Chas and Dave introduced this line to one of their commercials for Courage Best Bitter, *c* 1983. It emulates talkative women who interrupt the pleasures of the drinking process. 'To rabbit', meaning 'to talk', comes from rhyming slang ('rabbit and pork').

rags-to-riches. *Cliché.* Usually in publishers' blurbs. A certain type of novel is inevitably dubbed a 'rags-to-riches saga'. After the story of Cinderella, of course.

rain in Spain, the. See under HOW NOW, BROWN COW?

rain is the best policeman of all. *Saying.* Heard from a senior police officer after the Notting Hill Carnival had been rained off on the Late Summer Bank Holiday in August 1986. Meaning that crime falls when the rain does (as also in cold weather).

rains. See IT NEVER ~ BUT IT POURS.

ranch. See MEANWHILE BACK AT THE ~ . . .

rat. See LIKE ~S DESERTING A SINKING SHIP; YOU DIRTY ~!

Ray's a Laugh. Comedian Ted Ray (1909–77) served his apprenticeship around the music-halls before becoming one of Britain's great radio comedians. His programme Ray's a Laugh ran from 1949 to 1960. He recalled one of the most famous of the show's *Catch Phrases* in his book *Raising the Laughs* (1952). It occurred in sketches between 'Mrs Hoskin' (played by Bob Pearson) and 'Ivy' (Ted Ray): 'George Inns [the producer] agreed that the climax of their original conversation should be the mention of a mystical "Dr Hardcastle" whom Ivy secretly adored . . . From the moment Bob, in his new role, had spoken the words, "I sent for young Dr Hardcastle", and we heard Ivy's excited little intake of breath, followed by, **"He's loo-vely, Mrs Hoskin . . . he's loo-oo-vely!"** a new phrase had come into being.'

Mrs Hoskin would also say, famously, **Ee, it was agony, Ivy!** – however, it has been suggested that this had earlier origins in music-hall.

I recall people in the mid-1950s saying the name **Jen-nif-er** in a special way. This appears to have grown out of an exchange between Ted Ray and a little girl (again played by Bob Pearson). Ray would ask what her name was and she would lisp the reply.

The only other of the show's phrases I would mention is **if you've never been to Manchester, you've never lived!** Or perhaps it was, 'If you haven't been . . . you haven't lived'? Either way, it was said by Tommy Trafford (Graham Stark). Probably, one has here another *Format Phrase* – 'If/Until you've . . . you haven't lived'. From the *Observer* (15 January 1989) on the George Formby Appreciation Society: 'Until you have seen this herd of wallies, all long past their sell-by dates and playing their ukuleles in time to a film of their diminutive hero, you haven't lived.' Compare, too, the Spanish proverb that Mencken records: 'He who has not seen Seville has seen nothing.'

reach for the sky/stars! (sometimes just **reach for it!**) *Idiom*. This is what a character in a Western movie says to someone when he wants him to 'put his hands up'. However, when Paul Brickhill entitled

his biography of Douglas Bader, the legless flying ace, *Reach for the Sky* (1954) he was no doubt alluding to the RAF motto *'per ardua ad astra'* ('through striving to the stars').

'Reach for the *Star*' was a line used in promoting the newspaper (current February 1989).

read. See I'M SORRY I'LL ~ THAT AGAIN.

read any good books lately? See under *MUCH BINDING IN THE MARSH*.

read my lips. *Catch Phrase*. Although popularized by George Bush in his speech accepting the Republican nomination on 19 August 1988, the phrase was not new. Bush wanted to emphasize his pledge not to raise taxes, whatever pressure Congress applied, so what he said was, 'I'll say no, and they'll push, and I'll say no, and they'll push again, and I'll say to them, "Read my lips, no new taxes".' Although this became the only part of the speech to make any impact (apart from THOUSAND POINTS OF LIGHT), the phrase was excluded from the lengthy texts given by *The Times*, the *Guardian* and the *Independent*! According to William Safire in an article in the *New York Times* (September 1988), the phrase is rooted in 1970s rock music (despite there being a song with the title copyrighted by Joe Greene in 1957). The British actor/singer Tim Curry used the phrase as the title of an album of songs in 1978. Curry said he took it from an Italian-American recording engineer who used it to mean, 'Listen and listen very hard, because I want you to hear what I've got to say.'

Several lyricists in the 1980s used the phrase for song titles. A football coach with the Chicago Bears became nick-named Mike (Read My Lips) Ditka. There has been a thoroughbred race horse so named. Safire also cites a number of American politicians, also in the 1980s.

ready for Freddie. See under ARE YOU READY, EDDIE?

real. See WILL THE ~ . . . ?

realization. See DESPERATION . . .

real thing, it's the. *Slogan.* There have been so many rivals to Coca-Cola that there has been a continuing necessity to maintain that 'Coke' is the 'real' one. This idea appeared in 1942 in the form, 'The only thing like Coca-Cola is Coca-Cola itself.' 'It's the real thing' followed in 1970, and has proved one of the most enduring of the Coca-Cola slogans.

Tom Stoppard's play *The Real Thing* (1982) was more about love (as in 'It's the real thing this time'), but could hardly fail to remind one of the slogan. *OED* has an example of this use – ie true love as distinct from infatuation – in 1857.

See also COME ALIVE – YOU'RE IN THE PEPSI GENERATION.

rears. See SEX ~ ITS UGLY HEAD.

recipe. See WHAT'S THE ~ TODAY, JIM? under MORNING ALL!

red. See BETTER ~ THAN DEAD; LIKE A ~ RAG TO A BULL.

refreshes. See HEINEKEN ~ THE PARTS . . .

refusal. See PLEASE DO NOT ASK FOR CREDIT . . .

refuse. See I'M GOING TO MAKE HIM AN OFFER . . .

regret. See DEEPLY ~ ANY . . .

Reilly. See LIFE OF ~.

related. See I WONDER IF THEY ARE . . . ?

Renaissance man. *Idiom > Cliché.* Used to describe anyone who is accomplished in more than one field, but (these days) rather less than a polymath. Originally used to describe anyone who displayed the educated, civilized, practical virtues of the idealized Renaissance man. From *Time* (8 August 1977): 'At 50, Hood is the Renaissance man of sailing; he designed, cut the sails and outfitted *Independence*, the first man in history to control every aspect of a 12-tonner from drawing-board to helm.' From a letter in *Radio Times* (11 February 1989): 'I once told him [actor David Buck] that he was "the Renaissance man of radio". He thought that uproarious.'

I once heard a Radio 2 trailer for 'Renaissance man, Humphrey Lyttelton'. While admiring his ability to play the trumpet and to write and talk wittily (though not simultaneously), I couldn't help but feel this was pushing it a bit.

repetition. See WITHOUT HESITATION . . .

reporter. See OUR ~ MADE AN EXCUSE . . .

rest is history, the. *Cliché.* An ending to a biographical anecdote. Russell Grant, *TV Times* (15 October 1983): 'There across all the papers was the photograph of me presenting the Queen Mother with her chart, under the caption "Astrologer

Royal". Well, the rest, as they say, is history.'

Alan Bennett played delightfully on the phrase in *Oxford Today*, Michaelmas 1988, having described his transition from Oxford history don to Broadway revue artist: 'The rest, one might say pompously, is history. Except that in my case the opposite was true. What it had been was history. What it was to be was not history at all.'

rest of your life, the. See TODAY IS THE FIRST DAY . . .

restored. See THIS HAS ~ MY FAITH . . .

results. See I'LL GIVE YOU THE ~ . . .

resumed. See NORMAL SERVICE WILL BE ~ . . . under DO NOT ADJUST YOUR SET.

retire immediately. See LIGHT THE BLUE TOUCHPAPER . . . under *BAND WAGGON*.

return with us now to those thrilling days . . . See under HI-YO, SILVER!

return you to the studio. See under *BEYOND OUR KEN*.

reverse order. See I'LL GIVE YOU THE RESULTS IN . . .

—— **revisited.** *Format Phrase > Cliché*. In January 1989, Channel 4 showed a programme marking the fiftieth anniversary of the publication of a John Steinbeck novel, with the title 'The Grapes of Wrath' Revisited. In 1989, the South Bank Centre ran a commemoration of the 200th anniversary of the French Rev-olution under the blanket title 'Revolution Revisited'.

All such uses owe something to the title of Evelyn Waugh's novel *Brideshead Revisited* (1945), and especially to the TV adaptation in 1981, though the format was well-established before Waugh got hold of it. William Wordsworth wrote poems entitled 'Yarrow Visited', 'Yarrow Unvisited' and 'Yarrow Revisited' (the latter in 1831).

rewrite. See YOU DON'T ~ A HIT.

rhubarb, rhubarb! *Stock Phrase*. Actors mumble this in crowd scenes to give the impression of speech, as a background noise, without actually producing coherent sentences. I suppose some unwise actors might think they could actually get away with saying 'rhubarb', but the idea is to repeat a word, which uttered by various voices, adds together to sound like the noise a crowd makes. I am not sure that this custom dates from much before this century but it is a well-known concept now, as demonstrated by the use of the verb 'to rhubarb', meaning to talk nonsense.

Another phrase said to have been repeated by actors in this situation is 'My fiddle, my fiddle, my fiddle' and, I am assured, there is a phrase used by Russian actors meaning, literally, 'I speak and I don't speak'.

One wonders whether the adoption of the word 'rhubarb' in the English version has anything to do with its slang use to denote the male (and occasionally female) genitals. Or could there have been some rhyming slang phrase, ie rhubarb (tart) = fart (akin to raspberry tart = fart)? The rhyming slang books I have consulted do not support me in this, however.

rich. See IT'S ALL PART OF LIFE'S ~ PAGEANT.

rich and famous. *Cliché*. Designated a cliché on the basis that the words are always and inevitably put together. The first example I have noted was in the film *Breakfast at Tiffany's* (1961). The usage has become set in concrete since a film with the title *Rich and Famous* (1981). An American TV series *Lifestyles of the Rich and Famous* was established by 1986. From the *Independent* (4 April 1989): 'The [Press] Council's assistant director, said yesterday that lawyers acting for the rich and famous were becoming aware of the fast track system for getting speedy corrections of untruths.'

Richard. See OPEN THE DOOR, ~! under *ITMA*.

riches. See RAGS-TO-~.

ride off into the sunset. See DRIVE OFF INTO THE SUNSET.

right. See AM I ~ OR . . . ?; BANG TO ~S; CUSTOMER IS ALWAYS ~; IN YOUR HEART YOU KNOW . . . ; I THINK THAT SHOWS . . . ; IT'S WHAT YOUR ~ ARM'S FOR; ONE INSTINCTIVELY KNOWS . . . ; ~ ONE 'ERE under *EDUCATING ARCHIE*; SOMEWHERE TO THE ~ OF GENGHIS KHAN.

right Charlie. See PROPER CHARLIE.

right monkey! *Catch Phrase*. Al Read (1909–87), the northern comedian, was big on radio in the 1950s and then disappeared almost completely. His speciality was monologues – or, rather, dialogues –

with him playing all the parts. He used a number of standard Lancashire expressions and made them for a while his own – 'give over!', 'you'll be lucky . . . I say, you'll be lucky', and so on.

Above all, Read was known for two catch phrases – 'right monkey!' and **cheeky monkey!** For example: 'She said, "Did he say anything about the check suit?" and I thought, "Right monkey!"' '

From a theatre poster once seen in Blackpool: 'HENRY HALL PRESENTS AL READ IN *RIGHT MONKEY*.'

right stuff, the. *Idiom*. Tom Wolfe helped re-popularize the phrase 'the right stuff' when he chose to use it as the title of a book (1979, filmed 1983). He employed it to describe the qualities needed by test pilots and would-be astronauts in the early years of the US space programme.

But the 'right sort of stuff' had been applied much earlier to qualities of manly virtue, of good officer material and even of good cannon fodder. Partridge/*Slang* has an example from the 1880s. In this sense, the phrase was used by Ian Hay as the title of a novel – 'some episodes in the career of a North Briton' – in 1908.

It is now a handy journalistic device. An *Independent* headline over a story about the ballet *Ondine* (13 May 1988) was, 'The Sprite Stuff'; the same month, *The Magazine* had 'The Right Stuff' as the title of an article on furnishing fabrics; in 1989, there was an ITV book programme called *The Write Stuff*.

It has also been used as an expression for alcohol.

Riley. See LIFE OF ~.

ring. See DON'T CALL US . . .

ring of steel, a. *Idiom > Cliché*. Reporter on BBC TV *Nine O'Clock News* (17 December 1981): 'The place [Warsaw] is just a ring of steel.' From a report on the Falklands War in *The Times* (30 April 1982): 'RING OF STEEL AROUND ISLANDS'. From the *Sunday Express* (8 October 1983): 'SYRIAN STEEL RINGS ARAFAT'.

Somewhat earlier, Adolf Hitler had said in a speech on the Italian armistice in 1943: 'Tactical necessity may compel us once and again to give up something on some front in this gigantic fateful struggle, but it will never break the ring of steel that protects the Reich.' (Translation from *Hitler's Words*, Gordon W. Prange, 1944.)

road. See KEEP DEATH OFF THE ~.

roar. See STOP THE MIGHTY ~ under *IN TOWN TONIGHT*.

robbed. See WE WUZ ~.

Robinson, Jack. See BEFORE ONE CAN SAY ~.

rocking-horse manure. See under AS BUSY AS . . .

rock'n'roll. See IT'S ONLY ~; SEX'N'DRUGS'N'~.

Rodney, hello. See under *BEYOND OUR KEN*.

rogue's gallery, a/ the. *Idiom*. A group of disreputable people as shown in a photograph or picture (eg wanted criminals) but also used humorously of quite inoffensive people so portrayed. The criminal use was prevalent in the US in the mid- to late nineteenth century. The allusive twentieth-century UK use derives, in part, I think, from a Latin school textbook *The Rogue's Gallery* (current by the 1950s, at least) which included classical descriptions of notable Roman villains.

From an *Independent* report of a speech in the House of Lords by Lord Stevens of Ludgate (on 26 April 1989): 'For most people, the *Sun* and the *News of the World* were the starring exhibits in the Rogues Gallery of the Press, but each paper appeared to thrive on its notoriety, he said.'

roll over in one's grave. See TURN OVER. . . .

Rolls-Royce, loudest noise in a. See under AT 60 MILES AN HOUR . . .

Ron, oh. See under *TAKE IT FROM HERE*.

rose garden. See I NEVER PROMISED YOU A ~.

round hole. See SQUARE PEG IN A ~.

Round the Horne. More or less the same team as in *BEYOND OUR KEN* manifested itself from 1965–9 in *Round the Horne* – this time with somewhat broader and zanier scripts by Marty Feldman and Barry Took. Took told me: 'Marty and I went all out to avoid catch phrases but the cast kept pencilling them in. Eventually we gave up the unequal struggle.'

The new approach was typified by the introduction of two stock figures, the gay ex-chorus boys, Julian and Sandy. **Oh, hello, I'm Julian and this is my friend, Sandy** was how Hugh Paddick would refer to Kenneth Williams, opening the routines. From their first appearances, they larded their speech with bits of camp *parlare* (talk) from the *omipalomi* (homosexual) subculture of actors and dancers. Fantabulosa! One of their incarnations was as film producers:

Sandy: Mr Horne, we are in the forefront of your *Nouvelle Vague*. **That's your actual French**.

Julian: It means we are of the New Wave.

Sandy: And very nice it looks on you, too.

(Peter Cook claims to have launched **your actual** as a turn of phrase, however.) **Ooh, bold! Very bold!** was their standard exclamation.

Betty Marsden played Lady Beatrice Counterblast (née Clissold) and would say **many, many times!** (originally in answer to a query as to how many times she had been married). Spasm, her butler (played by Kenneth Williams), would wail **we be doomed, we all be doomed!** (a line shared with the John Laurie character in TV's *Dad's Army*, who would exclaim, 'Doomed I am, doomed!').

Rowan and Martin's Laugh-In. See LAUGH-IN.

rubbish! See under MORECAMBE AND WISE SHOW.

—— **rules OK.** *Catch Phrase > Cliché.* This curious affirmative is said to have begun in gang-speak of the late 1960s in Scotland and Northern Ireland, though some would say it dates back to the 1930s. Either a gang or a football team or the Provisional IRA would be said to 'rule OK'. Later this was turned into a joke with numerous variations – 'Queen Elizabeth rules UK', 'Rodgers and Hammerstein rule OK, lahoma', and so on.

It soon became an all but unstoppable cliché. In 1981, Virginian rubbed tobacco was advertised beneath the slogan 'Virginian Rolls OK' and a French cigarette beneath *'Gauloises à rouler, OK'*. In 1982, I was asked by BBC Radio to present a series on local government. 'Yes,' I said, 'I will – as long as you don't call it "Town Hall Rules OK".' Two weeks later, they rang back to say, 'We've chosen that title you suggested.' And they had. I only spoke it through gritted teeth.

'GOLF RULES OK?' appeared as an *Observer* headline (13 November 1983). With luck, the phrase is now on the way out.

run. See TAKE THE MONEY AND ~; THIS ONE WILL ~ AND ~; WHAT A WAY TO ~ . . . ; YOU CAN ~ BUT YOU CAN'T HIDE.

running. See HIT THE GROUND ~.

safe. See JUST WHEN YOU THOUGHT . . .

sail off into the sunset. See DRIVE OFF INTO THE SUNSET.

sailor. See HELLO, ~!; ENOUGH BLUE TO . . .

saloon must go, the. See —— MUST GO!

Sam. See PLAY IT AGAIN, ~.

same. See THEY ALL LOOK THE ~ . . . ; WILL NEVER BE THE ~ AGAIN.

sand. See SUN, ~ AND SEA.

sand-box, cat in a. See under AS BUSY AS . . .

sandboy. See HAPPY AS A ~.

sandwiches. See BEER AND ~ AT NO. 10.

Sandy. See OH, HELLO, I'M JULIAN . . . under *ROUND THE HORNE*.

sapristi! See under *GOON SHOW*.

satirical. See HO-HO, VERY ~.

savage story of lust and ambition, a. *Cliché.* Of the type used to promote films and books. This was actually used on posters for the film *Room at the Top* (1958).

say. See AND SO WE ~ FAREWELL; I MEANTER ~; I ~, I ~, I ~!; I ~ WHAT A SMASHER; I ~ YOU FELLOWS!; ~ NO MORE under *MONTY PYTHON'S FLYING CIRCUS*.

say goodnight, Dick/Gracie. See under *LAUGH-IN*.

say it with flowers. *Slogan > Catch Phrase.* Henry Penn of Boston, Massachusetts, was chairman of the National Publicity Committee of the Society of American Florists in 1917. He was discussing the need for a slogan with Major Patrick O'Keefe, head of an advertising agency. O'Keefe suggested, 'Flowers are words that even a babe can understand' – a line he had found in a poetry book. Penn considered that too long. O'Keefe, agreeing, rejoined, 'Why, you can say it with flowers in so many words'. Mr Penn's hand went bang! on the table. They had found their slogan.

Later came several songs with the title.

scale. See ON A ~ OF ONE TO TEN.

scarce. See under AS BUSY AS . . .

scholar. See GENTLEMAN AND A ~.

schoolboy. See AS EVERY ~ KNOWS.

schoolgirl. See KEEP THAT ~ COMPLEXION.

school of hard knocks, the. *Idiom.* Ie experience, hardship, considered as an educative force. The *OED Supp.* calls this 'US Slang' and finds it in 1912. *The Complete Naff Guide* (1983) has as a 'naff boast': 'But then, of course, I left university without a degree. I like to think I have a First from the School of Hard Knocks.'

Receiving an honorary doctorate in the humanities from the University of Nevada in May 1976, Frank Sinatra said, 'I am a graduate of the school of hard knocks.' At least, he didn't say he had attended **the university of life**. (Partridge/*Slang* prefers 'the university of hard knocks' and dates it *c* 1910.) Lord Baden-Powell

wrote a book called *Lessons from the 'Varsity' of Life* (1933).

scorcher. See PHEW, WHAT A ~!

scot-free. See GET AWAY WITH SOMETHING ~.

Scott. See GREAT ~!

Scottish play. See under BREAK A LEG.

Scotty. See BEAM ME UP, ~.

screaming. See DRAGGED KICKING AND ~ . . .

sea. See SUN, SAND AND ~.

seasons. See MAN FOR ALL ~.

seats. See YOU WANT THE BEST ~ . . .

see. See AND WHEN DID YOU LAST ~ YOUR FATHER?; BELIEVE ONLY HALF OF WHAT YOU ~; COME UP AND ~ ME SOMETIME; JOIN THE ARMY AND ~ THE WORLD; MY EYES ARE DIM . . . ; NICE TO ~ YOU . . .

seen. See YOU AIN'T ~ NOTHIN' YET!

see you later, alligator. *Catch Phrase.* Note how a phrase develops: according to Flexner, the simple 'See you later', as a form of farewell, entered American speech in the 1870s. By the 1930s, it had some 'jive use' as 'See you later, alligator'. To this was added the response, 'In a while, crocodile'.

This exchange became known to a wider public through the song 'See You Later, Alligator', sung by Bill Haley and his Comets in the film *Rock Around the Clock* (1956), which recorded the origins of rock'n'roll. Princess Margaret and her set became keen users. There was even a sudden vogue for keeping pet alligators.

The next stage was for the front and back of the phrase to be dropped off, leaving the simple 'Lay-tuh' as a way to say goodbye.

sell. See PILE IT HIGH . . .

send in/on the clowns. *Stock Phrase.* The tradition that the **show must go on** grew out of circus. Whatever mishap occurred, the band was told to go on playing and the cry went up 'send in/on the clowns' – for the simple reason that panic had to be avoided, the audience's attention had to be diverted, and the livelihood of everybody in the circus depended on not having to give the audience its money back. So, like 'send in the clowns', 'the show must go on' seems primarily a circus phrase, though no one seems able to turn up a written reference much before 1930.

In 1950, 'the show must go on' is spoken in the film *All About Eve* and, in the same decade, Noël Coward wrote a song which posed the question '*Why* Must the Show Go On?'

Stephen Sondheim chose the 'Send in . . .' form as the title of a song in *A Little Night Music* 1974. Perhaps 'send in' was right for the circus, 'send on' for the stage?

sends. See IT ~ ME.

sense. See YOU *KNOW* IT MAKES ~.

serious. See JUST HOW S . . . ?; YOU CANNOT BE ~!

seriously, though, he's doing a grand job. *Catch Phrase.* After a satirical attack on a person in BBC TV's *That Was The Week That Was* (1962–3), David Frost would proffer this pretend conciliation. I can remember it being taken up by clergymen and others but Ned Sherrin, the show's producer, claims that the phrase was used no more than half a dozen times in all.

serious money. *Colloquialism.* Meaning 'money in excessive amounts'. Long-man/*Register* correctly surmises that this 'facetious usage seems to have started life among the fast-burning earners of the post-BIG BANG, pre-Bust city of London, who when speaking of salaries in the six-figure bracket would concede that this was "serious money"'. Long-man/*Register* also notes that the usage might spread to other areas: 'Annie's – a bar favoured by serious drinkers' (*Sunday Times*, 28 August 1988).

The phrase was helped to stick by its use as the title of Caryl Churchill's satirical play about the City (1987).

serve that lady with a crusty loaf! See under BAND WAGGON.

service. See NORMAL ~ WILL BE RESUMED . . . under DO NOT ADJUST YOUR SET.

sesame. See OPEN, ~!

set. See DO NOT ADJUST YOUR ~; FINE ~S THESE FERGUSONS.

set alarm bells ringing, to. *Cliché.* Of journalism. Meaning 'to alert'. 'The trio moved off in a yellow Mini and as they drove west the resemblance between Mr

Waldorf and Martin began to ring alarm bells among the police' (*The Times*, 20 October 1983). 'The committee chairman, Mr Sam Nunn . . . interrupted a committee hearing on nuclear weapons to make the announcement, immediately setting off alarm bells in Washington' (*Guardian*, 3 February 1989).

set the Thames on fire, to. *Idiom.* Usually in the negative: 'Well, he didn't exactly set the Thames on fire' – meaning, 'he failed to make an impression'. However, W.S. Gilbert in *Princess Ida* (1884) has:
They intend to send a wire?
To the moon – to the moon
And they'll set the Thames on fire
Very soon – very soon.
Versions of this saying date back to the eighteenth century, and similar things have been said about the Rhine, Seine and Liffey in the appropriate languages. The Romans had the expression, *'Tiberium accendere nequaquam potest'* [it isn't at all possible to set the Tiber on fire].
The Thames, famously, once used to freeze over, which would only serve to increase the achievement should anyone manage to set it on fire.

settlement. See JUST AND LASTING ~.

sevens. See SIXES AND ~.

seven stone weakling. See under YOU, TOO, CAN HAVE A BODY LIKE MINE.

seven year itch, the. *Idiom.* Ie the urge to be unfaithful to a spouse after a certain period of matrimony. The *OED Supp.* provides various examples of this phrase going back from the mid-twentieth to the

mid-nineteenth century, but without the specific matrimonial context. For example, the 'seven year itch' describes a rash from poison ivy which was believed to recur every year for a seven-year period. Then one has to recall that since biblical days seven-year periods (of lean or fat) have had especial significance, and there has also been the army saying, 'Cheer up – the first seven years are the worst!'
But the specific matrimonial use was not popularized until used as the title of George Axelrod's play (1952) and then film (1955). 'Itch' had long been used for the sexual urge but, as Axelrod commented on my *Quote . . . Unquote* programme (BBC Radio 4, 1979): 'There was a phrase which referred to a somewhat unpleasant disease but nobody had used it in a sexual [I think he meant 'matrimonial'] context before. I do believe I invented it in that sense.'
Oddly, I can find no mention in any reference book I have consulted of 'itch' being used in connection with venereal diseases. Nonetheless, I was interested to come across the following remark in *W.C. Fields: His Follies and Fortunes* (Robert Lewis Taylor, published as early as 1950): 'Bill exchanged women every seven years, as some people get rid of the itch.'

sex'n'drugs'n'rock'n'roll. *Catch Phrase.* Ie what young people are supposed to be preoccupied with. From a 1977 song by Ian Dury and Chaz Jankel (written as 'Sex & Drugs & Rock & Roll'), which continues, '. . . is [*sic*] all my brain and body need . . . is very good indeed'.
'Nostalgia for the 1960s, call it sex and drugs and rock and roll (and high

purpose) is rife in *Hot Flashes*' (*Guardian*, 25 January 1989). 'Aurum Press is shortly to publish [Lord Whitelaw's] memoirs . . . "It's not exactly sex, drugs and rock-and-roll", Aurum's Tim Chadwick tells me' (*Observer*, 26 February 1989).

sex rears its ugly head. *Idiom > Cliché*. And how curious. Why? Because the penis rises? If so, then why ugly? A very odd usage, except that the construction 'to raise/rear its ugly head' was probably used about other matters before sex. The image is presumably of a Loch Ness-type monster, perhaps, emerging from the deep.

The 'sex-' form has been current since at least 1930 when James R. Quirk used it in a *Photoplay* editorial about the film *Hell's Angels*. It is used both as an explanation for people's behaviour (like '*cherchez la femme*') and as a complaint of the intrusion of sex in books, TV programmes, etc where the speaker would rather not find it.

shadow. See AVOID FIVE O'CLOCK ~.

shaken not stirred. See MARTINI - ~.

shame. See AIN'T IT A ~ under *ITMA*; NICE ——, ~ ABOUT THE ——.

shame of our ——, the. *Cliché*. Of tabloid journalism. But 'THE SHAME OF OUR PRISONS' was a headline in the *Observer*, 3 May 1981.

shattering. See THE EFFECT IS ~ under I THOUGHT —— UNTIL I DISCOVERED ——.

she knows, you know! *Catch Phrase*. Diminutive northern comedienne Hylda Baker (1908–86) used to say this about Cynthia, her mute giraffe-like butt. Her other phrase **be soon!** was used as the title of a TV series in the 1950s.

Shell. See THAT'S ~.

shell-like. See IN YOUR ~ EAR.

she should lie back and enjoy it. *Saying*. This is best described – as it is in Paul Scott's novel *The Jewel in the Crown* (1966) – as 'that old, disreputable saying'. Daphne Manners, upon whose 'rape' the story hinges, adds: 'I can't say, Auntie, that I lay back and enjoyed mine.'

It is no more than a saying – a 'mock-Confucianism' is how Partridge/*Slang* describes it, giving a date *c* 1950, and one is unlikely ever to learn when, or from whom, it first arose.

A word of caution to anyone thinking of using it. An American broadcaster, Tex Antoine, said in 1975: 'With rape so predominant in the news lately, it is well to remember the words of Confucius: "If rape is inevitable, lie back and enjoy it." ' ABC News suspended Antoine for this remark, then demoted him to working in the weather department and prohibited him from appearing on the air.

she who must be obeyed. *Idiom*. The original 'she' in the novel *She* (1887) by H. Rider Haggard was the all-powerful Ayesha, 'who from century to century sat alone, clothed with unchanging loveliness, waiting till her lost love is born again'. But also, 'she was obeyed throughout the length and breadth of the land, and to question her command was certain death'.

From the second of these two quotations we get the use of the phrase by barrister Horace Rumpole with regard to his formidable wife in the 'Rumpole of the Bailey' stories by John Mortimer (in TV plays since 1978, and novelizations therefrom). Hence, too, one of the many nicknames applied to Margaret Thatcher – 'The great she-elephant, she who-must-be-obeyed' (Denis Healey, quoted in the *Observer*, 4 March 1984).

shift the goalposts. See MOVE THE GOAL-POSTS.

ship. See LIKE RATS DESERTING A SINKING ~.

shipping. See ATTENTION ALL ~.

shirt. See STUFFED ~.

shock, horror! *Catch Phrase*. Reaction expressed in parody of tabloid newspaper-speak, from the 1970s onwards. In form it is, of course, similar to 'Shock, horror, probe, sensation!' promoted by *Private Eye* as a stock sensational newspaper headline. 'Shock probe' has been, I think, a type of *News of the World* headline.

shome mistake shurely? (or **shurely shome mistake?**) *Catch Phrase*. Written as such and interpolated as an editorial query in *Private Eye* copy (from the 1980s) – compare WHO HE? – this reproduces the spraying vocal style of William Deedes, editor of the *Daily Telegraph*, 1974–86.

—— **shopping days to Christmas.** *Slogan*. This may have been one of the coin-

ages of H. Gordon Selfridge (1856–1947). At least, when he was still in Chicago he sent out an instruction to heads of departments and assistants at the Marshall Field store there: 'The Christmas season has begun and but twenty-three more shopping days remain in which to make our holiday sales record.'

short, fat, hairy legs. See under MORE-CAMBE AND WISE SHOW.

shot. See WHO ~ J.R.?

show. See LET'S DO THE ~ . . . ; GREATEST ~ ON EARTH; ~ MUST GO ON under SEND IN THE CLOWNS.

shows. See I THINK THAT ~ . . .

shut that door! *Catch Phrase*. Larry Grayson (*b* 1930) came to prominence on TV in the 1970s. The first time he used the phrase was on stage at the Theatre Royal, Brighton in 1970: 'when I felt a terrible draught up my trouser legs. I turned to the wings and said it. I really meant it, but the only response was giggles from the wings and a roar of laughter from the audience. So I kept it in my act. I can't go anywhere now without taxi-drivers or shopkeepers telling me to "shut that door".'

shut up, Eccles! See under GOON SHOW.

sick and tired. *Colloquialism > Cliché*. Why always these two words together? There is a 1783 example. In May 1988, Terry Dicks, a Conservative MP and self-proclaimed tribune of the plebs, spoke during a Commons debate on the arts, and said: 'Ordinary people are sick and tired of people who can well afford to pay the full going rate for attendance at the theatre and ballet getting away with being subsidized by the rest of us.' This seems a fairly classic context for the phrase to be used – and spoken by just the type of person one would expect to use it.

From the *Independent* (7 March 1989): 'President Bush complained he was "sick and tired" of attacks on Defence Secretary-designate John Tower.'

sick as a parrot. See under OVER THE MOON.

sick-bag. See PASS THE ~, ALICE.

Sidi Barrani. See DID I EVER TELL YOU . . . under *MUCH BINDING IN THE MARSH*.

silly Billy. *Nickname/ Idiom*. For a foolish person. The most notable person to be given it as a nickname was William Frederick, 2nd Duke of Gloucester (1776–1834), uncle of William IV – though it was also applied to the king himself. In the wrangles between Whigs and Tories, when the king supported the former, Gloucester is reported to have asked, 'Who's Silly Billy now?'

Partridge/*Slang* has Henry Mayhew in 1851 finding 'Silly Billy . . . very popular with the audience at the fairs' (as a name used by a clown for his stooge).

In the 1970s, Mike Yarwood, the TV impressionist, put it in the mouth of the Labour politician Denis Healey, because it went rather well with the Healey persona and distinctive vocal delivery. Healey then imitated art by saying it himself.

According to Alan Watkins in the *Observer* (13 January 1985), Randolph Churchill, the Conservative politician

(and son of Winston), was also noted for using the expression.

silly little man. See under BAND WAGGON.

silly (old) moo. *Stock Phrase*. Alf Garnett (Warren Mitchell) in the BBC TV comedy series *Till Death Us Do Part* would say either form of this to his wife (Dandy Nichols) – a euphemism for 'cow'. Dandy Nichols said that people used to call it out to her in the street – affectionately, nonetheless. The series ran from 1964 to 1974.

Silver. See HI-YO, ~.

sinking. See BOVRIL PREVENTS THAT ~ FEELING; LIKE RATS DESERTING A ~ SHIP.

sitting. See ARE YOU ~ COMFORTABLY? . . . ; NO MORE LATIN . . .

—— situation, a. *Format Phrase > Cliché*. For several years in the 1970s and 80s, *Private Eye* waged a campaign against the unnecessary addition of the word 'situation' in situations where the speaker thought it added something to the sentence. This succeeded in making the matter a well-known joke but did not entirely put an end to the practice. Two ripe examples from my own reading: an employee of the Royal Borough of Windsor and Maidenhead wrote to a householder in 1981 and asked him to trim a hedge. He did so in these words: 'Whereas a hedge situation at Altwood Road, Maidenhead in Berkshire, belonging to you overhangs the highway known as Altwood Road, Maidenhead aforesaid, so as to endanger or obstruct the passage of pedestrians . . .'

And Yoko Ono is quoted in *The Love You Make*, Peter Brown and Steven Gaines, 1983, as saying: '[John Lennon] asked if I had ever tried [heroin]. I told him that while he was in India with the Maharishi, I had a sniff of it in a party situation . . .'

Oddly, as long ago as 22 August 1934, *The Times* was drawing attention to the trend: 'A popular dodge at present is to add the word "situation" or "position" to a noun; by this means, apparently, it has been discovered that the most pregnant meanings can be expressed with the least effort. The "coal situation" remains unchanged; the "herring position" is grave.'

sixes and sevens, to be at. *Idiom.* Meaning 'to be confused, in an unresolved situation'. The usual origin given for this expression (by, for example, Ewart) is that in the days when the medieval guilds of London took pride in their order of precedence, the Merchant Taylors and the Skinners could not agree who should be sixth, and who seventh. After an intervention by the Lord Mayor, they agreed to take it in turns – as they do to this day.

Morris, on the other hand, supports the theory that it dates from a dice game (as mentioned by Chaucer in one of his poems) in which the dice bore marks up to seven, if not further: 'Only a confused or disorganized person would roll for this point' (ie a 'six and seven'). This is the origin supported by the *OED*.

I note that Shakespeare's only use of the phrase occurs in *King Richard II* (II.ii.122): 'All is uneven,/ And everything is left at six and seven' – though it strikes me that in *Pericles* (IV.vi.74) he may be making a punning allusion to it when (in

a sexual context) Lysimachus says: 'Did you go to't [copulate] young? Were you a gamester at five or at seven?'

six of one. See under I'M NOT A NUMBER . . .

sixpence. See BANG GOES SAXPENCE.

sixty-four (thousand) dollar question, the. *Catch Phrase/Idiom.* 'Ah, that's the sixty-four dollar question, isn't it?' some people will exclaim, when surely they mean 'sixty-four *thousand*'. Or do they? Put it down to inflation. *Webster's Dictionary* says that $64 *was* the highest award in a CBS radio quiz called *Take It or Leave It* which ran from 1941–8 and in which the value of the prize doubled every time the contestant got a right answer (in the progression 1–2–4–8–16–32–64 – hence the title *Double Your Money* given to the first of the British TV versions). This is how the saying entered common parlance, meaning 'that is the question which would solve all our problems if only we knew the answer to it'.

An example of the original use in the 1950s is contained in a *Daily Express* article about P.G. Wodehouse written by Rene McColl (undated): ' "Wodehouse, Esq.", I observed, "Could I, to use the vernacular of this our host nation, pop the jolly old 64-dollar question? If you were back in Germany, a prisoner, and you had it all to do again – would you do it?" '

Subsequently, in the US TV version of the show (1955–7), the top prize did go up to $64,000 – though, cunningly, when ITV imported the show for British viewers shortly afterwards, the title was simply *The 64,000 Question* or *Challenge*, making no mention of the denomination of currency involved.

In February 1989, I heard a female weather forecaster on ITV being asked, 'Is the mild weather going to continue?' She replied, 'That's the sixty-four million dollar question.' So inflation is still rampant.

Skegness is so bracing. See IT'S SO BRACING.

sky. See REACH FOR THE ~.

sleep. See WE NEVER ~.

slept. See QUEEN ELIZABETH ~ HERE.

sliced bread. See GREATEST THING SINCE ~.

slow down. See NATURE'S WAY OF TELLING YOU TO ~.

slowly. See TWIST ~, ~, IN THE WIND.

slow, slow, quick, quick, slow. *Stock Phrase*. Dance tempo spoken by Victor Sylvester (1902–78), ballroom dance instructor and band leader, on radio from 1941 and on TV from the 1950s. The tempo is for the quickstep.

In December 1988, poster advertisements for the Rover 200 series compared start-up speeds for two Rover models and a BMW under the heading, 'Quick, Quick, Slow'.

small. See ONE ~ STEP FOR . . .

small, but perfectly formed. *Catch Phrase/Idiom.* I can remember quite clearly the time when this phrase first registered with me. It was at a one-man show performed by Tim Thomas at the tiny Soho Poly theatre in about 1975. Addressing the diminutive audience at a lunch-hour performance, he informed us we were 'small . . . but perfectly formed'.

As such, it was an idiom which I vaguely thought to be theatrical, possibly American showbiz, in origin. I am sure, too, that I have heard variations, of the 'small, but exquisitely talented' variety.

Then, in 1983, I was intrigued when Artemis Cooper published *A Durable Fire – The Letters of Duff and Diana Cooper 1913–50*. In a letter from Duff to Diana in October 1914, he writes: 'That is the sort of party I like . . . You must think I have enjoyed it too, with your two stout lovers frowning at one another across the hearth rug, while your small, but perfectly formed one kept the party in a roar.'

From the use of fashionable slang elsewhere in the letters, I would suppose that this coinage was not original to Cooper but drawn from the smart talk of the period. If there is an earlier example of the phrase in use, however, I wait with bated breath to hear of it.

The 'small, but . . .' construction appears earlier in the German saying '*klein, aber mein*' ('small, but my own') and in the line from 'Ode to Evening' (1747) by William Collins: 'Or where the beetle winds/ His small but sullen horn' (where 'sullen' = 'of a deep, dull or mournful tone' – *OED*).

I might mention, also, that Richard Lowe has sent me this entry from the Skipton Town Council Yearbook: 'The following remarkable record is taken from a gravestone at the east end of Christ Church burial ground: "In memory of Edwin Calvert, son of Richard Calvert, of Skipton, known by the title of the

'Commander in Chief'. He was the *smallest and most perfect* human being in the world, being under 36 inches in height, and weighing 25 lb.. He died much lamented and deeply regretted by all who knew him, August 7th 1859, aged 17 years".'

small is beautiful. *Slogan.* The title of the book published in 1973 by Professor E.F. Schumacher (1911–77) provided a *Catch Phrase* and a slogan for those who were opposed to an expansionist trend in business and organizations that was very apparent in the 1960s and 70s and who wanted 'economics on a human scale'. However, it appears that he very nearly didn't come up with the phrase. According to his daughter and a correspondent (*Observer*, 29 April/ 6 June 1984), the book was going to be called 'The Homecomers'. His publisher, Anthony Blond suggested 'Small*ness* is Beautiful', and then Desmond Briggs, the co-publisher, came up with the eventual wording.

smarter than the average bear, (Booboo). *Catch Phrase.* Said of himself by Yogi Bear to his sidekick, Booboo, in the American Yogi Bear cartoon TV series (1958–). The character was voiced by Charles 'Daws' Butler. At his death in May 1988, it was suggested, perhaps mistakenly, that he had coined the phrase as well.

smasher. See I SAY, WHAT A ~!

smile on your face. See under COME ALIVE . . .

smile, you're on *Candid Camera*! *Stock Phrase.* American Allen Funt translated

his practical joke radio programme *Candid Microphone* to TV and it ran from 1948–78 (there was a British version, too). On revealing to members of the public that they had been hoaxed, this was the somewhat hopeful greeting – hopeful that they would not take it badly.

snap! crackle! pop! *Slogan.* For Kellogg's Rice Krispies, in the US from *c* 1928, later in the UK. There has been more than one version. An early one: 'It pops! It snaps! It crackles!'

sneezes. See COUGHS AND ~ SPREAD DISEASES.

snook. See COCK A ~.

snowball/snowflake's chance in Hades, a. See NO MORE CHANCE THAN A SNOWBALL IN HELL.

snow-storm in Karachi. See under AS BUSY AS . . .

sock. See PUT A ~ IN IT!

sock it to me! See under LAUGH-IN.

Sod's Law. See IF ANYTHING CAN GO WRONG, IT WILL.

so, farewell then. *Catch Phrase.* From the drab poems of 'E.J. Thribb' which have graced *Private Eye*'s 'Poetry Corner' since the 1970s. Most of them celebrate, in an off-hand way, the recent deaths of famous people, and usually began, 'So, farewell then . . .'
From the *Observer* (17 April 1988): 'So farewell then Kenneth Williams . . .'
Compare AND SO WE SAY FAREWELL . . .

soft as a brush. See DAFT AS A BRUSH.

soil. See ANSWER LIES IN THE ~ under *BEYOND OUR KEN*.

soldiers. See OLD ~ NEVER DIE . . .

somebody up there likes me. See SOME-ONE . . .

some mothers do 'ave 'em. See under DON'T SOME MOTHERS HAVE 'EM.

some of my best friends are ——. *Format Phrase.* Most commonly ending with 'Jews/Jewish'. A self-conscious (and occasionally jokey) disclaimer of prejudice. In a May 1946 letter, Somerset Maugham replied to charges that he was anti-semitic and said: 'God knows I have never been that; some of my best friends in England and America are Jews . . .'
So, clearly, at that date the phrase could be used without irony. However, the line may – according to one source – have been rejected as a cartoon caption by the *New Yorker* prior to the Second World War and presumably dates, in any case, from the Nazi persecution of the Jews from the 1930s on.
In the (Jewish) Marx Brothers film *Monkey Business* (as early as 1931), there is the line, 'Some of my best friends are *housewives.*'
The Russian Prime Minister, Alexei Kosygin, was apparently unaware of the phrase's near-cliché status in 1971 when he said, 'There is no anti-semitism in Russia. Some of my best friends are Jews.'

someone isn't using Amplex. See under EVEN YOUR BEST FRIENDS . . .

someone somewhere wants a letter from you. *Slogan.* For the Post Office, current in the early 1960s.

someone up there likes me. *Catch Phrase.* Shortly before he was elected leader of the Labour Party in 1983, Neil Kinnock emerged unscathed from his car when it inexplicably turned over on the M4 motorway. He remarked, 'My escape was miraculous. It's a word which is somewhat over-used, but I know what it means. Someone up there likes me.'
Somebody Up There Likes Me was the title of a 1956 film written by Ernest Lehman. It starred Paul Newman and was based on the life of the World Middle-weight Boxing Champion of 1947–8, Rocky Graziano (not to be confused with Rocky Marciano). I believe Graziano's autobiography had the same title. There was a title song from the film – also, in 1957, a song called 'Somebody Up There Digs Me'.

something. See AND NOW FOR ~ COMPLETELY DIFFERENT; GOOD MORNING, SIR! . . . under *MUCH BINDING IN THE MARSH*.

somewhere in England. *Stock Phrase.* In 1986, I received a jokey birthday card which announced in small letters on the back that it was printed 'somewhere in England'. There was a film *Somewhere in England* (1940) which begot a series of British regional comedies (Halliwell lists *Somewhere in Camp/ on Leave/ in Civvies* and *in Politics*).
The construction originated in the First World War, for security reasons (eg 'somewhere in France . . .'), and its use came to be broadened to anywhere one

cannot, or one does not want to, be too precise about.

somewhere to the right of Genghis Khan. *Cliché.* As a description of someone's politics. Arthur Scargill, president of the National Union of Mineworkers, told John Mortimer in the *Sunday Times* (10 January 1982): 'Of course, in those days, the union leaders were well to the right of Genghis Khan.' An allusion from the *Independent* (28 January 1989): 'Close friends say he [Kenneth Clarke] has been an emollient force behind the doors of the Department of Health, but Genghis Khan would have looked like a calming influence alongside his ebullient ministers David Mellor and Edwina Currie.'

Genghis Khan (*c* 1162–1227) was a Mongol ruler who conquered large parts of Asia and, whether rightly or not, is always portrayed as a brutal pillager.

son. See A GOOD IDEA . . . under *EDUCATING ARCHIE*; ONE DAY ALL THIS WILL BE YOURS, MY ~.

son and heir, the. *Idiom.* Now used only jokingly to describe one's eldest son. Charles Dickens has 'together with the information that the Son and Heir would sail in a fortnight' in *Dombey and Son* (Chapter 17) (1846–8). Shakespeare has 'the son and heir to that same Faulconbridge' (*King John*, I.i.56) but here quotation marks are not yet quite around the phrase.

son of ——. *Format Phrase.* Used, particularly, as the title of sequels in American films, emphasizing how they are the derivatives of (usually) superior origin-als. The *OED Supp.* cites the first such book as *Son of Tarzan* by Edgar Rice Burroughs. The first such film was probably *Son of the Sheik* (1926), with Rudolph Valentino, following *The Sheik* (1921). Then *Son of Kong* (1933) followed *King Kong*. Others have been: *Son of Ali Baba/ Captain Blood/ Dr Jekyll/ Dracula/ Frankenstein/ Geronimo/ Lassie/ Monte Cristo/ Paleface/ Robin Hood/ Zorro.*

Alternatively, you could stage a return: *The Return of Dracula/ the Scarlet Pimpernel/ a Man Called Horse.* And then merely add a number. Following the example of *The Godfather, Part II* (1974), we have had not only *Rocky II – IV* but also *Jaws II,* and *French Connection II/ Death Wish II/ Damien: Omen II/ Friday the Thirteenth, Part II/ Crocodile Dundee 2,* and so on.

There were exceptions, of course. The sequel to *American Graffiti* was *More American Graffiti.* Forswearing 'Pink Panther 2 etc', Blake Edwards gave us *The Pink Panther Strikes Again, The Revenge of the Pink Panther, The Return of the Pink Panther.* The *Airport* sequels followed their own peculiar sequence of titles – from *Airport 1975* to *Airport '77* and then *Airport '80 – The Concorde.*

soot, juggling with. See under AS BUSY AS . . .

sorry. See I'M ~ I'LL READ THAT AGAIN.

space. See WATCH THIS ~.

speak as you find, that's my motto. *Catch Phrase.* In a 1950s radio series *Hello Playmates!* featuring Arthur Askey, this catch phrase was spoken not by him but by Nola Purvis (Pat Coombs), the daughter of the studio cleaner (Irene Handl). This was her smug excuse for the appalling insults she hurled. In 1955, *Hello Playmates!* won the *Daily Mail* Radio Award as the year's top show and the catch phrase was inscribed on the presentation silver microphone – which didn't go down too well with Askey who had never uttered it. (Source Bob Monkhouse, who with Denis Goodwin wrote the show.)

special. See AND A ~ GOODNIGHT TO *YOU*.

speeding bullet. See under *SUPERMAN*.

spelled. See THAT ~ ——.

spend a penny, to. *Idiom*. Euphemism for 'to go to the lavatory'. The first public convenience to charge one penny opened in London in 1855. So I am curious about this from Chapter 6 of Charles Dickens's *Dombey and Son* (1846–8): 'The young Toodles, victims of a pious fraud, were deluded into repairing in a body to a chandler's shop in the neighbourhood, for the ostensible purpose of spending a penny.' (*OED Supp.* does not find it before 1945.)

spend, spend, spend!, I'm going to. *Catch Phrase*. Viv Nicholson (*b* 1936) and her husband Keith, a trainee miner, were bringing up three children on a weekly wage of £7 in Castleford, Yorkshire. Then, in September 1961, they won £152,000 on Littlewoods football pools. Arriving by train to collect their prize (as Viv recalled in her autobiography, *Spend, Spend, Spend*, 1977), they were confronted by reporters. One

asked: 'What are you going to do when you get all this money?' Viv said, 'I'm going to spend, spend, spend, that's what I'm going to do.' She says it was just an off-the-cuff remark, but it made newspaper headlines and was later used as the title not only of her book but of a TV play about her.

As a phrase it still lingers, not least because of the tragic overtones to Viv's use of it. Keith died in a car crash and Viv worked her way through a series of husbands until the money had all gone. From the *Daily Mail* (4 March 1989): 'The Sixties were indeed "a low dishonest decade" . . . We thought the great post-war boom would go on for ever, that both individuals and the state could spend, spend, spend without the smallest concern for tomorrow.'

spirit of ——, the. *Cliché*. Of politics. Like MESSAGE OF ——, this is a highly versatile phrase. 'The Spirit of '76' came into use following the American Revolution in the eighteenth century. Later, President Eisenhower was very fond of the format, several times speaking of 'the Spirit of Geneva' in 1955, and 'the Spirit of Camp David' in 1959. Michael Foot, the Labour politician, combined it with another political cliché following a by-election victory, and said that Labour would, 'get the spirit of Darlington **up and down the country** [another politician's favourite]'. (The Darlington win was reversed at the General Election the following month . . .)

spit. See DOESN'T IT MAKE YOU WANT TO ~! under *BAND WAGGON*; DON'T ~ . . .

Spode's Law. See IF ANYTHING CAN GO WRONG, IT WILL . . .

sponned. See I'VE BEEN ~ under *GOON SHOW*.

sponsor. See AND NOW A WORD FROM OUR ~.

sport of kings, the. *Idiom*. In the seventeenth century it was war-making. William Somerville described hunting as 'the sport of kings' in *The Chase*, 1735. But in the twentieth century horse racing has tended to be the sport so described. So, too – with what justification, I know not – has surf-riding.

spot. See A ~ OF HOMELY FUN under *HAVE A GO; DID YOU ~ . . . ?*

spreading alarm and despondency. *Idiom > Cliché*. The *ODQ* quotes Vladimir Peniakoff (1897–1951) who in his book *Private Army* wrote: 'A message came on the wireless for me. It said 'SPREAD ALARM and DESPONDENCY . . . The date was, I think, May 18th, 1942.' It also draws attention to the Army Act of 1879: 'Every person subject to military law who . . . spreads reports calculated to create unnecessary alarm or despondency . . . shall . . . be liable to suffer penal servitude.'

square one. See BACK TO ~.

square peg in a round hole, a. (or *vice versa*) *Idiom*. Meaning 'someone badly suited to their job or position'. Mostly the twentieth century, but note this from Sydney Smith, *Lectures on Moral Philosophy*, 1804: 'If you choose to represent the various parts in life by holes upon a table, of different shapes – some circular, some triangular, some square, some oblong – and the persons acting these parts by bits of wood of similar shapes, we shall

generally find that the triangular person has got into the square hole, and a square person has squeezed himself into the round hole.'

stage, kindly leave the. See I DON'T WISH TO KNOW THAT . . .

stain. See HOLD IT UP TO THE LIGHT . . .

stairs. See GET UP THEM ~!

stamp. See WE MUST ~ OUT THIS EVIL IN OUR MIDST.

stand. See WILL THE REAL ——, PLEASE ~ UP?

star. See YOU'RE GOING OUT A YOUNGSTER . . . ; REACH FOR THE SKY.

started. See I'VE ~, SO I'LL FINISH!

starts. See WEEKEND ~ HERE.

starving. See WHEN PEOPLE ARE ~ IN INDIA.

stay, can't you. See MUST YOU GO . . . ?

steel. See RING OF ~.

step. See ONE SMALL ~ . . . ; ONE ~ FORWARDS . . .

stetson. See KEEP IT UNDER YOUR HAT.

still going strong. See BORN 1820 . . .

stirred. See DOWN IN THE FOREST SOMETHING ~; MARTINI SHAKEN NOT ~.

stone. See LEAVE NO ~ UNTURNED.

stone me! See under *HANCOCK'S HALF-HOUR*.

stop. See AND WHEN THE MUSIC ~S under ARE YOU SITTING COMFORTABLY?; BUCK ~S HERE; ~ THE MIGHTY ROAR . . . under *IN TOWN TONIGHT*; WHEN DID YOU ~ BEATING YOUR WIFE?

stop me and buy one. *Slogan.* Lionel and Charles Rodd were on the board of T. Wall & Sons, the ice cream manufacturers, and are believed to have come up with this slogan in 1923. 8500 salesmen with the words on their tricycles pedalled round Britain out of a national network of 136 depots.

In the 1970s, there followed the graffito on contraceptive vending machines, 'Buy me and stop one'.

stop messin abaht! See under *HANCOCK'S HALF-HOUR*.

stopping. See I WON'T TAKE ME COAT OFF . . .

Stork. See CAN YOU TELL ~ FROM BUTTER?

story. See COCK AND BULL ~; EVERY PICTURE TELLS A ~; I WANNA TELL YOU A ~; ~ REALLY BEGINS under *GOON SHOW*; SAVAGE ~ OF LUST . . .

straight out of Central Casting. *Idiom.* Meaning 'a person who conforms to type, or to what you would expect'. From the *Observer* (19 March 1939): 'If you had asked Central Casting, or Equity, to provide an archetypal bigot, it's unlikely they could come up with someone as perfect as Jan van der Berg . . . owner of one of the better restaurants in Windhoek, the capital of Namibia.'

Central Casting was set up in 1926 and maintained by all major Hollywood studios as a pool for supplying extras for films. David Niven, for example, claimed to have been listed on their books in the mid-1930s as 'Anglo-Saxon Type No. 2008'.

Strand. See YOU'RE NEVER ALONE WITH A ~.

street. See MAN IN THE ~; THERE'LL BE DANCING IN THE ~S TONIGHT.

streets paved with gold, to find the. *Idiom.* When Hollywood was in its heyday, many writers were reluctant to go there, fearing how badly they would be treated. According to Arthur Marx in *Son of Groucho* (1973), his father tried very hard to persuade the dramatist George S. Kaufman to join him out on the West Coast.

'No, no,' said Kaufman. 'I don't care how much they pay me. I hate it out there.'

'But, George,' pleaded Groucho, 'the streets out here are paved with gold.'

There was a moment's pause, and then Kaufman said, 'You mean, you have to bend down and pick it up?'

But where did this near-cliché originate? In the story of Dick Whittington, he makes his way to London from Gloucestershire because he hears the streets are paved with gold and silver. The actual Dick Whittington was thrice Lord Mayor of London in the late fourteenth and early fifteenth centuries. The popular legend does not appear to have been told before 1605.

The streets of heaven are also sometimes said to be paved with gold – though not in the Bible. There is, however, a Negro spiritual where the 'streets in heaven am paved with gold'.

strike it out. See IF IN DOUBT . . .

string, piece of. See under HOW MANY BEANS . . . ?

studio, return you to the. See under *BEYOND OUR KEN*.

stuff. See RIGHT ~.

stuffed shirt, a. *Idiom*. There seems to be an urge among obituary writers to credit the recently deceased with the coining of phrases, even where the facts do not really support it. Patrick Brogan writing of Mrs Clare Boothe Luce in the *Independent* (12 October 1987) stated: 'She wrote a series of articles poking fun at the rich and pompous, coining for them the descriptive phrase "stuffed shirts", a title she used for her first book.'

That book was published in 1933, but the *OED Supp.* has an example of the phrase dating from 1913 (when Luce was a mere ten), which makes it clear that by then it was already current US usage for a pompous person. So though she may have re-popularized the phrase she certainly didn't coin it.

stupid. See VERY INTERESTING . . . BUT ~! under *LAUGH-IN*.

success. See IT WENT FROM FAILURE TO CLASSIC . . .

suck eggs. See DON'T TEACH YOUR GRANDMOTHER . . .

suck it and see. *Catch Phrase/Idiom*. Meaning 'try out'. It was used as a catch phrase by Charlie Naughton of the Crazy Gang, though of music-hall origin (Partridge/*Slang* dates it from the 1890s).

suitable. See NOT ~ FOR THOSE . . .

summer. See LONG HOT ~.

Sunny Jim. *Catch Phrase/Idiom*. One might say, 'Ah, there you are . . . I've been looking for you, Sunny Jim' – even if the person isn't called Jim. It is a name applied to a cheerful person but can also be a slightly patronizing expression, and thus was aptly applied to James Callaghan, when Prime Minister, who was nothing if not patronizing in return with his air of a bank manager who knew best (an *Observer* headline of 18 March 1979 stated, 'Sunny Jim tires of wheeler-dealing').

Few who use the name know that it originated with a character who appeared in ads for Force breakfast cereal from about 1903. He was the invention of two young American women, a Miss Ficken and Minnie Maud Hanff (usually credited with the phrase), who came up with a jingle and rough sketch of the character for the Force Food Company.

sun, sand and sea. *Cliché*. Used in travel promotion. In 1972, I interviewed a group of children born in London of West Indian parents, who were about to pay their first visit to Barbados. When I asked one of them what he expected to find there, he quite spontaneously said, 'All I know is, it's sun, sand and sea.' We used this line as the title of a Radio 4 programme which reported their reactions before and after the visit.

Clearly, the child had absorbed this alliterative phrase at an early age. It is never very far away. Several songs have the title. From a photo caption in the *Observer* (26 June 1988): 'Sun, sand and sea are no longer enough for the Yuppie generation of fun-seekers.'

sunset. See DRIVE . . . OFF INTO THE ~.

Superman. The comic-strip hero was the brainchild of a teenage science-fiction addict, Jerry Siegel, in 1933. Five years later, Superman appeared on the cover of No. 1 of *Action Comics*. In 1940, he took to the radio airwaves in the US on the Mutual Network, with Clayton 'Bud' Collyer as the journalist Clark Kent who can turn into the Man of Steel whenever he is in a tight spot: 'This looks like a job for . . . Superman! Now, off with these clothes! **Up, up and awa-a-a-ay!**' After appearing in film cartoons, Superman finally appeared as a live-action hero on the screen in a 1948 fifteen-episode serial. He was still on the big screen in the 1970s and 80s.

It was from the radio series, however, that the exciting phrases came:

Announcer: Kellogg's Pep . . . the super-delicious cereal . . . presents . . . *The Adventures of Superman!* **Faster than a speeding bullet!** [*ricochet*] More powerful than a locomotive! [*locomotive roar*] Able to leap tall buildings at a single bound! [*rushing wind*] Look! Up in the sky!
Voice 1: **It's a bird!**
Voice 2: **It's a plane!**
Voice 3: **It's Superman!**
Announcer: Yes, it's Superman – a strange visitor from another planet, who came to earth with powers and abilities far beyond those of mortal men. Superman! – who can change the course of mighty rivers, bend steel with his bare hands, and who – disguised as Clark Kent, mild-mannered

reporter for a great metropolitan newspaper – fights **a never-ending battle for truth, justice and the American way.**

'Up, up, and away!' was used by Jim Webb as the title of a song in 1967 and, in the same year, was incorporated in the slogan 'Up, up and away with TWA'.

—— **superstar.** *Format Phrase.* The suffix '—— Superstar' became fashionable following the success of the musical *Jesus Christ Superstar* (1970). Tim Rice, its lyricist, tells me that he and the composer, Andrew Lloyd Webber, settled on the title after seeing a 1960s Las Vegas billing for 'Tom Jones – Superstar'.

The showbiz use of the term 'superstar' although very much a 1960s thing – it was also used by Andy Warhol – has been traced back to 1925 by the *OED Supp.* which finds in that year talk of 'cinema super-stars'.

support your local ——. *Slogan > Format phrase.* From the US, I think. The format was established before the 1968 film *Support Your Local Sheriff* (which was followed three years later by *Support Your Local Gunfighter*). In 1969 there was a police bumper sticker in the US, 'Support your local police, keep them independent'.

Compare YOUR FRIENDLY NEIGHBOURHOOD ——.

sur le continong/telephoneo. See under MORNING ALL!

surrender. See NO ~!

swap. See NEVER ~ HORSES IN MIDSTREAM.

sweat. See HORSES ~ . . .

sweeps. See IT BEATS, AS IT ~ . . .

sweet. See HOW ~ IT IS under AND AWA-A-AAY WE GO!

sweet Fanny Adams/ sweet F.A./ sweet fuck-all. *Idiom.* Ie nothing at all. There actually was a person called Fanny Adams. Her gravestone in the cemetery at Alton in Hampshire records: 'Sacred to the memory of Fanny Adams, aged 8 years and 4 months, who was cruelly murdered on Saturday, August 21, 1867.' She was the victim of Frederick Booth, a 29-year-old solicitor's clerk, who grotesquely mutilated the body. His diary entry for the day read, 'Killed a young girl – it was fine and hot'. He was executed on Christmas Eve, 1867.

At about the same time, tinned meat was introduced to the Royal Navy and sailors, unimpressed, said it was probably made up from the remains of the murdered girl. 'Fanny Adams' became the naval nickname for mutton or stew, and then the meaning was extended to cover anything that was worthless.

The abbreviation 'Sweet F.A.' being re-translated as 'Sweet Fuck-All' is a more recent coinage.

swim. See CAN A DUCK ~?

swine. See YOU DIRTY ROTTEN ~, YOU under *GOON SHOW*.

swinging! See under DODGY!

swinging London/the Swinging Sixties. *Catch Phrase/Nickname.* 'Swinging' had been a musician's commendation for many years before it was adopted to describe the free-wheeling, uninhibited atmosphere associated with the 1960s. By extension, 'swinging' came to denote sexual promiscuity. 'A swinger' was one who indulged in such activity.

How the word caught on is not totally clear. In the early 1960s, the comedian Norman Vaughan would say it (see DODGY!) But Frank Sinatra had had an album entitled *Songs for Swinging Lovers* (1958), Peter Sellers, *Songs for Swinging Sellers* (1959), and Diana Dors *Swinging Dors*.

The coming together of 'swinging' and 'London' may first have occurred in an edition of the *Weekend Telegraph* magazine on 30 April 1965 in which the words of the American fashion journalist Diana Vreeland (c 1903–89) were quoted: 'I love London. It is the most swinging city in the world at the moment.' In addition, a picture caption declared, 'London is a swinging city'. Almost exactly one year later, *Time* magazine picked up the angle and devoted a cover-story to the concept of 'London: The Swinging City' (edition dated 15 April 1966).

T

Taffia, the. *Nickname.* Used for a group of Welshmen looking after their own interests. For example, in the media, one might have said that the founders of Harlech TV in 1968 were members of the Taffia – including Richard Burton, Sir Geraint Evans, John Morgan and Wynford Vaughan-Thomas. The word is an obvious combination of 'Taffy' (the traditional nickname for a Welshman, from the supposed Welsh pronunciation of Davy = David) and *mafia*, the Sicilian-Italian word which means 'bragging', applied to the organized body of criminals among Italian immigrants in the US.

From the *Sun* (2 April 1979): 'Terror of the Taffia! The militants who'll black out your telly for their cause' – ie rather the opposite of the above-described HTV mob.

Similar light-hearted coinages are **the Murphia** (from Murphy, the typical Irish name and nickname of a potato), applied to the band of Irish broadcasters in the UK headed by Terry Wogan, and **kosher nostra**, for the Jewish 'mafia'.

Take It From Here. The radio programme in which **anything can happen and probably will** was first broadcast on 23 March 1948 and ran until 1959. It was based on literate scripts by Frank Muir and Denis Norden, and featured Jimmy Edwards (1920–88), Dick Bentley (*b* 1907) and June Whitfield (*b* 1927) (who succeeded Joy Nichols). A few of the phrases that came out of it:

black mark, Bentley! Edwards referring to Dick B. Muir told me that it arose from the use of 'black mark!' by James Robertson Justice in Peter Ustinov's film of *Vice Versa*.

gently, Bentley! Edwards to Dick B.

oh, Ron!/Yes, Eth? The immortal exchange between a swooning Whitfield and a gormless Bentley as the lovers in the segment of the show known as 'The Glums'. A stock phrase originally rather than a catch phrase, but it caught on because of Eth's rising inflection and Ron's flat response.

ullo, ullo, ullo, what's this? Edwards as Pa Glum (usually interrupting son Ron as he attempted to kiss fiancée Eth). Muir says: 'It was not meant to be a catch phrase but as Pa Glum always said it on his entrance – and it was so useful a phrase in everyday life – it caught on.' It also, of course, echoes the traditional inquiry of a policeman encountering something suspicious going on.

wake up at the back there! Muir: 'This was a line I always used in writing Jim's schoolmaster acts. It was technically very useful in breaking up his first line and getting audience attention.'

Jim: They laughed at Suez, but he went right ahead and built his canal – wake up at the back there!

Compare WAKE UP THERE! under YOU 'ORRIBLE LITTLE MAN!

take it in. See CAN DISH IT OUT . . .

take the mickey, to. *Idiom.* Meaning 'to send up, tease'. From rhyming slang, 'Mickey Bliss' = 'piss'. From the 1950s – though later, 'are you by any chance extracting the Michael', became common.

Who was Mickey Bliss to be so honoured, I wonder?

take the money and run, to. *Idiom.* Meaning 'to settle for what you've got and not hang about'. Or it might be advice given to people worried about the worth of the job of work they were doing. One might also say, 'I should take the money and run, if I were you.' I have no citations for this other than the title of Woody Allen's film 1968 film *Take the Money and Run*.

tale. See AND THEREBY HANGS A ~.

talent will out. *Saying.* Meaning that if a person has talent, a way of expressing it will be found. The only citation I have here is from an advertisement for Lloyds Bank Young Theatre Challenge (June 1988): 'Talent will out, they say. But only under the right conditions.'

As such, this is a perfectly reasonable adaptation of the proverb 'Murder will out' (ie will be found out, will reveal itself) which goes back at least to 1325, and of 'Truth will out' which goes back to 1439.

talk. See WE HAVE WAYS . . .

tall, dark and handsome. *Cliché.* This description of a romantic hero's attributes (as likely to be found especially in women's fiction) seems to have surfaced in the early 1900. Flexner puts it in the late 1920s as a Hollywood term referring to Rudolph Valentino (though, in fact, he was not particularly tall). Cesar Romero played the lead in the 1941 film *Tall, Dark and Handsome* which no doubt helped fix the phrase in popular use. However, in a piece called 'Loverboy of the Bourgeoisie' (collected in 1965), Tom Wolfe writes: 'It was Cary Grant that Mae West was talking about when she launched the phrase "tall, dark and handsome" in "She Done Him Wrong" (1933).'

tank. See PUT A TIGER IN YOUR ~.

tante. See *PLUME DE MA* ~.

Tarzan. See ME, ~ . . .

taste. See IT'S ALL DONE IN THE BEST POSSIBLE ~.

taxi. See FOLLOW THAT ~!

tea. See I WANT MY ~.

teach. See DON'T ~ YOUR GRANDMOTHER . . .

tea-party. See LIKE A VICARAGE ~.

teeth. See OLD AS MY TONGUE . . .

telephoneo, sur le. See under MORNING ALL!

television. See TIT, TOTE AND ~.

tell. See EVERY PICTURE ~S A STORY; IT'S THE WAY I ~ 'EM!; I WANNA ~ YOU A STORY!; ONLY TIME WILL ~.

telling. See WHY ARE YOU ~ . . . under AR-CHERS.

tell-tale tit. *Idiom.* The title of the spicy memoirs of the actress Fiona Richmond (published 1987) probably seemed to promise more lubricity than the phrase was originally meant to deliver. As Iona & Peter Opie record in *The Lore and Language of Schoolchildren:*

Tell tale tit
Your tongue shall be slit,

And all the dogs in the town
Shall have a little bit
– has been 'stinging in the ears of blabbers for more than two hundred years' (or since 1780, at least).

ten. See NINE OUT OF ~; ON A SCALE OF ONE TO ~.

tender loving care. *Catch Phrase/Idiom.* Understandably, this is a phrase that appears irresistible to song-writers. The catalogue of the BBC Gramophone Library reveals a considerable list:

As 'T.L.C.', there is a song by Lehman: Lebowsky: C. Parker dating from 1960 (and translated as 'Tender loving *and* care'). Also with this title, there is a Motown song by Jones: Sawer: Jerome (1971), an instrumental by R.L. Martin: Norman Harris (1975); and a song by the Average White band and Alan Gorrie.

As 'Tender Lovin' Care' there is a song written by Brooks: Stillman (1966) and one written and performed by Ronnie Dyson (1983).

As 'Tender Loving Care', there is a song written by Mercer: Bright: Wilson, and recorded in 1966 by Nancy Wilson. It was also used as the title of an album by her.

It has also been suggested to me that 't.l.c.' was used in advertisements for BUPA, the medical insurance scheme, or for Nuffield Hospitals. Have I imagined it being used in washing powder ads, too – for Dreft perhaps? The *OED Supp.* recognizes the phrase as a colloquialism denoting, 'especially solicitous care such as is given by nurses' and cites the *Listener* (12 May 1977): 'It is in a nurse's nature and in her tradition to give the sick what is well called "TLC", "tender loving care", some constant little service to the sick.'

The earliest use of the phrase, in this sense, that I have come across occurs in the final chapter, 'T.L.C. TREATMENT', of Ian Fleming's *Goldfinger* (1959). James Bond says to Pussy Galore, 'All you need is a course of TLC.' 'What's TLC,' she asks. 'Short for Tender Loving Care Treatment,' Bond replies. 'It's what they write on most papers when a waif gets brought in to a children's clinic.'

Well, there's no phrase like a good phrase. In Shakespeare *2 King Henry VI* (III.ii.277/9) we read:

Commons. (Within): [ie a rabble off-stage] An answer from the King, or we will all break in!

King: Go, Salisbury, and tell them all from me,
I thank them for their tender loving care.

tenderness. See TRY A LITTLE VC 10DERNESS under BOAC TAKES GOOD CARE OF YOU.

ten-four! *Stock Phrase.* In the American TV cop series *Highway Patrol* (1955–9), Chief Dan Matthews (Broderick Crawford) was always bellowing this into his radio. It signifies agreement and conforms to the 'ten-code' of radio communication used by US police, especially from the 1960s onwards.

tennis, anyone? See under ANYONE FOR TENNIS?

terrible. See BOSS, BOSS . . . under *ITMA*.

terrific. See THE ——FULNESS IS ~ under YAROOOO; IT'S ~ under *EDUCATING ARCHIE*.

T.G.I.F. *Catch Phrase.* Short for 'Thank God It's Friday'. I heard first it in 1967 though it was current in the 1940s. It is amusing to see how broadcasters have shrunk from spelling it out when using it for Friday night programmes. Granada TV in Manchester had *At Last It's Friday* in 1968 and Capital Radio, *T.G.I.F.* in 1983. In the early 1970s, on the other hand, BBC TV did have *Thank God It's Sunday*, appropriately.

Compare P.O.E.T.S.' DAY.

Thames. See SET THE ~ ON FIRE.

thank. See AY THANG YEW under *BAND WAG-GON*.

thank you, music-lovers! *Stock Phrase.* The American musician Spike Jones (1911–64) specialized in comedy arrangements on radio, records and films from the late 1930s onwards. After massacring some well-known piece of music like 'The Dance of the Hours' he would come forward and say this.

thar. See THERE'S GOLD IN THEM ~ HILLS.

—— that almost got away. *Format Phrase > Cliché.* Based on 'This was the fish that almost got away'. A British film with the title *The One That Got Away* (about an escaped prisoner) was released in 1957.

—— that is ——, the. *Format Phrase > Cliché.* Portentousness-enabler. An advert for some old Alfred Hitchcock film shown in London (November 1983) ran thus: 'This is a unique opportunity to see these classic films and either re-live or experience for the first time the genius that is Hitchcock.'

Perhaps this use derives from the format used so notably by Edgar Allan Poe in *To Helen* (1831): 'The glory that was Greece/ And the grandeur that was Rome.'

that'll do nicely, sir. *Slogan > Catch Phrase.* A fawning line from an American Express TV ad of the late 1970s.

that man. See under *ITMA*.

that's all, folks! *Stock Phrase.* The concluding line – not spoken, but written on the screen – of *Merry Melodies*, the Warner Bros. cartoon series, from 1930. When Mel Blanc (1908–89), the voice behind so many cartoon characters, was asked for an epitaph, he plumped for the following 'in joined-up handwriting' – 'That's All, Folks!'

that spelled ——, the ——. *Cliché.* From the *Sun*, 15 October 1983: 'The Ding-Ding special that spelled love for Sid and Jan Parker will take a trip DOWN MEMORY LANE . . . to celebrate their 25th wedding anniversary. The happy couple will kiss and cuddle on the top deck of the No. 44 bus, just like they did when they were courting.'

that's Shell – that was! *Slogan.* For Shell petrol, from the early 1930s. Two one-headed men with the slogan 'That's Shell – that is!', current in 1929, were developed into one seemingly two-headed man (his head sweeping from left-profile to right) with the more widely-known slogan. A possibly apocryphal story is that the two-headed man was devised by

a member of the public called Horsfield, who received £100 for his trouble.

that's the way it crumbles, cookie-wise. *Catch Phrase.* Meaning 'that's the way it is, there's no escaping it'. Bartlett describes the basic 'that's the way the cookie crumbles' as an anonymous phrase from the 1950s. It was, however, given a memorable twist in Billy Wilder's film *The Apartment* (1960). The main characters make much use of the suffix '-wise', as in 'promotion-wise' and 'gracious-living-wise'. Then Miss Kubelik (Shirley MacLaine) says to C.C. Baxter (Jack Lemmon): 'Why can't I ever fall in love with somebody nice like you?' Replies Baxter: 'Yeah, well, that's the way it crumbles, cookie-wise.'

A joke translation of the original phrase – '*Sic biscuitus disintegrat*' – occurred in an Iris Murdoch novel, I believe, before 1978. A showbiz variant I heard in 1988 was 'That's the way the mop flops'.

that's what —— is all about. *Format Phrase > Cliché.* This appears most frequently in sporting contexts. The basic notion is 'Winning is what it's all about' (and never mind all that nonsense of the Olympic motto). Often ascribed to Vince Lombardi, coach and general manger of the Green Bay Packers pro-football team from 1959, in the form 'Winning isn't everything, it's the only thing', it was nevertheless said by John Wayne as a football coach in the 1953 movie *Trouble Along the Way*. President Nixon's notorious Committee to Re-Elect the President in 1972 had as its motto: 'Winning in politics isn't everything; it's the only thing'.

The format can handily be used in any sport – 'Whoever plays best is going to win . . . this is what the game is all about', Peter Purves, commentating on BBC TV *Championship Darts*, 22 September 1983 – and in other contexts, of course. 'That's what love is all about' is a line in the song 'The Love Bug Will Bite You' by Pinky Tomlin (1937).

. . . that's you and me. *Cliché*. Ingratiating way that some broadcasters adopt to involve the listener or viewer. Eg 'The Chancellor of the Exchequer today imposed a swingeing new tax on everybody whoever downed a well-earned pint, put a pony on a gee-gee, or lit up a Christmas cigar – that's you and me.'

that's your actual French. See under *ROUND THE HORNE*.

that was the —— that was. *Format Phrase*. The BBC TV satire show *That Was The Week That Was* (1962–3) launched this one. The programme's title was apparently modelled on THAT'S SHELL – THAT WAS!
Headline in the *Evening Standard* (25 January 1989) about a programme to mark the tenth anniversary of Mrs Thatcher's government: 'That Was the Ten Years, That Was'.

theatre. See FUNNY THING HAPPENED . . . ; DOCTOR GREASEPAINT WILL CURE ME.

——: the Movie. *Format Phrase*. I think the first film to be so labelled was *Abba: The Movie* in 1977. In these days of 'concepts' and 'merchandising' in pop music, perhaps the idea was to distinguish this product from 'the tour', 'the TV series', 'the book' and 'the album' (in 1978 'Abba: The Album' did indeed appear). The format has subsequently been used to poke fun at exploitation, self-promotion, and self-aggrandizement in certain quarters. For example, a Cambridge Footlights show in the mid-1980s was called *Ian Botham: The Movie*. In 1985, Michael Rogin, a professor of political science at Berkeley, California, entitled his exploration of President Reagan's (sometimes) unattributed borrowings of film-quotes, 'Ronald Reagan: The Movie'. Headline over an article in the *Observer* (30 April 1989) suggesting that a film would one day be made of a certain actress's life: 'Meryl Streep: The Movie?'

there. See ALL HUMAN LIFE IS ~; BECAUSE IT IS ~.

thereby. See AND ~ HANGS A TALE.

there is no alternative. *Slogan/Catch Phrase*. When asked for the origin of Margaret Thatcher's famously nannyish phrase in 1984, her then political secretary replied: 'I am not sure that the Prime Minister ever actually used the phrase . . . and my suspicion, shared by others, is that TINA was coined by those who were pressing for a change of policy.'
However, in 1986, I happened to stumble upon a report of a speech Mrs Thatcher made to the Conservative Women's Conference, on 21 May 1980, marking the end of her first year in office. Describing the harsh economic measures already set in train by her government, she said: 'There is no easy popularity in that, but I believe people accept *there is no alternative*.'

So, there, she *had* said it, and publicly, too. I don't know whether this was the first time – in fact, I think she may well have said it at some stage in 1979.

The acronym 'TINA', said to have been coined by Young Conservatives, was flourishing by the time of the Party Conference in September 1981.

A correspondent suggests that I compare it to an old Hebrew catch phrase '*ain breira*' ('there is no choice').

there'll be dancing in the streets tonight. *Cliché.* In journalism – to signify elation. Tom Stoppard in an extended parody of sports journalism in the play *Professional Foul* (1978) has: 'There'll be Czechs bouncing in the streets of Prague tonight as bankruptcy stares English football in the face.'

there'll never be another! *Stock Phrase.* Max Miller (1895–1963), 'The Cheeky Chappie', had stock phrases rather than phrases that caught on. **When I'm dead and gone, the game's finished!** was one. Rather on the same theme was ingratiating stuff like, 'Miller's the name, lady. There'll never be another!'

there's gold in them thar hills. *Saying.* Meaning 'there are opportunities in the way indicated'. Presumably this phrase was established in US gold-mining by the end of the nineteenth century. It seems to have had a resurgence in the 1930s/40s, probably through use in Western films. Frank Marvin wrote and performed a song with the title in (I think) the 1930s. A Laurel and Hardy short called *Them Thar Hills* appeared in 1934. The melodrama *Gold in the Hills* by J. Frank Davis has been performed

every season since 1936 by the Vicksburg Theatre Guild in Mississippi.

The phrase now has a jokey application to any enterprise which contains a hint of promise.

there's no answer to that! See under *MORECAMBE AND WISE SHOW.*

these are dynamite! *Cliché.* The sort of thing journalists think real people say, or which people say because journalists expect it of them. From the *Sun* (10 December 1984): 'Mr Little rushed to the Sun offices to study the photographs and said: "These are dynamite".'

these foolish things. *Catch Phrase.* Best known as the title of a popular song ('These foolish things/ Remind me of you', lyrics by Eric Maschwitz, 1936), picked up by Michael Sadleir for a book called *These Foolish Things* in 1937.

they all look the same in the dark. *Catch Phrase.* Contemptuous male view of women as sexual objects. Ovid in his *Ars Amatoria* says much the same thing more diplomatically: 'The dark makes every woman beautiful.'

they call/called/are calling ——. *Cliché.* Whoever 'they' may be, they certainly do a lot of it and are most helpful to journalists in search of a tag. Eg '[Of a mining disaster] . . . in what they are calling the South African Aberfan' (Martyn Lewis, ITN's *The Making of '81*); 'Alfredo Astiz drank free champagne in seat 9A of the executive suite on a British Caledonian DC10 flight to Rio yesterday. The man they call Captain Death was being returned to his homeland via Brazil' (*Daily*

Mail, 12 June 1982); 'They call it paradise. Now burnt-out cars litter the roads, some the tombs of drivers who could not beat the flames' (*The Times*, 19 February 1983); 'They called him [Bjorn Borg] "The Iceberg" ' (ITN report, 7 February 1989).

they came . . . *Cliché*. Of funeral journalism. The chief thing is to start with the word 'They'. From the opening of the *Observer* report on the funeral of Jennie Lee (27 November 1988): 'They scattered the ashes of a proud Scots lassie yesterday on a cold Welsh hillside . . .' But much better to put 'They came . . .' From *The Times* (11 April 1983): 'They came, 541 of them, across half a world [to the Falklands] to dedicate the war memorial on a treeless hillside above Blue Beach, where British forces first stepped ashore.' Also useful: 'They buried their own . . .'

they don't make —— like that any more. *Format Phrase*. From an *Independent* obituary (26 January 1989): ' "They don't make them like that any more" said Danny La Rue of Freddie Carpenter, a director who was equally at home with both the traditional and the modern musical.' From the *Guardian* (30 January 1989): 'Paying the keenest attention to the oil painting, when he delivered his judgement it was one that carried enormous authority. "They don't," he said, "make pigs like that any more".'

Especially applied to songs in the form, 'They don't write songs like that any more!' – to which the joke response is, 'Thank goodness!'

they laughed when I sat down at the piano, but when I started to play . . . ! *Slogan*. For the US School of Music piano tutor, from 1925. The copy underneath this headline includes the following: 'As the last notes of the Moonlight Sonata died away, the room resounded with a sudden roar of applause . . . Men shook my hand – wildly congratulated me – pounded me on the back in their enthusiasm! . . . And then I explained [how] I saw an interesting ad for the US School of Music . . .'

This ad gave rise to various jokes: 'They laughed when I sat down to play – someone had taken away the stool/ how did I know the bathroom door was open/ etc.' John Caples, the copywriter, also came up with, 'They grinned when the waiter spoke to me in French – but their laughter changed to amazement at my reply' (presumably for another client).

they're playing our tune, darling. *Catch Phrase*. I suppose this must come from romantic fiction when (presumably married and ageing) lovers hear a tune that makes them nostalgic. But I do not have any citations. All I can recall is a joke about the Queen saying it to Prince Philip when the National Anthem struck up. A musical *They're Playing Our Song* (by Marvin Hamlisch and Carole Bayer Sager) was presented in New York in 1979.

thing. See JUST ONE OF THOSE ~S; REAL ~.

things ain't what they used to be. *Saying > Catch Phrase*. The title of the Frank Norman/Lionel Bart's musical *Fings Ain't Wot They Used T'be* (1959) – which popularized an already existing catch phrase in a particular form – gave rise to one of the nicest juxtaposition jokes I have spotted. In an edition of the *Liverpool Echo* of c 1960, an advertisement for the Royal Court Theatre announced:

THIS WEEK & NEXT
THEATRE CLOSED FOR ALTERATIONS
Box Office Now Open for
Lionel Bart's Smash Hit Musical
'FINGS AIN'T WOT THEY USED T'BE'

It should be remembered that a song by Mercer Ellington and Ted Persons, published in 1939, was called 'Things Ain't What They Used To Be'.

things I've done for England, the. *Catch Phrase.* In Sir Alexander Korda's film *The Private Life of Henry VIII* (1933), Charles Laughton as the King is just about to get into bed with one of his many wives when, alluding to her ugliness, he sighs: 'The things I've done for England.' The screenplay was written by Lajos Biro and Arthur Wimperis.

This became a catch phrase, to be used ironically when confronted with any unpleasant task. In 1979, Prince Charles on a visit to Hong Kong sampled curried snake meat and, with a polite nod towards his forebear, exclaimed, 'Boy, the things I do for England . . .'

thinking man's/person's/woman's ——, the. *Format Phrase.* As long ago as 1931, Pebeco toothpaste in the US was being promoted as 'The Toothpaste for Thinking People'. However, I think it was Frank Muir who set the more recent trend (now almost a cliché) when he talked of Joan Bakewell as 'the thinking man's crumpet'. Much later, Chantal Cuer, a French-born broadcaster in Britain, said she had

been described as 'the thinking man's croissant'.

And how about these for originality? 'Frank Delaney – the thinking man's Russell Harty (*Sunday Times*, 16 October 1983); 'Frank Delaney – the thinking man's Terry Wogan' (*Guardian*, 17 October 1983); 'the thinking woman's Terry Wogan, TV's Frank Delaney' (*Sunday Express*, 30 October 1983).

And still it goes on. Janet Suzman, the actress, tells me she has been described as 'the thinking man's Barbara Windsor'. From the *Independent* (28 January 1989): 'One member of the Government said: "[Kenneth Clarke's] the thinking man's lager lout".' From the *Observer* (29 January 1989): 'It was chaired by Nick Ross, the thinking woman's newspaper boy.'

Also, from the *Observer* (13 September 1987): 'His performance as a trendy and hung-up LA painter in *Heartbreakers* made him the thinking woman's West Coast crumpet' – which brings us back more or less to where we started.

In February 1989, the American magazine *Spy* drew up a long list of examples of American variations on the theme: *Hobbies* magazine in 1977 described Descartes as 'The thinking man's philosopher'; *Boating Magazine* (1984) described the Mansfield TDC portable toilet as 'the thinking man's head'; *Horizon* (1965) called Lake Geneva, 'the thinking man's lake'; and, *Esquire* (1986) called actor William Hurt, 'the thinking man's asshole'.

thinks . . . thanks to Horlicks. *Slogan.* During the 1950s, Horlicks was promoted in comic-strip sagas, emphasizing the refreshing qualities of the milk drink for tired housewives, run-down executives, etc. Customarily, these would end with the hero/heroine offering thanks within a think bubble. But the idea was an old one. 'Thinks . . . thanks to *Radio Times*' was running in the 1930s.

thirteen years of Tory misrule. *Slogan* – or, rather, political *Catch Phrase* with the force of a slogan. Uttered in the run-up to the 1964 General Election, which Labour won, it may be said to have had some effect. Also in the form 'thirteen wasted years', with which compare Churchill's remark about 'four wasted years' (to Denis Kelly, in private conversation, 1949 – quoted in Martin Gilbert's *Never Despair*).

thirty-five years! See under BEYOND OUR KEN.

this ad insults women. *Slogan*. Usually attached to the offending sexist ad with a sticker, this is a comment from the women's movement in the 1970s. I recall an Elliott shoe shop ad in 1979 which showed a pair of models wearing woollen thigh boots – upon which someone had written 'This insults and degrades sheep'.

this great movement of ours. *Catch Phrase*. A Labour Party phrase – or so it was noted in the early 1980s. Sometimes abbreviated to 'THIGMOU'.

this has restored my faith in British justice. *Cliché*. What members of the public say, when prompted by journalists, after winning a court case.

this is a free country. (or **it's a . . .**) *Catch Phrase*. Partridge/*Slang* dates this as 'late C19' and calls it 'expressive of tolerance (or apathy depending on points of view').

this is beautiful downtown Burbank. See under LAUGH-IN.

this is Funf speaking! *Catch Phrase*. Spoken sideways into a glass tumbler on *ITMA*, this phrase was 'the embodiment of the nation's spy neurosis' (according to the producer, Francis Worsley). The first time Funf appeared was in the second edition of the show on 26 September 1939, just after the outbreak of the Second World War. Initially, he said, 'Dees ees Foonf, your favourite shpy!' Jack Train recalled that when Worsley was searching for a name for the spy, he overheard his six-year-old son, Roger, trying to count in German: '*Ein, zwei, drei, vier, funf*' – and that's where he always got stuck.

For a while it became a craze to start phone conversations with the words.

this is the city. See under DRAGNET.

this is/ was war. *Cliché*. Meaning 'this is very serious, and justifies the particular course adopted'. Wilson Goode, Mayor of Philadelphia, defending a police fire-bombing raid that went disastrously wrong: 'This was not child's play. This was war' (*Time*, 15 May 1985). Front page headline from the *Daily Express*, 24 May 1985: 'Drug menace: now it's WAR'. After the Heysel football stadium disaster: 'Said a Belgian Red Cross rescue worker: "This is not sport. This is war" ' (*Time*, 10 June 1985). Sign outside the Las Vegas Hilton promoting a big fight (February 1989): 'THIS TIME IT'S WAR. TYSON VS. BRUNO'.

this is where we came in. *Catch Phrase*. Meaning 'I am/you are beginning to repeat myself/yourself. This is where we should stop whatever it is we are doing.' From the remark uttered in cinemas when continuous performances were the order of the day – from the 1920s to the 1970s.

this must be ——. See IF IT'S ——, ~ ——.

this one will run and run. *Cliché*. One of *Private Eye*'s collection of phrases – this one (said of anything, but especially of a political dispute) was originally the sort of extract from theatrical criticism that managements like to display outside the theatre to promote a show. Said originally to have derived from a review by Fergus Cashin of the *Sun*.

this play what I have wrote. See under *MORECAMBE AND WISE SHOW*.

this thing is bigger than both of us. *Catch Phrase* > *Cliché*. ('This thing' = 'our love'.) A whopping film cliché which I can hardly believe was ever uttered – at least, I am unable to give a citation. All I have examples of is the ironic use of the phrase. I am told that Milton Berle popularized it, satirically, in his American radio and TV shows in the US of the 1940s and 50s. In Britain, Frank Muir and Denis Norden did a similar job in their scripts for radio's TAKE IT FROM HERE (1947–58). For example, in this extract from their *Hamlet* with Hollywood subtitles: 'Oh, dear Ophelia, I have not art to reckon my groans but that I love thee best ("DON'T FIGHT THIS THING, KID, IT'S BIGGER THAN BOTH OF US.").'

In the 1976 re-make of *King Kong*, with the giant ape brushing against the side of the house they are in, Jeff Bridges as 'Jack Prescott' says to Jessica Lange as 'Dwan', 'He's bigger than both of us, know what I mean?'

thought. See I ~ —— UNTIL I DISCOVERED ——; JUST WHEN YOU ~ IT WAS SAFE . . .

thousand. See DEATH OF A ~ CUTS; CAST OF ~S.

thousand points of light, a. *Slogan* – or, rather, a political *Catch Phrase* written for George Bush by Peggy Noonan in the 1988 presidential election campaign. He used it on the campaign trail and in his acceptance speech for the Republican nomination ('I will keep America moving forward, always forward – for a better America, for an endless enduring dream and a thousand points of light'). On the eve of his inauguration in January 1989, a crowd of 40,000 people in Washington switched on pen-torches (handed out beforehand) to dramatize the phrase.

But what did it mean? It was said to symbolize individual endeavour, voluntary charity efforts, across the country. In June 1989, President Bush announced details for his 'Points of Light Programme', costing $25m, to encourage a voluntary crusade to fight poverty, drugs and homelessness. But even Mr Bush never seemed too sure. On one occasion, he called it '1000 points of life'. Herblock, the cartoonist, drew a drunk at a bar pledging his vote to Bush because he had promised '1000 pints of Lite'.

Perhaps it was supposed to echo Shakespeare, *The Merchant of Venice* (V.1.90): 'How far that little candle throws his beams!/ So shines a good deed in a naughty world.' Light often comes in thousands: 'It was but for an instant that I seemed to struggle with a thousand mill-weirs and a thousand flashes of light' (Charles Dickens, *Great Expectations*, 1860–1, Chapter 54). At the time of writing it is impossible to say how much more life the Bush phrase has in it.

three most useless things in the world, the. *Saying*. Paul Beale's version in Partridge/*Slang* has the definition: 'The Pope's balls, a nun's cunt – and a vote of thanks'. He dates this 1950. In about 1971 I recall hearing (from a well-known comic actor) the showbiz version which is 'a nun's tits, the Pope's balls, and a rave review in the *Stage* [the trade paper]'.

thrilling days of yesteryear. See HI-YO, SILVER!

throw in one's chips. See CASH ONE'S CHIPS.

thus. See 'TWAS EVER ~.

thus far shalt thou go and no further. *Saying/Catch Phrase*. Hearing the Rev. Ian Paisley, the Ulster loyalist, booming this out in 1974 (in the form, 'So far and no further'), I was not entirely surprised to find that the apparent 'first use' seemed also to lie in an Anglo-Irish context. Charles Stewart Parnell, the champion of Irish Home Rule, said in Cork in 1885: 'No man has a right to fix the boundary of the march of a nation; no man has a right to say to his country, Thus far shalt thou go and no further.'
On the other hand, George Farquhar, the (Irish-born) playwright has this in

The Beaux' Stratagem (1707): 'And thus far I am a captain, and no farther' (Act III, Scene 2). And then again, the Book of Job 38:11 has: 'Hitherto shalt thou come, but no further: and here shall thy proud waves be stayed.'

tidy. See KEEP BRITAIN ~.

tiger. See PUT A ~ IN YOUR TANK.

time. See ANY ~ . . . ; AT THIS MOMENT IN ~; MANY, MANY ~S under *ROUND THE HORNE*; ONCE UPON A ~; ONLY ~ WILL TELL.

time has passed by ——. *Catch Phrase > Cliché*. Probably from travel-writing, film travelogues. Memorably completed in the commentary to Muir & Norden's 'Bal-ham, Gateway to the South' (*c* 1948): 'Time has passed by this remote corner. So shall we.'

time marches on. *Catch Phrase/Stock Phrase > Slogan*. 'Time . . . Marches On' was a line used in – and to promote – the 'March of Time' news-documentary-dramas which ran on American radio for fourteen years from 1931. The programmes were sponsored by *Time* magazine. I'm not sure to what extent the phrase existed before then as a way of saying, 'It's getting on, time is moving forward . . .'

Times, The. See TOP PEOPLE TAKE ~.

tiny. See OUT OF YOUR ~ CHINESE MIND.

tired. See SICK AND ~

tired and emotional, to be. *Idiom*. Meaning 'drunk'. A pleasant euphemism, ideally suited to British newspapers which have to operate under libel laws effectively preventing any direct statement of a person's fondness for the bottle. The expression 't. and e.' (to which it is sometimes abbreviated) is said to have arisen when *Private Eye* printed a spoof Foreign Office memo suggesting it was a useful way of describing the antics of George Brown when he was Foreign Secretary (1966–8). An *Eye* cover showed him gesticulating while Harold Wilson explained to General de Gaulle: '*George est un peu fatigué, votre Majesté.*' Ironically, there was never any question that Brown *did* get drunk.

I am not convinced that *Private Eye* actually coined the phrase, though it undoubtedly popularized it. It has been suggested that a BBC spokesman said of Brown 'He was very tired and emotional' after the much criticized appearance he made on TV on the night of President Kennedy's death in November 1963. In fact, it was ITV Brown appeared on and I cannot trace the remark, even if it was made.

tiswas, all of a. *Idiom*. Meaning 'confused, in a state'. This might be from an elaboration of 'tizz' or 'tizzy' and I suspect there is a hint of 'dizziness' trying to get in somewhere. But no one really knows. The acronym 'Today Is Saturday, Wear A Smile' seems not to have anything to do with the meaning of the word and to have been imposed later. The acronym-slogan was the apparent reason for the title *Tiswas* being given to a children's ITV show of the 1970s, famous for its bucket-of-water-throwing and general air of mayhem. Broadcast on Saturday mornings, its atmosphere was certainly noisy and confused.

tit. See I HAVEN'T BEEN SO HAPPY SINCE . . . ; MANNERS PLEASE, ~S FIRST . . . ; TELL-TALE ~.

tit, tote and television. *Saying*. In the days when newspapers were still produced in Fleet Street, tabloid hacks would remind themselves that the chief preoccupations were encapsulated in this phrase (though I did not hear it myself until 1984).

An alternative recipe that I heard a year later is: 'Bosoms, QPR [Queen's Park Rangers football team] and "WHERE ARE THEY NOW?" '

In 1978, Derek Jameson, then editor-in-chief of Express Newspapers (though he denied saying it) was quoted as remarking of the launch of the *Daily Star*: 'It'll be all tits, bums, QPR and roll your own fags.'

t.l.c. See TENDER LOVING CARE.

toaster. See FEW VOUCHERS SHORT OF A POP-UP ~.

to boldly go where no man has gone before. See under BEAM ME UP, SCOTTY!

today. See I DIDN'T GET WHERE I AM ~.

today is the first day of the rest of your life. *Slogan*. Attributed to one Charles Dederich, founder of anti-heroin centres in the US, in *c* 1969, this has also occurred in the form 'Tomorrow is etc' as a wall slogan.

'Today Is the First Day of the Rest of My Life' was apparently sung in a late 1960s musical *The Love Match*.

today ——, tomorrow ——. *Slogan >
Format Phrase.* A foreign-language slogan occasionally impinges upon English
speech. Such a construction capable of
innumerable variations is 'Today ——,
tomorrow the world!'

The concept can be glimpsed in embryo
in the slogan for the National Socialist
Press in Germany of the early 1930s:
'*Heute Presse der Nationalsozialisten,
Morgen Presse der Nation*' [Today the
press of the Nazis, tomorrow the nation's
press]. This reaches its final form in
'*Heute gehört uns Deutschland – morgen die ganze Welt*' [Today Germany belongs to us – tomorrow the whole world].
Although John Colville in *The Fringes of
Power* states that by 3 September 1939,
Hitler 'had already . . . proclaimed that
"Today Germany is ours; tomorrow the
whole world",' I have not found an
example of Hitler actually saying it. However, in *Mein Kampf* (1925) he had said:
'If the German people, in their historic
development, had possessed tribal unity
like other nations, the German Reich
today would be the master of the entire
world.'

The phrase seems to have come from
the chorus of a song in the Hitler Youth
'songbook':

  *Wir werden weiter marschieren
  Wenn alles in Scherben fällt
  Denn heute gehört uns Deutschland
  Und morgen die ganze Welt.*

Which may be roughly translated as:

  We shall keep marching on
  Even if everything breaks into frag-
  ments,
  For today Germany belongs to us
  And tomorrow the whole world.

Another version replaces the second
line with '*Wenn Scheiße vom Himmel

fällt' [When shit from Heaven falls]. Sir
David Hunt tells me he recalls hearing
the song in 1933 or possibly 1934.

By the outbreak of the Second World
War, it was sufficiently well-known, as
John Osborne recalled in *A Better Class
of Person* (1981), for an English school
magazine to be declaring: 'Now soon it
will be our turn to take a hand in the
destinies of Empire. Today, scholars; tomorrow, the Empire.' In the 1941 British
film *Forty-Ninth Parallel*, Eric Portman
as a German U-boat commander gets to
say, 'Today, Europe . . . tomorrow the
whole world!'

So common is the construction now
that a New York graffito (reported in
1974) stated: 'Today Hollywood, tomorrow the world', and one from El Salvador
(March 1982) ran: '*Ayer Nicaragua, hoy
El Salvador, mañana Guatemala!*' [Yes-
terday Nicaragua, today El Salvador, tomorrow Guatemala!]. The *Guardian* (6
July 1982) carried an advertisement with
the unwieldy headline: 'Self-managing
Socialism: Today, France – Tomorrow,
the World?'

A variation: from the black MP Paul
Boateng's victory speech in the Brent
South constituency (June 1987): 'Brent
South today – Soweto tomorrow!' See
also, for a 1932 example, LIFE BEGINS AT
FORTY.

told. See I THINK WE SHOULD BE ~.

tomorrow. See AND THE NEXT *TONIGHT* WILL
BE ~ NIGHT; EAT, DRINK AND BE MERRY . . . ;
TODAY ——, ~ ——.

tomorrow belongs to me/us. *Slogan.*
Has this ever been used as a political
slogan, either as 'Tomorrow belongs to

me' or 'to us'? What one can say is that in the musical *Cabaret* (1968, filmed 1972), Fred Ebb (words) and John Kander (music) wrote a convincing pastiche of a Hitler Youth song:

The babe in his cradle is closing his eyes, the blossom embraces the bee,
But soon says a whisper, 'Arise, arise',
Tomorrow belongs to me.
O Fatherland, Fatherland, show us the sign your children have waited to see,
The morning will come when the world is mine, Tomorrow belongs to me.

The idea seems definitely to have been current in Nazi Germany. A popular song, '*Jawohl, mein Herr*', featured in the 1943 episode of the German film chronicle *Heimat* (1984), includes the line, 'For from today, the world belongs to us'.

The nearest the slogan appears to have been actually used by (an admittedly right-wing) youth organization is referred to in this report from the *Guardian* (30 October 1987): 'Contra leader Adolfo Calero . . . was entertained to dinner on Wednesday by Oxford University's Freedom Society, a clutch of hoorays . . . A coach-load of diners . . . got "hog-whimpering" drunk . . . and songs like "Tomorrow Belongs To Us" and "Miner, Cross that Picket Line" were sung on the return coach trip.'

The same paper, reporting a meeting of the SDP leader, Dr David Owen, on 1 February 1988 noted: 'Down, sit down, he eventually gestured; his eyes saying Up, stay up. It reminded you of nothing so much as a Conservative Party conference in one of its most Tomorrow-belongs-to-us moods.'

It is perhaps an obvious slogan for a young people's political organization. I

have a note of something once said by Saint-Simon: 'The future belongs to us. In order to do things one must be enthusiastic.'

tongue. See OLD AS MY ~ . . .

Toni. See WHICH TWIN HAS THE ~?

tonight. See NOT ~, JOSEPHINE; THERE'LL BE DANCING IN THE STREETS ~.

Tonight. See AND THE NEXT ~ . . .

too clever by half. *Idiom.* To say that someone is 'too clever by half' is to show that you think they are more clever than wise, and are overreaching themselves. As such, this is a fairly common idiom. However, the most notable political use of the phrase was by the 5th Marquess of Salisbury (1893–1972), a prominent Conservative, about another such, Iain Macleod. In a speech to the House of Lords in 1961, he said: 'The present Colonial Secretary has been too clever by half. I believe he is a very fine bridge player. It is not considered immoral, or even bad form to outwit one's opponents at bridge. It almost seems to me as if the Colonial Secretary, when he abandoned the sphere of bridge for the sphere of politics, brought his bridge technique with him.'

The remark seems to run in the family. The 3rd Marquess had anticipated him in a debate on the Irish Church Resolutions in the House of Commons on 30 March 1868, when he said of an amendment moved by Disraeli: 'I know that with a certain number of Gentlemen on this side of the House this Amendment is popular. I have heard it spoken of as being very clever. It is clever, Sir; it is too clever by half.'

Rodney Ackland's version of an Alexander Ostrovsky play was presented as *Too Clever by Half* at the Old Vic, London, in 1988. Previously, the Russian title had been translated as *The Diary of a Scoundrel* and *Even the Wise Can Err, Even a Wise Man Stumbles*, and *Enough Stupidity in Every Wise Man*.

Of Dr Jonathan Miller, the polymath, in the mid-1970s, it was said, 'He's too clever by three-quarters.'

too little, too late. *Slogan.* The American Professor Allan Nevins wrote in an article in *Current History* (May 1935): 'The former allies had blundered in the past by offering Germany too little and offering even that too late, until finally Nazi Germany had become a menace to all mankind.' That was where the phrase began. On 13 March 1940, the former Prime Minister David Lloyd George said in the House of Commons: 'It is the old trouble – too late. Too late with Czechoslovakia, too late with Poland, certainly too late with Finland. It is always too late, or too little, or both.'

From there the phrase passed into more general use, though usually political. From the *Notting Hill & Paddington Recorder* (25 January 1989): 'Junior Transport Minister, Peter Bottomley, came to West London last week to unveil plans for a £250m. relief road that will cut a swathe through the heart of the area . . . But Hammersmith and Fulham councillors are furious about the government consultation exercise which they claim is "too little too late".'

From the *Guardian* (30 January 1989): 'The Home Office is preparing a video to warn prisoners of the dangers [of AIDs] – but is it too little, too late?'

top. See OVER THE ~.

top people take *The Times. Slogan.* In the mid-1950s, *The Times* was shedding circulation, the end of post-war newsprint rationing was in sight, and an era of renewed competition in Fleet Street was about to begin. In 1954, the paper's agency, the London Press Exchange, commissioned a survey to discover people's attitudes to 'The Thunderer'. They chiefly found it dull, but the management was not going to change anything, least of all allow contributors to be identified by name. The paper would have to be promoted for what it was. A pilot campaign in provincial newspapers included one ad showing a top hat and pair of gloves with the slogan 'Men who make opinion read *The Times*'.

It was not the London Press Exchange but an outsider who finally encapsulated that superior view in a memorable way. G.H. Saxon Mills was one of the old school of advertising copywriters. But he was out of a job when he bumped into Stanley Morison of *The Times*. As a favour, Mills was asked to produce a brochure for visitors to the paper's offices. When finished, it contained a series of people who were supposed to read the paper – a barrister, a trade-union official and so on. Each was supported by the phrase, 'Top People take *The Times*'.

The idea was adopted for a more public promotional campaign and first appeared on posters during 1957, running into immediate criticism of its snob-appeal. But sales went up and, however toe-curling it may have been, the slogan won attention for the paper and was allowed to run on into the early 1960s.

Tory. See THIRTEEN YEARS OF ~ MISRULE.

tote. See TIT, ~ AND TELEVISION.

touch of hello folks and what about the workers, a. See under *BAND WAGGON*; WHAT ABOUT THE WORKERS?

touch of the ——, a. See under DODGY!

touchpaper. See LIGHT THE BLUE ~ . . . under *BAND WAGGON*.

tough. See WHEN THE GOING GETS ~ . . .

tour. See MAGICAL MYSTERY ~.

train. See AGE OF THE TRAIN under WE'RE GETTING THERE.

train, put it on the. See under LET'S —— AND SEE IF ——.

travel. See HAVE GUN WILL ~.

trick or treat? *Catch Phrase*. One of the least welcome imports to Britain from the US in recent years has been the Hallowe'en custom of children, suitably dressed up, knocking on the doors of complete strangers and demanding a 'trick or treat' – ie that the house owners should hand over some small present (sweets, money) or have a trick played on them (a message written on the front door in shaving foam, for example). Fairly harmless in essence, the practice soon led to horror stories reaching the UK of children playing 'tricks' which did real damage and of their being given poisoned sweets as 'treats'.

The American origins of the custom seem somewhat obscure (*OED Supp.* does not find the phrase before 1947). In the North of England, the traditional Mischief Night may have given rise to the same sort of demands, and may also have given rise to the jingle ending:

If you haven't got a penny, a ha-penny will do,
If you haven't got a ha'penny, your door's going through

– though, on the other hand, that appears to be a version of 'Christmas is coming'. As I write (January 1989), an ITV quiz has just been launched called *Trick or Treat* which aims to do one or the other to its contestants.

trip. See CLUNK, CLICK, EVERY ~.

trolley. See OFF ONE'S ~.

trowel. See LAY IT ON WITH A ~.

truckin'. See KEEP ON ~.

true, O king! *Catch Phrase*. When I have made an obvious statement, perhaps even a pompous one, my wife has a way of saying to me, 'True, O King!' I wondered where she had picked up this habit until one day I happened to see an old film of Charles Laughton indulging in a public reading from the Bible, as he was latterly wont to do. He was telling the story of Nebuchadnezzar and the gentlemen who were cast into the burning fiery furnace. 'Did not we cast three men bound into the midst of fire?' Nebuchadnezzar asks (Daniel 3:24). 'They answered and said unto the king, True, O king.'

The nearest Shakespeare gets is the ironical ' "True"? O God!' in *Much Ado About Nothing* (IV.i.68), though he has any number of near misses like 'true, my liege', 'too true, my lord' and 'true, noble prince.'

Just to show that my wife is not alone – Mrs H. Joan Langdale of Tunbridge Wells wrote to me in June 1988 to say, 'My father, a Classical Scholar and an Anglican priest, used to use your wife's quotation "True, O King!" and always added, "Live for ever".'

trumpet. See BLOW ONE'S OWN ~.

trust. See IN GOD WE ~ . . .

truth. See ECONOMICAL WITH THE ~; ~, JUSTICE AND THE AMERICAN WAY under *SUPERMAN*; MOMENT OF ~.

try. See I'LL ~ ANYTHING ONCE.

try a little VC 10derness. See under BOAC TAKES GOOD CARE OF YOU.

T.T.F.N. See under *ITMA*.

Tunbridge Wells. See DISGUSTED, ~.

tune. See TURN ON, ~ IN . . . ; THEY'RE PLAYING OUR ~.

tunnel. See LIGHT AT THE END OF THE ~.

tuppence coloured. See PENNY PLAIN . . .

turned out nice. See IT'S ~ AGAIN!

turn on, tune in, drop out. *Slogan.* 'Tune in to my values, reject those of your parents, turn on [drug] yourself; deal with your problems and those of society by running away from them' – this was the meaning of the hippie philosophy as encapsulated in a slogan by one of the movement's gurus, Dr Timothy Leary (*b* 1920). It was used as the title of a lecture by him in 1967, and the theme was explored further in his book *The Politics of Ecstasy*. I believe that more recently Leary has taken to attributing the origin of the phrase to Marshall McLuhan.

A joke variant of what was also known as 'the LSD motto', was: 'Turn on, tune in, drop dead'.

turn/roll over in one's grave, to. *Idiom.* Meaning that whichever dead person was likely to do this would be appalled by something that has just happened or been proposed. Mencken has 'It is enough to make —— turn over in his grave' as an 'English saying, not recorded before the nineteenth century'.

In about 1976, one of the idiocies attributed to President Gerald Ford was, 'If Abraham Lincoln was alive today, he'd be turning in his grave.'

tutti-frutti. *Idiom.* Meaning 'all the fruits' in Italian, this phrase was first applied early in the nineteenth century in the US to ice cream containing bits of various chopped-up fruits. Then it became the name of a proprietary brand of fruit-flavoured chewing gum.

More recently, it has been immortalized as the title of a rock'n'roll number written and sung by Little Richard (from 1957). Alas, the lyrics are impenetrable and almost certainly have nothing to do with ice cream or chewing gum.

'twas ever thus. *Catch Phrase.* An exclamation meaning almost the same as the more modern 'So what's new?' It does not occur in Shakespeare or the Bible. In fact, the only examples I have turned up so far are: as the first line of 'Disaster' by C.S. Calverley (*d* 1884): ''Twas ever thus from childhood's hour!' (This is a parody of lines from Thomas Moore's 'The Fire Worshippers' in *Lalla Rookh* (1817): 'Oh! ever thus from childhood's hour!'); and, as the title, ''Twas Ever Thus' given to the parody of the same poem by Henry S. Leigh (1837–83). His version begins, 'I never rear'd a young gazelle.'

twelve good men and true. *Saying.* 'It is a maxim of English law that legal memory begins with the accession of Richard I in 1189 . . . with the establishment of royal courts, giving the same justice all over the country, the old diversity of local law was rapidly broken down, and a law common to the whole land and to all men soon took its place . . . The truth of [witnesses'] testimony [was] weighed not by the judge but by twelve "good men and true"' (Winston Churchill, *A History of the English-Speaking Peoples*, Vol. 1.)

I think there are two issues here, and perhaps the twelve is an ancillary to the phrase 'good men and true'. Why are there twelve jurymen, I wonder? Because that was the number of Christ's disciples, the tribes of Israel, the signs of the zodiac? As for the rest, 'Are you good men and true' occurs on its own in Shakespeare's *Much Ado About Nothing* (III.iii.1). Dogberry puts the question,

and being a constable would naturally use legal terminology.

twelve o'clock in London. See under FAMILY FAVOURITES.

twentieth century. See DRAGGED KICKING AND SCREAMING . . .

twenty things you didn't know about ——. *Format Phrase.* Derived from a regular *Sun* feature of the 1980s (said to have been devised by Wendy Henry) in which trivia is displayed about celebrities. From the *Independent* (24 April 1989): '20 Things You Didn't Know About Mrs T.'

twin. See WHICH ~ HAS THE TONI?

Twinkletoes. See HELLO, IT'S ME, ~ under *EDUCATING ARCHIE*.

twist slowly, slowly in the wind, (to allow someone to). *Idiom.* From the *Guardian* (28 January 1989): 'The foreign press observed with admiration the way President Bush stressed in words that he was not ditching the beleaguered Mikhail Gorbachev by playing his China card, while making it clear he was doing exactly that, and leaving the Soviet leader to twist a little longer in the wind.'

Richard Nixon's henchmen may have acted wrongly and, for much of the time, spoken sleazily. Occasionally, however, they minted political phrases that have lingered on. John D. Ehrlichman (*b* 1925), Nixon's Assistant for Domestic Affairs until he was forced to resign over Watergate in 1973, came up with one saying that caught people's imagination. In a telephone conversation with John

Dean (Counsel to the President) on 7/8 March 1973 he was speaking about Patrick Gray (Acting Director of the FBI). Gray's nomination to take over the FBI post had been withdrawn by Nixon during Judiciary Committee hearings – though Gray had not been told of this. Ehrlichman said: 'I think we ought to let him hang there. Let him twist slowly, slowly in the wind.'

2–4–6–8, who do we appreciate?/ ——. *Format Phrase.* This widely-used chant was popularized in the *GOON SHOW.* In *c*

1954, for example, members of the Wallace Greenslade Fan Club [he was one of the show's announcers] had to cry: '2–4–6–8, who do we appreciate? GREENSLADE!'

Compare, '2–4–6–8, gay is just as good as straight, 3–5–7–9, lesbians are mighty fine' – a chant of the Gay Liberation Front in the 1970s.

twopence coloured. See PENNY PLAIN . . .

two-way family favourite. See under - *FAMILY FAVOURITES.*

U

Ugandan. See DISCUSSING ~ AFFAIRS.

ugly. See SEX REARS ITS ~ HEAD.

ullo, ullo, ullo. See under *TAKE IT FROM HERE*.

unacceptable face of ——, the. *Format Phrase*. In 1973, it was revealed that a former Tory Cabinet minister, Duncan Sandys, had been paid £130,000 in compensation for giving up his £50,000 a year consultancy with the Lonrho company. The money was to be paid, quite legally, into an account in the Cayman Islands to avoid British tax. This kind of activity did not seem appropriate when the Government was promoting a counter-inflation policy. Replying to a question from Jo Grimond MP in the House of Commons on 15 May, Edward Heath, the Prime Minister, created a format phrase which has been used to describe almost anything. He said, 'It is the unpleasant and unacceptable face of capitalism, but one should not suggest that the whole of British industry consists of practices of this kind.'

unaccustomed as I am to public speaking. *Catch Phrase > Cliché*. On 26 July 1897, Winston Churchill made his first political speech at a Primrose League gathering near Bath: 'If it were pardonable in any speaker to begin with the well worn and time honoured apology, "Unaccustomed as I am to public speaking", it would be pardonable in my case, for the honour I am enjoying at this moment of addressing an audience of my fellow-countrymen and women is the first honour of the kind I have ever received.'

It is somehow reassuring that even an orator of future greatness should have fallen back on the dreadful cliché to begin his first effort. I wonder how long it had really been used as a speech-maker's introductory gambit?

Opening a Red Cross bazaar at Oxford, Noël Coward once began: 'Desperately *accustomed* as I am to public speaking . . .'

uncle. See BOB'S YOUR ~!; I'M A MONKEY'S ~.

under. See UP AND ~; KEEP IT ~ YOUR HAT.

undersold. See NEVER KNOWINGLY ~.

university of life, the. See under SCHOOL OF HARD KNOCKS.

unknown. See JOURNEY INTO THE ~.

unpunished. See NO GOOD DEED GOES ~.

unturned. See LEAVE NO STONE ~.

up. See ~ A BIT under BERNIE, THE BOLT!; SOMEONE ~ THERE LIKES ME.

up and down the country. See under SPIRIT OF ——.

up and under. *Stock Phrase.* This is a rugby football term for a short, high kick which sends the ball high in the air enabling the kicker and his team-mates to run forward and regain possession of the ball. But to TV viewers it was inseparably linked to the commentator Eddie Waring (1909–86). He broadcast commentaries, in his distinctive and highly imitable voice, for twenty years before he retired

in 1981. Another of his expressions was **an early bath** – for a player being sent off the field early.

up the wooden hill to Bedfordshire. *Idiom.* Originally a nursery euphemism, I think this has become part of grown-up 'golf-club slang', as someone once termed it – ie a conversational cliché. Sir Hugh Casson and Joyce Grenfell included it in their *Nanny Says* (1972), together with 'Come on, up wooden hill, down sheet lane'. 'Up the Wooden Hill to Bedfordshire' was the title of the first song recorded by Vera Lynn, in 1936. The 'bed – fordshire' joke occurs in a synopsis of *Ali Baba and the Forty Thieves; or, Harlequin and the Magic Donkey* staged at the Alexandra Theatre, Liverpool, in 1868. Indeed, as so often, Swift found it even earlier. In *Polite Conversation* (1738), the Colonel says, 'I'm going to the Land of Nod.' Neverout replies: 'Faith, I'm for *Bedfordshire.*' But then again, the poet Charles Cotton had used it in 1665.

up, up and away. See under *SUPERMAN.*

upwards. See ONWARDS AND ~!

us. See IS HE ONE OF ~?

used car. See WOULD YOU BUY A ~ . . .

useless. See THREE MOST ~ THINGS IN THE WORLD; ~ AS A CHOCOLATE KETTLE under AS BUSY AS . . .

usual. See BUSINESS AS ~.

vague. See DON'T BE ~ . . .

van. See FOLLOW THAT TAXI!

varieties. See HEINZ 57 ~.

vegetable. See ANIMAL, ~ OR MINERAL.

venture. See NOTHING ~.

very interesting . . . but stupid! See under *LAUGH-IN*.

vicarage tea-party. See LIKE A ~.

victory. See DIG FOR ~.

vital. See IT'S ABSOLUTELY ~ . . .

vouchers. See FEW ~ SHORT OF A POP-UP TOASTER.

waiting. See ACCIDENT ~ TO HAPPEN.

wake up at the back there! See under *TAKE IT FROM HERE*.

wakey-wakey! *Stock Phrase/Catch Phrase. The Billy Cotton Band Show* ran on radio and TV for over twenty years. For one seven-year period it was broadcast on radio without a break for fifty-two weeks of the year. First would come a fanfare, then Billy Cotton's cry (without any 'rise and shine') would be followed by a brisk, noisy rendering of 'Somebody Stole My Gal'. The programme was first broadcast on 6 February 1949 at 10.30 am. Because of this unsocial hour, rehearsals had to begin at 8.45 – not the best time to enthuse a band which had just spent six days on the road. 'Oi, come on,' said Cotton, on one occasion, 'Wakey-wakey!' It worked, and eventually led to such a cheerful atmosphere that the producer said the show might as well start with it. Said Cotton (1899–1969): 'I thought of all those people lying in their beds and I remembered the sergeant who used to kick my bottom when I was a kid – and out came the catchword.' So it remained – even when the programme moved to its better-remembered spot at Sunday lunchtime.

walk. See HE CAN'T ~ AND CHEW GUM . . . under HE CAN'T FART . . .

Walker, Johnnie. See BORN 1820 . . .

walkies! *Catch Phrase.* If proof were needed that life can begin at seventy, it was provided by Barbara Woodhouse (1910–88). In 1980, after much badgering, she persuaded the BBC that she should present a programme called

Training Dogs the Woodhouse Way (and training the owners, too). She instantly became a national figure of the eccentric kind the British like to have from time to time, and also found fame in the US. Her authoritative delivery of such commands as 'Ssssit!' and 'Walkies!' were widely imitated. However, by December 1981 she was a telling a newspaper that she was going to retreat a fraction from the public eye: 'It's just that I'm getting tired of people saying "Walkies!" to me wherever I go. Even in a village of 300 inhabitants in Queensland.'

walking. See LET YOUR FINGERS DO THE ~.

wall. See BACKS TO THE ~; WRITING ON THE ~.

walls have ears. *Slogan*. This was the neatest encapsulation of the security theme in the Second World War. Others were 'Careless talk costs lives', 'Enemy ears are listening', 'Tittle Tattle lost the battle', and KEEP IT UNDER YOUR HAT.

The idea of inanimate objects being able to hear is a very old one – even beyond 1727, when Jonathan Swift wrote, 'Walls have tongues, and hedges ears.' In Vitzentzos Kornaros's epic poem *Erotokritos* (c 1645) there is the following couplet (here translated from the Greek):

> For the halls of our masters have ears and hear,
> And the walls of the palace have eyes and watch.

(I am indebted to George Macdonald Ross for this reference.)

More recently I have been told of a joke which went: 'Walls have ears – I know, I've just found one in my ice-cream.'

wanna. See I ~ TELL YOU A STORY.

want. See IF YOU ~ ANYTHING . . . ; I ~ . . .

war. See ALL IS FAIR IN . . . ; DADDY, WHAT DID YOU DO IN THE GREAT ~?; DAY ~ BROKE OUT; DON'T YOU KNOW THERE'S A ~ ON?; GOOD ~; MAKE LOVE, NOT ~; NO MORE ~; THIS IS ~.

warm. See WET AND ~.

war's over, you know, the. *Catch Phrase*. Said to someone who is being noticeably and unnecessarily careful about wasting food, power etc. Current since the Second World War and a natural replacement for DON'T YOU KNOW THERE'S A WAR ON?

was it good for you, too? *Catch Phrase* (and, if one could believe that anyone has ever said it except in jest > *Cliché*). What one is supposed to say to one's sexual partner (or at least to the one who is nearest to the earth) after intercourse. (Compare DID THE EARTH MOVE FOR YOU?) Indications that the phrase had 'arrived' came when Bob Chieger so entitled a book of quotations about love and sex (1983) and Maureen Lipman, the actress, a book of funny pieces, ditto (1985).

——watch. *Format Phrase > Cliché*. The addition of the suffix '——watch' to signify any kind of regular attention to something began in earnest in 1985. However, it stemmed from Neighbourhood Watch (sometimes Home Watch) schemes which had been started by the police a year or two before this – schemes in which residents are encouraged to 'police' their own and each other's properties.

In 1985 I noted the TV programme titles *Drugwatch, Nature Watch, Newswatch, Crimewatch UK, Firewatch,* not to mention a feature called 'Wincey's Animal Watch' on TV-am. In 1986 came *Birdwatch UK* and *Childwatch* (on TV). Since then I have become aware of *Railwatch* (BBC TV, 1989), *Weather Watch* (ITV, 1989), 'Longman Wordwatch', a scheme for readers to contribute to the *Longman Register of New Words,* and something called the Worldwatch Institute in Washington – which seems to be the ultimate in ——watches.

watching. See BIG BROTHER IS ~ YOU.

watch the birdie! (also **watch the dicky bird!**) *Catch Phrase.* What photographers say to gain the attention of those they are photographing (especially children) and to make them look at the same point. I suppose originally they held a toy bird near the camera lens. A song 'Watch the Birdie' appeared in the film *Helzapoppin* (1942).

To obtain the semblance of a smile, the photographer says, 'Smile, please!' or 'Say "cheese!"' ' Cecil Beaton is reported to have encouraged (some of) his subjects to, 'Say "lesbian!"' '

'Smile, please – watch the birdie!' was adopted as one of the many *ITMA* catch phrases.

watch this space. *Stock Phrase* – almost a *Slogan,* in a way. Now used mainly as a light-hearted way of saying, 'further details will follow'. I expect this probably came out of the US, though I can't work out quite how. Perhaps it would be put on advertisement hoardings to await the arrival of a poster? From there transferred to newspaper, even broadcasting, use – meaning 'pay attention to this slot'? The *OED Supp.*'s earliest example is, however, taken from an advertisement in the *B.E.F. Times* [British Expeditionary Force] in 1917.

water. See COME HELL AND HIGH ~; DON'T GO NEAR THE ~; HE'S FALLEN IN THE ~ under *GOON SHOW*; LEAVE IT IN THE ~ under LET'S —— AND SEE IF ——.

Watergate. See ——GATE.

Watson. See ELEMENTARY, MY DEAR ~.

way. See AND THAT'S THE ~ IT IS; IT'S THE ~ I TELL 'EM!; THAT'S THE ~ IT CRUMBLES, COOKIE-WISE; WE HAVE ~S OF MAKING YOU TALK; WHAT A ~ TO RUN A ——.

we are just good friends. *Cliché.* The standard way of expressing to a newspaper that your relationship with another is not romantic. From *Vivien: The Life of Vivien Leigh* by Alexander Walker (1987): 'At Cherbourg, Jack [Merivale – Vivien's lover as her marriage to Laurence Olivier was ending in 1960] experienced for the first time the bruising intrusiveness of the British Press who boarded the ship *en masse* to interrogate Vivien's handsome travelling companion. In self-defence, he fell back on the old "just good friends" cliché.'

Now only used as a consciously humorous evasion, especially when not true. A BBC sitcom current in 1984 was called *Just Good Friends* and several songs about that time also had the title.

weasel. See POP GOES THE ~.

we be doomed, we all be doomed! See under ROUND THE HORNE.

weekend starts here, the. *Slogan.* Associated-Rediffusion's TV pop show *Ready, Steady, Go* was transmitted live on Friday evenings in the mid-1960s. The slogan was current by 1964. For some reason it stuck, and has been used by other programmes since.

week is a long time. See —— IS A LONG TIME IN ——.

weep. See LAUGH AND THE WORLD LAUGHS WITH YOU . . .

we have ways (and means) of making you talk. *Catch Phrase > Cliché.* The threat by evil inquisitor to victim appears to have come originally from 1930s Hollywood villains and was then handed on to Nazi characters from the 1940s onwards.

Halliwell found Douglas Dumbrille, as the evil Mohammed Khan, saying 'We have ways of making *men* talk' in *Lives of a Bengal Lancer* (1935) – by forcing slivers of wood under the fingernails and setting fire to them . . . A typical 'film Nazi' use can be found in the British *Odette* (1950) in which the French Resistance worker (Anna Neagle) is threatened with unmentioned nastiness by one of her captors. Says he: 'We have ways and means of making you talk.' Then, after a little stoking of the fire with a poker, he urges her on with: 'We have ways and means of making a woman talk.'

Later, used in caricature, the phrase saw further action in TV programmes like *LAUGH-IN* (*c* 1968) – invariably pronounced with a German accent. Frank Muir presented a comedy series for London Weekend Television with the title *We Have Ways of Making You Laugh* (1968).

welcome. See HELLO, GOOD EVENING, AND ~.

well. See ALIVE AND ~ AND LIVING IN ——.

well, he would, wouldn't he? *Catch Phrase.* An innocuous enough phrase but one still used allusively because of the way it was spoken by Mandy Rice-Davies (*b* 1944) in 1963. A 'good time girl' and friend of Christine Keeler's, she was called as a witness when Stephen Ward, the ponce-figure in the Profumo Affair [Secretary of State for War John Profumo carried on with Keeler who was allegedly sharing her favours with the Soviet military attaché] was charged under the Sexual Offences Act.

During the preliminary Magistrates' Court hearing on 28 June 1963, she was questioned about the men she had had sex with. When told by Ward's defence counsel that Lord Astor – one of the names on the list – had categorically denied any involvement with her, she replied, chirpily: 'Well, he would, wouldn't he?'

The court burst into laughter, the expression passed into the language, and is still resorted to because – as a good catch phrase ought to be – it is bright, useful in various circumstances, and tinged with innuendo.

well to the right of Genghis Khan. See SOMEWHERE TO THE RIGHT OF GENGHIS KHAN.

we must stamp out this evil in our midst. *Stock Phrase > Cliché.* Of journalism. In June 1967, Chris Welch of *Melody Maker* wrote: 'We can expect a deluge of drivel about the new people [proponents of Flower Power, peace and love] any day now from the Sunday papers, with demands to "stamp out this evil in our midst".'

we name the guilty men. *Cliché.* Of journalism. From the *Observer* (16 April 1989): 'Like all the best Sunday journalists, I name the guilty men, and one guilty woman, if we include Mrs Shirley Williams.'

Guilty Men was the title of a tract 'which may rank as literature' (A.J.P. Taylor). It was written by Michael Foot, Frank Owen and Peter Howard using the pseudonym 'Cato'. Published in July 1940, it taunted the appeasers who had brought about the situation where Britain had had to go to war with Germany. The preface contains this anecdote: 'On a spring day in 1793 a crowd of angry men burst their way through the doors of the assembly room where the French Convention was in session. A discomforted figure addressed them from the rostrum. "What do the people desire?" he asked. "The Convention has only their welfare at heart." The leader of the angry crowd replied, "The people haven't come here to be given a lot of phrases. They demand a dozen guilty men."'

The phrase 'We *name* the guilty men' subsequently became a cliché of popular 'investigative' journalism. Equally popular was the similar, 'We name these *evil* men'.

The 'guilty men' taunt was one much used in the 1945 General Election by the Labour Party (and was referred to in a speech by Winston Churchill, House of Commons, 7 May 1947).

we never closed. *Slogan.* Coined by Vivien Van Damm, proprietor of the Windmill Theatre, London – a venerable comedy and strip venue – which was the only West End showplace to remain open during the Blitz. An obvious variant: 'We never clothed'.

we never sleep. *Slogan.* For Pinkerton's national detective agency which opened its first office in Chicago, 1850 (and which – through its open eye symbol *may* have given us the term 'private eye').

wept. See JESUS ~!

we're doomed! See under ROUND THE HORNE.

we're getting there. *Slogan.* For British Rail, rather questionably (current 1985). In 1980, the organization had been promoted by the even more questionable **this is the age of the train**, which it undoubtedly wasn't (attracting the comments: 'Yes, it takes an age to catch one', 'Ours was 104' etc).

we're in. See MEREDITH, ~!

we're with the Woolwich. *Slogan.* For the Woolwich Equitable Building Society. In the late 1970s, there was a series of TV ads which posed the question 'Are you with the Woolwich?' More than most advertising lines, these managed to work their way into jokes and sketches. Perhaps more correctly rendered as, 'No, I'm with the Woolwich' – in answer to such questions as, 'Are you with me?'

we shall not be moved. *Slogan/Catch Phrase.* Shout/chant of defiance.

According to Bartlett, originally from a negro spiritual (echoing more than one psalm): 'Just like a tree that's standing by the water/ We shall not be moved.' Later widely taken up as a song of the civil rights and labour movements, from the 1960s. In the UK, I fancy, only the simple slogan was chanted, not the whole spiritual.

we shall not see his like again. *Cliché.* In obituaries, and alluding to Shakespeare, *Hamlet* (I.ii.187), where the Prince says of his late father:

A was a man, take him for all in all;
I shall not look upon his like again.

In *Joyce Grenfell Requests the Pleasure* (1976), the actress recalls being rung by the United Press for a comment on the death of Ruth Draper, the monologist: 'My diary records: "I said we should not see her like again. She was a genius." Without time to think, clichés take over and often, because that is why they have become clichés, they tell the truth.'

Westchester. See under LET'S —— AND SEE IF ——.

wet and warm. *Catch Phrase.* On being offered a drink, one might say, 'I don't mind what it is, as long as it's wet and warm.' Almost a conversational cliché. Mencken cites a 'Dutch proverb': 'Coffee has two virtues: it is wet and warm.'

we've got a right one 'ere! See under *EDUCATING ARCHIE.*

we wuz robbed! *Catch Phrase.* A notable reaction to sporting defeat came from the lips of Joe Jacobs (1896–1940), American manager of the boxer Max Schmeling.

Believing his man to have been cheated of the heavyweight title in a fight against Jack Sharkey on 21 June 1932, Jacobs shouted his protest into a microphone – 'We wuz robbed!'

On another occasion, in October 1935, Jacobs left his sick-bed to attend the World Series (ball game) for the one and only time in Detroit. Having bet on the losers, he opined: '**I should of stood in bed.**'

whack. See 'AS 'E BIN IN, ~?

wharfies' picnic. See under AS BUSY AS . . .

what about the workers? *Catch Phrase.* Usually written, 'Wot abaht . . .', this is the traditional proletarian heckler's cry during a political speech. It is almost a *Slogan* in its own right, but is now only used satirically. It occurs along with other rhetorical clichés during the 'Party Political Speech' (written by Max Schreiner) on the Peter Sellers' comedy album 'The Best of Sellers' (1958). Also in the 1950s, Harry Secombe as 'Neddie Seagoon' on the BBC radio GOON SHOW would sometimes exclaim (for no very good reason), 'Hello, folks, and what about the workers?!' Later, in the 1970s, Eric Morecambe incorporated it in a nonsense phrase of sexual innuendo when referring to 'a touch of hello-folks-and-what-about-the-workers!'

In 1984, in a TV programme to mark his hundredth birthday, Manny Shinwell, the veteran Labour MP, appeared to be claiming that he had been asking 'What about the workers?' – seriously – in 1904, but whether he meant literally or figuratively wasn't clear.

See also *BAND WAGGON.*

what a difference a day makes! *Saying.* Almost proverbial, yet not listed in any proverb books. It either expresses surprise at someone's rapid recovery from some mood which had laid them low, or expresses the old thought that time is a great healer. Did it begin in a song? 'What a Difference a Day Made' was a hit for Esther Phillips in 1975 (though written in 1934).

what a way to run a ——. *Format Phrase.* A cartoon believed to have appeared in the American *Collier's* magazine (though *Ballyhoo* in 1932 has also been suggested) showed two trains about to collide. An American signalman is looking out of his box and the caption is: 'Tch-tch-what a way to run a railroad!'

The Boston & Maine railroad picked up this line when it sought, 'a statement which would explain some of the problems of the railroad in times of inclement weather'. It took the 'stock railroad phrase', derived from the cartoon, and put it between each paragraph of the advertisement in the form, 'That's A H**l of a Way to Run a Railroad!' Added at the foot of the ad was the line, 'But the railroad always runs.'

Thus the phrase came into the language as an exclamation concerning mismanagement or chaos of any kind, in the form, 'What a way (*or* hell of a way) to run a railroad/ railway.'

Echoes or developments of this construction occur in the title of G. F. Fiennes's *I Tried to Run a Railway* (1967) – he had worked for British Rail – and the Conservative Party 1968 poster: 'Higher unemployment . . . Higher unemployment . . . Higher taxation . . . Higher prices . . . What a way to run a country!'

And from the *Independent* Magazine (4 February 1989): 'The shop told me that it only had demonstration [satellite TV] dishes and suggested I call back in a fortnight. This is, surely, no way to run a revolution!'

what did *you* in the Great War, Daddy? See DADDY, WHAT DID YOU DO . . . ?

what do you think of it so far? See under MORECAMBE AND WISE SHOW.

whatever happened to ——? *Cliché.* The conversational query occurs, for example, in Noël Coward's song 'I Wonder What Happened to Him?' (from *Sigh No More*, 1945) in the form, 'Whatever became of old Bagot . . . ?' But the film title *Whatever Happened to Baby Jane?* (1962) fixed the phrase in the way most usually employed by journalists. Like WHERE ARE THEY NOW? this became a standard formula for feature-writing on a slack day. In the early 1980s, the *Sunday Express* ran a weekly column, disinterring the stars of yesteryear, sometimes under the heading 'Where are they now . . . ?' but more usually, 'What ever happened to . . . ?' (See TIT, TOTE AND TELEVISION.)

Coty perfume was advertised with the slogan 'Whatever Happened to Romance?' (quoted in 1984).

what me – in my state of health? See under *ITMA*.

what's a nice girl like you doing in a joint/place like this? *Cliché.* Of conversation/chatting up, and now used only in a consciously arch way. It is listed among the 'naff pick-up lines' in *The Naff Sex Guide* (1984). I suspect it may have arisen in Hollywood Westerns of the 1930s. It was certainly established as a film cliché by the 1950s when Frank Muir and Denis Norden included this version in a TAKE IT FROM HERE parody: 'Thanks, Kitty. Say, why does a swell girl like you have to work in a saloon like this?'

In 1973, *Private Eye* carried a cartoon of a male marijuana-smoker with a female, and the caption, 'What's a nice joint like you . . . ?'

what's new, pussycat? *Idiom.* Of Warren Beatty, the film actor, Sheilah Graham wrote in *Scratch an Actor* (1969): 'He uses the telephone as a weapon of seduction. He curls up with it, cuddles it, whispers into it, "What's new, pussycat?" (He coined the phrase, and the picture was originally written for him.)'

The film with the title (and the Tom Jones' song therefrom) came out in 1965. Perhaps Graham was right. Whatever the case, I would guess that the use of 'pussycat' to describe someone, particularly a woman, as 'attractive, amiable, submissive' (*OED Supp.*) probably emanates from the US, if not precisely from Hollywood.

what's on the table, Mabel? See under HAVE A GO.

what's the damage? *Catch Phrase.* Said when asking how much the bill is (eg for drinks) or establishing who should pay it. *The Hallamshire Glossary* by the Rev. Joseph Hunter (*b* 1784) records that this was in common use in the Sheffield area between 1790 and 1810. In fact, the *OED* has the word 'damage' = 'cost, expense' in 1755, and in 1852 'What's the damage, as they say in Kentucky' appears in Har-

riet Beecher Stowe's *Uncle Tom's Cabin* (though not concerning drink). Presumably, the use derives from legal damages.

what's the recipe today, Jim? See under MORNING ALL!

what's up, doc? *Catch Phrase.* The characteristic inquiry of Bugs Bunny, the cartoon character, in the film series which ran from 1937–63, addressed to Elmer Fudd, the doctor who devoted his life to attempting to destroy the rabbit. Bugs made his official debut in 1940. In full, the phrase, was 'Er, what's up, Doc?' – followed by a carrot crunch. The voices of both characters were done by Mel Blanc (1908–89) who, on emerging from a coma in 1983, inevitably put the question to his physician.

The phrase was used as the title of a film starring Barbra Streisand and Ryan O'Neal (1972).

what the butler saw. *Catch Phrase.* 'What the Butler Saw' was the name given to a type of penny-in-the-slot machine introduced in Britain *c* 1880. It was a frisky development of the very old peep show. The female so observed was probably doing something fairly mild in corsets and, if this was an early version of soft porn, it wasn't exactly decadent.

The Museum of the Moving Image in London contains a Mutoscope as invented by Herman Casler in 1897 and links it to the arrival of 'What the Butler Saw', although there had been earlier machines through which pictures on cards were flipped to give an impression of movement. The museum notes that these penny-in-the-slot machines were in Britain for some seventy years, finally disappearing with the arrival of decimal coinage in 1971.

I note that the phrase was used as the title of a comedy first performed at Wyndham's Theatre on 2 August 1905. An advertising postcard of the time shows a girl complaining to her parents, 'My dolly has been and broke itself!' which suggests that any butler in the piece was unlikely to have had his voyeuristic urge gratified.

The phrase was again used as a title by Joe Orton for his posthumously-produced farce about goings-on in a psychiatric clinic (1969). In this piece, a butler definitely makes no appearance, though the characters do tend to wander about in their underpants, or less.

Other uses include acting as the title for an instrumental number recorded by Lord Rockingham's XI (in 1958) and for a song recorded by Squeeze in 1980. Very much earlier than both these, Florrie Forde, the music-hall star, recorded a song called 'What the Curate Saw', which is clearly an allusion.

From the *Observer* (20 May 1989): [Headline to book review] 'What the Butler Didn't See'.

what would you do, chums? See under *BAND WAGGON*.

wheel has come full circle, the. *Cliché.* This expression probably owes its fame to the fact that Edmund the Bastard says it in Shakespeare's *King Lear* (V.iii.173). He is referring to the wheel of Fortune, being at that moment back down at the bottom where he was before it began to revolve.

whelk-stall. See COULDN'T RUN A ~.

when are you going to finish off that dress? *Cliché.* Used in chatting up, flirting. Addressed to a woman with skimpy decolletage. Tom Jones can be heard so addressing a member of the audience on the LP 'Tom Jones – Live at Caesar's Palace, Las Vegas' (1971).

when did you last see . . . ? See AND WHEN DID YOU LAST SEE . . . ?

when did you stop beating your wife? *Catch Phrase.* An example of a leading question (because by attempting to start answering it you admit that you *did* once beat your wife). Or, an example of an unanswerable question?

when I'm dead and gone the game's finished. See under THERE'LL NEVER BE ANOTHER.

when it rains, it pours. See under IT NEVER RAINS, BUT IT POURS.

when I was in Patagonia . . . *Stock Phrase.* A regular participant in the radio *Brains Trust* of the 1940s was Commander A.B. Campbell. His stock phrase arose in an earlier version of the programme when it was still called *Any Questions* (in 1941). Donald McCullough, the chairman, said: 'Mr Edwards of Balham wants to know if the members of the Brains Trust agree with the practice of sending missionaries to foreign lands.' Prof. Joad and Julian Huxley gave their answers and then Campbell began, 'When I was in Patagonia . . .'

In a book which used the phrase as its title, Campbell recalled: 'I got no further, for Joad burst into a roar of laughter and the other members of the session joined in. For some time the feature was held up while the hilarity spent itself. For the life of me I could not see the joke . . . Even today (1951), years after, I can raise a laugh if I am on a public platform and make an allusion to it.'

when people are starving in India . . . *Saying.* I am indebted to *The Complete Directory to Prime Time Network TV Shows* (1981) for the information that when a proposed US series called *B.A.D. Cats* crashed in 1980, Everett Chambers, its executive producer, said, 'We bought $40,000 worth of cars to smash up, and we never got a chance to smash them up. I think that's kind of immoral, $40,000 worth of cars to smash up when people are starving in India.'

I had always taken this to be a (British) nanny's expression, but the nearest I can find, recorded in *Nanny Says* by Sir Hugh Casson and Joyce Grenfell (1972) is, 'Think of all the poor starving children who'd be grateful for that nice plain bread and butter.'

Wasn't it also advised that it was polite to leave a little food on the side of the plate 'for the starving in India' if not for 'Mr Manners'?

Paul Beale in Partridge/*Catch Phrases*, commenting on the American 'Remember the starving Armenians' notes: 'The one used to exhort me as a child, late 1930s, to clear up my plate or to tackle something I found unpalatable was "think of all the poor starving children in China!"'

when the going gets tough, the tough get going. *Slogan/ Catch Phrase.* One of several axioms said to have come from the Boston–Irish political jungle or,

more precisely, from President Kennedy's father, Joseph P. Kennedy (1888–1969). At this distance, it is impossible to say for sure whether this wealthy, ambitious businessman/ ambassador/ politician originated the expression, but he certainly instilled it in his sons.

Subsequently, it was used as a slogan for the film *The Jewel of the Nile* (1985) and a song with the title sung by Billy Ocean and the stars of the film was a No. 1 hit in 1986. The joke slogan 'When the going gets tough, the tough go shopping' had appeared on T-shirts in the US by 1982.

when the music stops. See under ARE YOU SITTING COMFORTABLY? . . .

when the world was young. *Idiom.* I take this to be a wistful expression not only of 'long ago' but also of a time more innocent than the present. It may derive ultimately from this verse in the Bible: 'For the world has lost his youth, and the times begin to wax old' (2 Esdras 14:10).

Precisely as 'When the World Was Young', I have found it used as the title of a painting (1891) by Sir E.J. Poynter PRA which shows three young girls in a classical setting, relaxing by a pool. It was also used by Johnny Mercer as the title of his very popular version of a French song known as '*Le Chevalier de Paris*' or '*Ah! Les Pommiers Doux*' (c 1951).

Compare the lines 'When all the world is young, lad, / And all the trees are green/ . . . Young blood must have its course, lad,/ And every dog his day', from 'Young and Old' in the *Water Babies* (1863) by Charles Kingsley.

when you got it, flaunt it. *Slogan/Catch Phrase*. The Braniff airline in the US used this headline over ads in *c* 1969 featuring celebrities such as Sonny Liston, Andy Warhol and Joe Namath. Perhaps the line was acquired from the 1967 Mel Brooks movie *The Producers* where it appears as: 'That's it, baby! When you got it, flaunt it.'

where are they now? *Cliché*. Journalistic formula – compare WHATEVER HAPPENED TO ——? The rhetorical question occurs rather differently in Wordsworth's ode 'Intimations of Immortality' (1807):
Whither is fled the visionary gleam?
Where is it now, the glory and the dream?

——, where are you now? *Format Phrase/Catch Phrase*. I think this is usually employed as an ironical plea to someone who has long-since departed because one finds present circumstances as bad as when the person was around. And so, one might have said in the Reagan Irangate scandal, 'Richard Nixon, where are you now?'

As such, it is a truncation of '. . . where are you now that your country needs you?' or **come back ——, all is forgiven** which, once upon a time, might have been said about a warrior who had retired to his farm. It appeared ironically in the graffito 'Lee Harvey Oswald, where are you now that YOUR COUNTRY NEEDS YOU?' during the presidencies of both Lyndon Johnson and Richard Nixon.

where do we go from here? *Cliché*. A way of rounding off pompous broadcasting discussions about the future (or almost anything) is for the chairman to ask this question. Alternatively, it can be put to an individual (who has just been interviewed about his life and works) in the form, 'Well, where do you go from here?'

In politics, as a theme for debates, it tends to be put even more pompously (though now, with luck, only jokingly) in the form **whither —— ?** (eg 'Whither Democracy?' 'Whither Europe?' 'Whither the Labour Party?')

'Where Do We Go From Here?' was also a song of the 1940s, popular for a while in the army.

where have all the —— gone? *Format Phrase > Cliché*. Based on the title of the song 'Where Have All the Flowers Gone' by Pete Seeger (1961).

where is it all leading us, I ask myself? See under MORNING ALL!

where it's at. See —— IS THE NAME OF THE GAME.

where's the beef? *Slogan > Catch Phrase*. A classic example of an advertising slogan turning into a political catch phrase. The Wendy International hamburger chain promoted its wares in the US, from 1984, with TV commercials, one of which showed elderly women eyeing a small hamburger on a huge bun – a Wendy competitor's product. 'It certainly is a big bun,' asserted one. 'It's a very big fluffy bun,' the second agreed. But the third asked, 'Where's the beef?'

The line caught on hugely. Walter Mondale, running for the Democratic nomination, used it to question the substance of his rival Gary Hart's policies.

where that came from. See AND THERE'S MORE ~.

where were you when the lights went out? *Catch Phrase*. The 1968 film *Where Were You When the Lights Went Out?* was inspired by the great New York blackout of 1965 when the electricity supply failed and, it was popularly believed, the birth-rate shot up nine months later. The phrase echoes an old music-hall song and perhaps also the American nonsense rhyme 'Where was Moses when the light went out?/ Down in the cellar eating sauerkraut'. This last appears to have developed from the 'almost proverbial' riddle (as the Opies call it in *The Lore and Language of Schoolchildren,* 1959):

Q. Where was Moses when the light went out?

A. In the dark.

The Opies find this in *The Riddler's Oracle, c* 1821.

which twin has the Toni? *Slogan*. A headline that asks a question, a slogan that contains the brand name, and an idea that was dotty enough to be much copied. In the early 1950s, Toni home perms featured pairs of identical twins (real ones) who also toured doing promotional work for the product. One twin had a Toni home perm, the other a more expensive perm – a footnote explained which was which in answer to the question.

During the 1970 General Election, the Liberal Party produced a poster showing pictures of Harold Wilson and Edward Heath with the slogan, 'Which twin is the Tory?'

whistle. See BLOW THE ~ ON; IF YOU WANT ANYTHING, JUST ~.

whither. See WHERE DO WE GO FROM HERE?

—— who came in from the cold, the. *Format Phrase > Cliché*. John Le Carré's 1963 novel *The Spy Who Came in from the Cold* popularized this expression. From then on, any people coming in from any kind of exposed position, or returning to favour, might find themselves described as 'coming in from the cold'.

who dares wins. *Slogan*. The SAS (Special Air Service regiment) was founded by Col. David Stirling in 1950 although its origins lay in the Second World War. Its motto became famous after members of the crack regiment had shot their way into the Iranian embassy in London, in May 1980, to end a siege (when wags suggested the motto should really be, 'Who dares use it [fire-power], wins'). A feature film about the supposed exploits of the SAS was made, using the motto as its title in 1982 and the *Daily Mirror* labelled its 'Win a Million' bingo promotion 'Who Dares Wins' in 1984.

The motto appears to have been borrowed from the Alvingham barony, created in 1929.

who do I have to fuck to get out of this —— ? *Catch Phrase*. Presumably, from showbiz. Having, as legend would have it, had to fuck to get cast in a show or picture, the speaker is wondering how the process can be reversed – because the show is having problems or turns out to be no good. Bob Chieger in *Was It Good For You, Too?* ascribes to 'Shirley Wood, talent coordinator for NBC's *The Tonight Show* in the 1960s', the quote: 'Who do you have to fuck to get *out* of show business?' The line 'Listen, who do I have to fuck to get *off* this picture?' occurs in Terry Southern's *Blue Movie* (1970). Steve Bach in *Final Cut* (1985) ascribes 'Who do I fuck to get off this picture?' simply to 'Anonymous Hollywood starlet (circa 1930)'.

who he? *Stock Phrase*. Popularized by *Private Eye* in the 1980s, this editorial interjection after a little-known person's name shows some signs of catching on: 'This month, for instance, has been the time for remembering the 110th anniversary of the birth of Grigori Petrovsky. Who he?' – *New Statesman*, 26 February 1988. I suspect Richard Ingrams, former editor of the *Eye*, consciously borrowed the phrase from Harold Ross (1892–1951), editor of the *New Yorker*. James Thurber, in *The Years with Ross* (1959), describes how Ross would customarily add this query to manuscripts (though not for publication) on finding a name he did not know in an article (sometimes betraying his ignorance). He said the only two names everyone knew were Houdini and Sherlock Holmes.

A book with the title *Who He? Goodman's Dictionary of the Unknown Famous* was published in 1984. The phrase echoes the Duke of Wellington's peremptory 'Who? Who?' on hearing the names of ministers in Lord Derby's new administration (1852).

whole new ball game, it's a. *Cliché*. From American business jargon. 'Mr Gerry Fernback, chairman of ABTA's retail travel agents' council said last week: "For the first time British Airways is making the right noises. It's a whole new ball game now . . . it's in their interest and ours that cheap tickets are available to the public" ' (*Observer*, 26 September 1983).

who loves ya, baby? *Catch Phrase*. Telly Savalas, as the lollipop-sucking New York police lieutenant in the TV series *Kojak* (1973–7) created a vogue for this phrase. Inevitably, there was also a song with the title (1975).

who's for tennis? See under ANYONE FOR ~?

who shot J.R.? *Catch Phrase*. The hero/villain J.R. Ewing (played by Larry Hagman) of the top-rated soap opera *Dallas* was shot in the cliff-hanging last episode of the programme's 1979–80 season. For reasons not entirely clear, the question of who had inflicted this far from mortal wound caused a sensation in the US and UK. Consequently, the first episode of the next series attracted 53.3% of the American viewing audience, the highest-ever rating. All those who had posed the question, or sported bumper-stickers declaring **I hate J.R.**, discovered that the guilty party was a jilted lover.

why are you telling me all this? See under ARCHERS.

width, feel the. See NEVER MIND THE QUALITY . . .

wife. See ALL THE WORLD AND HIS ~; MEET THE ~ under 'AS 'E BIN IN, WHACK?; WHEN DID YOU STOP BEATING YOUR ~?

—— will never be the same again. *Cliché*. Any change, however unremarkable, requires this journalistic phrase.

'The Broadway musical would never be the same again' – TV promo, New York 1983. 'Life for George Bush will never be the same again' – Tim Ewart, ITN news, 20 January 1989 (the day of the president's inauguration).

will the real ——, please stand up? *Stock Phrase > Catch Phrase*. In the American TV game *To Tell the Truth*, devised by Goodson-Todman Productions and shown from 1956–66, a panel had to decide which of three contestants, all claiming to be a certain person, was telling the truth. After the panellists had interrogated the challenger and the 'impostors', they had to declare which person they thought was the real one. MC Bud Collyer would then say: 'Will the real —— ——, please stand up!' and he or she did so. The game was revived in the UK as *Tell the Truth* in the 1980s.

In March 1984, Elizabeth Taylor, the actress, was quoted as saying: 'I'm still trying to find the real Elizabeth Taylor and make her stand up.'

win. See NOTHING VENTURE, NOTHING ~; WHO DARES ~S.

wind. See TWIST SLOWLY, SLOWLY IN THE ~.

wind of change, a/the. *Cliché*. Speaking to both houses of the South African parliament on 3 February 1960, Prime Minister Harold Macmillan gave his hosts a message they cannot have wanted to hear: 'The most striking of all the impressions I have formed since I left London a month ago is of the strength of this African national consciousness. In different places it may take different forms, but it is happening everywhere. The wind of change is blowing through this continent. Whether we like it or not, this growth of national consciousness is a political fact.'

The phrase 'wind of change' – though not, of course, original – was contributed to the speechwriting team by the diplomat (later Sir) David Hunt. The *OED Supp.* acknowledges that the use of the phrase 'wind(s) of change' increased markedly after the speech. When Macmillan sought a title for one of his volumes of memoirs he plumped for the more common, plural, usage – *Winds of Change*.

In a similar windy metaphor Stanley Baldwin had said in 1934: 'There is a wind of nationalism and freedom round the world, and blowing as strongly in Asia as elsewhere.' President George Bush made 'a new breeze is blowing' the theme of his inauguration speech on 20 January 1989.

wind-storm, fart in a. See under AS BUSY AS . . .

wink-wink. See under *MONTY PYTHON'S FLYING CIRCUS*.

winter of discontent, a/the. *Saying > Cliché*. Shakespeare's *Richard III* begins, famously, with Gloucester's punning and original metaphor:

Now is the winter of our discontent
Made glorious summer by this son of York;
And all the clouds that lour'd upon our House
In the deep bosom of the ocean buried

– even if the editor of the Arden edition does describe the entire image as 'almost proverbial'. Probably made all the more memorable by Laurence Olivier's delivery of these lines in the 1955 film, the phrase 'winter of discontent' suffered the unpleasant fate of becoming a politician's and journalist's cliché following the winter of 1978/9 when British life was disrupted by all kinds of industrial protests against the Labour government's attempts to keep down pay rises. Most notably, rubbish remained uncollected and began to pile up in the streets and a grave-diggers' strike in one area reputedly left bodies unburied.

This 'winter of discontent' (as it is still referred to) may perhaps have contributed to the Conservative victory at the May 1979 General Election. The question I have been asked is, who first referred to it as such?

Mrs Margaret Thatcher, opening her election campaign on TV (2 April 1979) said, 'We have just had a devastating winter of industrial strife – perhaps the worst in living memory, certainly the worst in mine', which is almost it, but not quite.

The first actual use I have found in a far-from-exhaustive search through the files is in the *Sun* (30 April 1979). As part of a series on the issues of the election in the week before polling, the paper splashed across two pages the words: 'WINTER OF DISCONTENT. Lest we forget . . . the *Sun* recalls the long, cold months of industrial chaos that brought Britain to its knees.' If this *is* the first use of the phrase, it almost ranks with the *Sun*'s made-up quote from James Callaghan, 'Crisis? What Crisis?' (headline, 11 January, 1979), which may be said to have helped topple the Labour Government and install the Tories.

Later on, the *Observer* (9 September) has as the subtitle to an article: 'Do we face a winter of discontent? Adrian Hamilton and Robert Taylor report on the union and employer mood.' The actual piece begins: 'To listen to the speeches at the annual conference of the Trades Union Congress at Blackpool this week was to believe that Britain is in for a winter of endless discontent and disruption.'

At the end of that same month, on the 26th, the *Daily Express* began a report of a speech by Mrs Thatcher at Milton Keynes, thus: 'STRIKE AT YOUR PERIL! Maggie spells out price of conflict this winter. Mrs Thatcher yesterday put a price on another winter of discontent. It would be lost jobs, she said.'

As far as I can make out, she never actually used the phrase itself. I rather think it was a journalistic imposition. In the last two instances, it is interesting to note that the 'winter' referred to is the forthcoming one of 1979/80 rather than 1978/9.

The *Observer* was still ringing changes on the original on 7 February 1982: 'WHY FOOTBALL MUST SURVIVE ITS WINTER OF PENURY AND DISCONTENT'.

——**wise.** See THAT'S THE WAY IT CRUMBLES.

wish. See I DON'T ~ TO KNOW THAT . . .

wish you were here! *Stock Phrase.* Although I have no citations for it in actual use, the cliché of holiday correspondence has been used as the title of songs (reaching the charts in 1953 and 1984) and of an ITV travel series (from 1973 onwards).

In the full form, '**Having a wonderful time**, wish you were here', Partridge/ *Catch Phrases* suggests a beginning in

Edwardian times. But why not earlier, at any time since the introduction of the postcard in Britain, which was in 1870? To be sure, cards on which you wrote your own message did not come on the scene until 1894 and the heyday of the picture postcard was in Edwardian times. In the early days, perhaps the message was already printed on the card by the manufacturer? Nowadays, probably, the wording is only used in jest or ironically.

Having Wonderful Time, a play about a holiday hotel in the Catskills, by Arthur Kober (1937) became, in an exchange of phrases, the musical *Wish You Were Here* in 1952. *Wish You Were Here* was also used in 1987 as the title of a British film about sexual awakenings in a seaside resort.

within. See ENEMY ~.

with —— like that, who needs ——? *Format Phrase*. In the form 'With friends like that, who needs enemies?' – said in desperation after one has been betrayed by a supporter – the earliest example I have is of something Richard Crossman said of certain Labour MPs in 1969. But it is of much older provenance. Charlotte Brontë said it, in a letter, concerning the patronizing reviewer of one of her books. Partridge/*Slang* compares it to the proverb, 'With a Hungarian for a friend, who needs an enemy.' George Canning, the nineteenth-century politician, wrote a verse ending, 'Save, save, Oh, save me from the candid friend'.

with one bound he was free. *Stock Phrase > Idiom*. Said now of anyone who escapes from a tricky situation or tight corner. I presume this comes either from cartoon strips or subtitles to silent films. It underlines the preposterousness of the adventures in which such lines can be 'spoken'.

without hesitation, deviation or repetition. *Stock Phrase > Catch Phrase*. In the radio panel game *Just a Minute* (1967–), devised by Ian Messiter, and of which versions have been played in fifty-seven countries, guests have to speak for one minute 'without hesitation, deviation or repetition'. From the *Independent* (6 September 1988): 'There is no protective, guiding commentary in Radio 1's new four-parter, in which youth speaks without hesitation, deviation or interruption about the things that really matter.' In 1982, an MP stood up in the House of Commons and said of a guillotine motion, that he thought all speeches on the Bill should be 'like those in that radio game "without deviation, repetition and . . . what was the other?' Prompts of: 'Hesitation!' from other MPs.

wogs begin at Barnet. *Saying*. An ironic view of the North/South divide in Britain (Barnet being on the outer edge of northwest London), clearly based on the old insular, foreigner-distrusting view that **wogs begin at Calais.** I first heard the Barnet version in 1964 (it was a motion for debate at the Oxford Union in the form 'When going North, the wogs begin at Barnet').

woman. See PUT A ~ ON TOP . . .

women. See HORSES SWEAT . . . ; THIS AD INSULTS ~.

women and children first! *Catch Phrase.* Used jokily in a situation where people might appear to be behaving as though caught in a shipwreck (in a crowded bus or train perhaps), this nevertheless has a sound historical origin.

HMS *Birkenhead* was one of the first ships to have a hull of iron. In 1852, she was taking 476 British soldiers to the eighth 'Kaffir War' in the Eastern Cape of South Africa when she ran aground fifty miles off the Cape of Good Hope. It was clear that the ship would go under but only three of the eight lifeboats could be used and these were rapidly filled with the twenty women and children on board. According to tradition, soldiers remained calm and did not even break ranks when the funnel and mast crashed down on to the deck. 445 lives were lost but the tradition of 'women and child' first was born. In naval circles, this is still known as the Birkenhead Drill.

Somerset Maugham said he always chose to sail on French ships: 'Because there's none of that nonsense about women and children first!'

wonder. See BOY ~ under *BATMAN*; DOUBLE DIAMOND WORKS ~S; I ~ IF THEY ARE . . . ?; NINE DAYS' ~.

wonderful. See HAVING A ~ TIME under WISH YOU WERE HERE!; YOUR POLICEMEN ARE ~.

wood. See YOU CAN'T GET THE ~ under GOON SHOW.

Woodbine. See AH, ~ . . .

wooden. See UP THE ~ HILL TO BEDFORD-SHIRE.

woodpile. See NIGGER IN THE ~.

Woolwich. See WE'RE WITH THE ~.

word. See AND NOW A ~ FROM OUR SPONSOR; PICTURE IS WORTH A THOUSAND ~S.

work. See GO TO ~ ON AN EGG; NEVER ~ WITH CHILDREN OR ANIMALS; ONLY FOOLS AND HORSES ~.

workers. See BLACK-COATED ~; WHAT ABOUT THE ~?

working classes. See ON BEHALF OF THE ~ . . .

works wonders. See DOUBLE DIAMOND ~.

world. See ALL THE ~ AND HIS WIFE; JOIN THE ARMY AND SEE THE ~; LAUGH AND THE ~ LAUGHS WITH YOU; MONEY MAKES THE ~ GO ROUND; THREE MOST USELESS THINGS IN THE ~; WHEN THE ~ WAS YOUNG.

world owes one a living, to believe the. *Saying.* I was first alerted to the provenance of this expression by its use in the epigraph to Graham Greene's novel *England Made Me* (1935):

'All the world owes me a living.'
– Walt Disney –
(*The Grasshopper and the Ants*)

Could Disney really claim credit for the phrase? Well, the cartoon in question – one of the first 'Silly Symphonies' – was released in 1934. It is based on the Aesop fable 'Of the ant and the grasshopper' (as it is called in Caxton's first English translation, 1484) which tells of a grasshopper asking an ant for corn to eat in winter. The ant asks, 'What have you done all the summer past?' and the grasshopper can only answer, 'I have sung.' The moral is that you should provide yourself in the summer with what you need in winter.

Disney turns the grasshopper into a fiddler and gives him a song to sing (written by Larry Morey to music by Leigh Harline):

Oh! the world owes me a living
Deedle, diedle, doedle, diedledum.
Oh! the world owes me a living
Deedle, diedle, doedle, diedleum, etc

I haven't seen the film, but I know this develops in time to:

Oh, the world owes us a living (*rpt*)
You should soil your Sunday pants
Like those other foolish ants,
So let's play and sing and dance . . .

And then, when the error of his ways has been pointed out to him, the grasshopper sings:

I owe the world a living (*rpt*)
I've been a fool the whole year long.
Now I'm singing a different song,
You were right and I was wrong.

This song became quite well known and presumably helped John Llewellyn Rhys choose *The World Owes Me a Living* for his 1939 novel about a redundant RFC hero who tries to make a living with a flying circus (filmed 1944).

It is a little odd rendered in this form, because on the whole it is not something people say about themselves. More usually, another would say, pejoratively, 'The trouble with you is, you think the world owes you a living.'

I have discovered the phrase used only once before Disney. In W.G. Sumner's *Earth Hunger* (1896), he writes: 'The men who start out with the notion that the world owes them a living generally find that the world pays its debt in the penitentiary or the poorhouse.' Sumner was an American author but I'm not to-

tally certain that the phrase originated in the US.

world's favourite airline, the. See under BOAC TAKES GOOD CARE OF YOU.

worried. See I'M ~ ABOUT JIM.

worry. See DON'T ~, BE HAPPY.

worse than the Blitz. See IT WAS ~ . . .

wotalotigot! *Slogan*. For Smarties chocolates, used from *c* 1958 to 1964. The slogan was found after taping children at play with them. At the end of the TV ads came the curious tag, **buy some for Lulu!**

wot no —— ? *Catch Phrase/Slogan*. The most common graffito of the past fifty years in Britain – apart from 'Kilroy was here' (with which it has sometimes been combined) – is the so-called figure of 'Chad', 'Mr Chad' or 'The Chad'. This is the large-nosed, bald, little figure who peers over walls with his hands resting either side of his head.

In Britain at least, there is no doubt Chad made his first appearance in the early stages of the Second World War, accompanied by protests about shortages of the time, such as, 'Wot no cake?', 'Wot no char?', 'Wot no beer?'

In my *Graffiti 3* (1981), I went into the possible origins of the name and the drawing at some length, though it was clear one was never really going to reach a final solution.

The phrase was used by Watneys London Ltd, the brewers, to promote their beer sometime in the 1940s or 50s. The slogan 'Wot no Watneys?' was written on a brick wall – or so everybody says. I wonder, though, whether people might be confusing this with the famous poster which showed graffiti on a brick wall declaring 'What we want is Watneys' or 'We want Watneys'? Alas, Watneys themselves have no copy of any of these adverts in their archives.

Having written the above, I now find that in 1933, at the end of Prohibition, Buster Keaton played in an American film farce with the title *What, No Beer?* As always, there's nothing new . . .

would. See WELL HE ~, WOULDN'T HE?

would you buy a used car from this man? *Saying.* Although attributed by some to Mort Sahl and by others to Lenny Bruce, and though the cartoonist Herblock denied that he was responsible (*Guardian*, 24 December 1975), this is just a joke and one is no more going to find an origin for it than for most such. The line accompanies a shifty looking picture of Richard Nixon and dates from 1952 at least (before any of the above-named humorists really got going). My authority for this is Hugh Brogan, writing in *New Society* (4 November 1982): 'Nixon is a double-barrelled, treble-shotted twister, as my old history master would have remarked; and the fact has been a matter of universal knowledge since at least 1952, when, if I remember aright the joke, "Would you buy a second-hand car from this man?" began to circulate.'

It was a very effective slur, and by 1968 – when Nixon was running (successfully)

for president – a poster was in circulation bearing a picture of him and the line.

One might use the phrase now about anybody one has doubts about. The *Encyclopedia of Graffiti* (1974) even finds: 'Governor Romney – would you buy a *new* car from this man?' In August 1984, John de Lorean said of himself – after being acquitted of drug-dealing – 'I have aged 600 years and my life as a hard-working industrialist is in tatters. Would you buy a used car from me?'

writing on the wall, the. *Idiom > Cliché.* Any hint, sign or portent, often doom-laden. The idea – though not the precise phrase – comes from the Bible (Daniel 5) where King Belshazzar is informed of the forthcoming destruction of the Babylonian Empire through the appearance of a man's hand writing on a wall.

I have often, in my role as graffiti-collector, been introduced as someone who saw 'the writing on the wall' – apparently an irresistible little joke. In a BBC broadcast to resistance workers in Europe (31 July 1941), 'Colonel Britton' (Douglas Ritchie) talked of the 'V for Victory' sign which was being chalked up in occupied countries: 'All over Europe the V sign is seen by the Germans and to the Germans and the Quislings it is indeed the writing on the wall . . .'

wrong. See IF ANYTHING CAN GO ~, IT WILL.

wrote. See THIS PLAY WHAT I HAVE ~ under *MORECAMBE AND WISE SHOW*.

Y

yaroooo! *Stock Phrase*. When Billy Bunter, the famous fat boy created by Frank Richards, came to be recreated for TV (1952–62), he was played by Gerald Campion. He gave a memorably metallic ring to the phrase **I say you fellows!** and to this one.

Also at Greyfriars School, the Indian boy, Hurree Jamset Ram (known as Inky), had a *Format Phrase*, **the ——fulness is terrific!**, as in 'the rottenfulness is terrific' or as in this example from one of the original stories by Richards (in *The Magnet* No. 401, October 1915): ' "Are we not in a state of warfulness?" [asked Inky]. Bob Cherry chuckled: "The warfulness is terrific, as terrific as your variety of the English language, Inky." '

years. See FIRST —— ~ ARE THE HARDEST.

yeh, yeh, yeh. *Catch Phrase*. 'Yeh' as a common corruption of 'yes' has been current (and derived from the US) since the 1920s. But whether spelt 'yeh-yeh-yeh', as in the published lyrics, or 'yeah-yeah-yeah' (which captures the Liverpudlian pronunciation better), this phrase became a hallmark of the Beatles after its use in their song 'She Loves You'. The single 'She Loves You' was in the UK charts for thirty-one weeks from August 1963 and was for fourteen years Britain's all-time best-selling 45 rpm record. But although most commonly associated with the Beatles, the phrase was not new. Some of the spadework in Britain had been done by the non-Liverpudlian singer Helen Shapiro who had a hit in September 1961 with 'Walking Back to Happiness' which included the refrain 'Whoop Bah Oh Yeah Yeah Yeah'. The Beatles had toured with Shapiro topping the bill before their own careers took off.

Following the Beatle use, there was a French expression in the early 1960s –

'*yé yé*' – to describe fashionable clothing.

yer plonker! *Catch Phrase*. Abusive epithet ('you idiot!') popularized by 'Del Boy' (David Jason) with reference to his younger brother, Rodney, in the BBC TV comedy series *Only Fools and Horses* (see ONLY FOOLS AND HORSES WORK) and current by 1986. In London dialect, 'plonker' = 'penis' (compare the epithets 'prick' and 'schmuck').

yesterday. See I WASN'T BORN ~.

yesterday's men. *Slogan/Idiom*. As a slogan, this had to be dropped for reasons of taste during the 1970 General Election campaign. The Labour Party issued a poster showing crudely-coloured models of Conservative politicians (Edward Heath, Iain Macleod, Lord Hailsham and others) and the additional line 'They failed before'. In fact, Labour lost the election to the men it had ridiculed as 'yesterday's' but the phrase continued to cause trouble. In 1971 it was used as the title of a BBC TV programme about how the defeated Labour leaders were faring in Opposition. This soured relations between the BBC and the Labour Party for a long while afterwards.

As an idiom, this could be applied to any ' has beens', and *OED Supp.* has a 1966 use, pre-dating the above.

yesteryear, thrilling days of. See under HI-YO, SILVER.

ying-tong-iddle-i-po! See under GOON SHOW.

yoo-hoo! See IT'S FOR ~!

you ain't seen nothin' yet! *Catch Phrase/Slogan*. President Ronald Reagan appropriated this catch phrase as a kind of slogan in his successful 1984 bid for re-election. He used it repeatedly during the campaign and, on 7 November, in his victory speech.

Partridge/*Catch Phrases* has a combined entry for 'you ain't seen nothin' yet' and 'you ain't heard nothin' yet', in which 'seen' is described as the commoner of the two versions. Both are dated from the 1920s. One could add that Bachman-Turner Overdrive, the Canadian pop group, had a hit with a song called 'You Ain't Seen Nothin' Yet' in 1974.

As for 'heard', it seems that when Al Jolson exclaimed 'You ain't heard nothin' yet!' in the first full-length talking picture *The Jazz Singer* (1927), he wasn't just ad-libbing as is usually supposed. He was promoting the title of one of his songs! He had recorded 'You Ain't Heard Nothing Yet', written by Gus Kahn and Buddy de Sylva, in 1919.

you and me. See THAT'S ~ . . .

you are what you eat. *Saying/ Slogan*. This neat encapsulation of a sensible attitude to diet was used as the title of an 'alternative' US film that was first shown in Britain in 1969. Of its content, *Films and Filming* (April 1969) noted: ' "You are what you eat," says an old hermit in a fairy-tale-painted wood; a band of blissfully beautiful people hopefully munch flowers in the park.' The BFI's *Monthly Film Bulletin* described the film as: 'A disjointed psychedelic picture of America's hippy revolution . . . The moralising note struck by the title is echoed nowhere else in the film.'

In other words, it was a load of 1960s tosh.

The idea behind the phrase has been around for many a year. Compare Brillat-Savarin in *La Physiologie du goût*: 'Tell me what you eat and I will tell you what you are' and L.A. Feuerbach: 'Man is what he eats (*Der Mensch ist, was er ißt*)' – in a review of Moleschott's *Lehre der Nahrungsmittel für das Volk* (1850). The German film chronicle *Heimat* (1984) included the version, '*Wie der Mensch ißt, so ist er*' [As a man eats, so he is].

you bet your sweet bippy! See under *LAUGH-IN*.

you cannot be serious! *Catch Phrase*. By 1980, John McEnroe, the American tennis-player and Wimbledon champion, had become celebrated for his 'Super-brat' behaviour towards umpires and linesmen – telling them 'You are the pits', and such like. 'You cannot be serious!' was elevated to catch phrase status through various showbiz take-offs, including Roger Kitter's record, 'Chalk Dust – The Umpire Strikes Back' (1982).

you can run but you can't hide. *Saying*. In the wake of the hijacking of a TWA airliner to Beirut in the summer of 1985, President Reagan issued a number of warnings to international terrorists. In October, he said that America had, 'sent a message to terrorists everywhere. The message: "You can run, but you can't hide." '

He was alluding to an utterance of the boxer Joe Louis who said of an opponent in a World Heavyweight Championship fight in June 1946, 'He can run, but he can't hide.' The opponent was Billy Conn

– who was a fast mover – and Louis won the fight on a knock-out.

I expect the saying probably pre-dates Louis, but it is very much associated with him.

you can't get the wood, you know! See under *GOON SHOW*.

you can't see the join. See under *MORECAMBE AND WISE SHOW*.

you dirty rat! *Catch Phrase*. Although impersonators of James Cagney (1899–1986) always have him saying 'You dirty rat!', it may be that he never said it like that himself. I am told, however, that in *Blonde Crazy* (1931) he calls someone a 'dirty, double-crossing rat' which amounts to much the same thing.

In Joan Wyndham's war-time diaries (*Love Lessons*, 1985) her entry for 1 October 1940 begins: 'Double bill at the Forum with Rupert. *Elizabeth and Essex*, and a gangster film where somebody actually *did* say "Stool on me would ya, ya doity rat!" ' Note her surprise that the line was uttered at all. Although it was a strange double-bill, I think she must have been watching a revival of *Taxi* (1931) which is about cabbies fighting off a Mob-controlled fleet. Cagney's exact words in that film are: 'Come out and take it, you dirty yellow-bellied rat, or I'll give it to you through the door.'

you dirty rotten swine you! See under *GOON SHOW*.

you don't have to be Jewish . . . *Slogan/Catch Phrase*. '. . . to love Levy's Real Jewish Rye' was how the slogan continued in the campaign current in the US in 1967. The point was reinforced by the words being set next to pictures of patently non-Jewish people (Indians, Chinese, Eskimos). There had been a show of Jewish humour with the title *You Don't Have to be Jewish* running on Broadway in 1965, which is probably where it all started.

Informal additions to the Levy bread posters were many. They included: '. . . to be offended by this ad/ . . . to be called one/ . . . to go to Columbia University, but it helps/ . . . to wear Levis/ . . . to be circumcised . . .'

you don't rewrite a hit. *Catch Phrase/ Idiom.* Meaning, you don't tamper with what is already established as successful. This showbiz phrase was used by Michael Grade in November 1987 when taking charge of the (rather unshowbiz) Channel 4.

you *know* it makes sense. *Slogan.* This was definitely the pay-off line to all road safety campaigns from 1968 to 1970, but the phrase had been used with emphasis on BBC TV's *TW3* in 1963, so I expect it must have been used somewhere else before this.

you know what comes between me and my Calvins? – nothing. *Slogan.* Brooke Shields, all of fifteen years of age, said this in a Calvin Klein jeans ad in 1980 and the line is remembered for its mild suggestiveness.

you know you're getting older when policemen look younger. *Saying.* The originator of this standard yardstick of age is sometimes supposed to have been Sir Arnold Bax (1883–1953), the composer. However – as with his other famous remark that 'You should make a point of trying every experience once, except incest and folk-dancing' – Bax was merely quoting someone else. In a footnote at the start of *Farewell, My Youth* (1943), Bax says: 'Arnold Bennett once remarked that his earliest recognition of his own middle age came at a certain appalling moment when he realized for the first time that the policeman at the corner was a mere youth.' Note that this applies to middle, rather than old, age.

To Sir Seymour Hicks (1871–1949), the actor-manager, is ascribed this: 'You will recognize, my boy, the first sign of old age; it is when you go out into the streets of London and realize for the first time how young the policemen look.'

I once invented for my father a yardstick for genuine old age: it is when the Pope looks – and is – younger than you.

you'll look a little lovelier each day (with fabulous Pink Camay). *Slogan.* One of the catchiest phrases from the early days of ITV, this one for Camay soap was around in *c* 1960. A year or two later, the BBC's *TW3* had a parody of it, about a Labour politician: 'You'll look a little lovelier each day/With fabulous Douglas Jay.'

you must have seen a lot of changes in your time? *Stock Phrase.* Conversation-starter supposedly much-used by members of the Royal Family. Noted by the early 1980s.

young. See WHEN THE WORLD WAS ~.

younger. See YOU KNOW YOU'RE GETTING OLDER . . .

young, gifted and black. *Catch Phrase*. From the title of a hit song recorded by the Jamaican duo Bob and Marcia in 1970. From the *Observer* (16 April 1989): 'They're young, gifted, and the hippest fun things since . . . CFC-free aerosols.' In June 1989, ITV was showing a comedy yarn about five young lads working on a Youth Training Scheme and called *Young, Gifted and Broke*.

youngster. See YOU'RE GOING OUT A ~ . . .

you 'orrible little man! *Catch Phrase*. Regimental Sergeant-Major Ronald Brittain (*c* 1899–1981) was reputed to have one of the loudest voices in the British Army. As his obituary in *The Times* put it: 'With his stentorian voice and massive parade ground presence [he] came to epitomise the British Army sergeant. Though he himself denied ever saying it, he was associated with the celebrated parade ground expression "You 'orrible little man" – in some quarters, indeed, was reputed to have coined it . . . His "**wake up there!**" to the somnolent after a command had in his opinion been inadequately executed was legendary – doubtless the ancestor of all the Wake Up Theres which have succeeded it.'

Compare WAKE UP AT THE BACK THERE! under *TAKE IT FROM HERE*.

your actual ——. See under *ROUND THE HORNE*.

your best friends won't tell you. See EVEN ~ . . .

your country needs *you*. *Slogan*. The caption to Alfred Leete's famous First World War recruiting poster showing Field Marshal Lord Kitchener pointing at *you* is a brilliant example of a slogan that is inseparable from a visual. It first appeared on the cover of *London Opinion* on 5 September 1914 and was taken up for poster use the following week. Earlier, a more formal advertisement bearing the words 'Your King and Country need you' with the royal coat of arms had been used. The idea was widely imitated abroad. In the USA, James Montgomery Flagg's poster of a pointing Uncle Sam bore the legend 'I want *you* for the US army'. There was also a version by Howard Chandler Christy featuring a woman with a mildly come-hither look saying, 'I want you for the Navy'.

'Your country needs you' became a *Catch Phrase* used in telling a man he had been selected for a dangerous or disgusting task.

you're famous when they can spell your name in Karachi. *Saying*. This comes from American showbiz and is quoted by Steve Aronson in *Hype* (1983).

you're going out a youngster – but you've gotta come back a star! *Cliché*. Not a cliché when new-minted in the film *42nd Street* (1933). Warren Baxter as a theatrical producer says the line to Ruby Keeler as the chorus girl who takes over at short notice from an indisposed star.

you're never alone with a Strand. *Slogan*. In a classic ad for a brand of cigarettes from W.D. & H.O. Wills which caught the public imagination and yet failed to sell the product. Devised in 1960 by John

May of S.H. Benson, the campaign was to launch a new, cheap, filter cigarette called Strand. May decided to appeal to the youth market by associating the product not with sex or social ease but with 'the loneliness and rejection of youth'. 'The young Sinatra was the prototype of the man I had in mind,' says May. 'Loneliness had made him a millionaire. I didn't see why it shouldn't sell us some cigarettes.'

And so, a Sinatra-clone was found in the twenty-eight-year-old actor, Terence Brook, who was also said to bear a resemblance to James Dean. He was shown mooching about lonely locations in raincoat and hat. In no time at all he had his own fan-club and the music from the TV ad – 'The Lonely Man Theme' – became a hit in its own right.

But the ads did not work. Viewers apparently revised the slogan in their own minds to mean, 'If you buy Strand, then you'll be alone'. However much the young may have wanted to identify with the figure, they did not want to buy him or his aura. Or perhaps it simply wasn't a very good cigarette? Either way, it hasn't been forgotten.

your friendly neighbourhood ——. *Format Phrase.* 'Usually ironic or facetious' notes *ODCIE* of this construction, and says it is derived from the slogan 'Your friendly neighbourhood policeman' in a police public-relations campaign of the 1960s. Myself, I would have suspected an American origin (compare SUPPORT YOUR LOCAL ——) but *ODCIE* may well be right.

your future is in your hands. *Slogan.* For the Conservative Party in the 1950 General Election. The Conservatives were returned to power under Churchill the following year. Churchill himself had used the idea in an address to Canadian troops aboard RMS *Queen Elizabeth* in January 1946: 'Our future is in our hands. Our lives are what we choose to make of them.'

your money or your life! *Stock Phrase/ Catch Phrase.* The highwayman's/ robber's challenge. In one of Jack Benny's most celebrated gags (playing on his legendary meanness), when the robber said this, Benny paused for a long time, and then replied, 'I'm thinking it over'. This was on American radio in the 1930s/40s.

'Your money *and* your life!' was an anti-smoking slogan in the UK in 1981.

your mother wouldn't like it. *Catch Phrase.* Ironic warning, used as the title of a rock-music programme on Capital Radio, presented by Nicky Horne, from 1973. Suzi Quatro recorded a song with the title 'Your Mama Won't Like Me' in 1975.

your own, your very own. *Stock Phrase.* Old-time music-hall from the Leeds City Varieties was a long-running TV favourite from 1953–83. As its chairman, Leonard Sachs spoke in a florid way, presumably reproducing traditional music-hall phrases. Before banging his gavel to bring on the next act, he would describe 'your own, your very own' artistes with alluring alliteration. At the end, the audience (all in period costume) would join in a sing-song: 'To conclude, we assemble the entire company, ladies and gentlemen – the entire company, the orchestra, but this time, ladies and gentlemen, **chiefly yourselves!'**

your policemen are wonderful. *Cliché*. What visiting American stars are traditionally supposed to say to London interviewers. From the *Guardian* (4 June 1983): 'When Kristina Wayborn [actress in James Bond film] said that she loved British fish and chips it seemed a simple kindness to ask what she thought of our policemen. "They are so wonderful. They make you feel so secure," she replied in the BEST POSSIBLE TASTE.'

yours. See ONE DAY ALL THIS WILL BE ~, MY SON.

yours to enjoy in the privacy of your own home. *Slogan*. A traditional advertising line, probably ex-US? *Private Eye*, in 1964, ran a spoof advertisement for a part-work, including the lure: 'Now experience the First World War in the privacy of your own home.'

you shouldn't be in the circus. See IF YOU CAN'T RIDE TWO HORSES AT ONCE . . .

you silly little man! See under *BAND WAGGON*.

you, too, can have a body like mine. *Slogan*. 'Charles Atlas' was born Angelo Siciliano in Italy in 1894 and died in America in 1972. He won the title of 'The World's Most Perfectly Developed Man' in a 1922 contest sponsored by Bernarr Macfaden and his *Physical Culture* magazine. Then he started giving mail-order body-building lessons. A famous promotional strip cartoon showed 'How Joe's body brought him FAME instead of SHAME.' 'Hey! Quit kicking sand in our face,' Joe says to a bully on the beach. Then he takes a Charles Atlas course and

ends up with a girl by his side who says, 'Oh, Joe! You are a real man after all!'

Like Joe, Atlas had himself been 'a skinny, timid weakling of only seven stone' (hence the expression **I was a seven stone weakling**. 'I didn't know what real health and strength were. I was afraid to fight – ashamed to be seen in a bathing costume.' But after watching a lion rippling its muscles at the zoo, he developed a method of pitting one muscle against another which he called 'Dynamic Tension'.

you've come a long way, baby (to get where you got to today). *Slogan*. For Virginia Slims cigarettes, in the US, from 1968. A slogan that rode on the feminist mood of the times in selling to women smokers. Indeed, the basic phrase has also been used on Women's Lib posters. One shows a woman giving a karate chop to a man's head. An article by Julie Baumgold with the title 'You've Come a Long Way, Baby' appeared in *New York* magazine on 9 June 1969.

A song with the title followed in 1971. After the failure of the US Equal Rights Amendment in 1982, a T-shirt appeared bearing the words, 'I Haven't Come A Long Way'.

you've made an old man very happy. *Catch Phrase*. As though said by an old man to a woman for sexual favours granted, now a humorous way of expressing thanks about anything. Neatly inverted in the film *The Last Remake of Beau Geste* (1977). Terry Thomas, as a prison governor, says to Ann-Margret, as a woman who has slept with him to secure an escape: 'Delighted you came, my dear, and I'd like you to know that you made a happy man feel very old.'

you've never had it so good. *Slogan.* This is the phrase that will forever be linked with the name of Harold Macmillan (later 1st Earl of Stockton)(1894–1986). It was first used by him in a speech at Bedford on 20 July 1957. He took pains to use the phrase not boastfully but as a warning: 'Let's be frank about it. Most of our people have never had it so good. Go around the country, go to the industrial towns, go to the farms, and you'll see a state of prosperity such as we have never had in my lifetime – nor indeed ever in the history of this country. What is beginning to worry some of us is "Is it too good to be true?" or perhaps I should say "Is it too good to last?" For amidst all this prosperity, there is one problem that has troubled us, in one way or another, ever since the war. It is the problem of rising prices. Our constant concern is: Can prices be steadied while at the same time we maintain full employment in an expanding economy? Can we control inflation?'

Macmillan is said to have appropriated the phrase from Lord Robens (a former Labour minister who had rejected social-ism and who had used the phrase in conversation with the Prime Minister not long before). However, as 'You Never Had It So Good', it had been a slogan used by the Democrats in the 1952 US presidential election.

In his memoirs, Macmillan commented: 'For some reason it was not until several years later that this phrase was taken out of its context and turned into a serious charge against me, of being too materialistic and showing too little of a spiritual approach to life . . . curiously enough these are the inevitable hazards to which all politicians are prone.'

Given the way the phrase came to dog him, it would have been surprising if it had ever been used as an official Tory party slogan. It was rejected – in so many words – for the 1959 General Election by the Conservatives' publicity group, partly because it 'violated a basic advertising axiom that statements should be positive, not negative'. There was, however, an official poster that came very close with, 'You're Having It Good, Have It Better'.

you want the best seats, we have them. *Slogan.* For the Keith Prowse ticket agency, from 1925 onwards.

Other reference books from Bloomsbury Publishing

Bloomsbury Dictionary of Quotations

The second edition of the most comprehensive new collection of quotations for over 40 years. With over 10,000 quotations, it includes biographies and detailed keywords index.

Bloomsbury Dictionary of Word Origins
John Ayto

This comprehensive new dictionary details the history of over 6,000 words.

Bloomsbury Guide to English Literature
Edited by Marion Wynne-Davies

The **new** authority on English literature, combining essays outlining the development of each genre with over 5,000 A-Z entries.

Bloomsbury Dictionary of Contemporary Slang
Tony Thorne

With over 6,000 entries and extensive cross-references, this book will tell you everything you've ever wanted to know about slang but were afraid to ask.

Bloomsbury Good Word Guide
Martin Manser

Now in its second edition, this is *the* accessible, practical manual for English usage in the 1990s.

Bloomsbury Good Reading Guide
Kenneth McLeish

With over 350 entries and thousands of reading suggestions, a fascinating way to (re)awaken the joy of reading.

For enquiries and further details please contact:

Reference Book Department, Bloomsbury Publishing Ltd,
2 Soho Square, London W1V 5DE